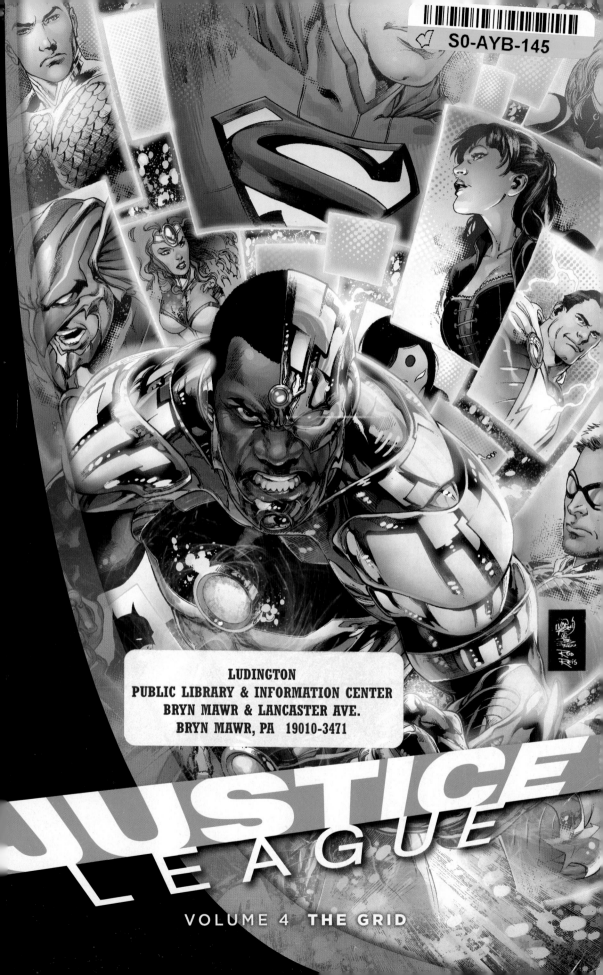

JUSTICE LEAGUE

VOLUME 4 THE GRID

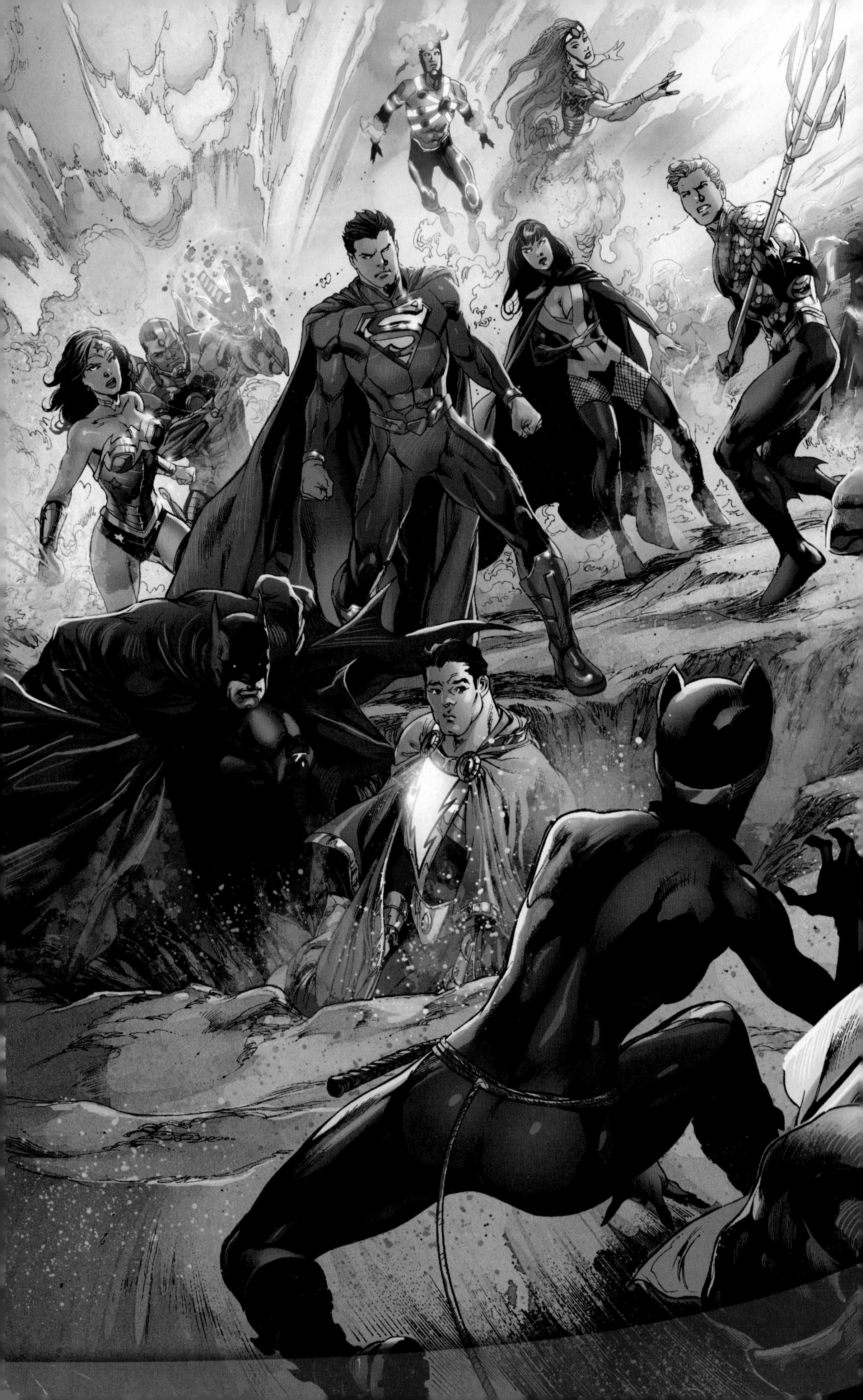

JUSTICE LEAGUE

VOLUME 4
THE GRID

GEOFF **JOHNS** writer

IVAN **REIS** JOE **PRADO** JESUS **SAIZ** OCLAIR **ALBERT**
JONATHAN **GLAPION** ZANDER **CANNON** GENE **HA**
ANDRES **GUINALDO** ROB **HUNTER** EBER **FERRIERA** artists

ROD **REIS** JEROMY **COX** ART **LYONS** HI-FI colorists

DEZI **SIENTY** NICK J. **NAPOLITANO** letterers

IVAN **REIS**, JOE **PRADO** & ROD **REIS**
collection cover artists

SUPERMAN created by JERRY **SIEGEL** & JOE **SHUSTER**
By special arrangement with the Jerry Siegel family

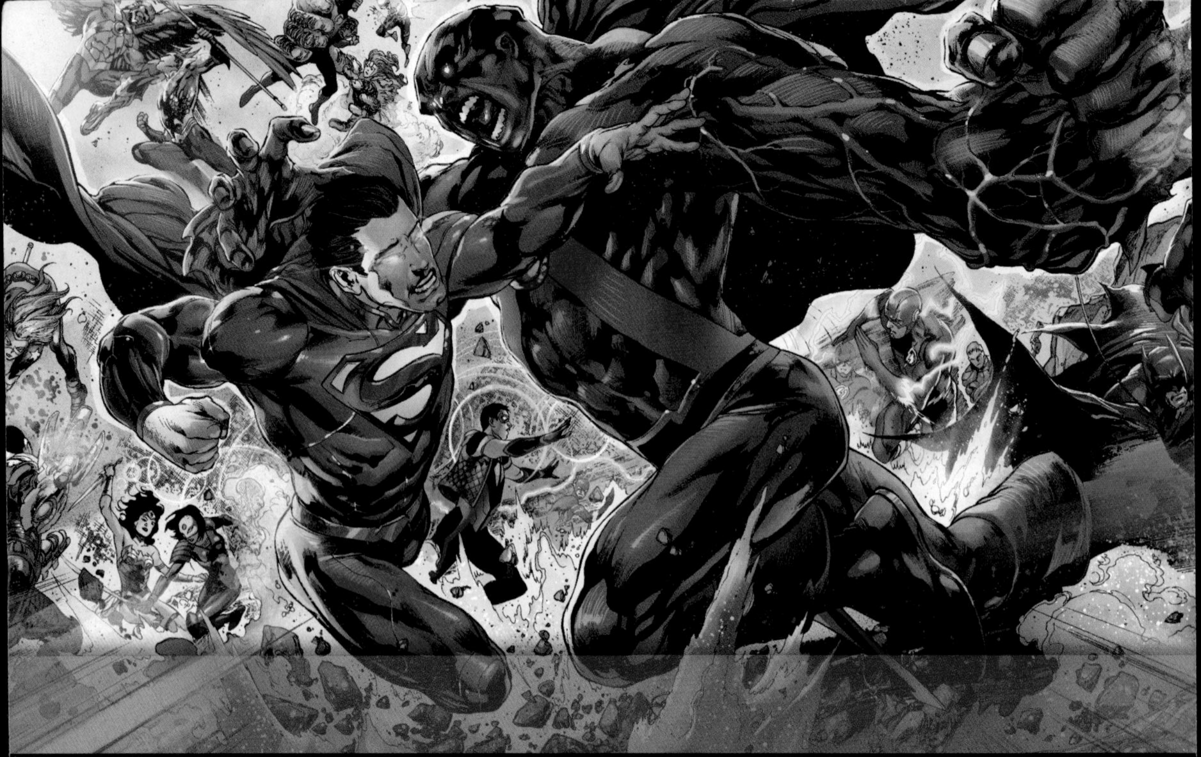

BRIAN CUNNINGHAM Editor – Original Series KATIE KUBERT Associate Editor – Original Series
KATE STEWART Assistant Editor – Original Series ROBIN WILDMAN Editor
ROBBIN BROSTERMAN Design Director – Books ROBBIE BIEDERMAN Publication Design

BOB HARRAS Senior VP – Editor-in-Chief, DC Comics

DIANE NELSON President DAN DIDIO and JIM LEE Co-Publishers GEOFF JOHNS Chief Creative Officer
AMIT DESAI Senior VP – Marketing and Franchise Management
AMY GENKINS Senior VP – Business and Legal Affairs NAIRI GARDINER Senior VP – Finance
JEFF BOISON VP – Publishing Planning MARK CHIARELLO VP – Art Direction and Design
JOHN CUNNINGHAM VP – Marketing TERRI CUNNINGHAM VP – Editorial Administration
LARRY GANEM VP – Talent Relations and Services ALISON GILL Senior VP – Manufacturing and Operations
HANK KANALZ Senior VP – Vertigo and Integrated Publishing JAY KOGAN VP – Business and Legal Affairs, Publishing
JACK MAHAN VP – Business Affairs, Talent NICK NAPOLITANO VP – Manufacturing Administration SUE POHJA VP – Book Sales
FRED RUIZ VP – Manufacturing Operations COURTNEY SIMMONS Senior VP – Publicity BOB WAYNE Senior VP – Sales

JUSTICE LEAGUE VOLUME 4: THE GRID

DC Comics, 1700 Broadway, New York, NY 10019
A Warner Bros. Entertainment Company.
Printed by RR Donnelley, Salem, VA, USA. 8/8/14. First Printing.

ISBN: 978-1-4012-5008-9

Library of Congress Cataloging-in-Publication Data

Johns, Geoff, 1973- author.
Justice League. Volume 4, The Grid / Geoff Johns ; [illustrated by] Ivan Reis.
pages cm. — (The New 52!)
ISBN 978-1-4012-4717-1 (hardback)
1. Graphic novels. I. Reis, Ivan, illustrator. II. Title. III. Title: Grid.
PN6728.J87J6543 2014
741.5'973—dc23
2013049803

SUSTAINABLE FORESTRY INITIATIVE
Certified Chain of Custody
20% Certified Forest Content,
80% Certified Sourcing
www.sfiprogram.org
SFI-01042
APPLIES TO TEXT STOCK ONLY

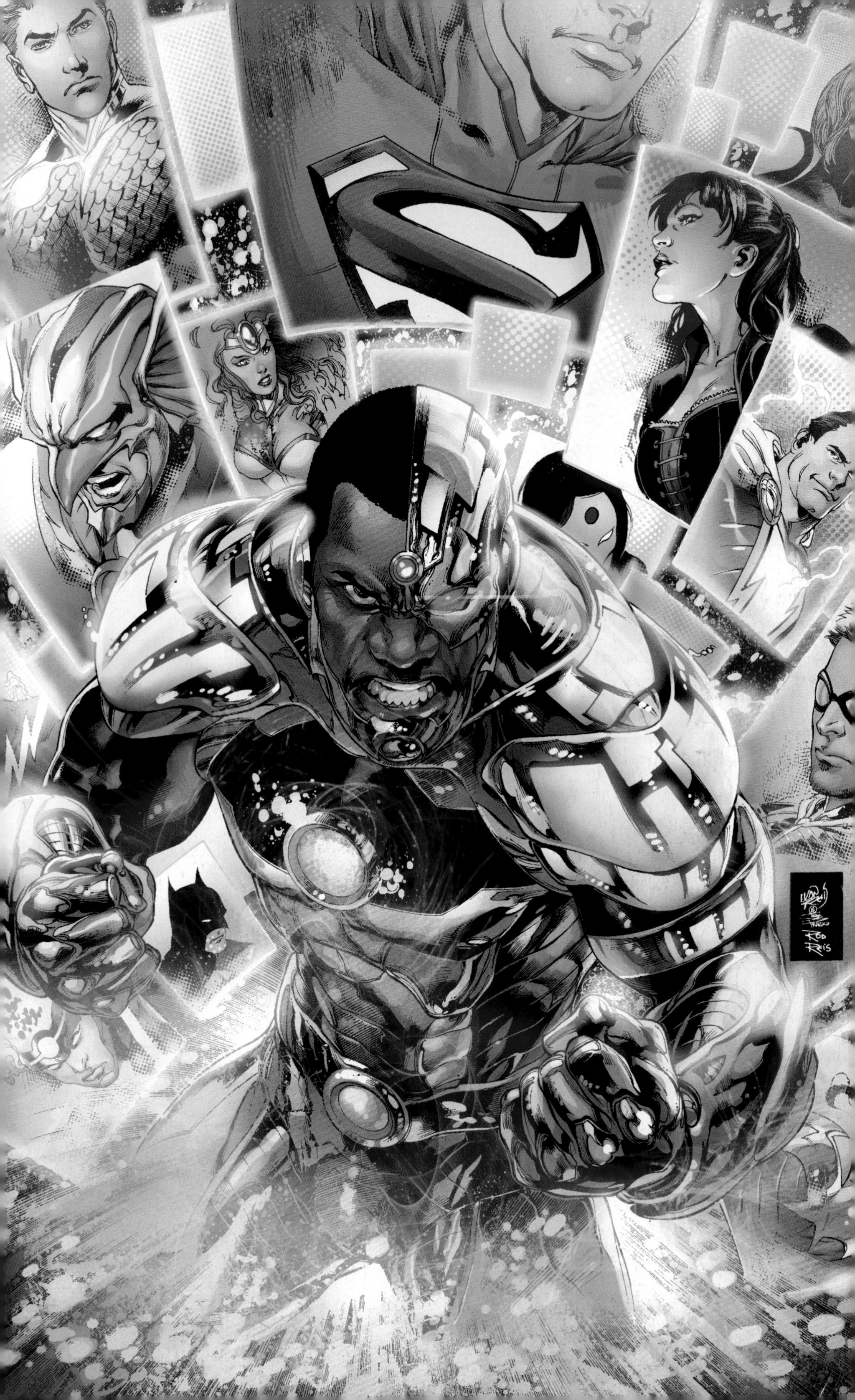

THE GRID

GEOFF JOHNS writer **JESUS SAIZ** artist **JEROMY COX** colorist **IVAN REIS, JOE PRADO** and **ROD REIS** cover artists

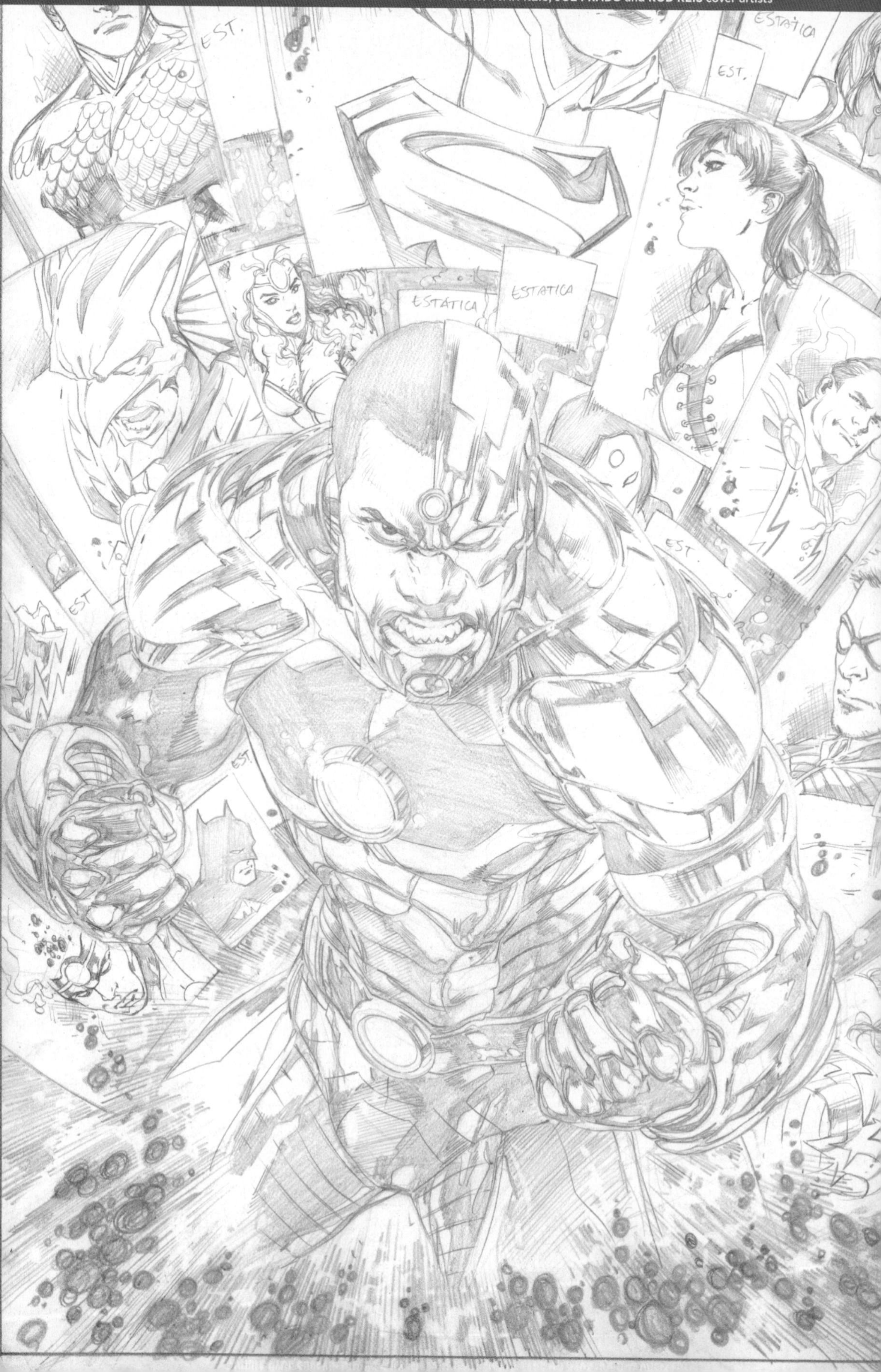
EST.
ESTÁTICA
EST.
ESTÁTICA
ESTÁTICA
EST.
EST
EST.

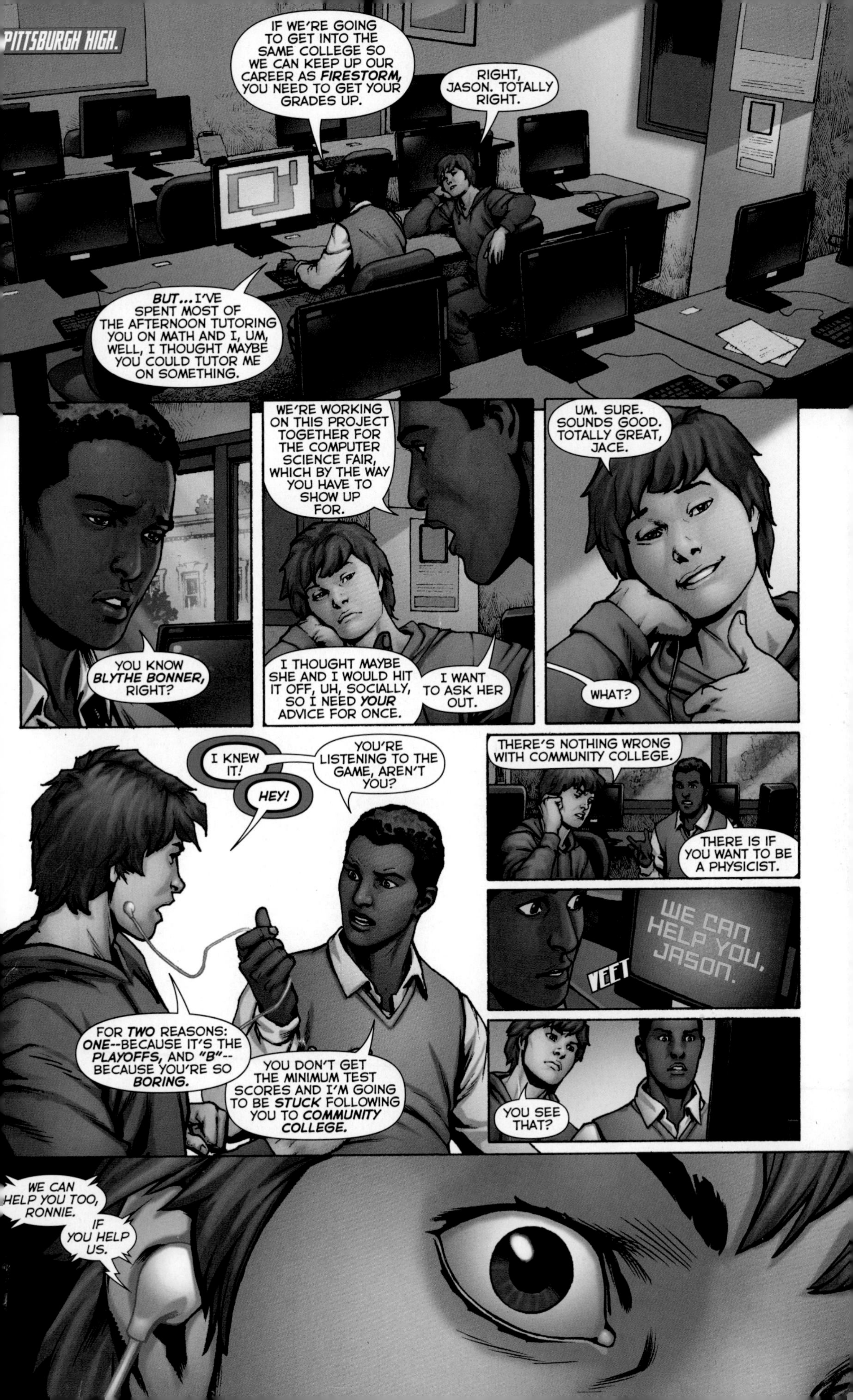

PITTSBURGH HIGH.
IF WE'RE GOING TO GET INTO THE SAME COLLEGE SO WE CAN KEEP UP OUR CAREER AS FIRESTORM, YOU NEED TO GET YOUR GRADES UP.
RIGHT, JASON. TOTALLY RIGHT.
BUT...I'VE SPENT MOST OF THE AFTERNOON TUTORING YOU ON MATH AND I, UM, WELL, I THOUGHT MAYBE YOU COULD TUTOR ME ON SOMETHING.
YOU KNOW BLYTHE BONNER, RIGHT?
WE'RE WORKING ON THIS PROJECT TOGETHER FOR THE COMPUTER SCIENCE FAIR, WHICH BY THE WAY YOU HAVE TO SHOW UP FOR.
I THOUGHT MAYBE SHE AND I WOULD HIT IT OFF, UH, SOCIALLY, SO I NEED YOUR ADVICE FOR ONCE.
I WANT TO ASK HER OUT.
UM. SURE. SOUNDS GOOD. TOTALLY GREAT, JACE.
WHAT?
I KNEW IT!
YOU'RE LISTENING TO THE GAME, AREN'T YOU?
HEY!
FOR TWO REASONS: ONE--BECAUSE IT'S THE PLAYOFFS, AND "B"--BECAUSE YOU'RE SO BORING.
YOU DON'T GET THE MINIMUM TEST SCORES AND I'M GOING TO BE STUCK FOLLOWING YOU TO COMMUNITY COLLEGE.
THERE'S NOTHING WRONG WITH COMMUNITY COLLEGE.
THERE IS IF YOU WANT TO BE A PHYSICIST.
WE CAN HELP YOU, JASON.
VEET
YOU SEE THAT?
WE CAN HELP YOU TOO, RONNIE.
IF YOU HELP US.

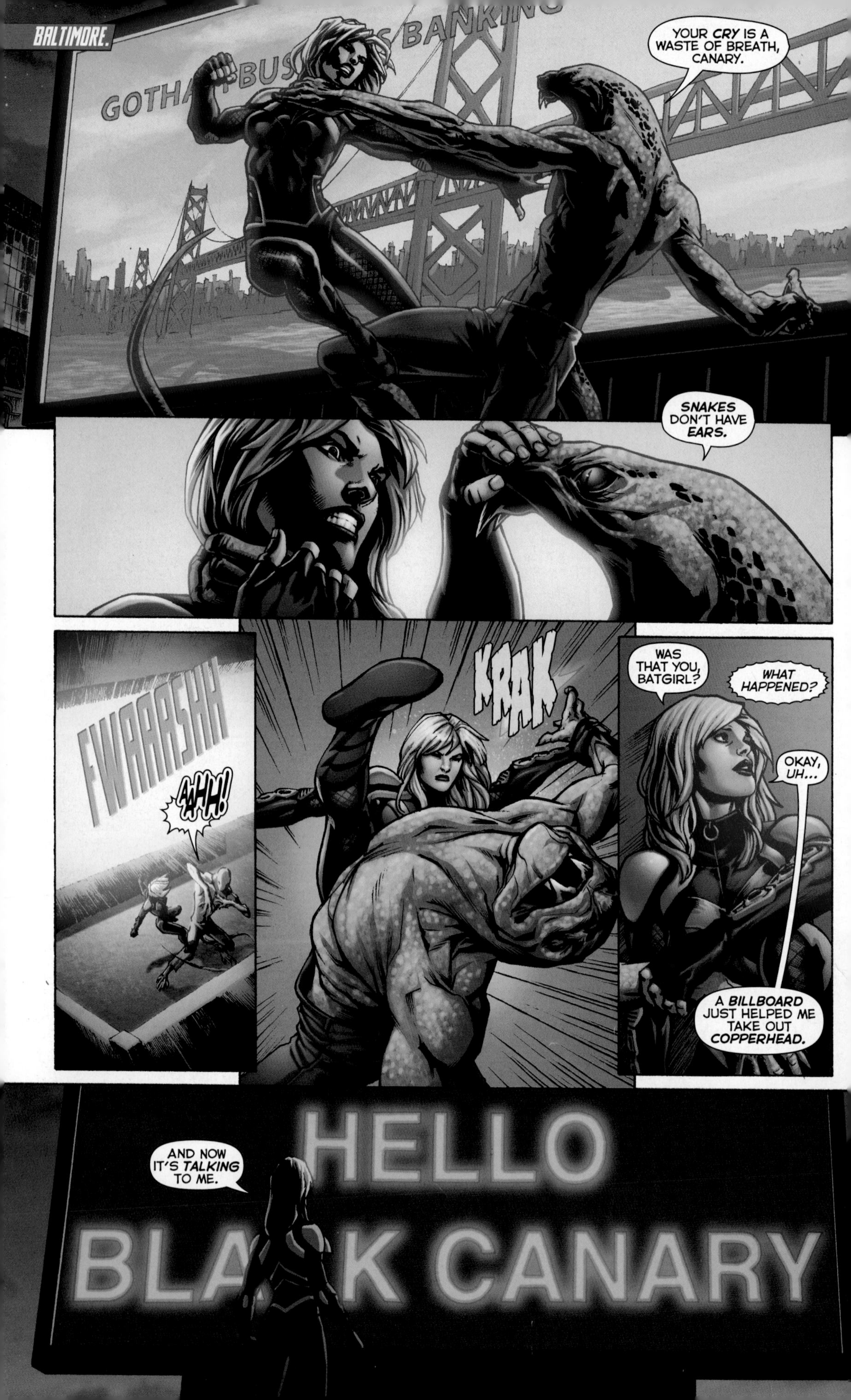
BALTIMORE.
YOUR CRY IS A WASTE OF BREATH, CANARY.
SNAKES DON'T HAVE EARS.
FWAARSHH
AAHH!
KRAK
WAS THAT YOU, BATGIRL?
WHAT HAPPENED?
OKAY, UH...
A BILLBOARD JUST HELPED ME TAKE OUT COPPERHEAD.
AND NOW IT'S TALKING TO ME.
HELLO
BLA K CANARY

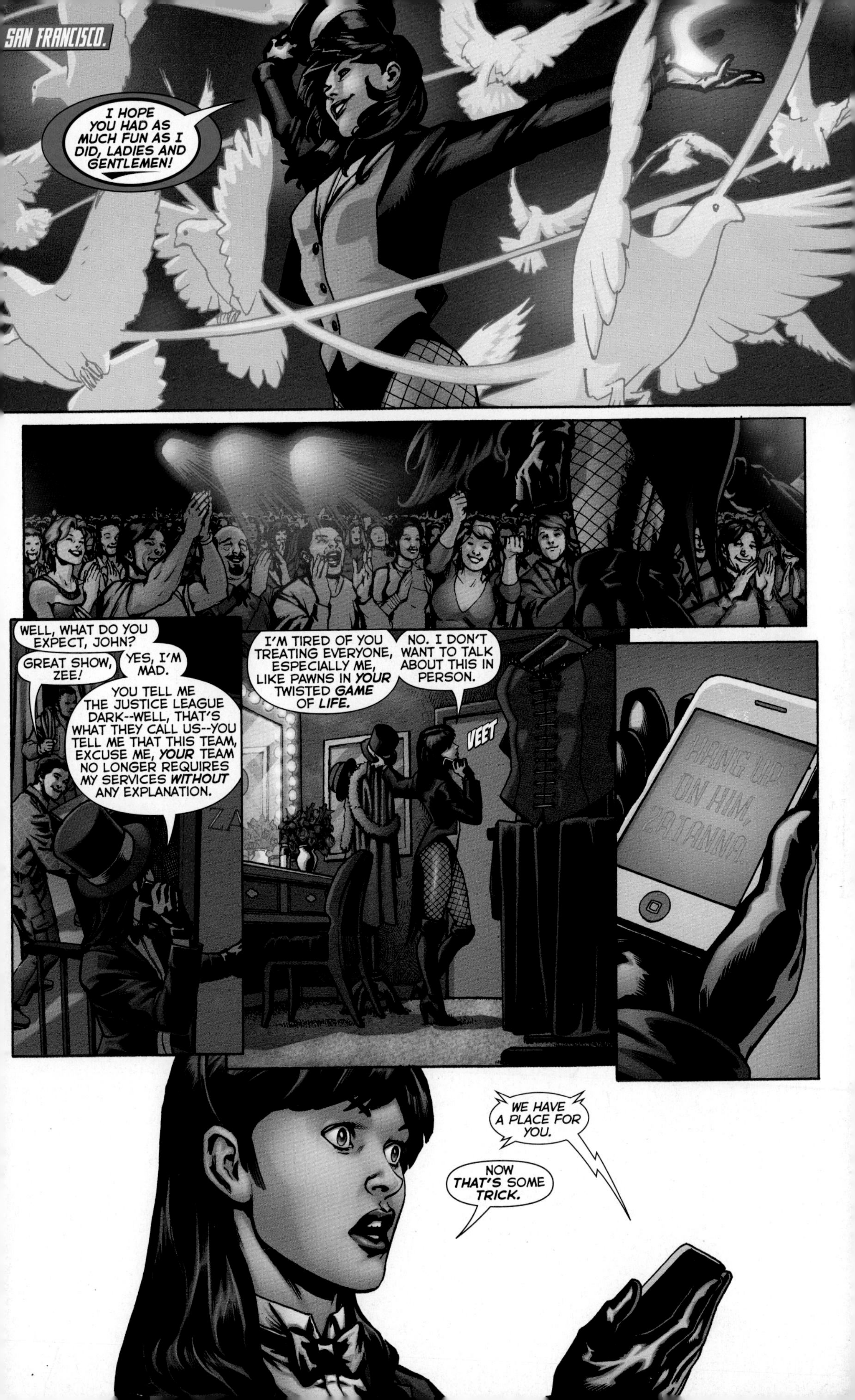
SAN FRANCISCO.
I HOPE YOU HAD AS MUCH FUN AS I DID, LADIES AND GENTLEMEN!
WELL, WHAT DO YOU EXPECT, JOHN?
GREAT SHOW, ZEE!
YES, I'M MAD.
YOU TELL ME THE JUSTICE LEAGUE DARK--WELL, THAT'S WHAT THEY CALL US--YOU TELL ME THAT THIS TEAM, EXCUSE ME, YOUR TEAM NO LONGER REQUIRES MY SERVICES WITHOUT ANY EXPLANATION.
I'M TIRED OF YOU TREATING EVERYONE, ESPECIALLY ME, LIKE PAWNS IN YOUR TWISTED GAME OF LIFE.
NO. I DON'T WANT TO TALK ABOUT THIS IN PERSON.
VEET
HANG UP ON HIM, ZATANNA.
WE HAVE A PLACE FOR YOU.
NOW THAT'S SOME TRICK.

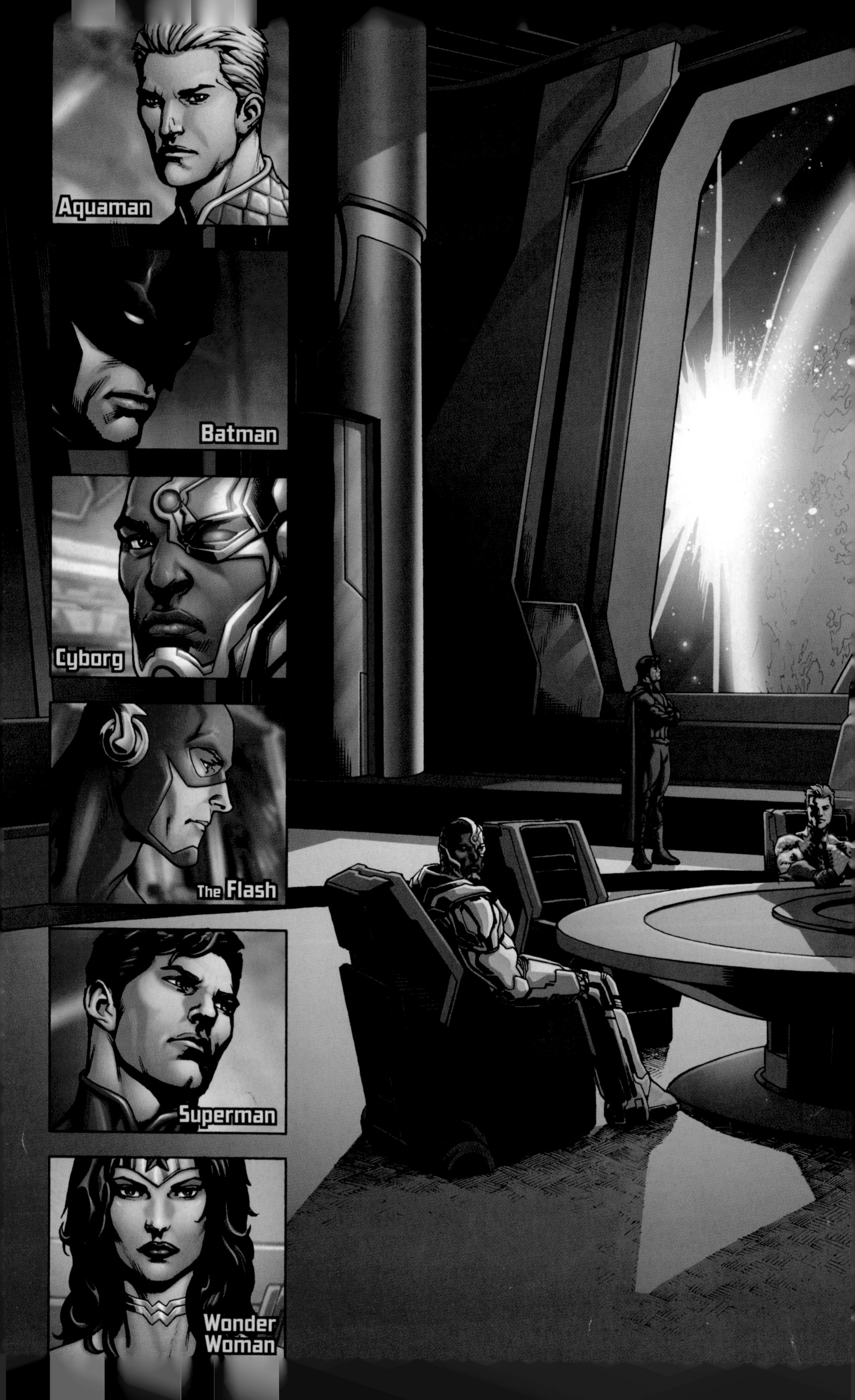
Aquaman
Batman
Cyborg
The Flash
Superman
Wonder Woman

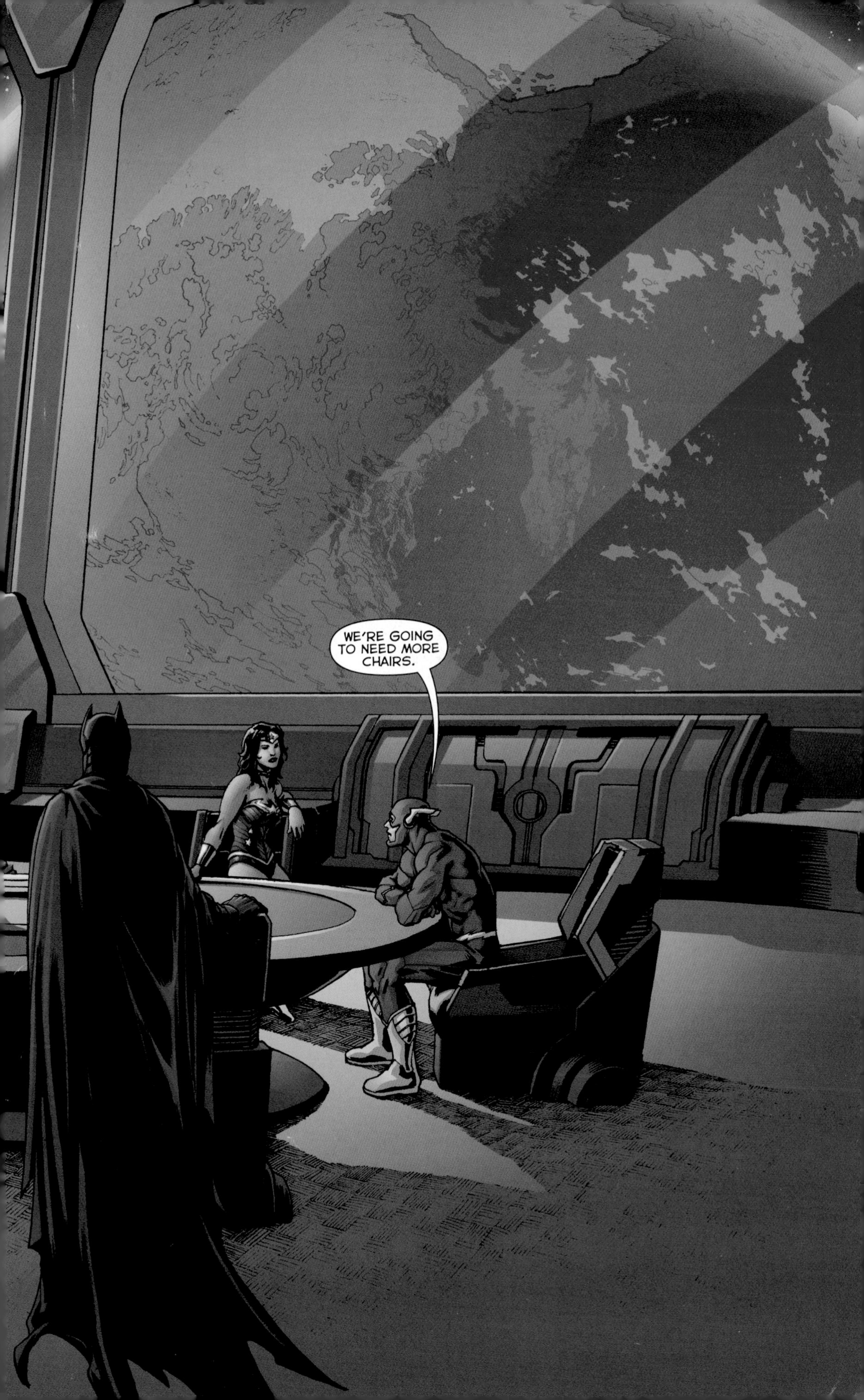
WE'RE GOING TO NEED MORE CHAIRS.

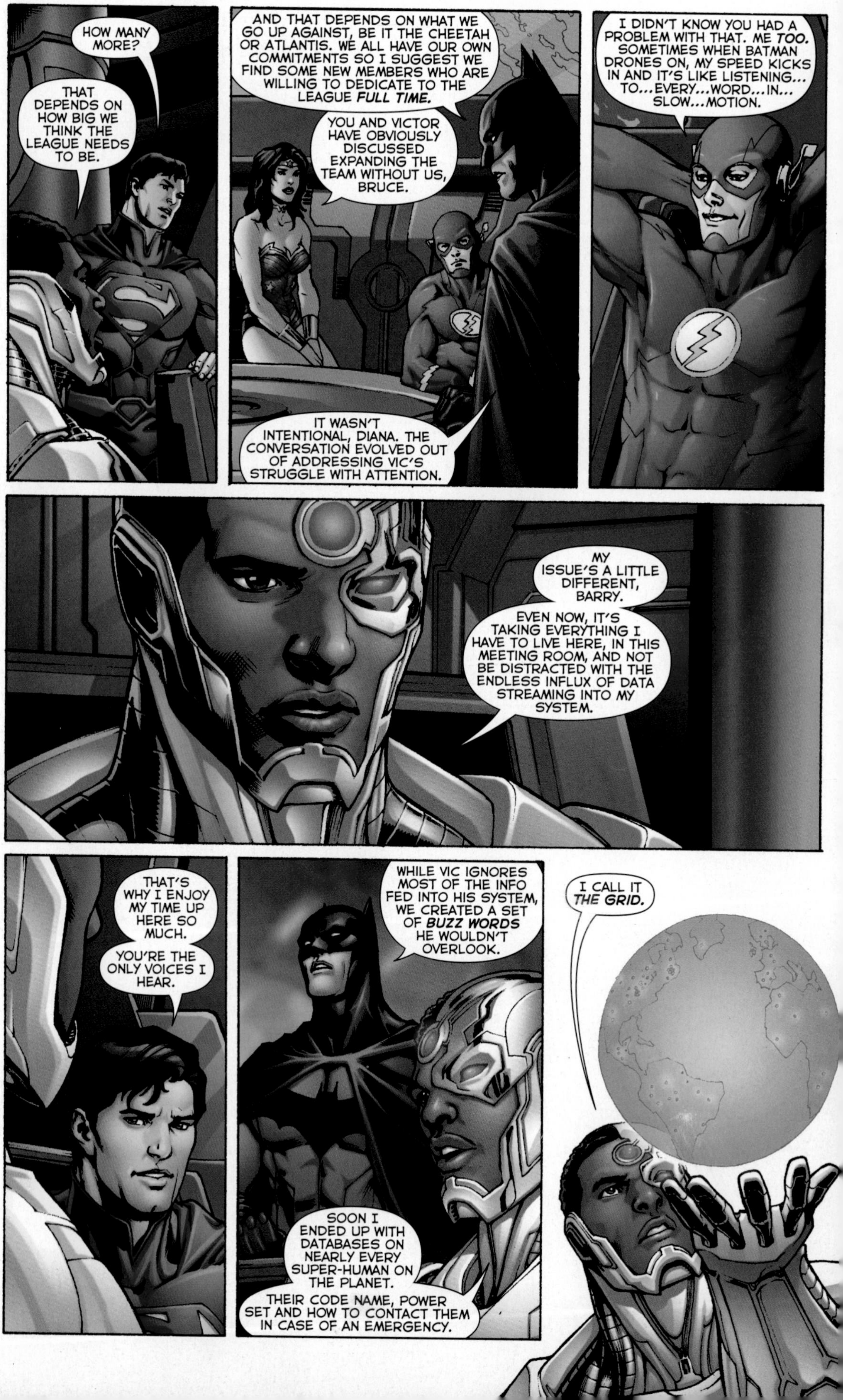
HOW MANY MORE?
THAT DEPENDS ON HOW BIG WE THINK THE LEAGUE NEEDS TO BE.
AND THAT DEPENDS ON WHAT WE GO UP AGAINST, BE IT THE CHEETAH OR ATLANTIS. WE ALL HAVE OUR OWN COMMITMENTS SO I SUGGEST WE FIND SOME NEW MEMBERS WHO ARE WILLING TO DEDICATE TO THE LEAGUE *FULL TIME.*
YOU AND VICTOR HAVE OBVIOUSLY DISCUSSED EXPANDING THE TEAM WITHOUT US, BRUCE.
IT WASN'T INTENTIONAL, DIANA. THE CONVERSATION EVOLVED OUT OF ADDRESSING VIC'S STRUGGLE WITH ATTENTION.
I DIDN'T KNOW YOU HAD A PROBLEM WITH THAT. ME *TOO.* SOMETIMES WHEN BATMAN DRONES ON, MY SPEED KICKS IN AND IT'S LIKE LISTENING... TO...EVERY...WORD...IN... SLOW...MOTION.
MY ISSUE'S A LITTLE DIFFERENT, BARRY.
EVEN NOW, IT'S TAKING EVERYTHING I HAVE TO LIVE HERE, IN THIS MEETING ROOM, AND NOT BE DISTRACTED WITH THE ENDLESS INFLUX OF DATA STREAMING INTO *MY* SYSTEM.
THAT'S WHY I ENJOY MY TIME UP HERE SO MUCH.
YOU'RE THE ONLY VOICES I HEAR.
WHILE VIC IGNORES MOST OF THE INFO FED INTO HIS SYSTEM, WE CREATED A SET OF *BUZZ WORDS* HE WOULDN'T OVERLOOK.
SOON I ENDED UP WITH DATABASES ON NEARLY EVERY SUPER-HUMAN ON THE PLANET.
THEIR CODE NAME, POWER SET AND HOW TO CONTACT THEM IN CASE OF AN EMERGENCY.
I CALL IT *THE GRID.*

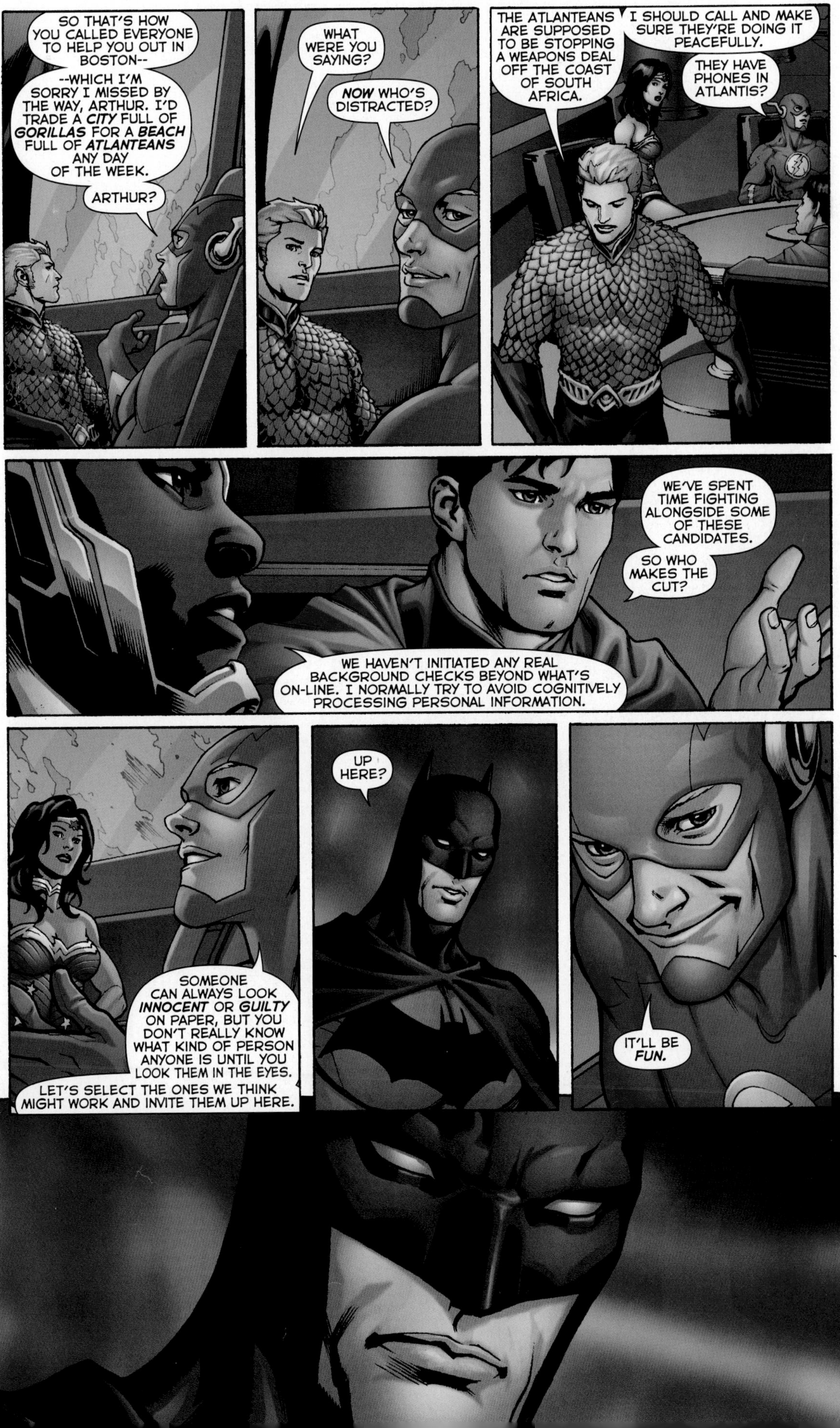
SO THAT'S HOW YOU CALLED EVERYONE TO HELP YOU OUT IN BOSTON--
--WHICH I'M SORRY I MISSED BY THE WAY, ARTHUR. I'D TRADE A *CITY* FULL OF *GORILLAS* FOR A *BEACH* FULL OF *ATLANTEANS* ANY DAY OF THE WEEK.
ARTHUR?
WHAT WERE YOU SAYING?
NOW WHO'S DISTRACTED?
THE ATLANTEANS ARE SUPPOSED TO BE STOPPING A WEAPONS DEAL OFF THE COAST OF SOUTH AFRICA.
I SHOULD CALL AND MAKE SURE THEY'RE DOING IT PEACEFULLY.
THEY HAVE PHONES IN ATLANTIS?
WE'VE SPENT TIME FIGHTING ALONGSIDE SOME OF THESE CANDIDATES.
SO WHO MAKES THE CUT?
WE HAVEN'T INITIATED ANY REAL BACKGROUND CHECKS BEYOND WHAT'S ON-LINE. I NORMALLY TRY TO AVOID COGNITIVELY PROCESSING PERSONAL INFORMATION.
SOMEONE CAN ALWAYS LOOK *INNOCENT* OR *GUILTY* ON PAPER, BUT YOU DON'T REALLY KNOW WHAT KIND OF PERSON ANYONE IS UNTIL YOU LOOK THEM IN THE EYES.
LET'S SELECT THE ONES WE THINK MIGHT WORK AND INVITE THEM UP HERE.
UP HERE?
IT'LL BE *FUN.*

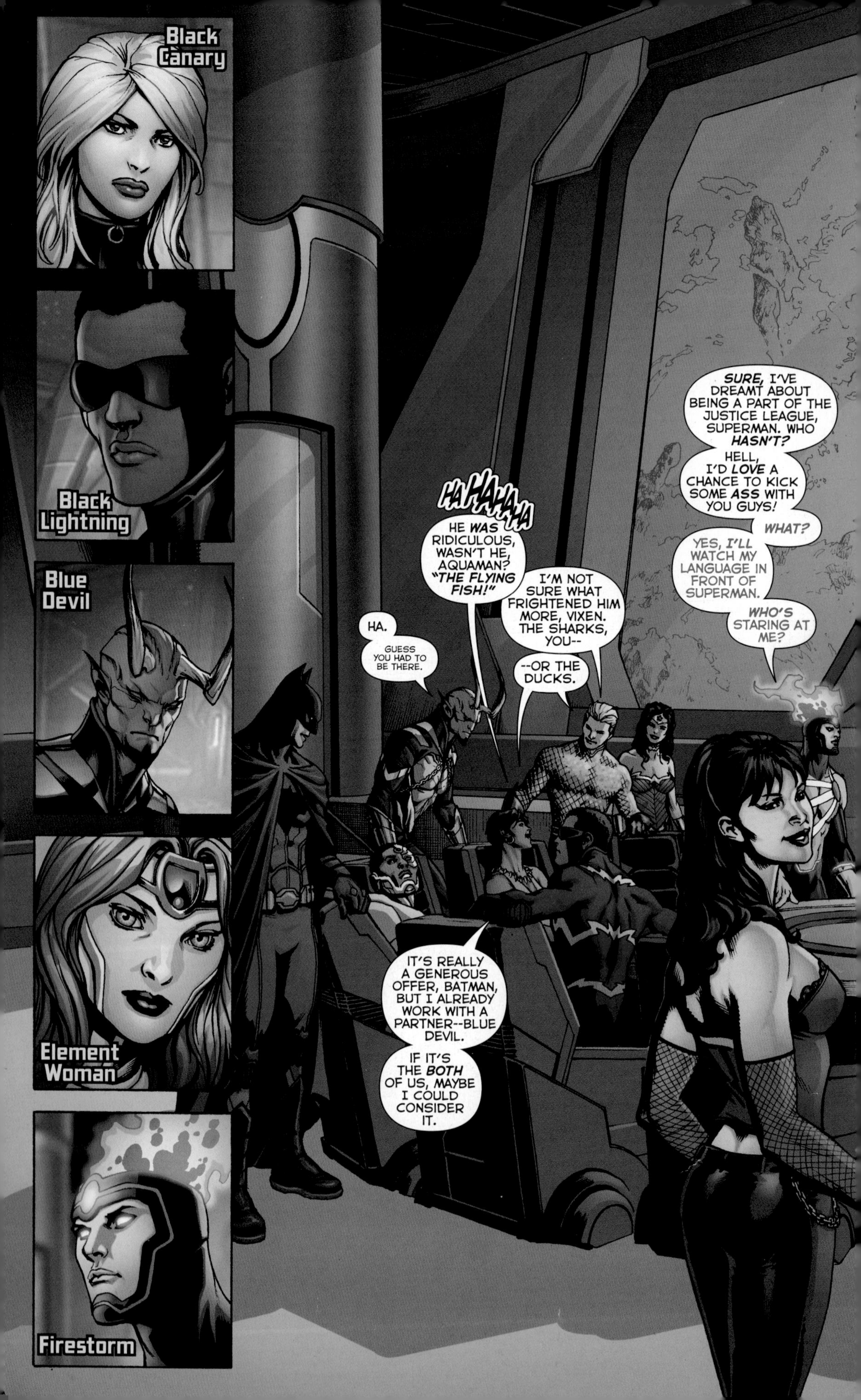
Black Canary
Black Lightning
Blue Devil
Element Woman
Firestorm
HAHAHAHA
HE WAS RIDICULOUS, WASN'T HE, AQUAMAN? "THE FLYING FISH!"
HA.
GUESS YOU HAD TO BE THERE.
I'M NOT SURE WHAT FRIGHTENED HIM MORE, VIXEN. THE SHARKS, YOU--
--OR THE DUCKS.
SURE, I'VE DREAMT ABOUT BEING A PART OF THE JUSTICE LEAGUE, SUPERMAN. WHO HASN'T?
HELL, I'D LOVE A CHANCE TO KICK SOME ASS WITH YOU GUYS!
WHAT?
YES, I'LL WATCH MY LANGUAGE IN FRONT OF SUPERMAN.
WHO'S STARING AT ME?
IT'S REALLY A GENEROUS OFFER, BATMAN, BUT I ALREADY WORK WITH A PARTNER--BLUE DEVIL.
IF IT'S THE BOTH OF US, MAYBE I COULD CONSIDER IT.

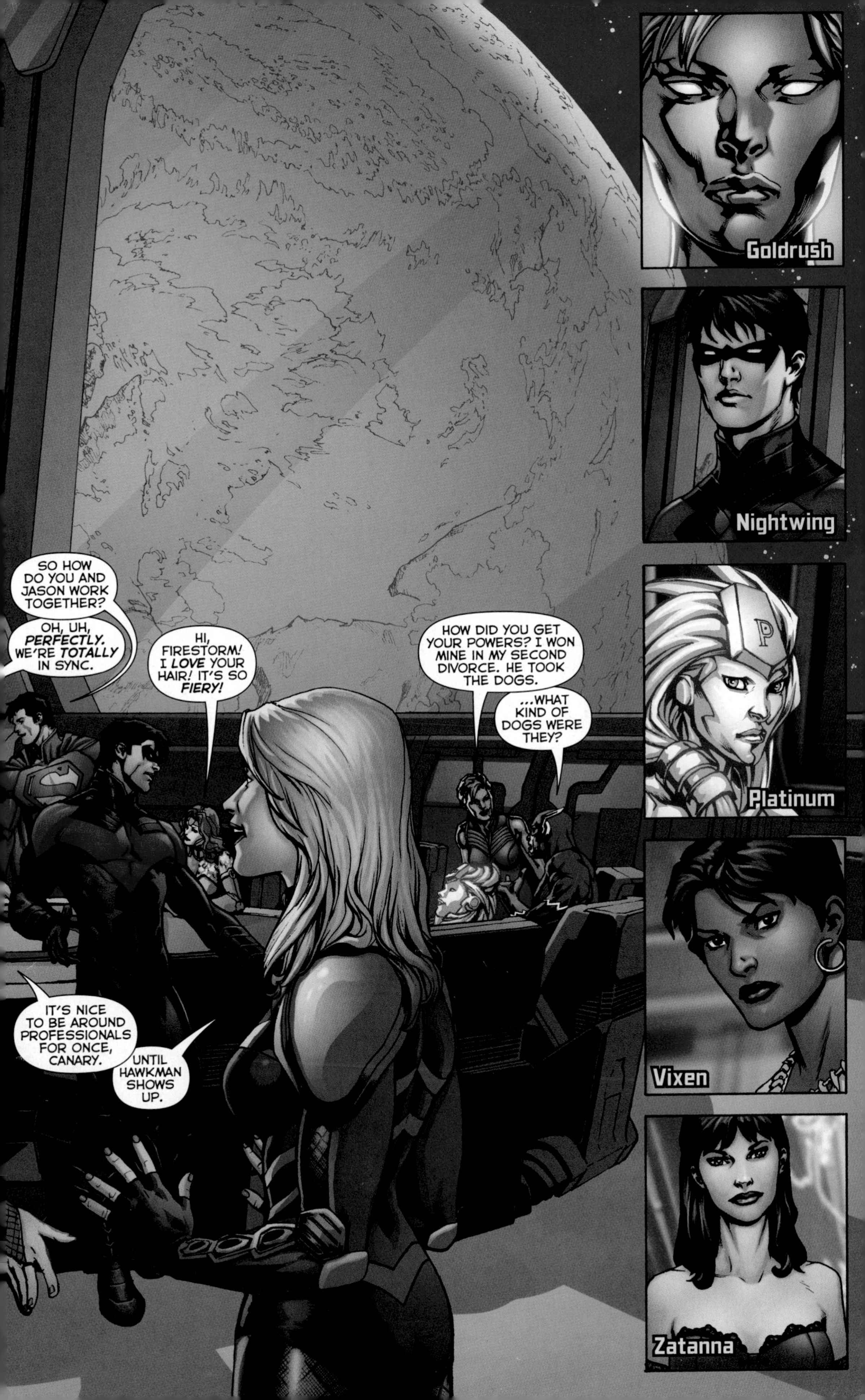
SO HOW DO YOU AND JASON WORK TOGETHER?
OH, UH, *PERFECTLY.* WE'RE *TOTALLY* IN SYNC.
HI, FIRESTORM! I *LOVE* YOUR HAIR! IT'S SO *FIERY!*
HOW DID YOU GET YOUR POWERS? I WON MINE IN MY SECOND DIVORCE. HE TOOK THE DOGS.
...WHAT KIND OF DOGS WERE THEY?
IT'S NICE TO BE AROUND PROFESSIONALS FOR ONCE, CANARY.
UNTIL HAWKMAN SHOWS UP.
Goldrush
Nightwing
Platinum
Vixen
Zatanna

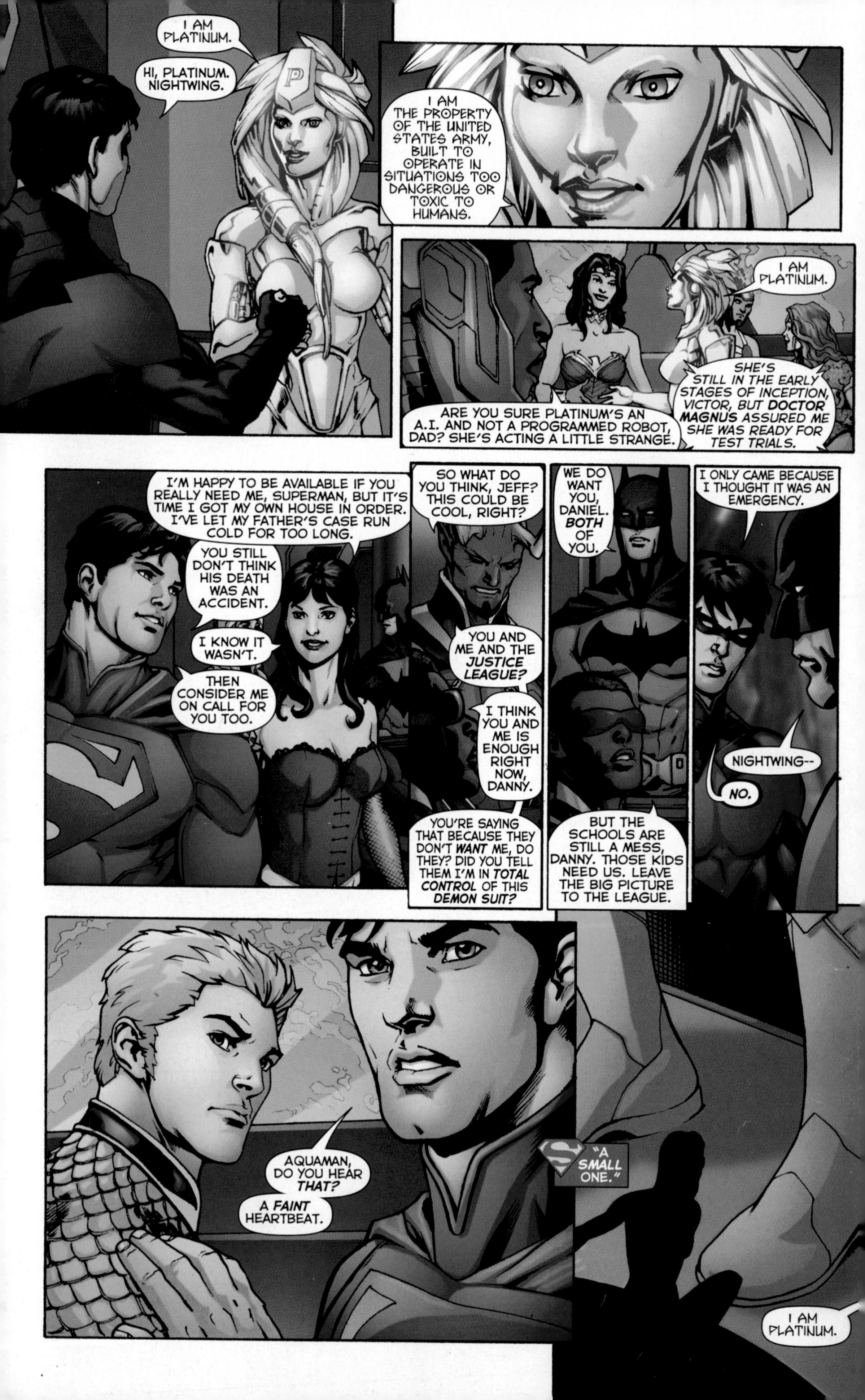
I AM PLATINUM.
HI, PLATINUM. NIGHTWING.
I AM THE PROPERTY OF THE UNITED STATES ARMY, BUILT TO OPERATE IN SITUATIONS TOO DANGEROUS OR TOXIC TO HUMANS.
I AM PLATINUM.
ARE YOU SURE PLATINUM'S AN A.I. AND NOT A PROGRAMMED ROBOT, DAD? SHE'S ACTING A LITTLE STRANGE.
SHE'S STILL IN THE EARLY STAGES OF INCEPTION, VICTOR, BUT DOCTOR MAGNUS ASSURED ME SHE WAS READY FOR TEST TRIALS.
I'M HAPPY TO BE AVAILABLE IF YOU REALLY NEED ME, SUPERMAN, BUT IT'S TIME I GOT MY OWN HOUSE IN ORDER. I'VE LET MY FATHER'S CASE RUN COLD FOR TOO LONG.
YOU STILL DON'T THINK HIS DEATH WAS AN ACCIDENT.
I KNOW IT WASN'T.
THEN CONSIDER ME ON CALL FOR YOU TOO.
SO WHAT DO YOU THINK, JEFF? THIS COULD BE COOL, RIGHT?
YOU AND ME AND THE JUSTICE LEAGUE?
I THINK YOU AND ME IS ENOUGH RIGHT NOW, DANNY.
YOU'RE SAYING THAT BECAUSE THEY DON'T WANT ME, DO THEY? DID YOU TELL THEM I'M IN TOTAL CONTROL OF THIS DEMON SUIT?
WE DO WANT YOU, DANIEL. BOTH OF YOU.
BUT THE SCHOOLS ARE STILL A MESS, DANNY. THOSE KIDS NEED US. LEAVE THE BIG PICTURE TO THE LEAGUE.
I ONLY CAME BECAUSE I THOUGHT IT WAS AN EMERGENCY.
NIGHTWING--
NO.
AQUAMAN, DO YOU HEAR THAT?
A FAINT HEARTBEAT.
"A SMALL ONE."
I AM PLATINUM.

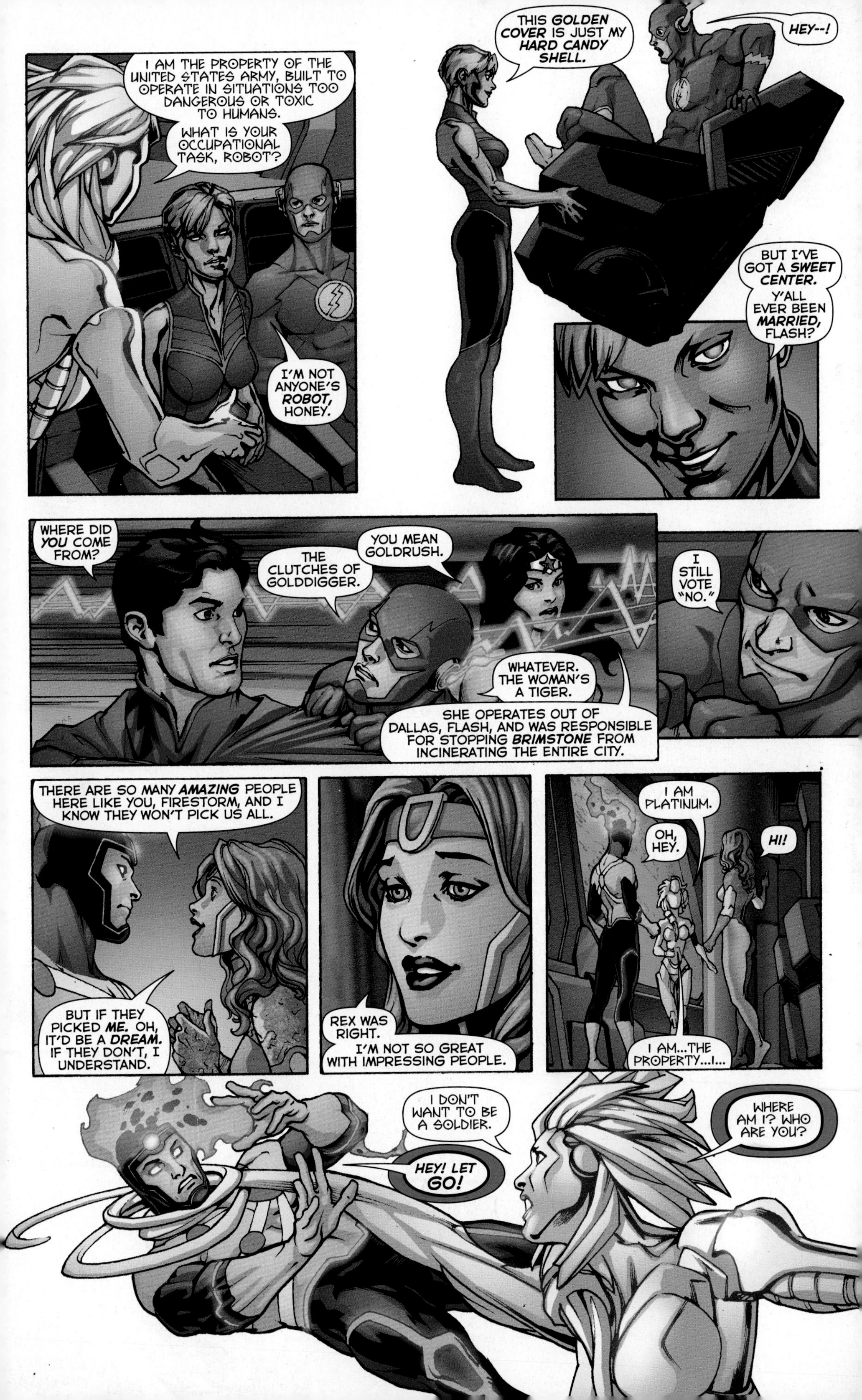
I AM THE PROPERTY OF THE UNITED STATES ARMY, BUILT TO OPERATE IN SITUATIONS TOO DANGEROUS OR TOXIC TO HUMANS.
WHAT IS YOUR OCCUPATIONAL TASK, ROBOT?
I'M NOT ANYONE'S ROBOT, HONEY.
THIS GOLDEN COVER IS JUST MY HARD CANDY SHELL.
HEY--!
BUT I'VE GOT A SWEET CENTER.
Y'ALL EVER BEEN MARRIED, FLASH?
WHERE DID YOU COME FROM?
THE CLUTCHES OF GOLDDIGGER.
YOU MEAN GOLDRUSH.
WHATEVER. THE WOMAN'S A TIGER.
SHE OPERATES OUT OF DALLAS, FLASH, AND WAS RESPONSIBLE FOR STOPPING BRIMSTONE FROM INCINERATING THE ENTIRE CITY.
I STILL VOTE "NO."
THERE ARE SO MANY AMAZING PEOPLE HERE LIKE YOU, FIRESTORM, AND I KNOW THEY WON'T PICK US ALL.
BUT IF THEY PICKED ME. OH, IT'D BE A DREAM. IF THEY DON'T, I UNDERSTAND.
REX WAS RIGHT.
I'M NOT SO GREAT WITH IMPRESSING PEOPLE.
I AM PLATINUM.
OH, HEY.
HI!
I AM...THE PROPERTY...I...
I DON'T WANT TO BE A SOLDIER.
HEY! LET GO!
WHERE AM I? WHO ARE YOU?

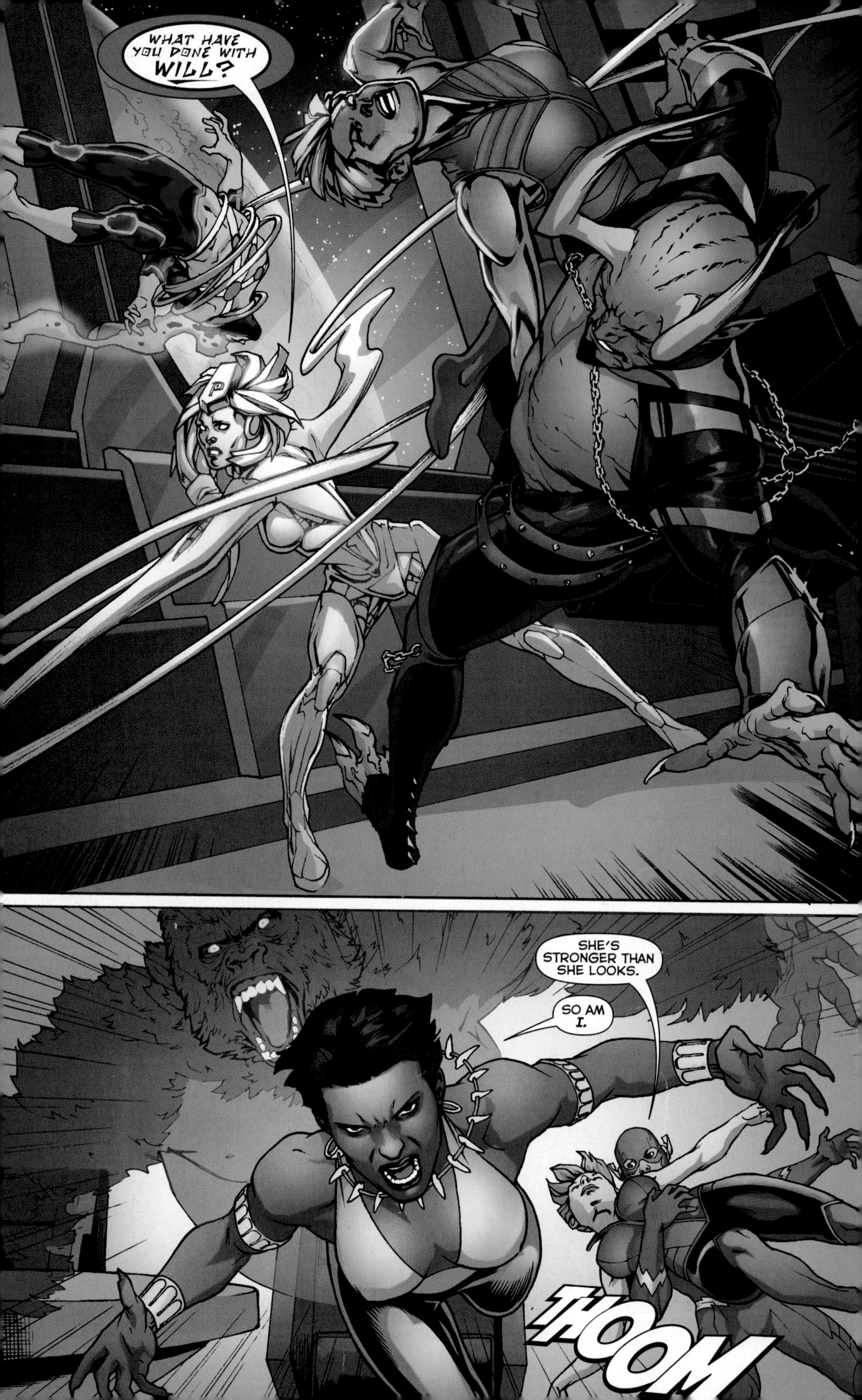
WHAT HAVE YOU DONE WITH WILL?
SHE'S STRONGER THAN SHE LOOKS.
SO AM I.
THOOM

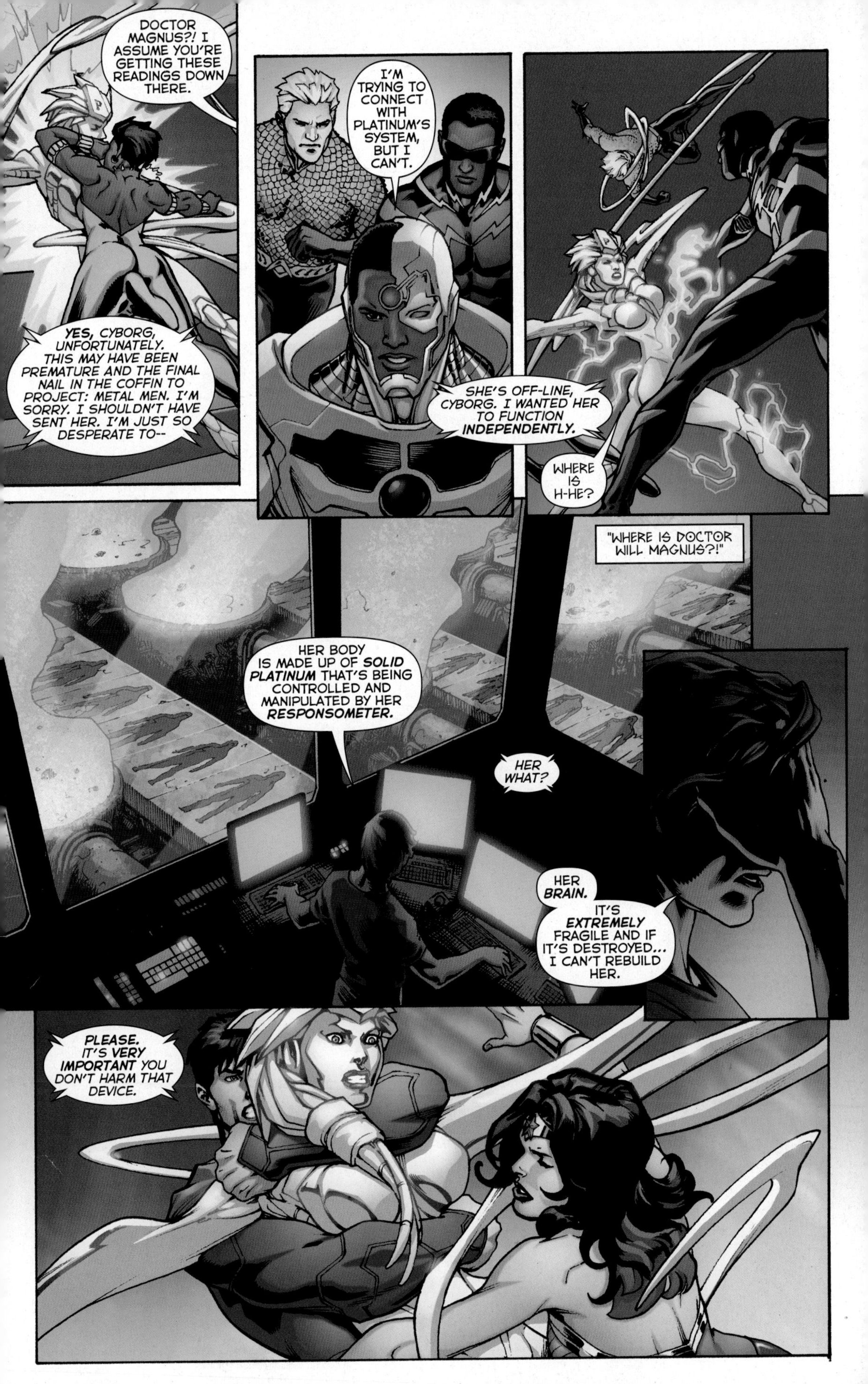
DOCTOR MAGNUS?! I ASSUME YOU'RE GETTING THESE READINGS DOWN THERE.
YES, CYBORG, UNFORTUNATELY. THIS MAY HAVE BEEN PREMATURE AND THE FINAL NAIL IN THE COFFIN TO PROJECT: METAL MEN. I'M SORRY. I SHOULDN'T HAVE SENT HER. I'M JUST SO DESPERATE TO--
I'M TRYING TO CONNECT WITH PLATINUM'S SYSTEM, BUT I CAN'T.
SHE'S OFF-LINE, CYBORG. I WANTED HER TO FUNCTION INDEPENDENTLY.
WHERE IS H-HE?
"WHERE IS DOCTOR WILL MAGNUS?!"
HER BODY IS MADE UP OF SOLID PLATINUM THAT'S BEING CONTROLLED AND MANIPULATED BY HER RESPONSOMETER.
HER WHAT?
HER BRAIN. IT'S EXTREMELY FRAGILE AND IF IT'S DESTROYED... I CAN'T REBUILD HER.
PLEASE. IT'S VERY IMPORTANT YOU DON'T HARM THAT DEVICE.

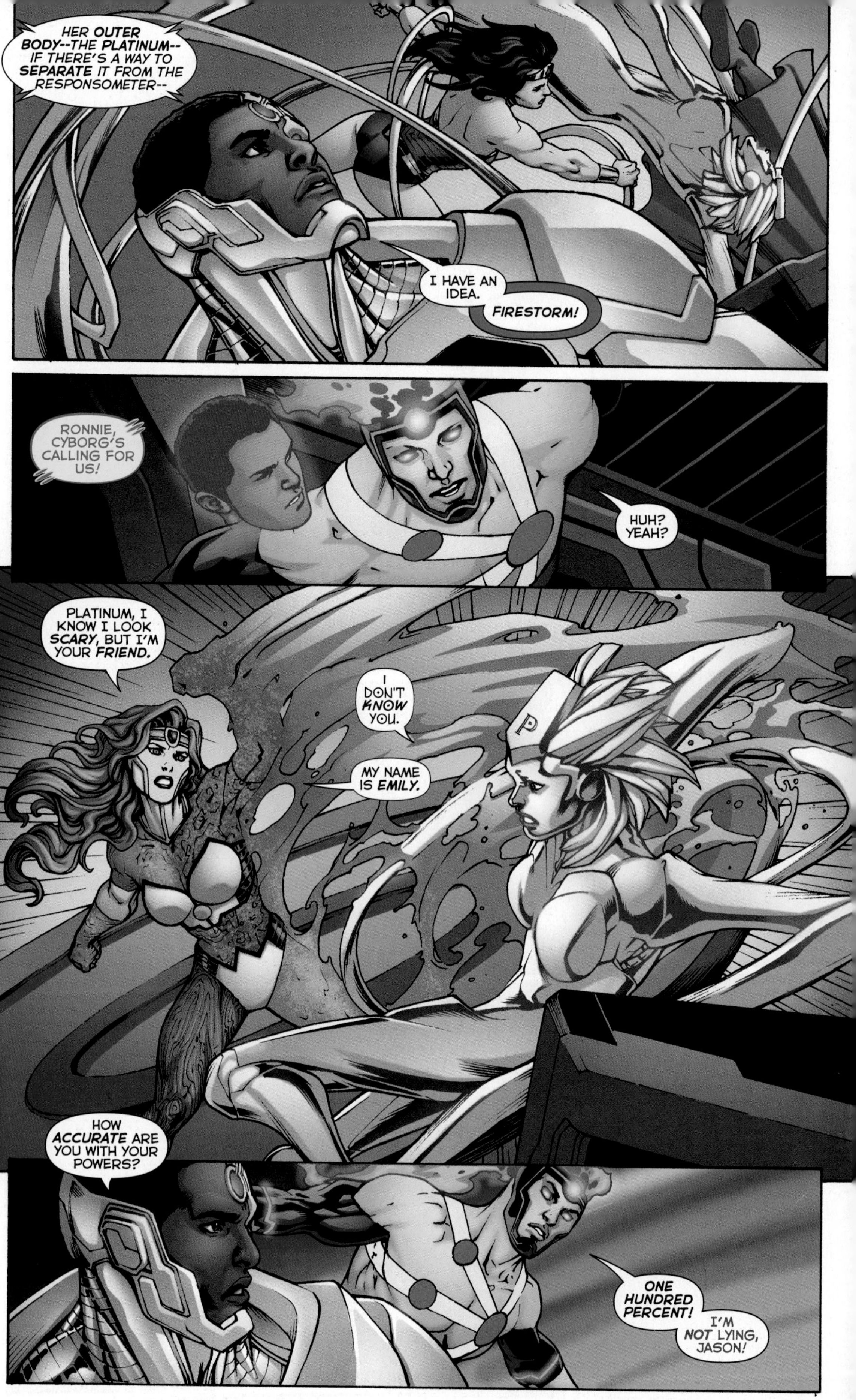
HER OUTER BODY--THE PLATINUM--IF THERE'S A WAY TO SEPARATE IT FROM THE RESPONSOMETER--
I HAVE AN IDEA.
FIRESTORM!
RONNIE, CYBORG'S CALLING FOR US!
HUH? YEAH?
PLATINUM, I KNOW I LOOK SCARY, BUT I'M YOUR FRIEND.
I DON'T KNOW YOU.
MY NAME IS EMILY.
HOW ACCURATE ARE YOU WITH YOUR POWERS?
ONE HUNDRED PERCENT!
I'M NOT LYING, JASON!

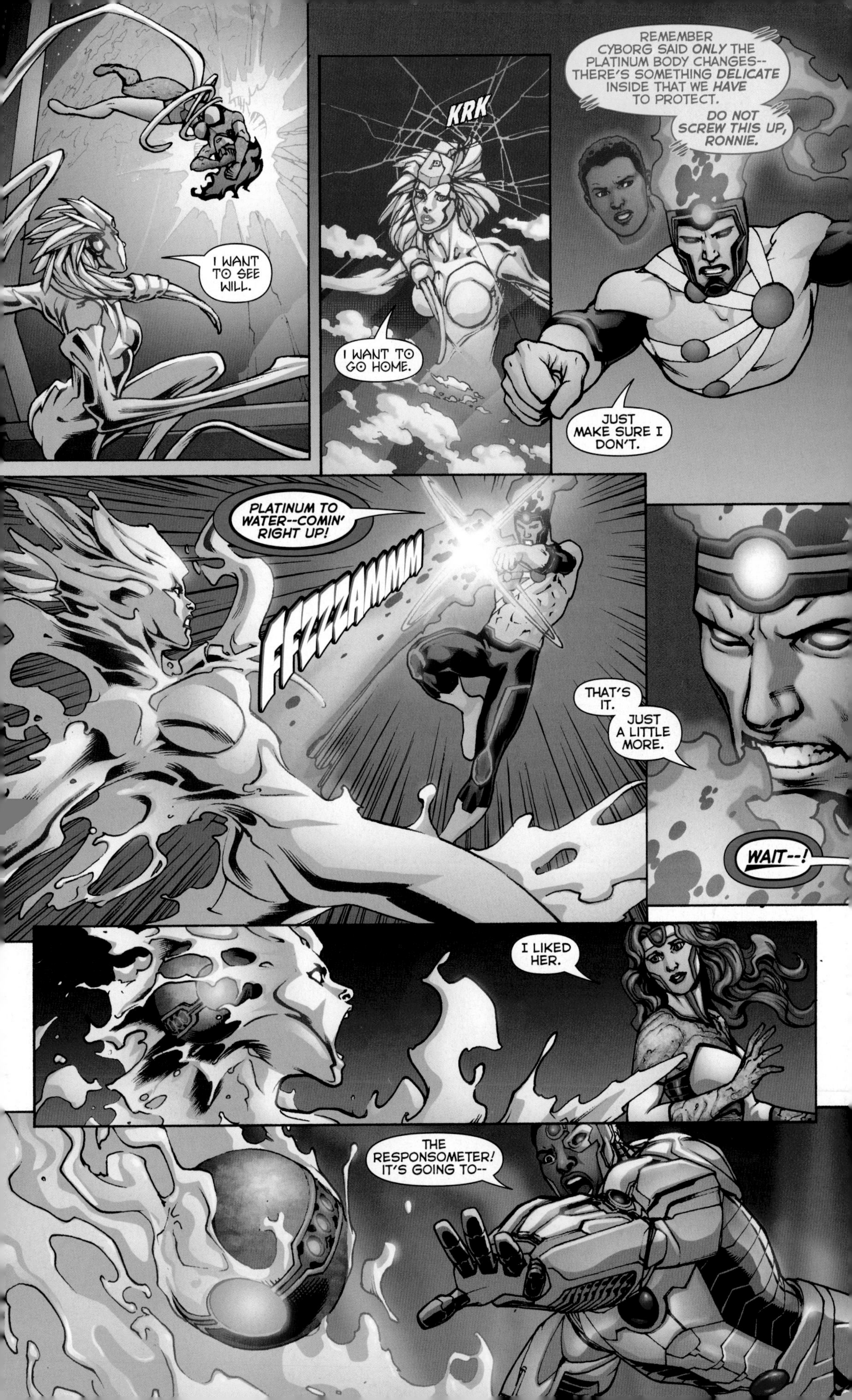

I WANT TO SEE WILL.
KRK
I WANT TO GO HOME.
REMEMBER CYBORG SAID ONLY THE PLATINUM BODY CHANGES-- THERE'S SOMETHING DELICATE INSIDE THAT WE HAVE TO PROTECT.
DO NOT SCREW THIS UP, RONNIE.
JUST MAKE SURE I DON'T.
PLATINUM TO WATER--COMIN' RIGHT UP!
FFZZZAMMM
THAT'S IT.
JUST A LITTLE MORE.
WAIT--!
I LIKED HER.
THE RESPONSOMETER! IT'S GOING TO--

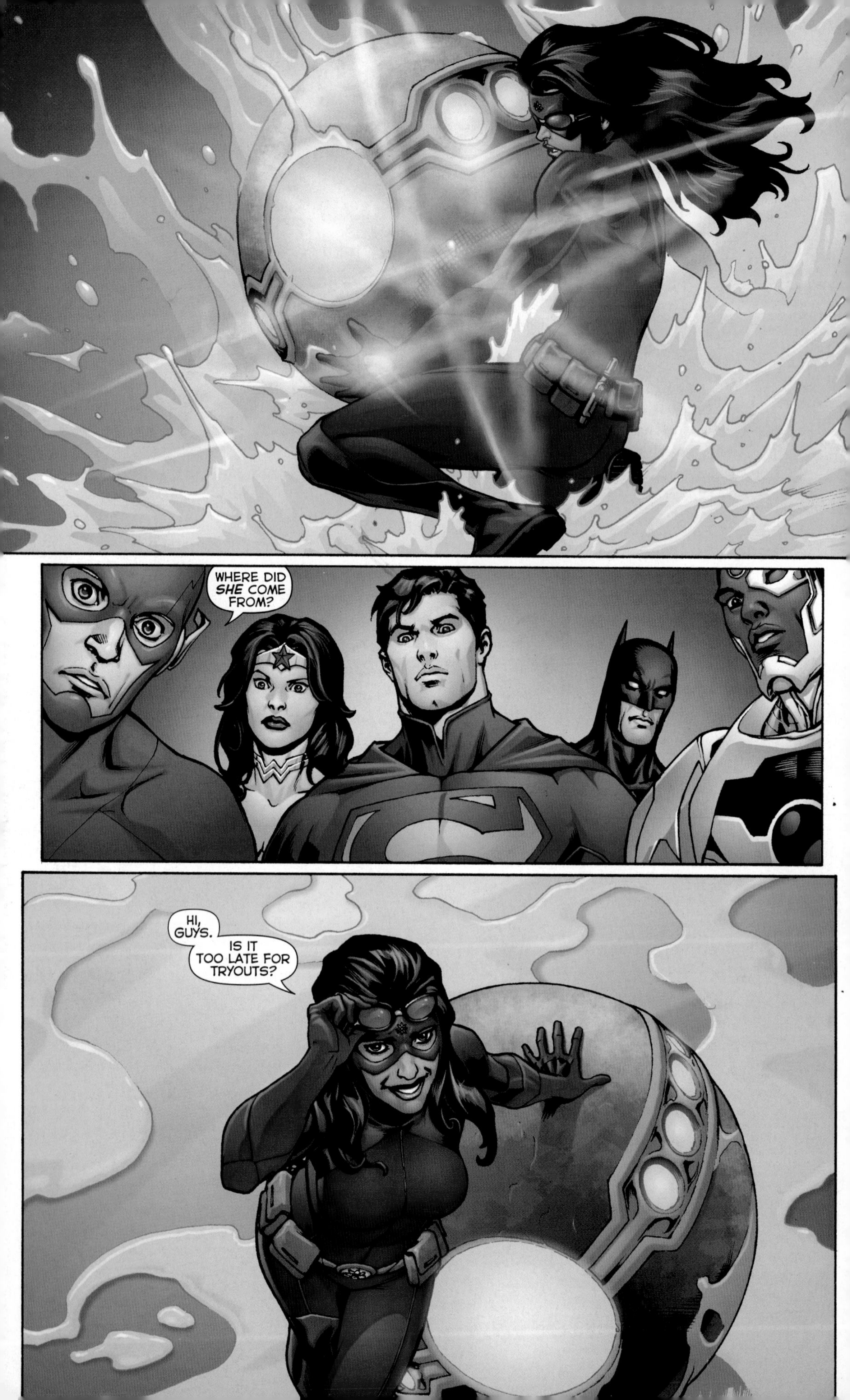
WHERE DID *SHE* COME FROM?
HI, GUYS.
IS IT TOO LATE FOR TRYOUTS?

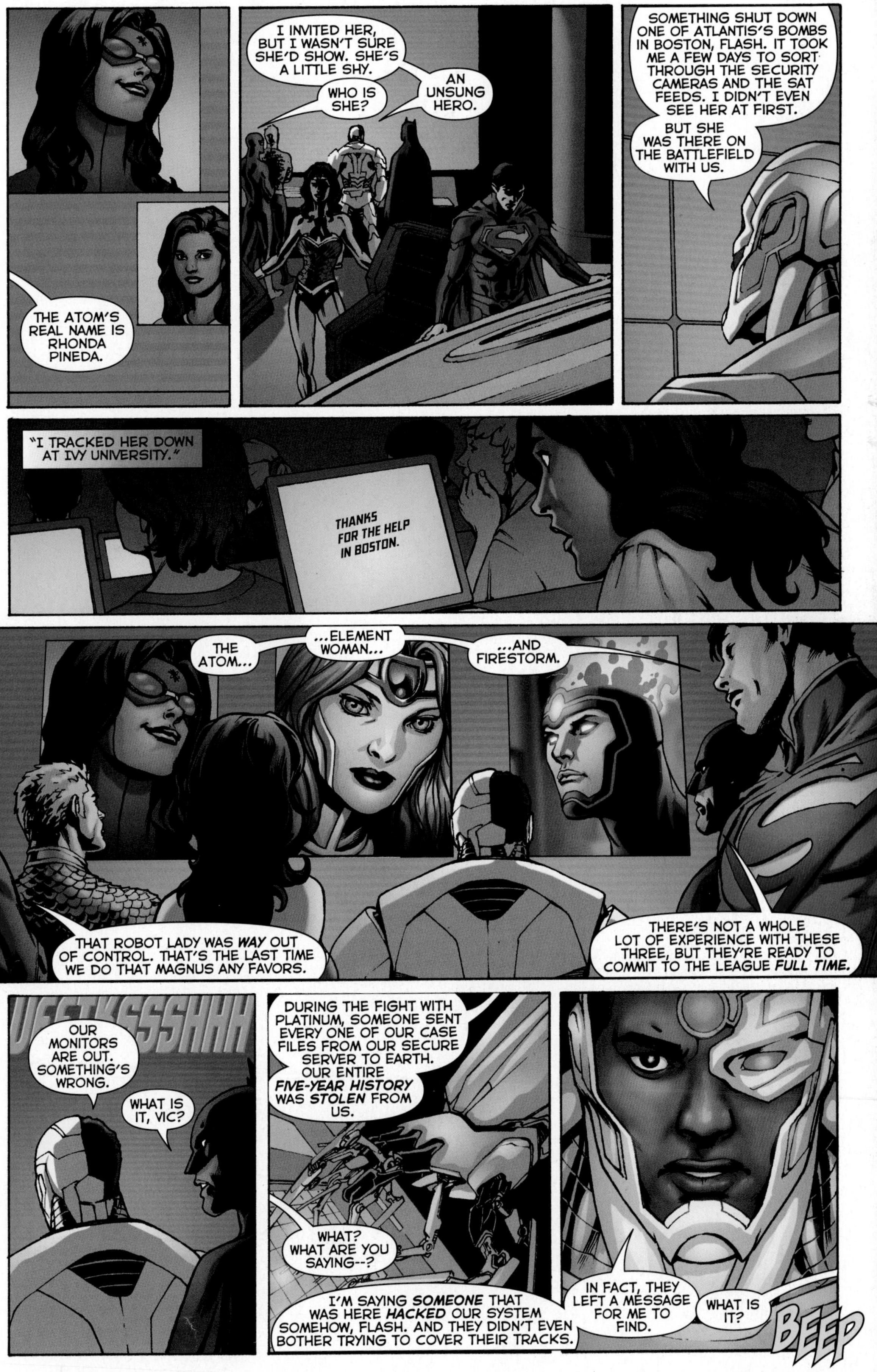
THE ATOM'S REAL NAME IS RHONDA PINEDA.
I INVITED HER, BUT I WASN'T SURE SHE'D SHOW. SHE'S A LITTLE SHY.
WHO IS SHE?
AN UNSUNG HERO.
SOMETHING SHUT DOWN ONE OF ATLANTIS'S BOMBS IN BOSTON, FLASH. IT TOOK ME A FEW DAYS TO SORT THROUGH THE SECURITY CAMERAS AND THE SAT FEEDS. I DIDN'T EVEN SEE HER AT FIRST.
BUT SHE WAS THERE ON THE BATTLEFIELD WITH US.
"I TRACKED HER DOWN AT IVY UNIVERSITY."
THANKS FOR THE HELP IN BOSTON.
THE ATOM...
...ELEMENT WOMAN...
...AND FIRESTORM.
THAT ROBOT LADY WAS *WAY* OUT OF CONTROL. THAT'S THE LAST TIME WE DO THAT MAGNUS ANY FAVORS.
THERE'S NOT A WHOLE LOT OF EXPERIENCE WITH THESE THREE, BUT THEY'RE READY TO COMMIT TO THE LEAGUE *FULL TIME.*
VFFTKSSSHHH
OUR MONITORS ARE OUT. SOMETHING'S WRONG.
WHAT IS IT, VIC?
DURING THE FIGHT WITH PLATINUM, SOMEONE SENT EVERY ONE OF OUR CASE FILES FROM OUR SECURE SERVER TO EARTH. OUR ENTIRE ***FIVE-YEAR HISTORY*** WAS ***STOLEN*** FROM US.
WHAT? WHAT ARE YOU SAYING--?
I'M SAYING ***SOMEONE*** THAT WAS HERE ***HACKED*** OUR SYSTEM SOMEHOW, FLASH. AND THEY DIDN'T EVEN BOTHER TRYING TO COVER THEIR TRACKS.
IN FACT, THEY LEFT A MESSAGE FOR ME TO FIND.
WHAT IS IT?
BEEP

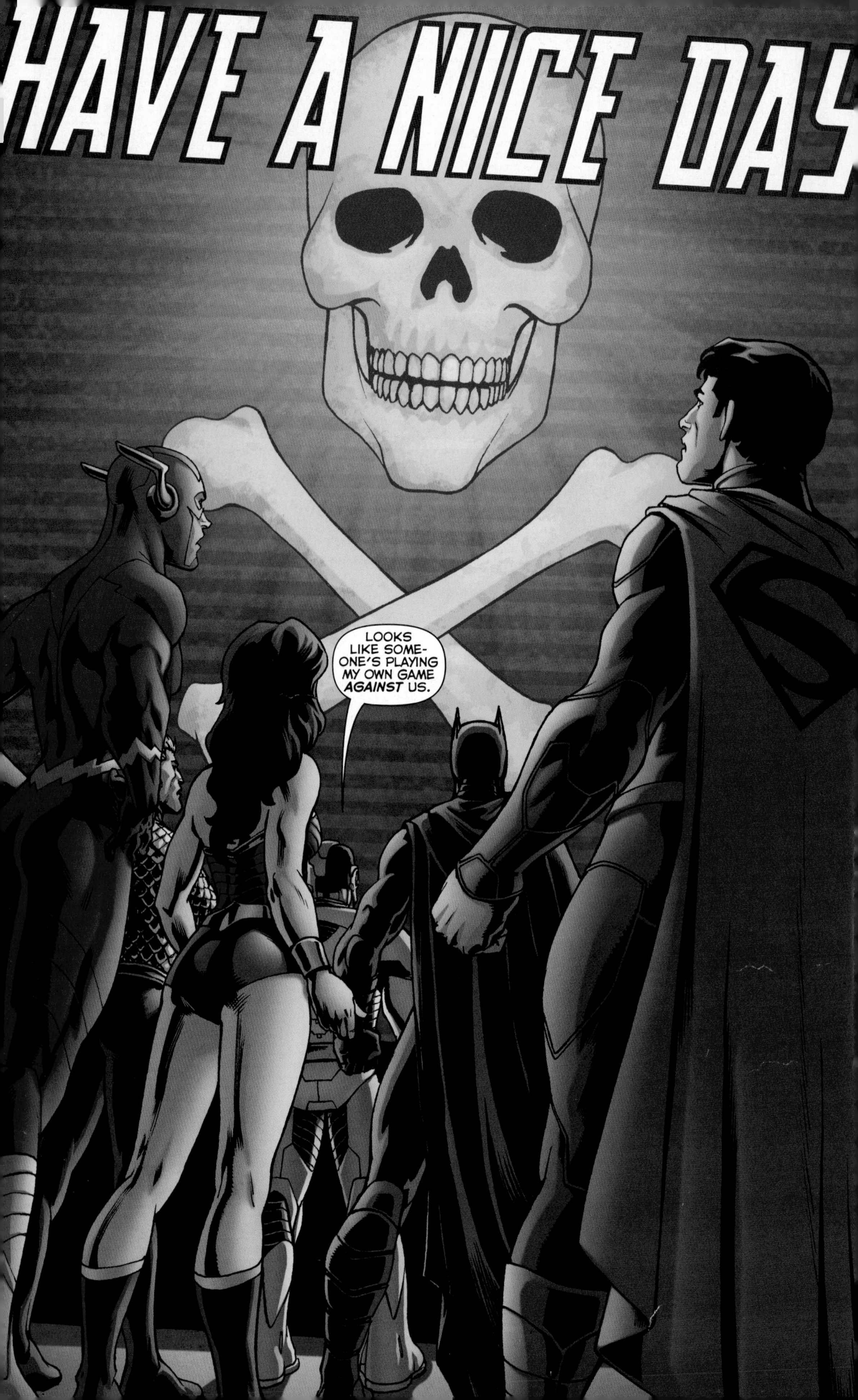
HAVE A NICE DAY
LOOKS LIKE SOME-ONE'S PLAYING MY OWN GAME *AGAINST* US.

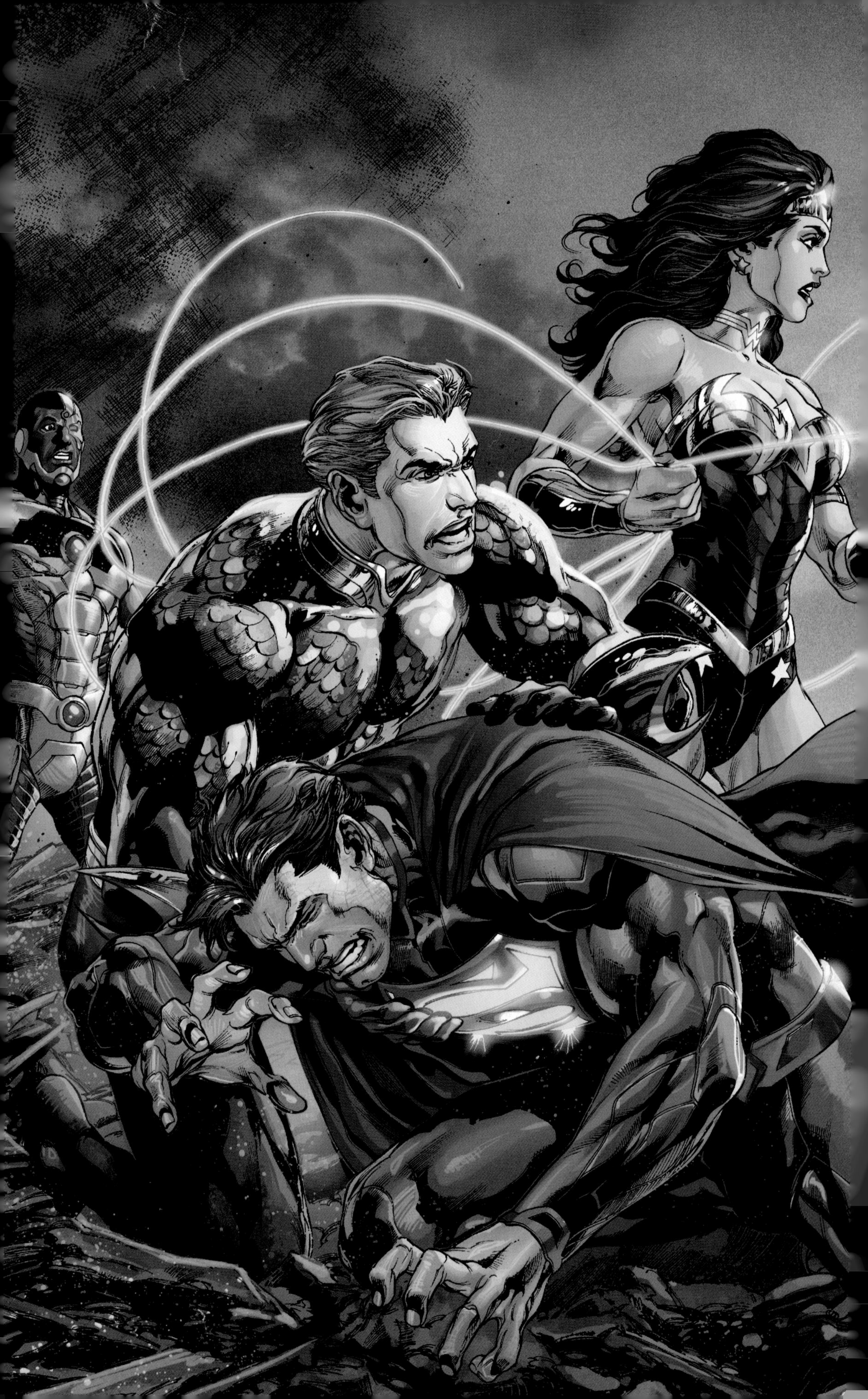

WAR GAMES

GEOFF JOHNS writer **IVAN REIS** penciller **JOE PRADO, OCLAIR ALBERT** and **JONATHAN GLAPION** inkers
ROD REIS colorist **IVAN REIS, JOE PRADO** and **ROD REIS** cover artists

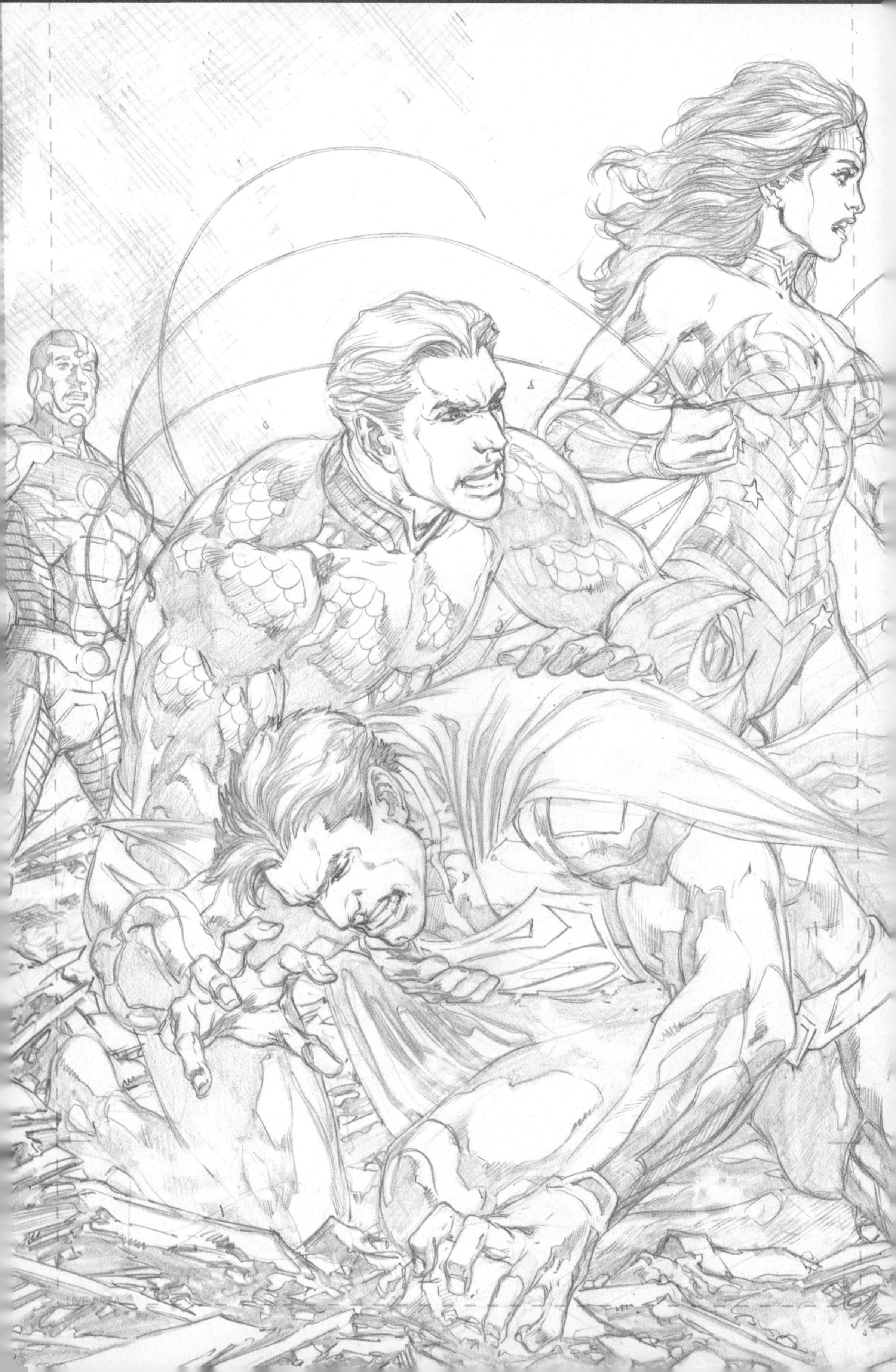

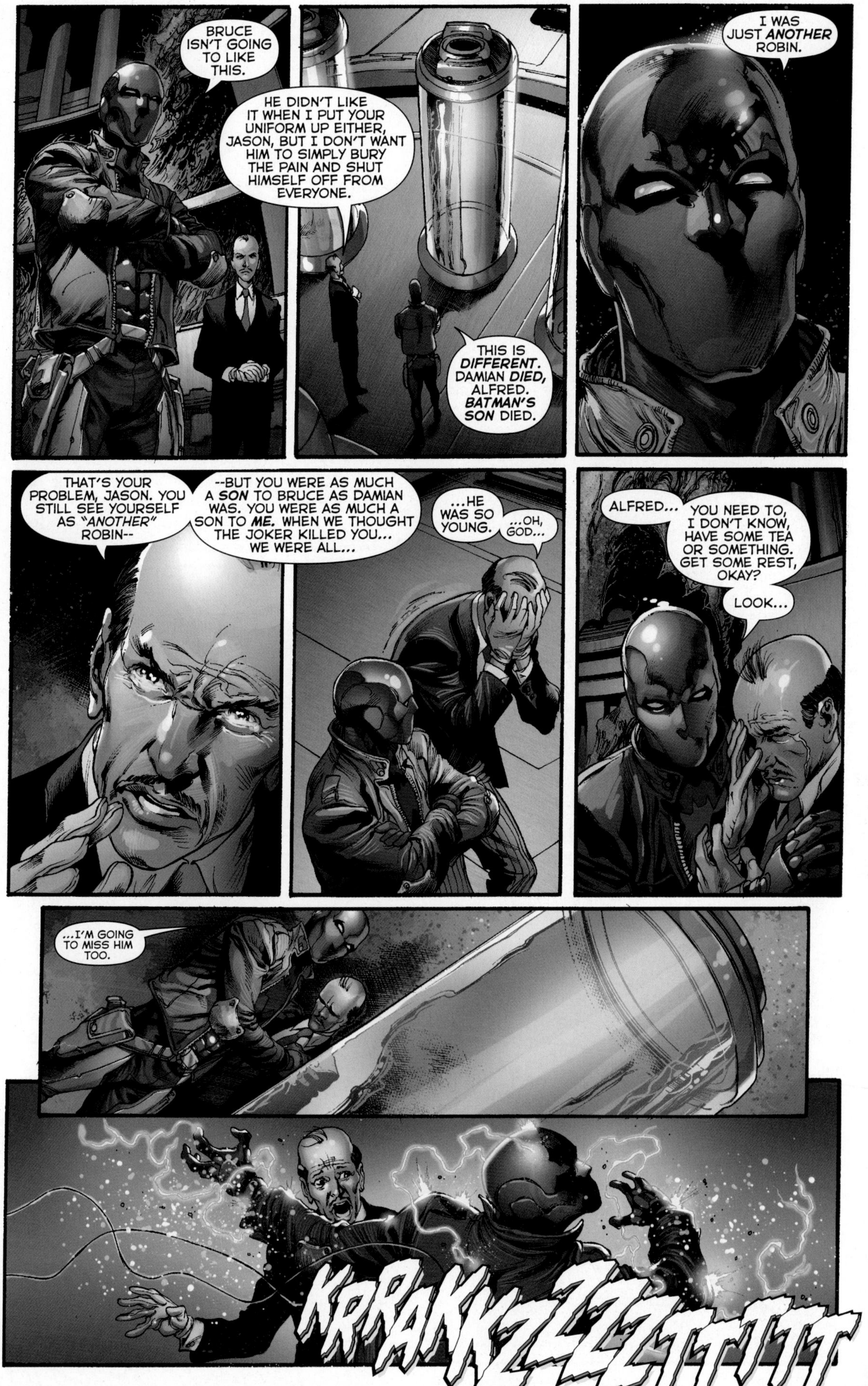
BRUCE ISN'T GOING TO LIKE THIS.
HE DIDN'T LIKE IT WHEN I PUT YOUR UNIFORM UP EITHER, JASON, BUT I DON'T WANT HIM TO SIMPLY BURY THE PAIN AND SHUT HIMSELF OFF FROM EVERYONE.
THIS IS *DIFFERENT*. DAMIAN *DIED,* ALFRED. *BATMAN'S SON* DIED.
I WAS JUST *ANOTHER* ROBIN.
THAT'S YOUR PROBLEM, JASON. YOU STILL SEE YOURSELF AS *"ANOTHER"* ROBIN--
--BUT YOU WERE AS MUCH A *SON* TO BRUCE AS DAMIAN WAS. YOU WERE AS MUCH A SON TO *ME.* WHEN WE THOUGHT THE JOKER KILLED YOU... WE WERE ALL...
...HE WAS SO YOUNG.
...OH, GOD...
ALFRED...
YOU NEED TO, I DON'T KNOW, HAVE SOME TEA OR SOMETHING. GET SOME REST, OKAY?
LOOK...
...I'M GOING TO MISS HIM TOO.
KRRAKKZZZZTTTTTT

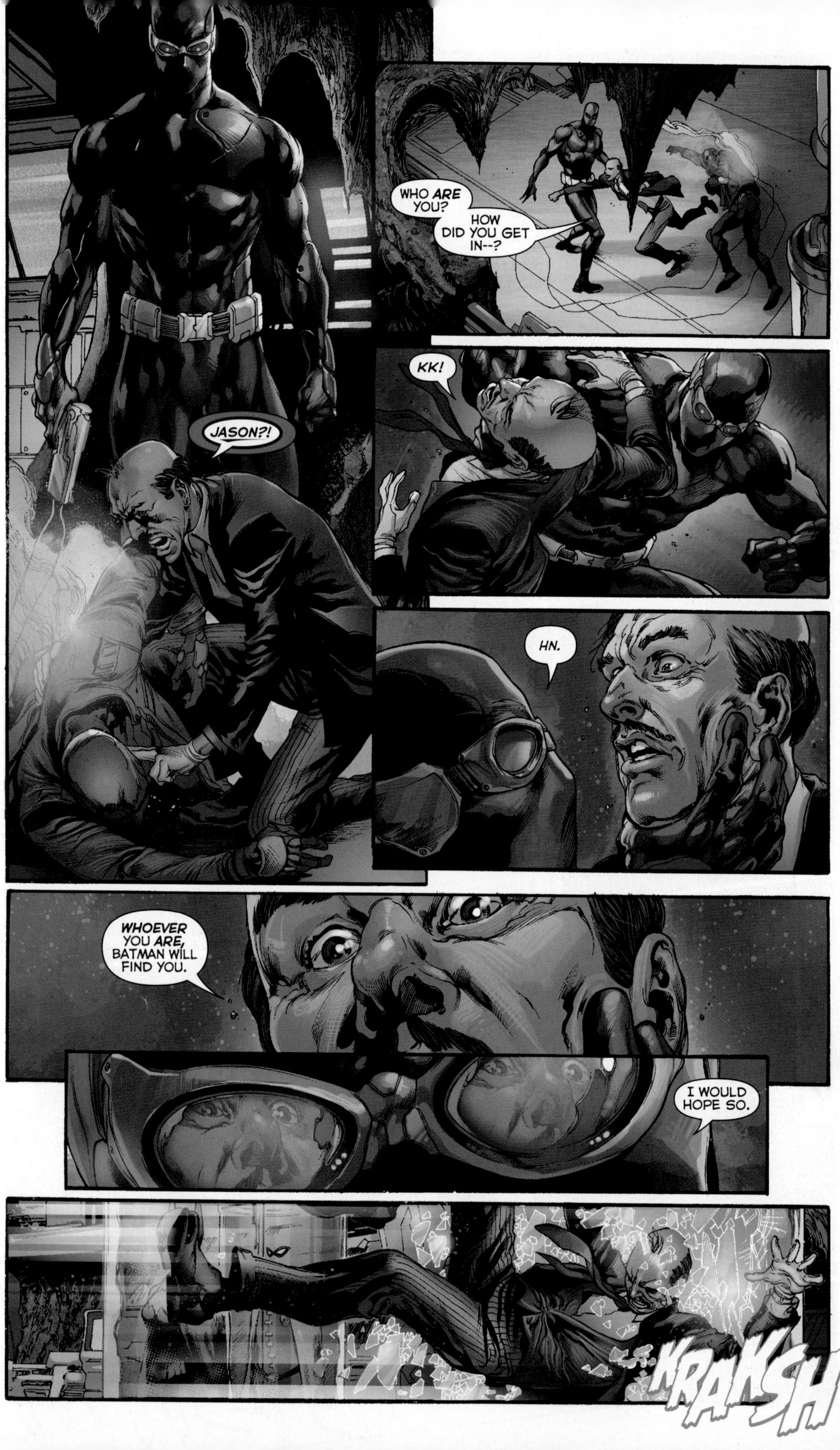
JASON?!
WHO ARE YOU?
HOW DID YOU GET IN--?
KK!
HN.
WHOEVER YOU ARE, BATMAN WILL FIND YOU.
I WOULD HOPE SO.
KRAKSH

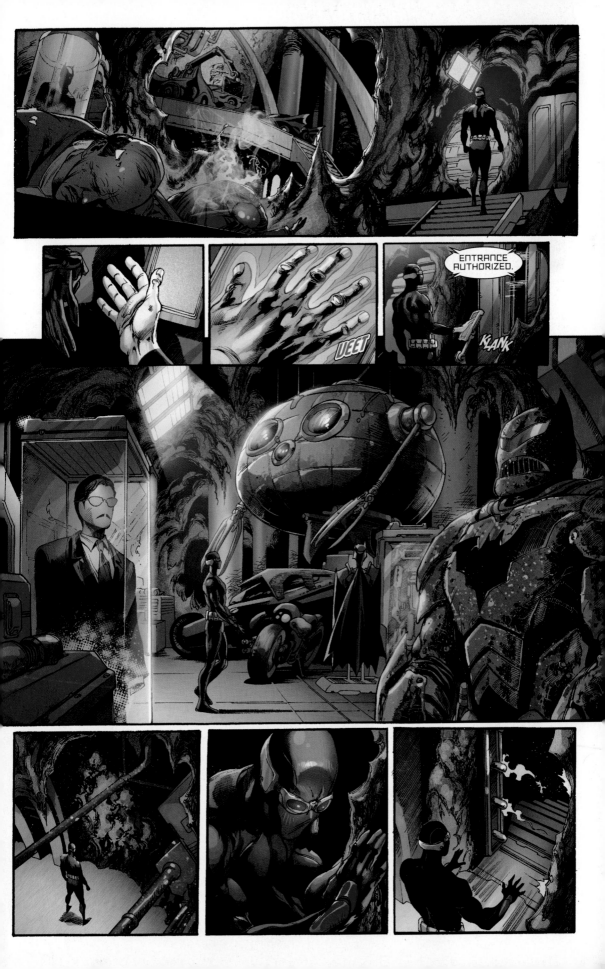

ENTRANCE
AUTHORIZED.

UEET

KLANK

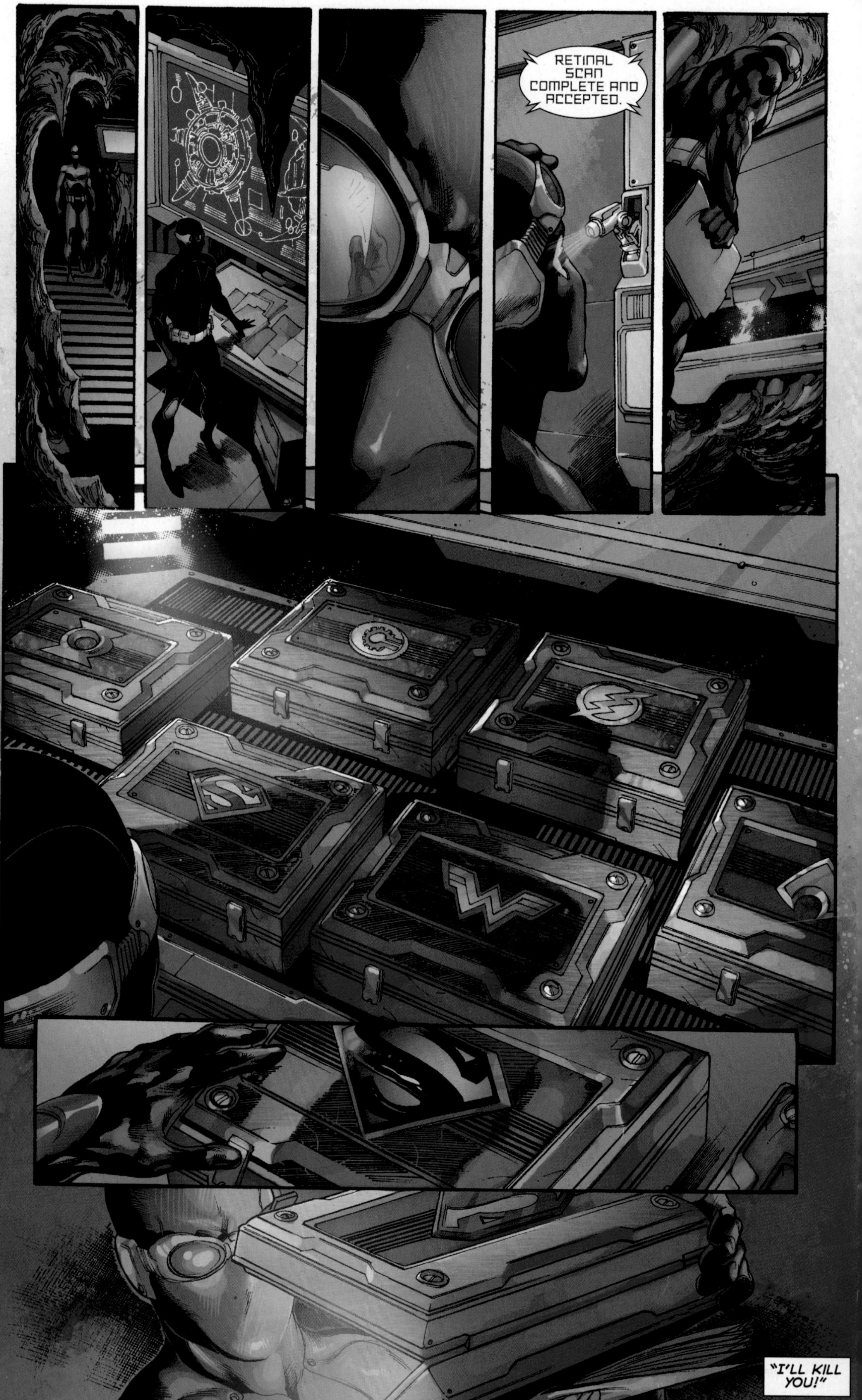
RETINAL SCAN COMPLETE AND ACCEPTED.
"I'LL KILL YOU!"

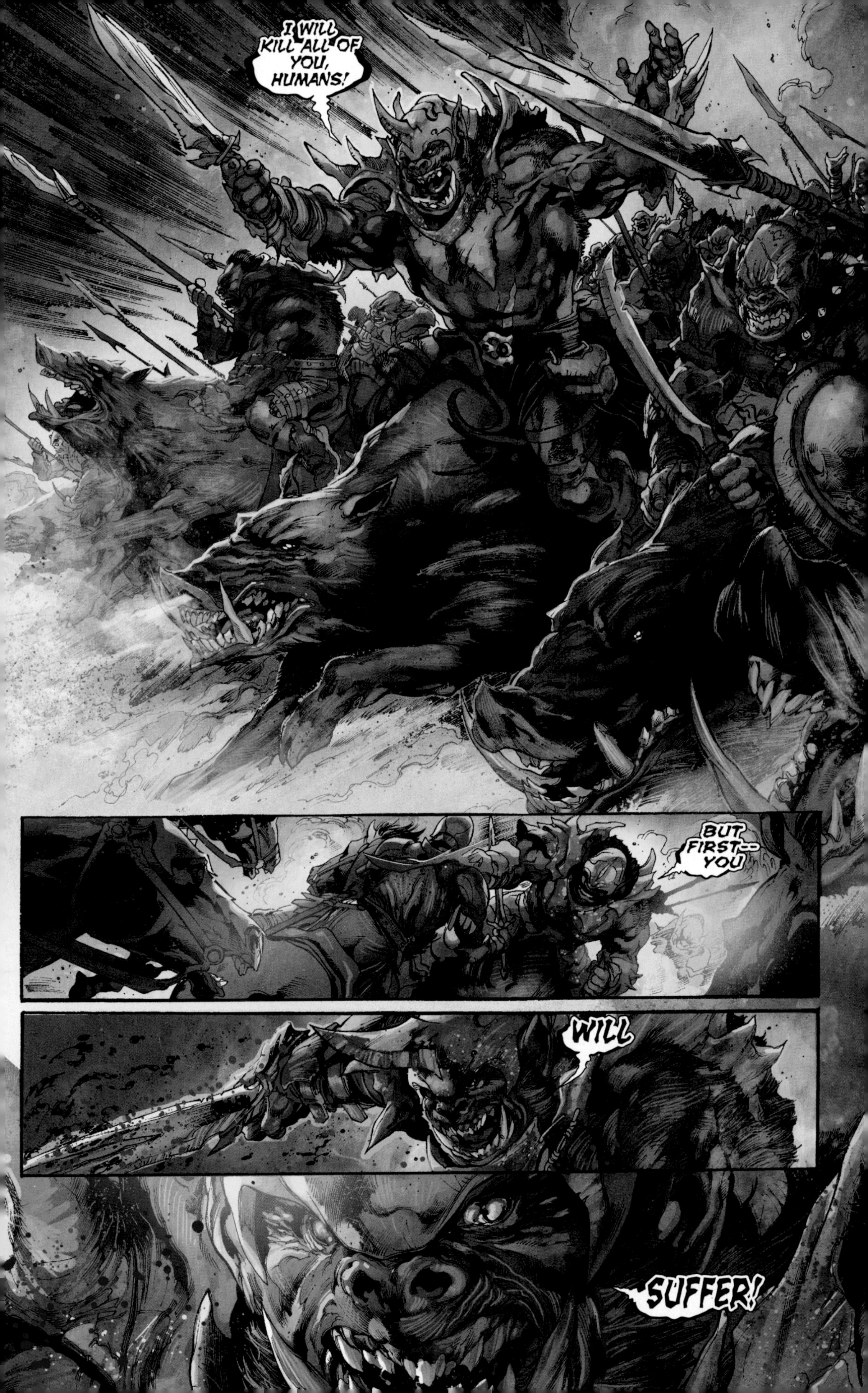
I WILL KILL ALL OF YOU, HUMANS!
BUT FIRST-- YOU
WILL
SUFFER!

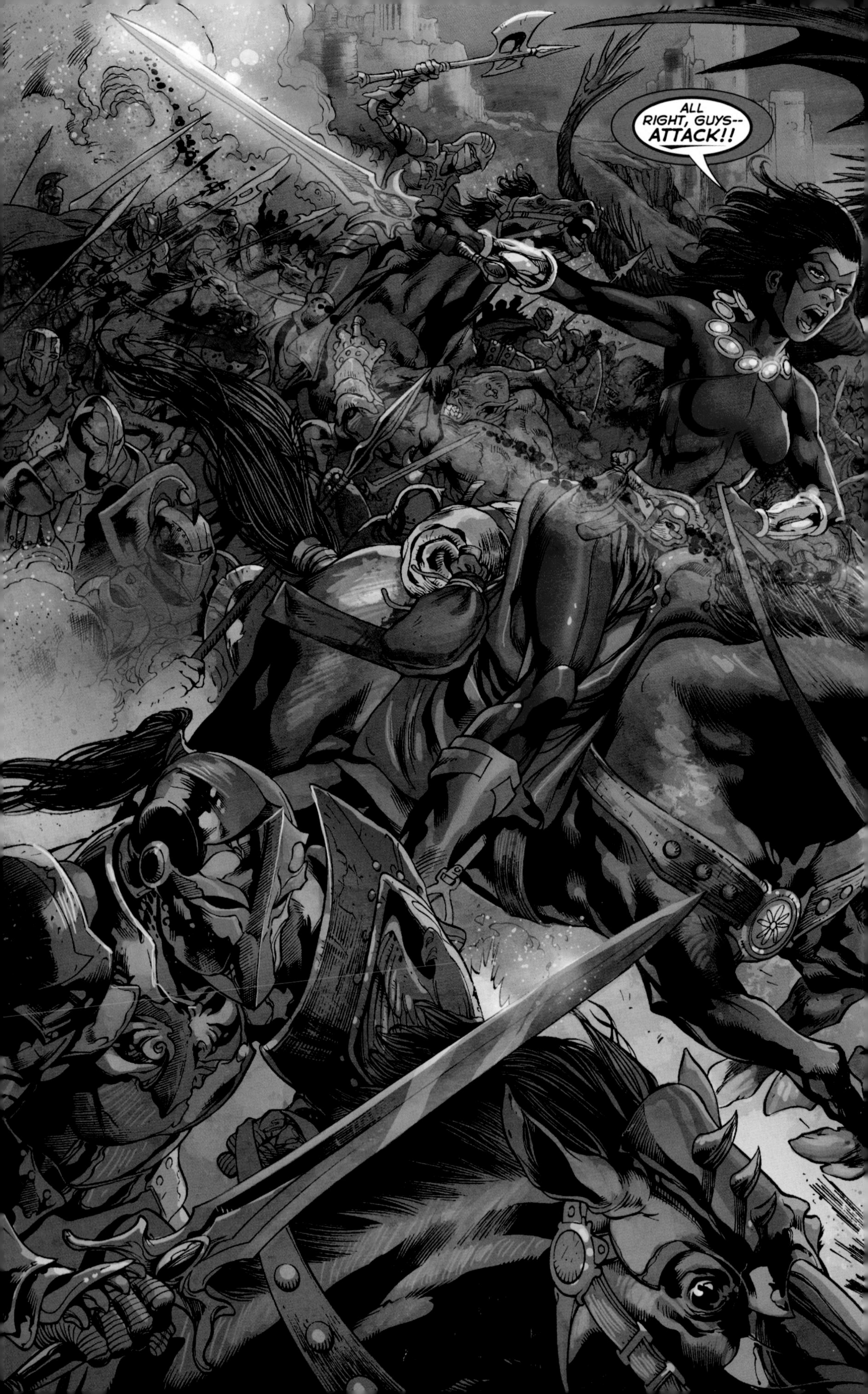
ALL RIGHT, GUYS-- ATTACK!!

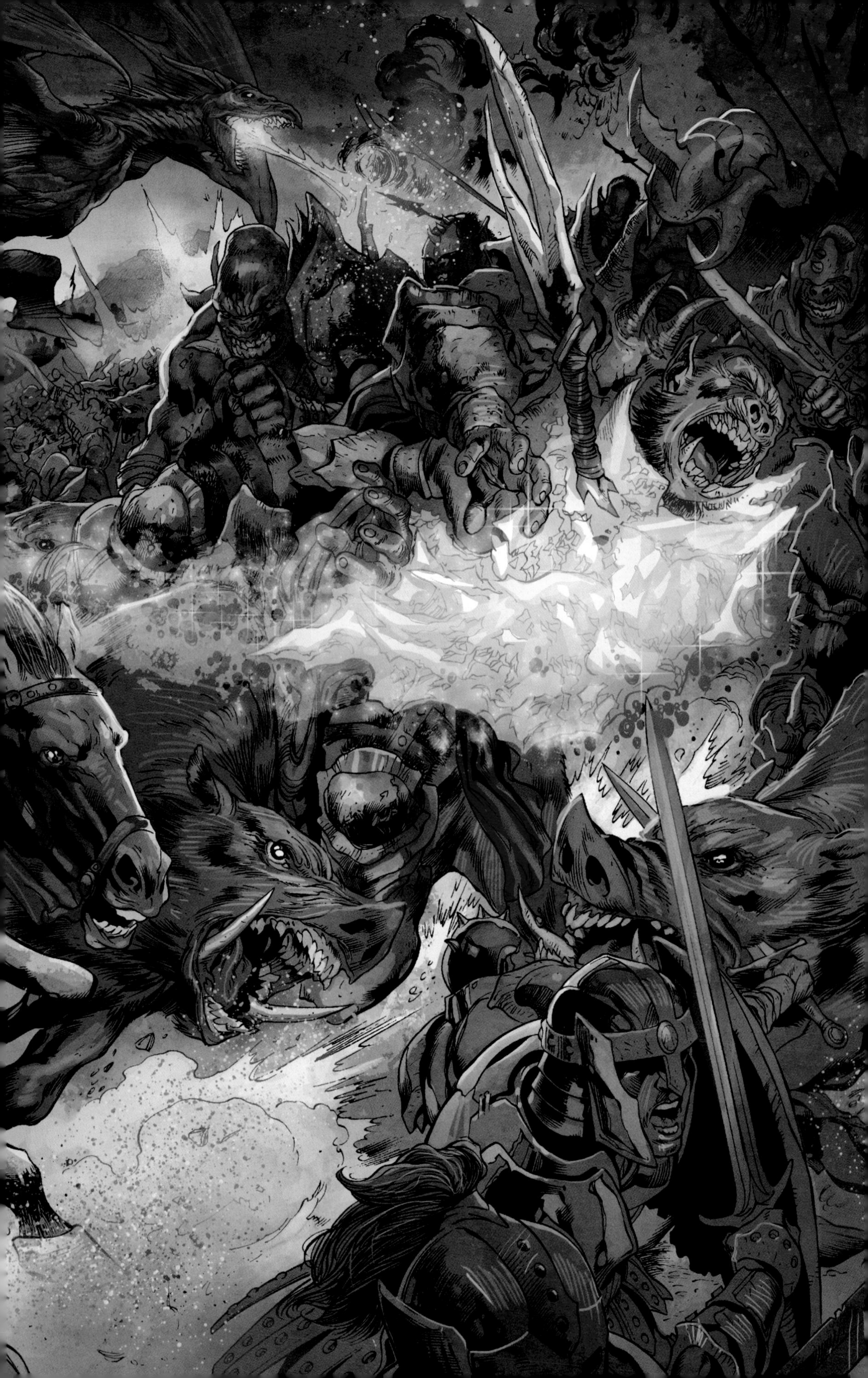

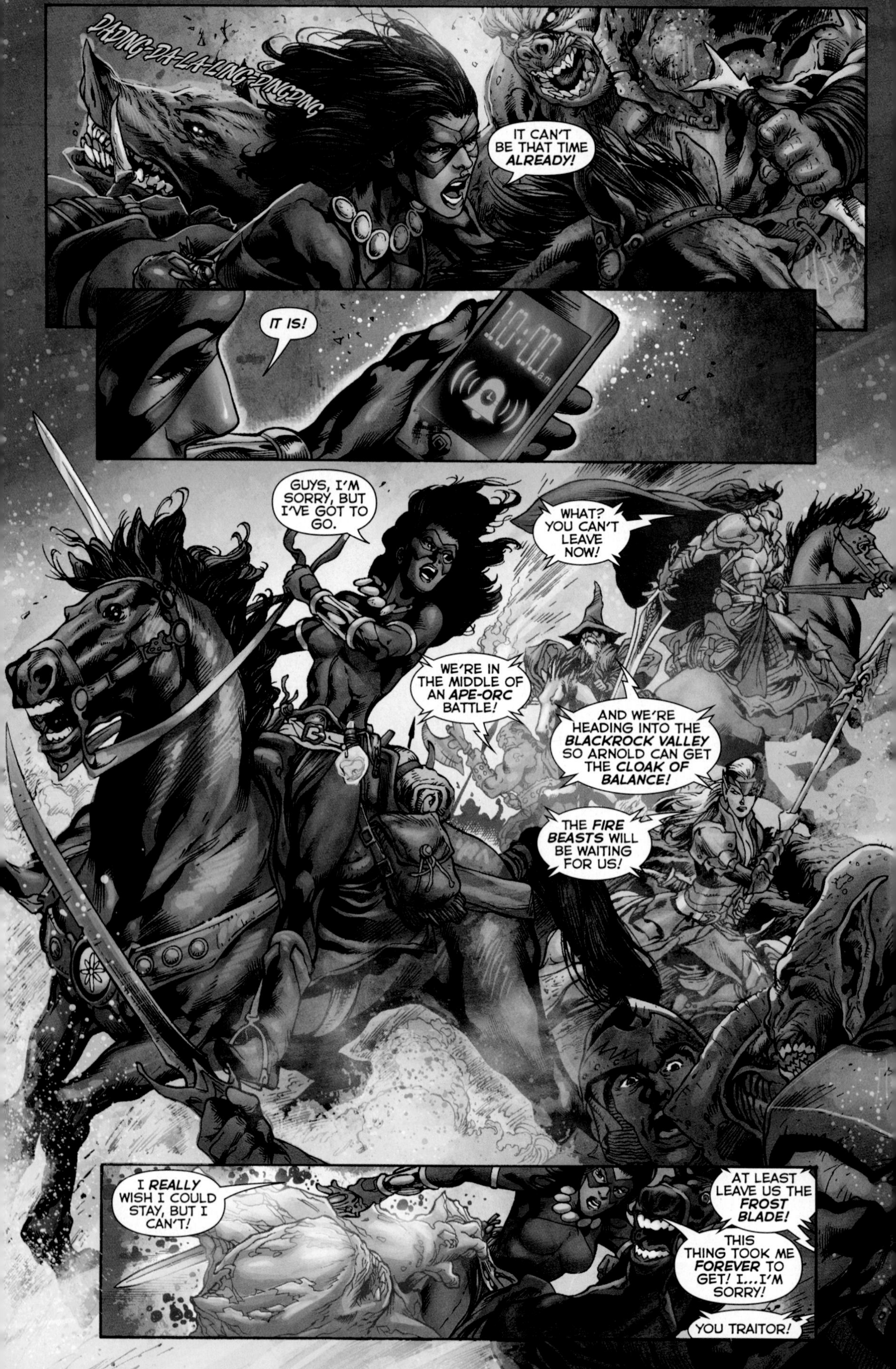
DADING-DA-LA-LING-DINGDING
IT CAN'T BE THAT TIME ALREADY!
IT IS!
10:00 a.m.
GUYS, I'M SORRY, BUT I'VE GOT TO GO.
WHAT? YOU CAN'T LEAVE NOW!
WE'RE IN THE MIDDLE OF AN APE-ORC BATTLE!
AND WE'RE HEADING INTO THE BLACKROCK VALLEY SO ARNOLD CAN GET THE CLOAK OF BALANCE!
THE FIRE BEASTS WILL BE WAITING FOR US!
I REALLY WISH I COULD STAY, BUT I CAN'T!
AT LEAST LEAVE US THE FROST BLADE!
THIS THING TOOK ME FOREVER TO GET! I...I'M SORRY!
YOU TRAITOR!

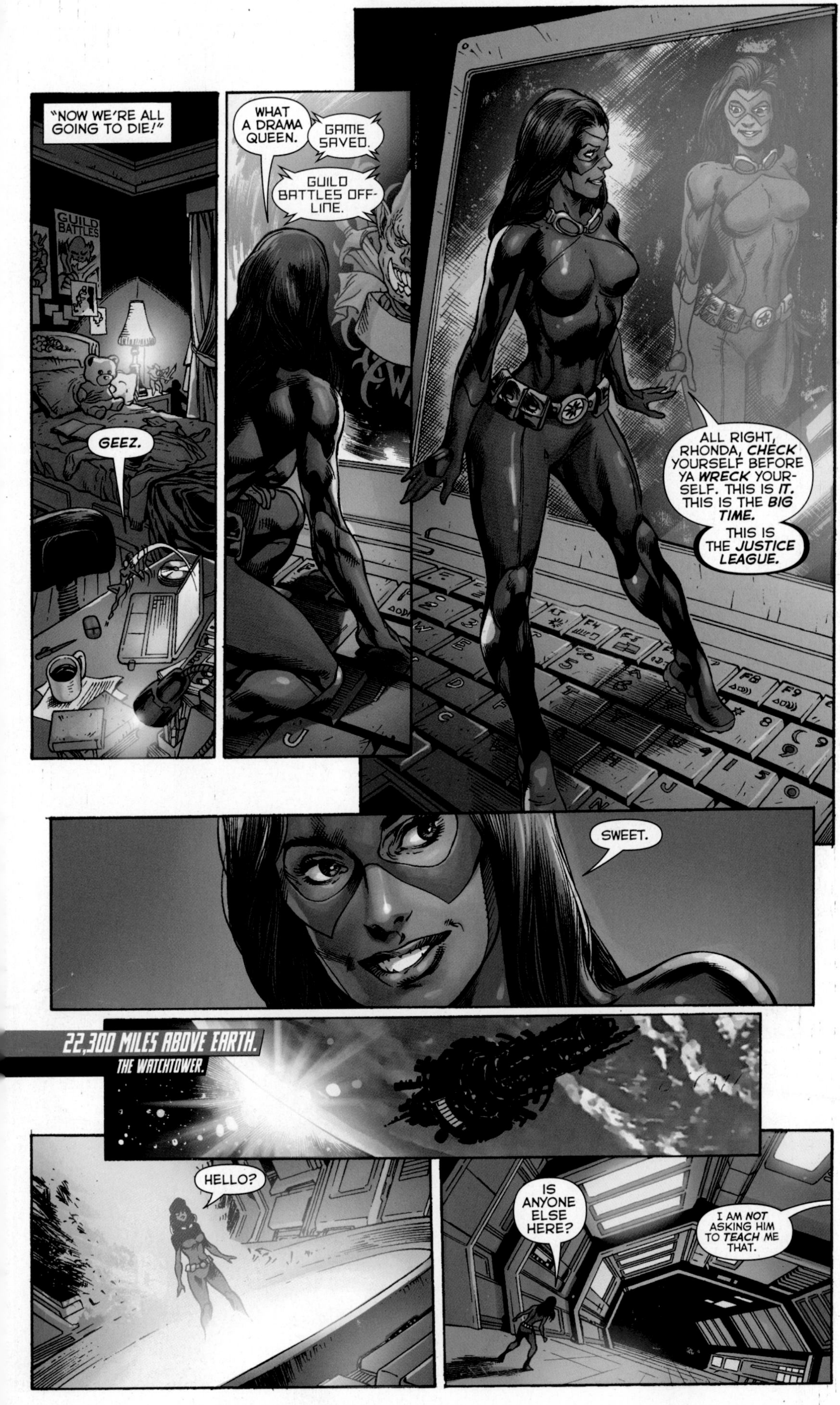
"NOW WE'RE ALL GOING TO DIE!"
GUILD BATTLES
GEEZ.
WHAT A DRAMA QUEEN.
GAME SAVED.
GUILD BATTLES OFF-LINE.
ALL RIGHT, RHONDA, CHECK YOURSELF BEFORE YA WRECK YOURSELF. THIS IS IT. THIS IS THE BIG TIME.
THIS IS THE JUSTICE LEAGUE.
SWEET.
22,300 MILES ABOVE EARTH.
THE WATCHTOWER.
HELLO?
IS ANYONE ELSE HERE?
I AM NOT ASKING HIM TO TEACH ME THAT.

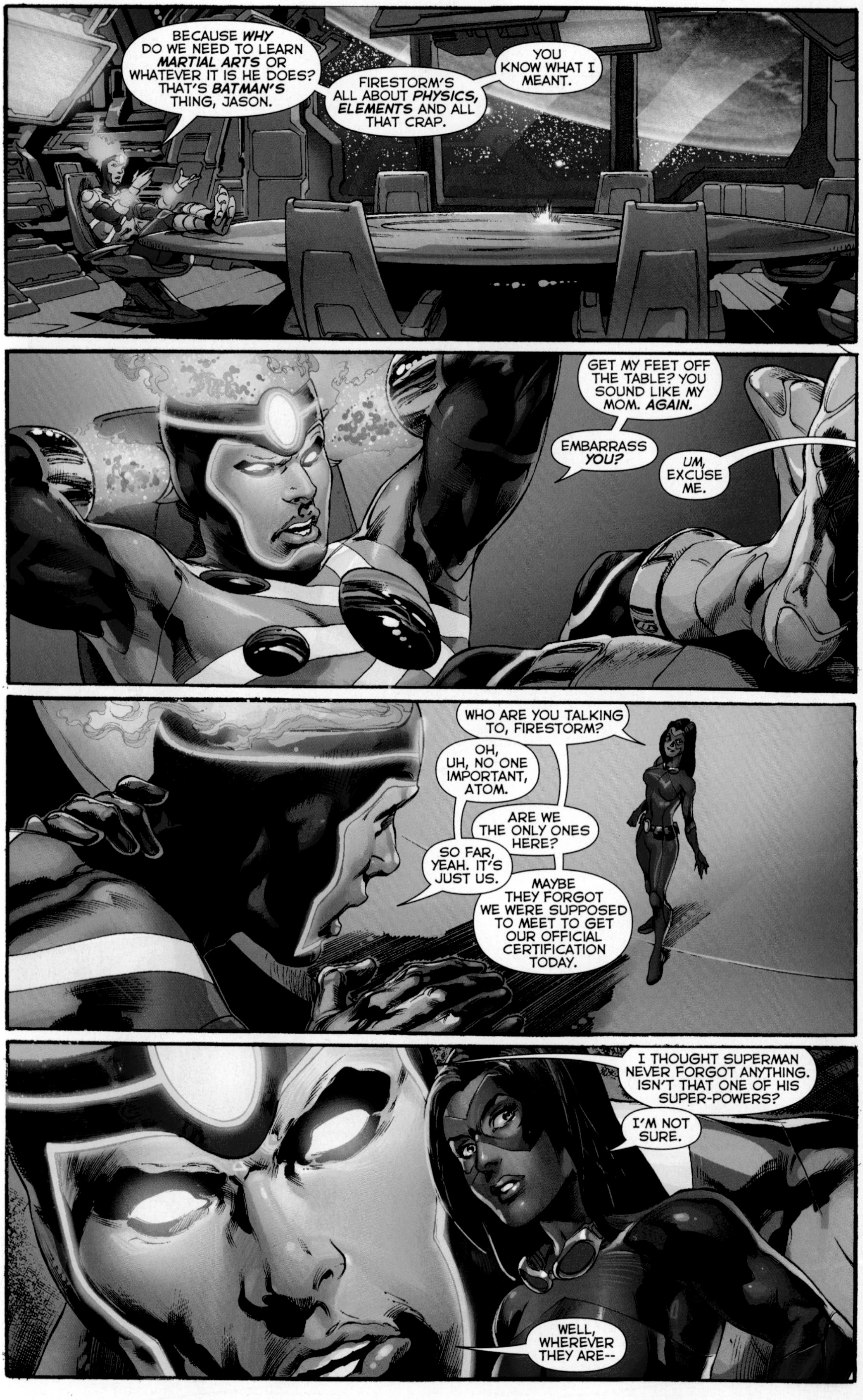
BECAUSE WHY DO WE NEED TO LEARN MARTIAL ARTS OR WHATEVER IT IS HE DOES? THAT'S BATMAN'S THING, JASON.
FIRESTORM'S ALL ABOUT PHYSICS, ELEMENTS AND ALL THAT CRAP.
YOU KNOW WHAT I MEANT.
GET MY FEET OFF THE TABLE? YOU SOUND LIKE MY MOM. AGAIN.
EMBARRASS YOU?
UM, EXCUSE ME.
WHO ARE YOU TALKING TO, FIRESTORM?
OH, UH, NO ONE IMPORTANT, ATOM.
ARE WE THE ONLY ONES HERE?
SO FAR, YEAH. IT'S JUST US.
MAYBE THEY FORGOT WE WERE SUPPOSED TO MEET TO GET OUR OFFICIAL CERTIFICATION TODAY.
I THOUGHT SUPERMAN NEVER FORGOT ANYTHING. ISN'T THAT ONE OF HIS SUPER-POWERS?
I'M NOT SURE.
WELL, WHEREVER THEY ARE--

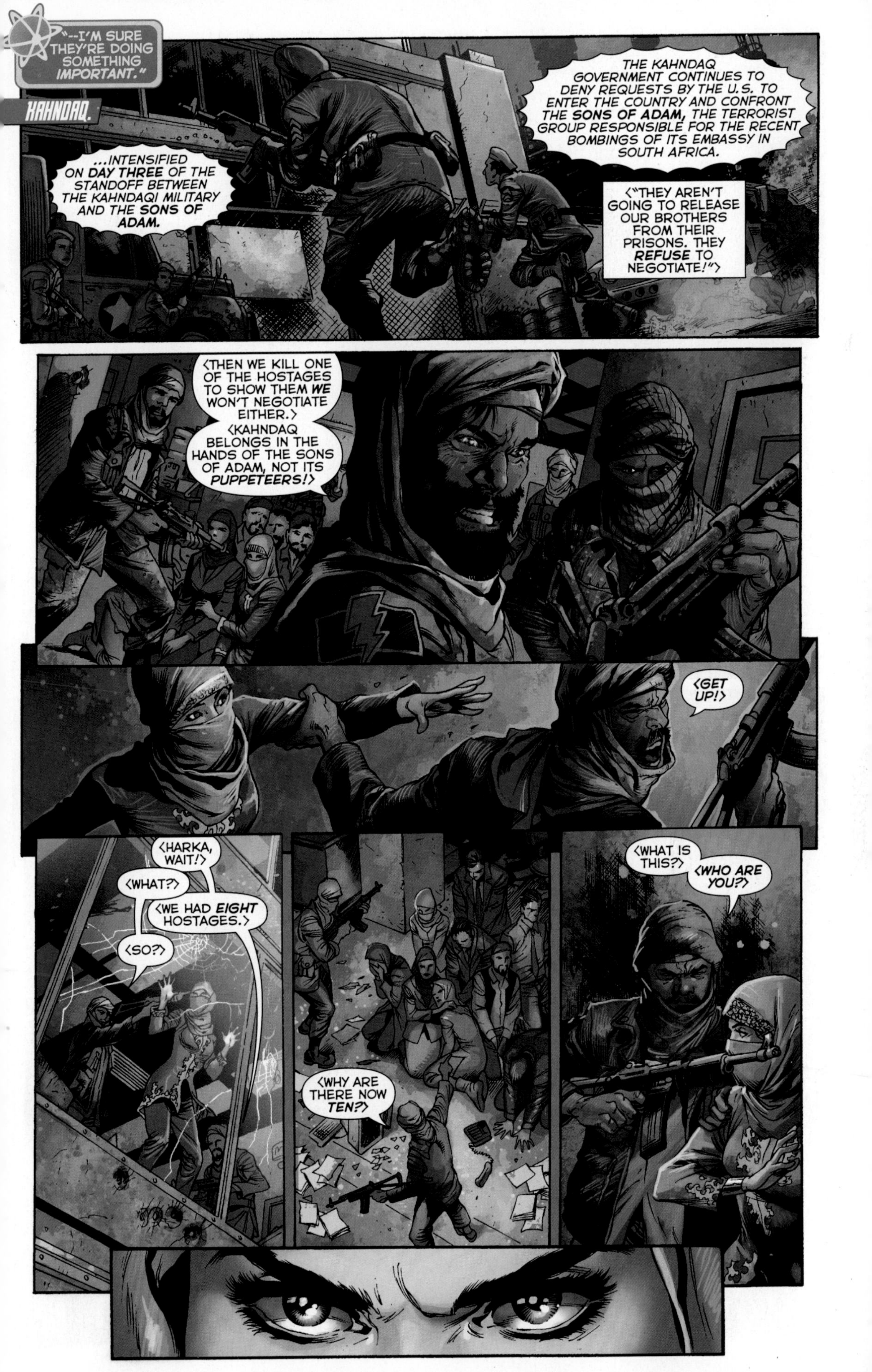
"--I'M SURE THEY'RE DOING SOMETHING IMPORTANT."
KAHNDAQ.
...INTENSIFIED ON DAY THREE OF THE STANDOFF BETWEEN THE KAHNDAQI MILITARY AND THE SONS OF ADAM.
THE KAHNDAQ GOVERNMENT CONTINUES TO DENY REQUESTS BY THE U.S. TO ENTER THE COUNTRY AND CONFRONT THE SONS OF ADAM, THE TERRORIST GROUP RESPONSIBLE FOR THE RECENT BOMBINGS OF ITS EMBASSY IN SOUTH AFRICA.
<"THEY AREN'T GOING TO RELEASE OUR BROTHERS FROM THEIR PRISONS. THEY REFUSE TO NEGOTIATE!">
<THEN WE KILL ONE OF THE HOSTAGES TO SHOW THEM WE WON'T NEGOTIATE EITHER.>
<KAHNDAQ BELONGS IN THE HANDS OF THE SONS OF ADAM, NOT ITS PUPPETEERS!>
<GET UP!>
<HARKA, WAIT!>
<WHAT?>
<WE HAD EIGHT HOSTAGES.>
<SO?>
<WHY ARE THERE NOW TEN?>
<WHAT IS THIS?>
<WHO ARE YOU?>

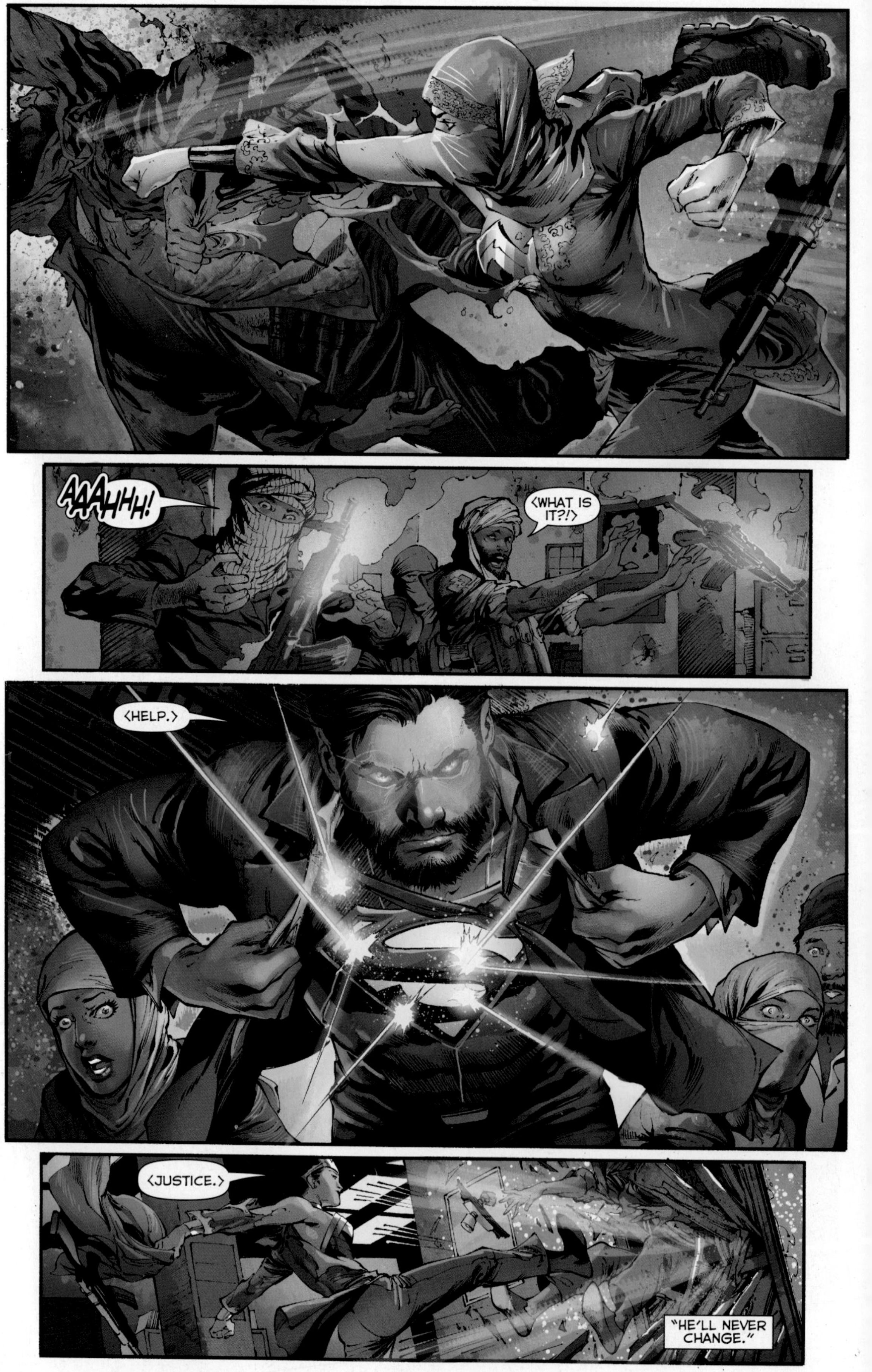
AAAHHH!
<WHAT IS IT?!>
<HELP.>
<JUSTICE.>
"HE'LL NEVER CHANGE."

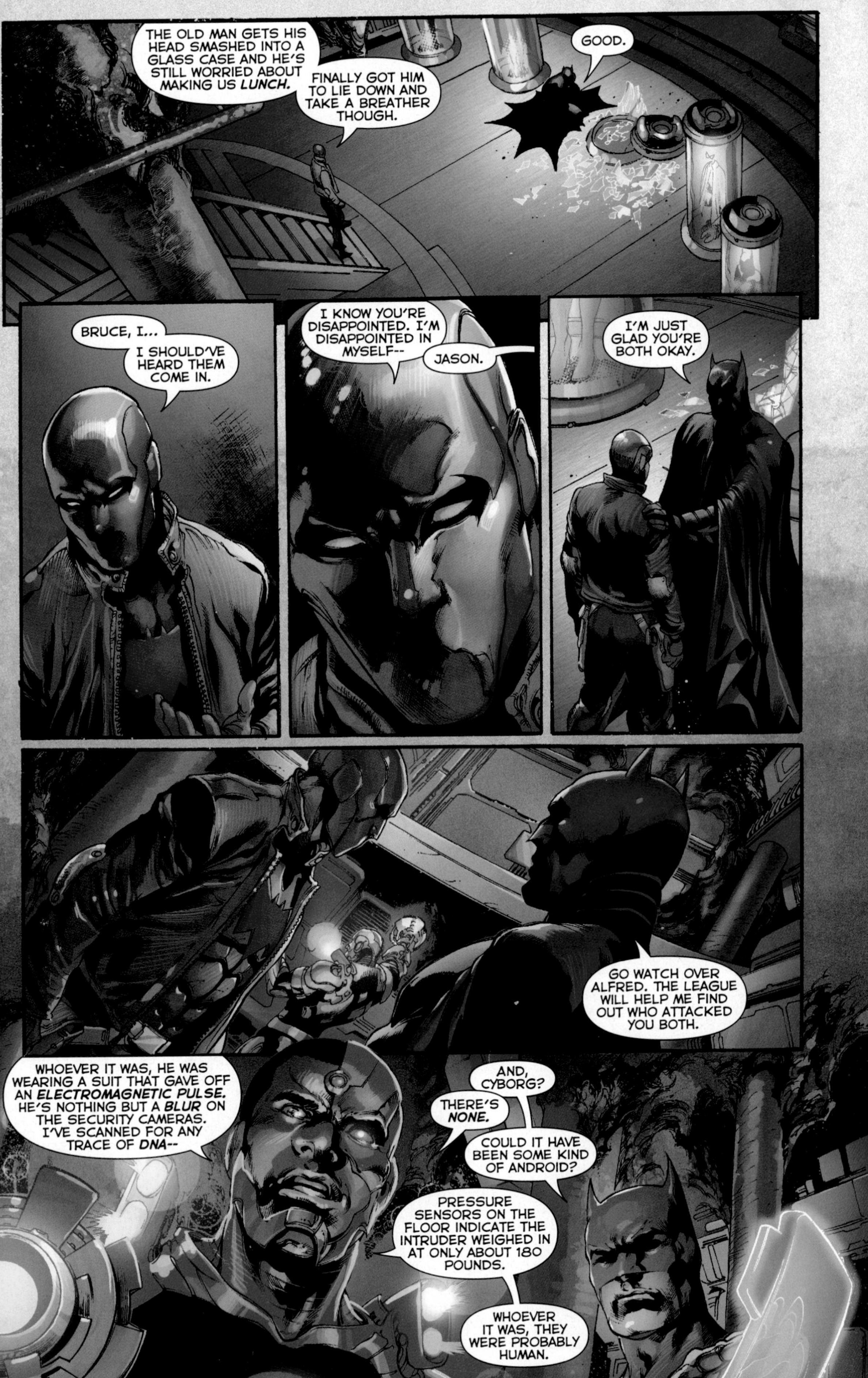
THE OLD MAN GETS HIS HEAD SMASHED INTO A GLASS CASE AND HE'S STILL WORRIED ABOUT MAKING US *LUNCH.*
FINALLY GOT HIM TO LIE DOWN AND TAKE A BREATHER THOUGH.
GOOD.
BRUCE, I...
I SHOULD'VE HEARD THEM COME IN.
I KNOW YOU'RE DISAPPOINTED. I'M DISAPPOINTED IN MYSELF--
JASON.
I'M JUST GLAD YOU'RE BOTH OKAY.
GO WATCH OVER ALFRED. THE LEAGUE WILL HELP ME FIND OUT WHO ATTACKED YOU BOTH.
WHOEVER IT WAS, HE WAS WEARING A SUIT THAT GAVE OFF AN *ELECTROMAGNETIC PULSE.* HE'S NOTHING BUT A *BLUR* ON THE SECURITY CAMERAS. I'VE SCANNED FOR ANY TRACE OF *DNA*--
AND, CYBORG?
THERE'S *NONE.*
COULD IT HAVE BEEN SOME KIND OF ANDROID?
PRESSURE SENSORS ON THE FLOOR INDICATE THE INTRUDER WEIGHED IN AT ONLY ABOUT 180 POUNDS.
WHOEVER IT WAS, THEY WERE PROBABLY HUMAN.

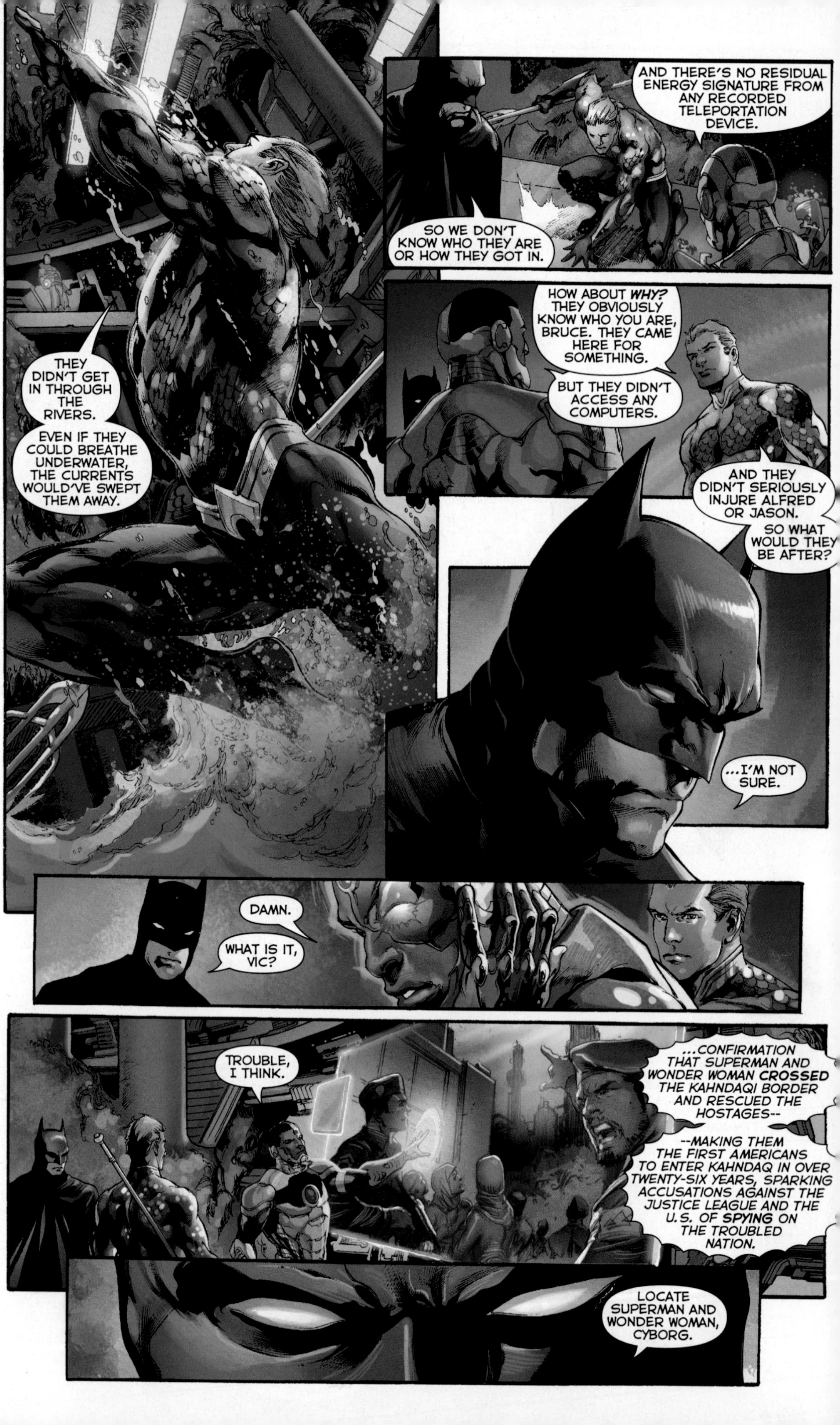
THEY DIDN'T GET IN THROUGH THE RIVERS.
EVEN IF THEY COULD BREATHE UNDERWATER, THE CURRENTS WOULD'VE SWEPT THEM AWAY.
AND THERE'S NO RESIDUAL ENERGY SIGNATURE FROM ANY RECORDED TELEPORTATION DEVICE.
SO WE DON'T KNOW WHO THEY ARE OR HOW THEY GOT IN.
HOW ABOUT **WHY?** THEY OBVIOUSLY KNOW WHO YOU ARE, BRUCE. THEY CAME HERE FOR SOMETHING.
BUT THEY DIDN'T ACCESS ANY COMPUTERS.
AND THEY DIDN'T SERIOUSLY INJURE ALFRED OR JASON.
SO WHAT WOULD THEY BE AFTER?
...I'M NOT SURE.
DAMN.
WHAT IS IT, VIC?
TROUBLE, I THINK.
...CONFIRMATION THAT SUPERMAN AND WONDER WOMAN ***CROSSED*** *THE KAHNDAQI BORDER AND RESCUED THE HOSTAGES--*
--MAKING THEM THE FIRST AMERICANS TO ENTER KAHNDAQ IN OVER TWENTY-SIX YEARS, SPARKING ACCUSATIONS AGAINST THE JUSTICE LEAGUE AND THE U.S. OF ***SPYING*** *ON THE TROUBLED NATION.*
LOCATE SUPERMAN AND WONDER WOMAN, CYBORG.

"AND TAKE ME THERE."

IT'S BEAUTIFUL, ISN'T IT?

IT IS.

I'VE BEEN ALL OVER THE WORLD, BUT NEVER KAHNDAQ.

THEY'VE BEEN BURIED BY *VIOLENCE* EVER SINCE THE U.S. TRIED TO APPOINT THEIR CHOICE OF LEADER.

THE PEOPLE REBELLED. THEN THE COUNTRY WAS DIVIDED BY CIVIL WAR. AND IT'S NEVER GOTTEN OUT.

WE COULD SAVE THEM, CLARK.

NOT JUST THE HOSTAGES, BUT THE ENTIRE COUNTRY.

IT'S NOT UP TO US TO CHANGE THE WORLD, DIANA.

WHY NOT?

I MADE THAT CHOICE A LONG TIME AGO AND IT WAS THE RIGHT CHOICE. I USE MY POWERS TO *INSPIRE*, NOT *INTERFERE*.

SOMETIMES THE WORLD *NEEDS* US TO INTERFERE.

WE COULD MAKE THINGS WORSE.

BY DELIVERING THE *WATER* THEY NEED? OR THE *FOOD* AND *SUPPLIES* THAT WOULD IMPROVE THEIR *LIVES*?

GOVERNMENT SANCTIONS MAY PREVENT OTHERS FROM COMING IN HERE, BUT NOT US.

NOTHING CAN STOP US, CLARK.

YOU DON'T WANT TO SAY THAT.

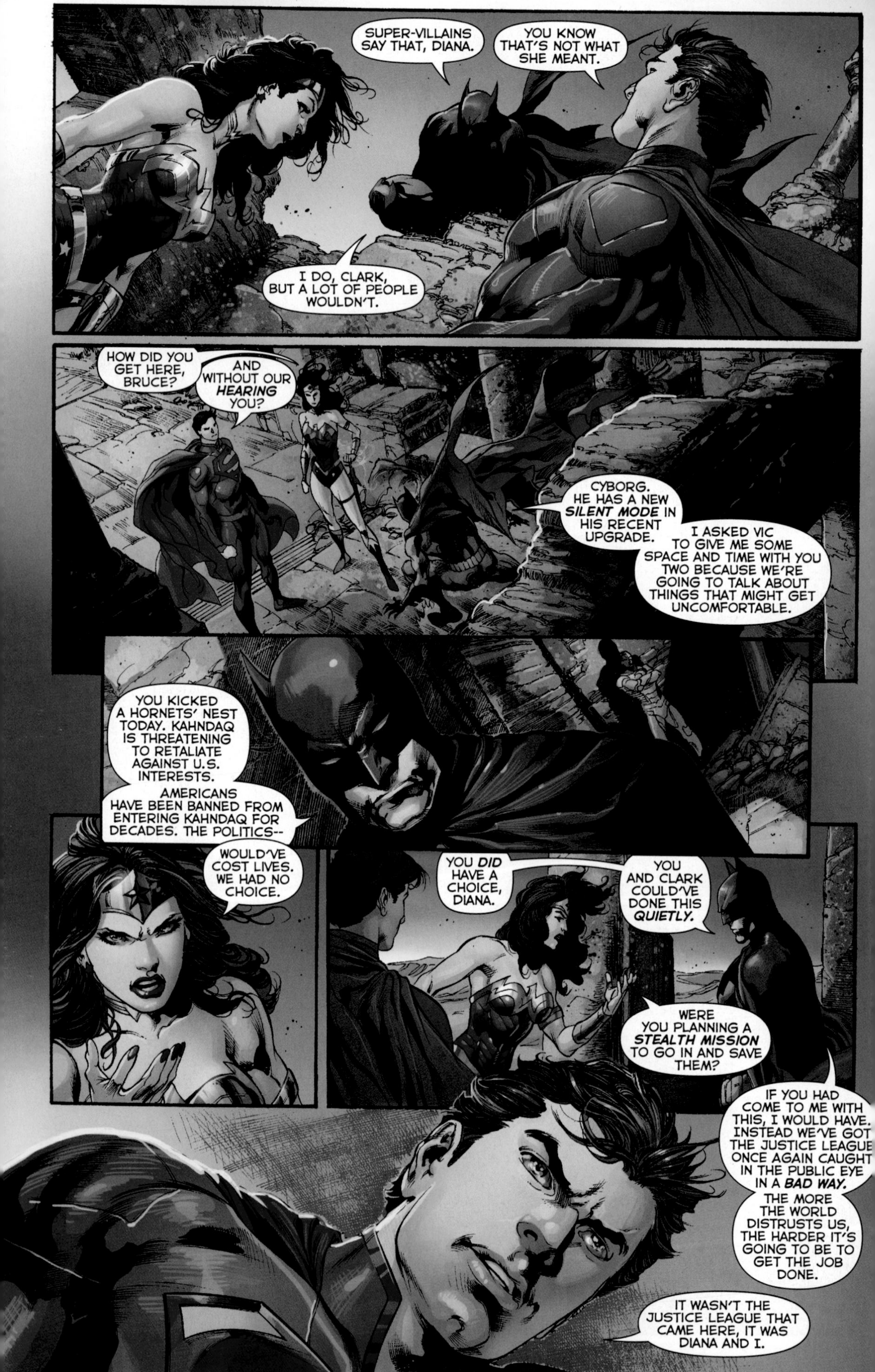
SUPER-VILLAINS SAY THAT, DIANA.
YOU KNOW THAT'S NOT WHAT SHE MEANT.
I DO, CLARK, BUT A LOT OF PEOPLE WOULDN'T.
HOW DID YOU GET HERE, BRUCE?
AND WITHOUT OUR *HEARING* YOU?
CYBORG. HE HAS A NEW *SILENT MODE* IN HIS RECENT UPGRADE.
I ASKED VIC TO GIVE ME SOME SPACE AND TIME WITH YOU TWO BECAUSE WE'RE GOING TO TALK ABOUT THINGS THAT MIGHT GET UNCOMFORTABLE.
YOU KICKED A HORNETS' NEST TODAY. KAHNDAQ IS THREATENING TO RETALIATE AGAINST U.S. INTERESTS.
AMERICANS HAVE BEEN BANNED FROM ENTERING KAHNDAQ FOR DECADES. THE POLITICS--
WOULD'VE COST LIVES. WE HAD NO CHOICE.
YOU *DID* HAVE A CHOICE, DIANA.
YOU AND CLARK COULD'VE DONE THIS *QUIETLY.*
WERE YOU PLANNING A *STEALTH MISSION* TO GO IN AND SAVE THEM?
IF YOU HAD COME TO ME WITH THIS, I WOULD HAVE. INSTEAD WE'VE GOT THE JUSTICE LEAGUE ONCE AGAIN CAUGHT IN THE PUBLIC EYE IN A *BAD WAY.*
THE MORE THE WORLD DISTRUSTS US, THE HARDER IT'S GOING TO BE TO GET THE JOB DONE.
IT WASN'T THE JUSTICE LEAGUE THAT CAME HERE, IT WAS DIANA AND I.

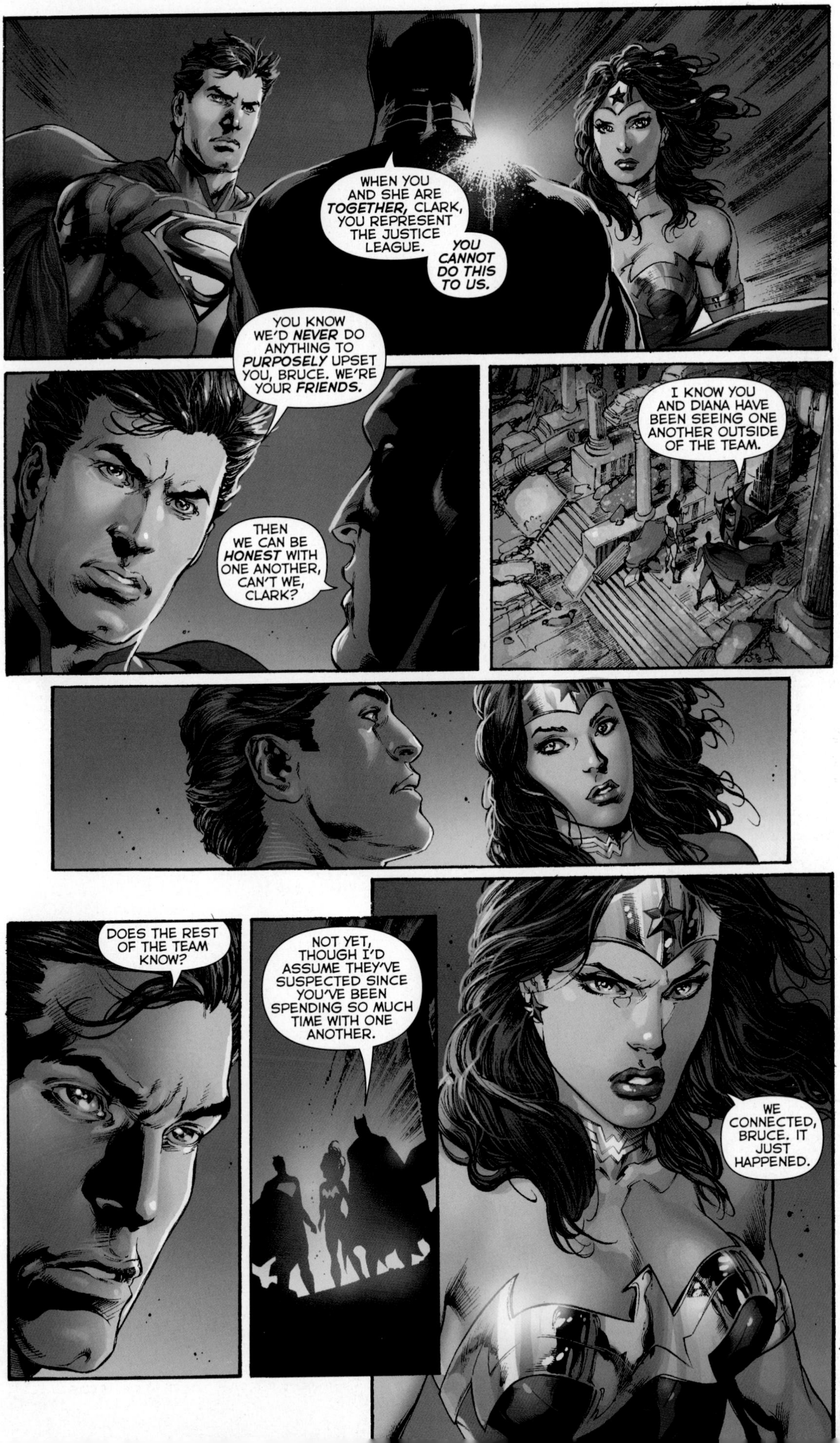
WHEN YOU AND SHE ARE *TOGETHER,* CLARK, YOU REPRESENT THE JUSTICE LEAGUE.
YOU CANNOT DO THIS TO US.
YOU KNOW WE'D *NEVER* DO ANYTHING TO *PURPOSELY* UPSET YOU, BRUCE. WE'RE YOUR *FRIENDS.*
THEN WE CAN BE *HONEST* WITH ONE ANOTHER, CAN'T WE, CLARK?
I KNOW YOU AND DIANA HAVE BEEN SEEING ONE ANOTHER OUTSIDE OF THE TEAM.
DOES THE REST OF THE TEAM KNOW?
NOT YET, THOUGH I'D ASSUME THEY'VE SUSPECTED SINCE YOU'VE BEEN SPENDING SO MUCH TIME WITH ONE ANOTHER.
WE CONNECTED, BRUCE. IT JUST HAPPENED.

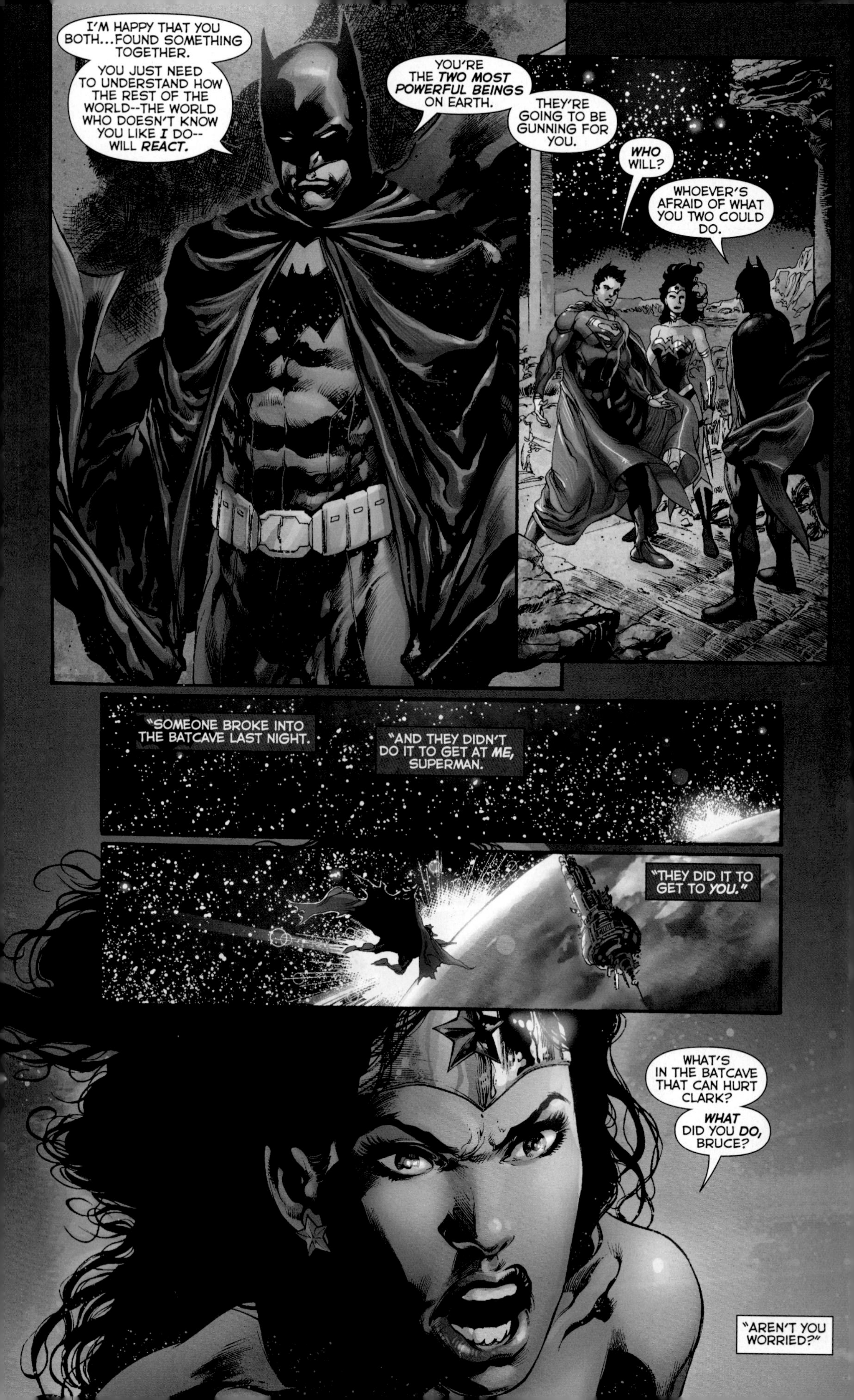
I'M HAPPY THAT YOU BOTH...FOUND SOMETHING TOGETHER.
YOU JUST NEED TO UNDERSTAND HOW THE REST OF THE WORLD--THE WORLD WHO DOESN'T KNOW YOU LIKE *I* DO--WILL *REACT.*
YOU'RE THE *TWO MOST POWERFUL BEINGS* ON EARTH.
THEY'RE GOING TO BE GUNNING FOR YOU.
WHO WILL?
WHOEVER'S AFRAID OF WHAT YOU TWO COULD DO.
"SOMEONE BROKE INTO THE BATCAVE LAST NIGHT.
"AND THEY DIDN'T DO IT TO GET AT *ME,* SUPERMAN.
"THEY DID IT TO GET TO *YOU.*"
WHAT'S IN THE BATCAVE THAT CAN HURT CLARK?
WHAT DID YOU *DO,* BRUCE?
"AREN'T YOU WORRIED?"

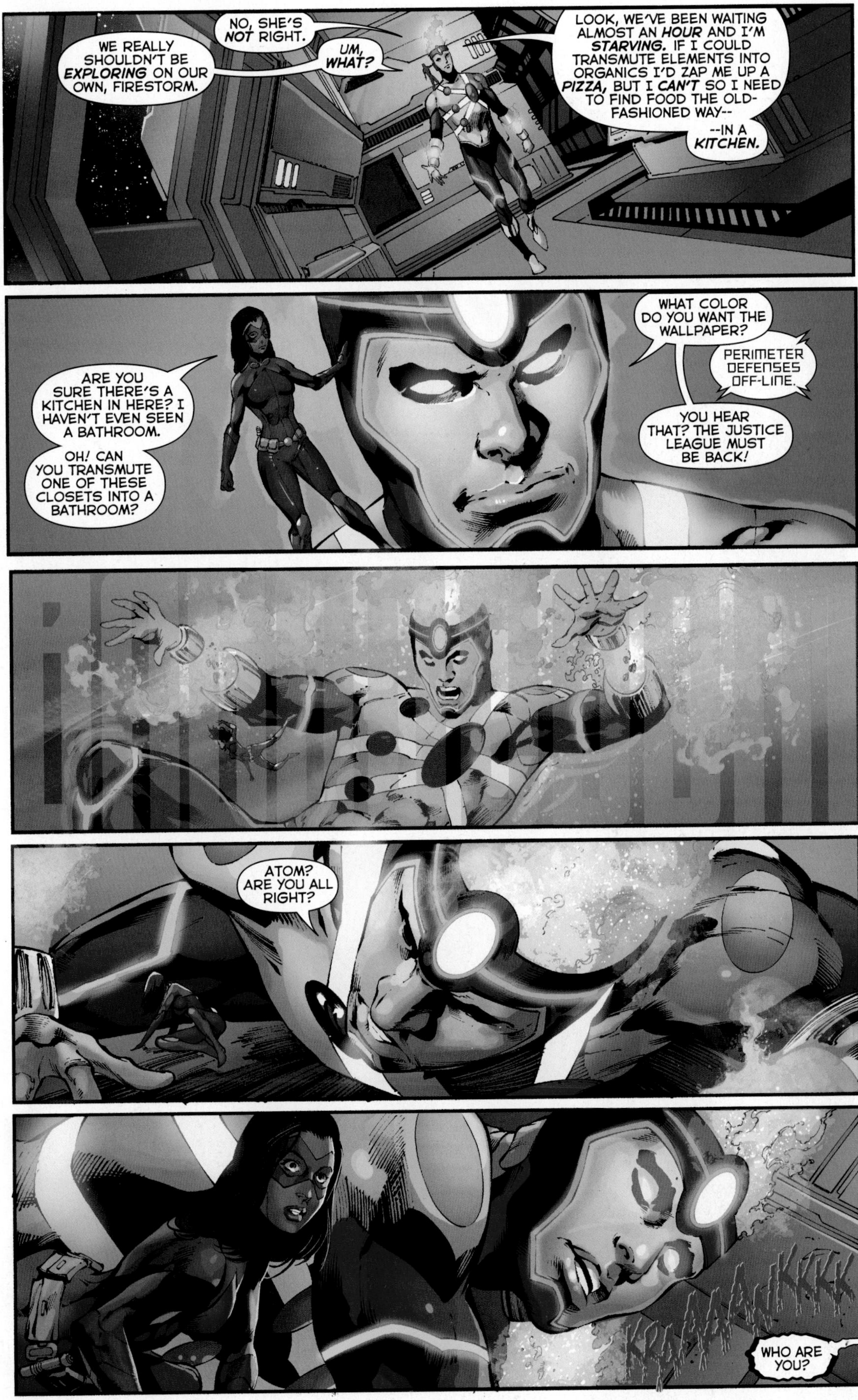
WE REALLY SHOULDN'T BE EXPLORING ON OUR OWN, FIRESTORM.
NO, SHE'S NOT RIGHT.
UM, WHAT?
LOOK, WE'VE BEEN WAITING ALMOST AN HOUR AND I'M STARVING. IF I COULD TRANSMUTE ELEMENTS INTO ORGANICS I'D ZAP ME UP A PIZZA, BUT I CAN'T SO I NEED TO FIND FOOD THE OLD-FASHIONED WAY--
--IN A KITCHEN.
ARE YOU SURE THERE'S A KITCHEN IN HERE? I HAVEN'T EVEN SEEN A BATHROOM.
OH! CAN YOU TRANSMUTE ONE OF THESE CLOSETS INTO A BATHROOM?
WHAT COLOR DO YOU WANT THE WALLPAPER?
PERIMETER DEFENSES OFF-LINE.
YOU HEAR THAT? THE JUSTICE LEAGUE MUST BE BACK!
ATOM? ARE YOU ALL RIGHT?
WHO ARE YOU?

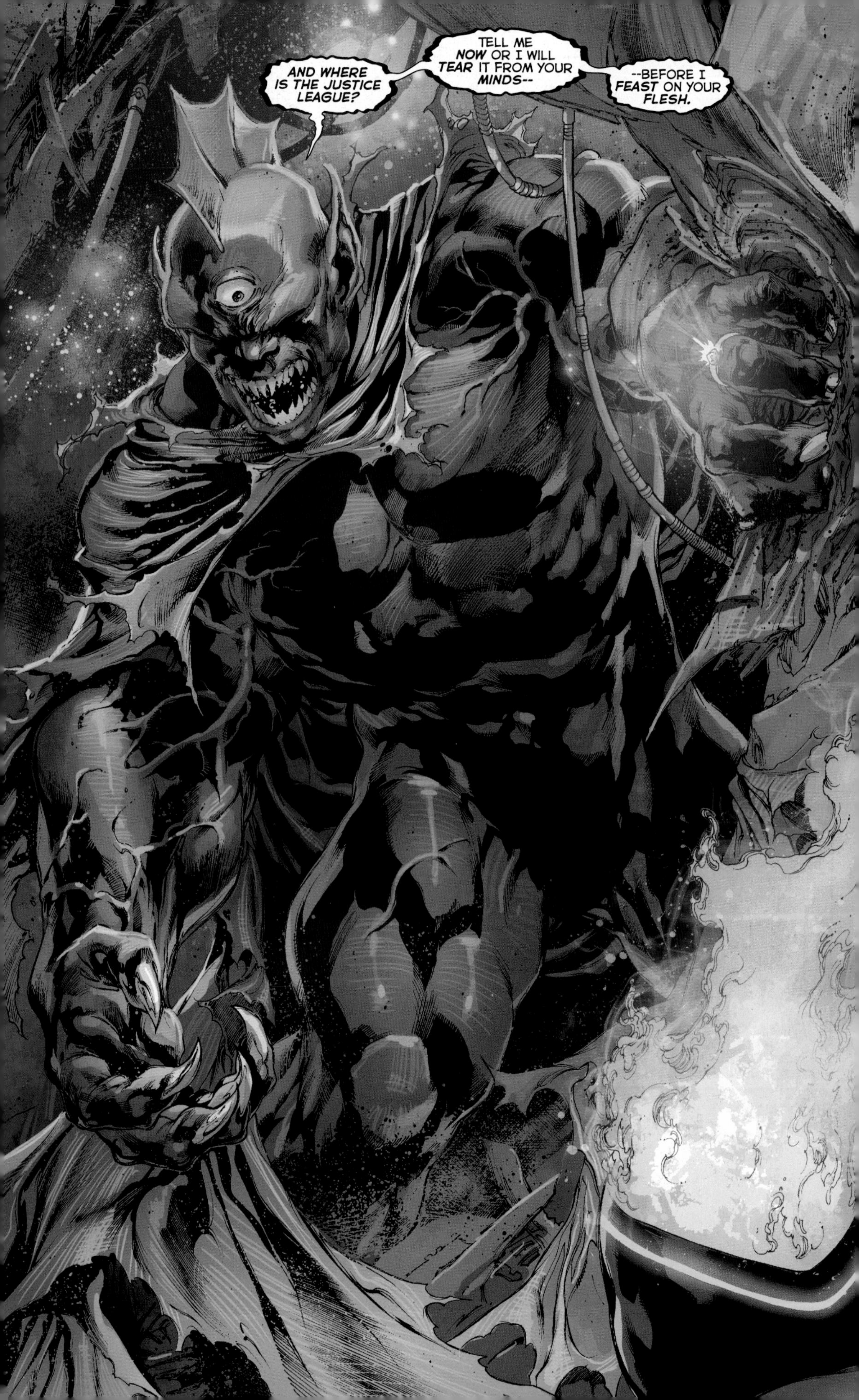
AND WHERE IS THE JUSTICE LEAGUE?
TELL ME NOW OR I WILL TEAR IT FROM YOUR MINDS--
--BEFORE I FEAST ON YOUR FLESH.

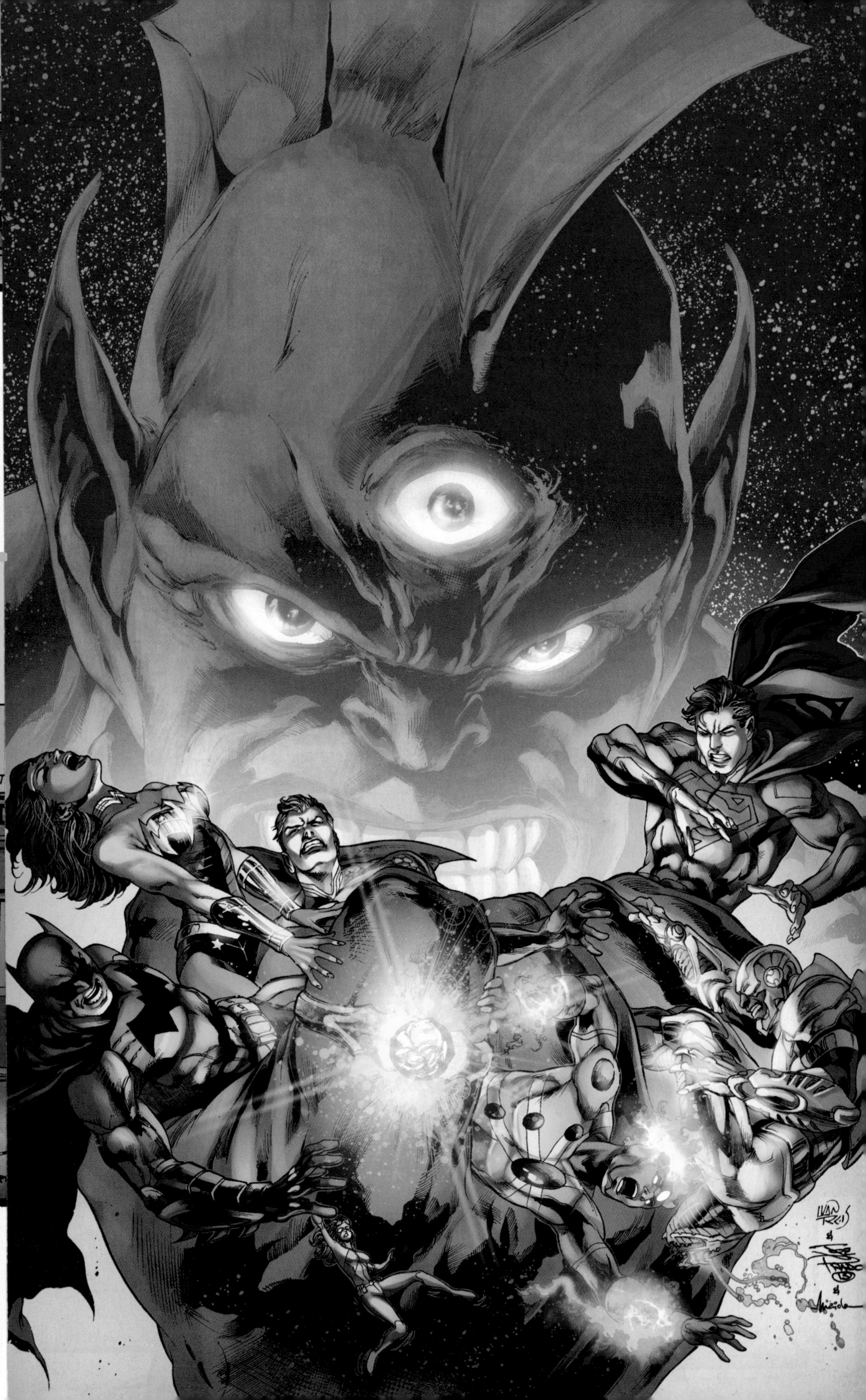

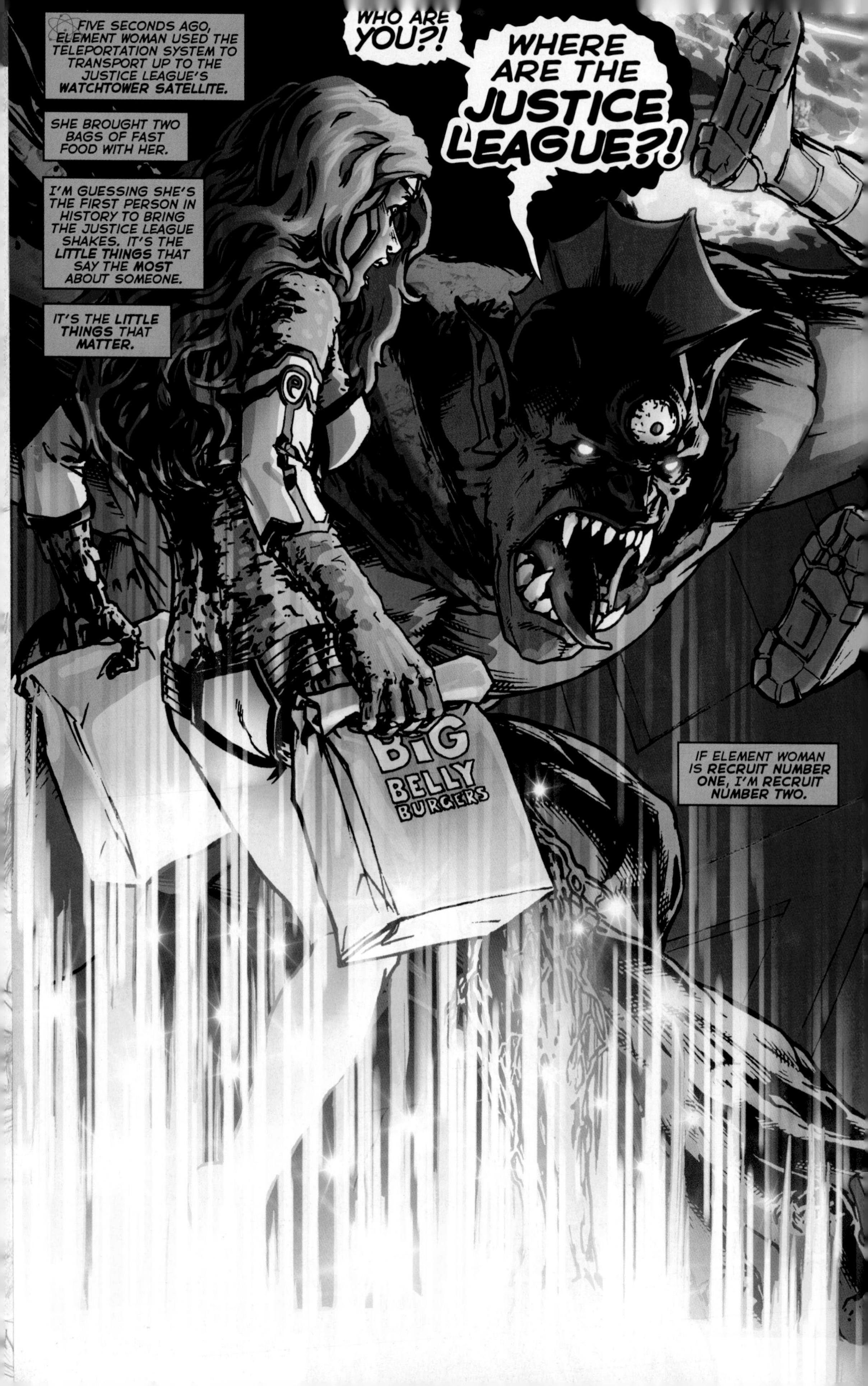
FIVE SECONDS AGO, ELEMENT WOMAN USED THE TELEPORTATION SYSTEM TO TRANSPORT UP TO THE JUSTICE LEAGUE'S WATCHTOWER SATELLITE.
SHE BROUGHT TWO BAGS OF FAST FOOD WITH HER.
I'M GUESSING SHE'S THE FIRST PERSON IN HISTORY TO BRING THE JUSTICE LEAGUE SHAKES. IT'S THE LITTLE THINGS THAT SAY THE MOST ABOUT SOMEONE.
IT'S THE LITTLE THINGS THAT MATTER.
WHO ARE YOU?!
WHERE ARE THE JUSTICE LEAGUE?!
BIG BELLY BURGERS
IF ELEMENT WOMAN IS RECRUIT NUMBER ONE, I'M RECRUIT NUMBER TWO.

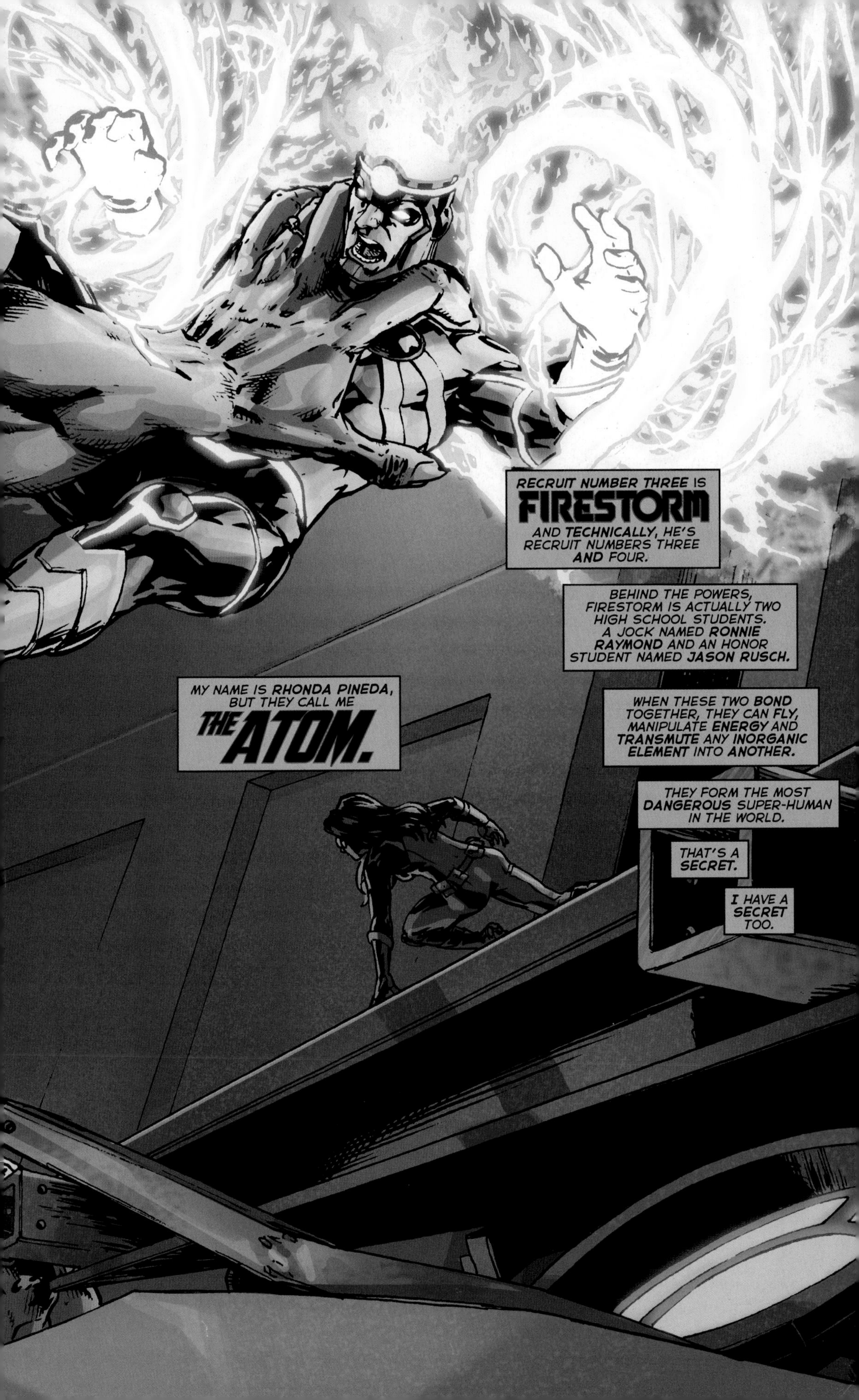
RECRUIT NUMBER THREE IS FIRESTORM AND TECHNICALLY, HE'S RECRUIT NUMBERS THREE AND FOUR.
BEHIND THE POWERS, FIRESTORM IS ACTUALLY TWO HIGH SCHOOL STUDENTS. A JOCK NAMED RONNIE RAYMOND AND AN HONOR STUDENT NAMED JASON RUSCH.
MY NAME IS RHONDA PINEDA, BUT THEY CALL ME THE ATOM.
WHEN THESE TWO BOND TOGETHER, THEY CAN FLY, MANIPULATE ENERGY AND TRANSMUTE ANY INORGANIC ELEMENT INTO ANOTHER.
THEY FORM THE MOST DANGEROUS SUPER-HUMAN IN THE WORLD.
THAT'S A SECRET.
I HAVE A SECRET TOO.

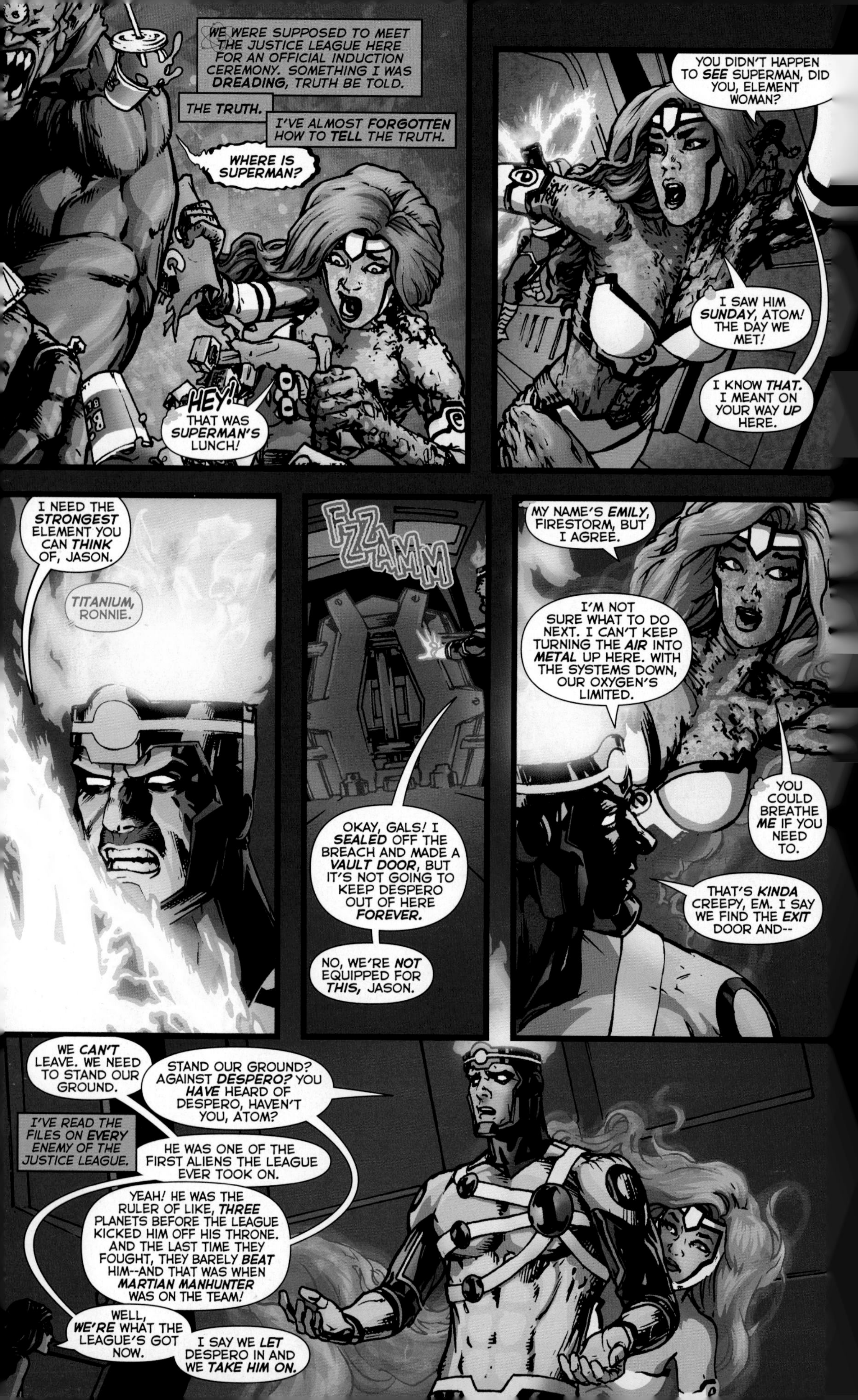

WE WERE SUPPOSED TO MEET THE JUSTICE LEAGUE HERE FOR AN OFFICIAL INDUCTION CEREMONY. SOMETHING I WAS DREADING, TRUTH BE TOLD.
THE TRUTH.
I'VE ALMOST FORGOTTEN HOW TO TELL THE TRUTH.
WHERE IS SUPERMAN?
HEY! THAT WAS SUPERMAN'S LUNCH!
YOU DIDN'T HAPPEN TO SEE SUPERMAN, DID YOU, ELEMENT WOMAN?
I SAW HIM SUNDAY, ATOM! THE DAY WE MET!
I KNOW THAT. I MEANT ON YOUR WAY UP HERE.
I NEED THE STRONGEST ELEMENT YOU CAN THINK OF, JASON.
TITANIUM, RONNIE.
FZZAMM
OKAY, GALS! I SEALED OFF THE BREACH AND MADE A VAULT DOOR, BUT IT'S NOT GOING TO KEEP DESPERO OUT OF HERE FOREVER.
NO, WE'RE NOT EQUIPPED FOR THIS, JASON.
MY NAME'S EMILY, FIRESTORM, BUT I AGREE.
I'M NOT SURE WHAT TO DO NEXT. I CAN'T KEEP TURNING THE AIR INTO METAL UP HERE. WITH THE SYSTEMS DOWN, OUR OXYGEN'S LIMITED.
YOU COULD BREATHE ME IF YOU NEED TO.
THAT'S KINDA CREEPY, EM. I SAY WE FIND THE EXIT DOOR AND--
WE CAN'T LEAVE. WE NEED TO STAND OUR GROUND.
STAND OUR GROUND? AGAINST DESPERO? YOU HAVE HEARD OF DESPERO, HAVEN'T YOU, ATOM?
I'VE READ THE FILES ON EVERY ENEMY OF THE JUSTICE LEAGUE.
HE WAS ONE OF THE FIRST ALIENS THE LEAGUE EVER TOOK ON.
YEAH! HE WAS THE RULER OF LIKE, THREE PLANETS BEFORE THE LEAGUE KICKED HIM OFF HIS THRONE. AND THE LAST TIME THEY FOUGHT, THEY BARELY BEAT HIM--AND THAT WAS WHEN MARTIAN MANHUNTER WAS ON THE TEAM!
WELL, WE'RE WHAT THE LEAGUE'S GOT NOW.
I SAY WE LET DESPERO IN AND WE TAKE HIM ON.

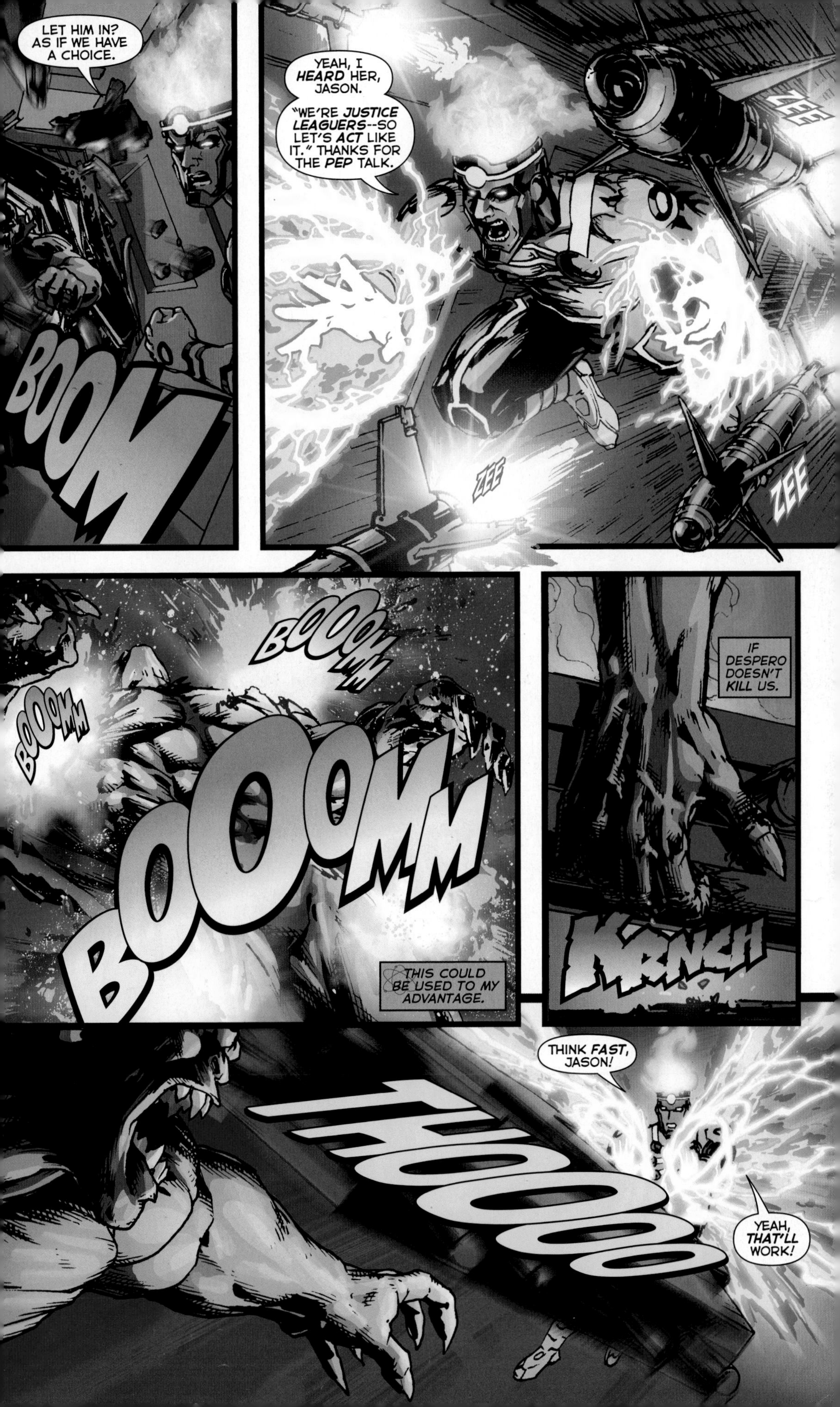
LET HIM IN? AS IF WE HAVE A CHOICE.
BOOM
YEAH, I HEARD HER, JASON.
"WE'RE JUSTICE LEAGUERS--SO LET'S ACT LIKE IT." THANKS FOR THE PEP TALK.
ZEE
ZEE
ZEE
BOOOMM
BOOOMM
BOOOMM
THIS COULD BE USED TO MY ADVANTAGE.
IF DESPERO DOESN'T KILL US.
KRNCH
THOOOOO
THINK FAST, JASON!
YEAH, THAT'LL WORK!

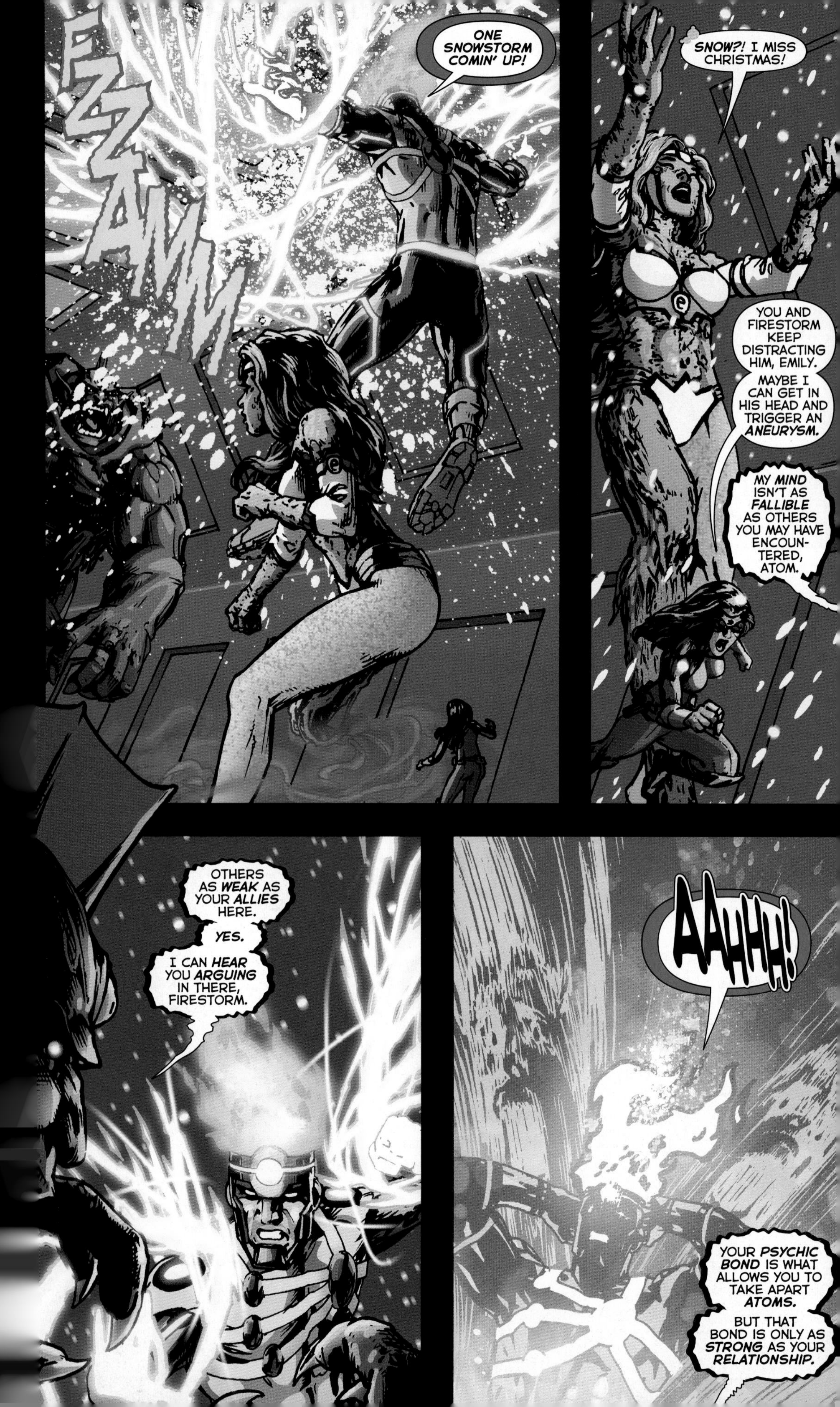
FZZAMM
ONE SNOWSTORM COMIN' UP!
SNOW?! I MISS CHRISTMAS!
YOU AND FIRESTORM KEEP DISTRACTING HIM, EMILY.
MAYBE I CAN GET IN HIS HEAD AND TRIGGER AN ANEURYSM.
MY MIND ISN'T AS FALLIBLE AS OTHERS YOU MAY HAVE ENCOUN-TERED, ATOM.
OTHERS AS WEAK AS YOUR ALLIES HERE.
YES.
I CAN HEAR YOU ARGUING IN THERE, FIRESTORM.
AAHHH!
YOUR PSYCHIC BOND IS WHAT ALLOWS YOU TO TAKE APART ATOMS.
BUT THAT BOND IS ONLY AS STRONG AS YOUR RELATIONSHIP.

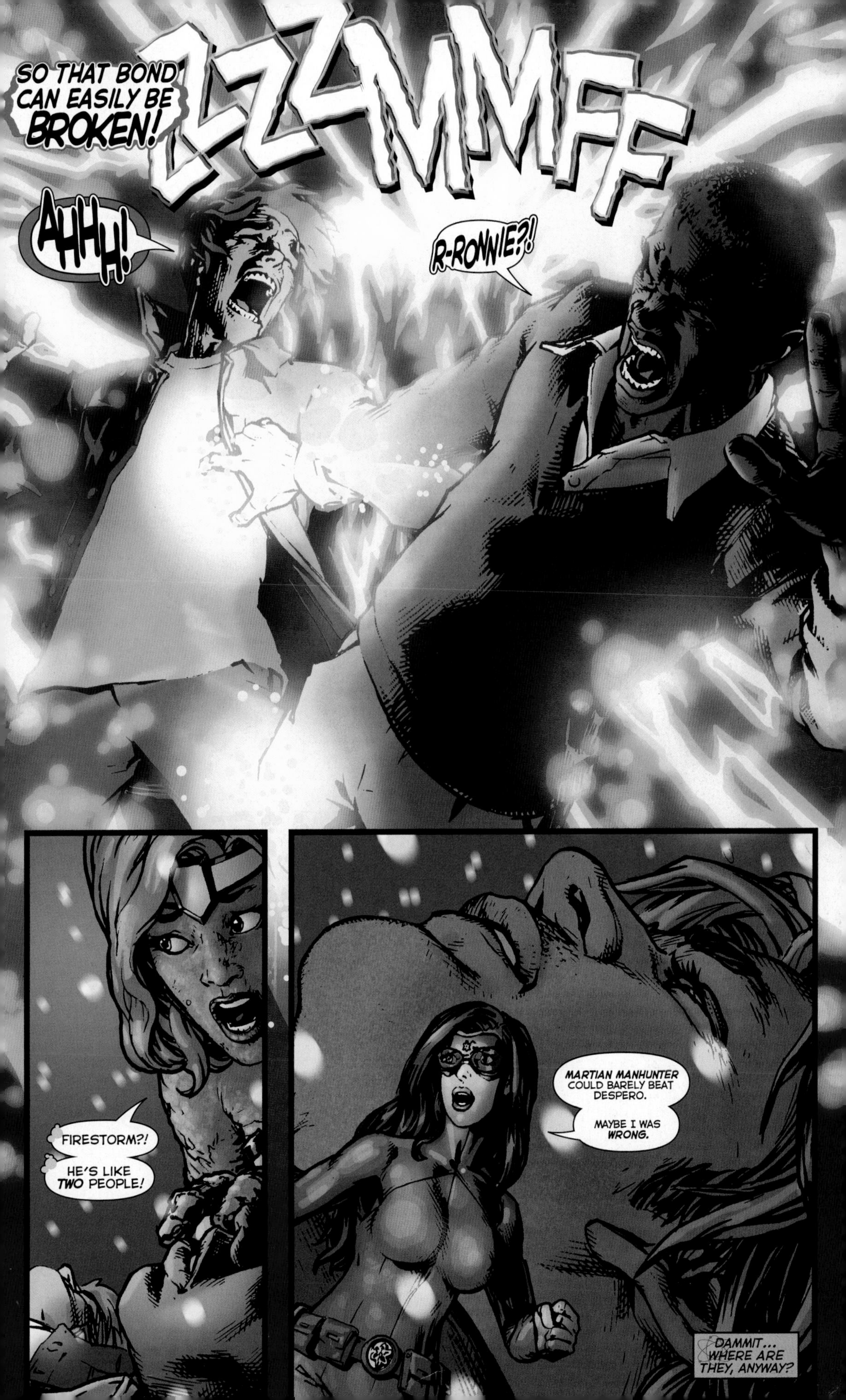
SO THAT BOND CAN EASILY BE BROKEN!
ZZZMMFF
AHHH!
R-RONNIE?!
FIRESTORM?!
HE'S LIKE TWO PEOPLE!
MARTIAN MANHUNTER COULD BARELY BEAT DESPERO.
MAYBE I WAS WRONG.
DAMMIT... WHERE ARE THEY, ANYWAY?

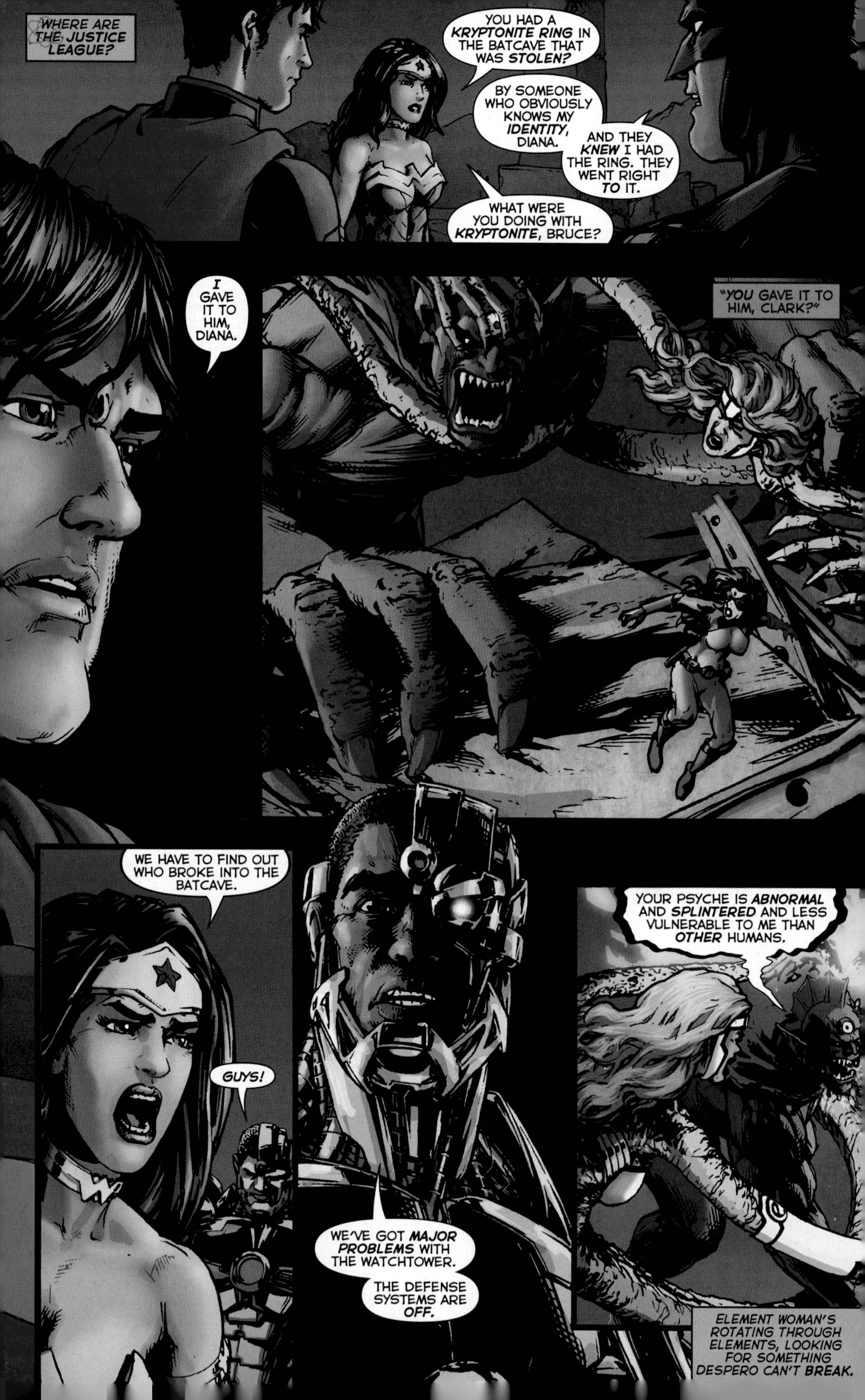
WHERE ARE THE JUSTICE LEAGUE?
YOU HAD A KRYPTONITE RING IN THE BATCAVE THAT WAS STOLEN?
BY SOMEONE WHO OBVIOUSLY KNOWS MY IDENTITY, DIANA.
AND THEY KNEW I HAD THE RING. THEY WENT RIGHT TO IT.
WHAT WERE YOU DOING WITH KRYPTONITE, BRUCE?
I GAVE IT TO HIM, DIANA.
"YOU GAVE IT TO HIM, CLARK?"
WE HAVE TO FIND OUT WHO BROKE INTO THE BATCAVE.
GUYS!
WE'VE GOT MAJOR PROBLEMS WITH THE WATCHTOWER.
THE DEFENSE SYSTEMS ARE OFF.
YOUR PSYCHE IS ABNORMAL AND SPLINTERED AND LESS VULNERABLE TO ME THAN OTHER HUMANS.
ELEMENT WOMAN'S ROTATING THROUGH ELEMENTS, LOOKING FOR SOMETHING DESPERO CAN'T BREAK.

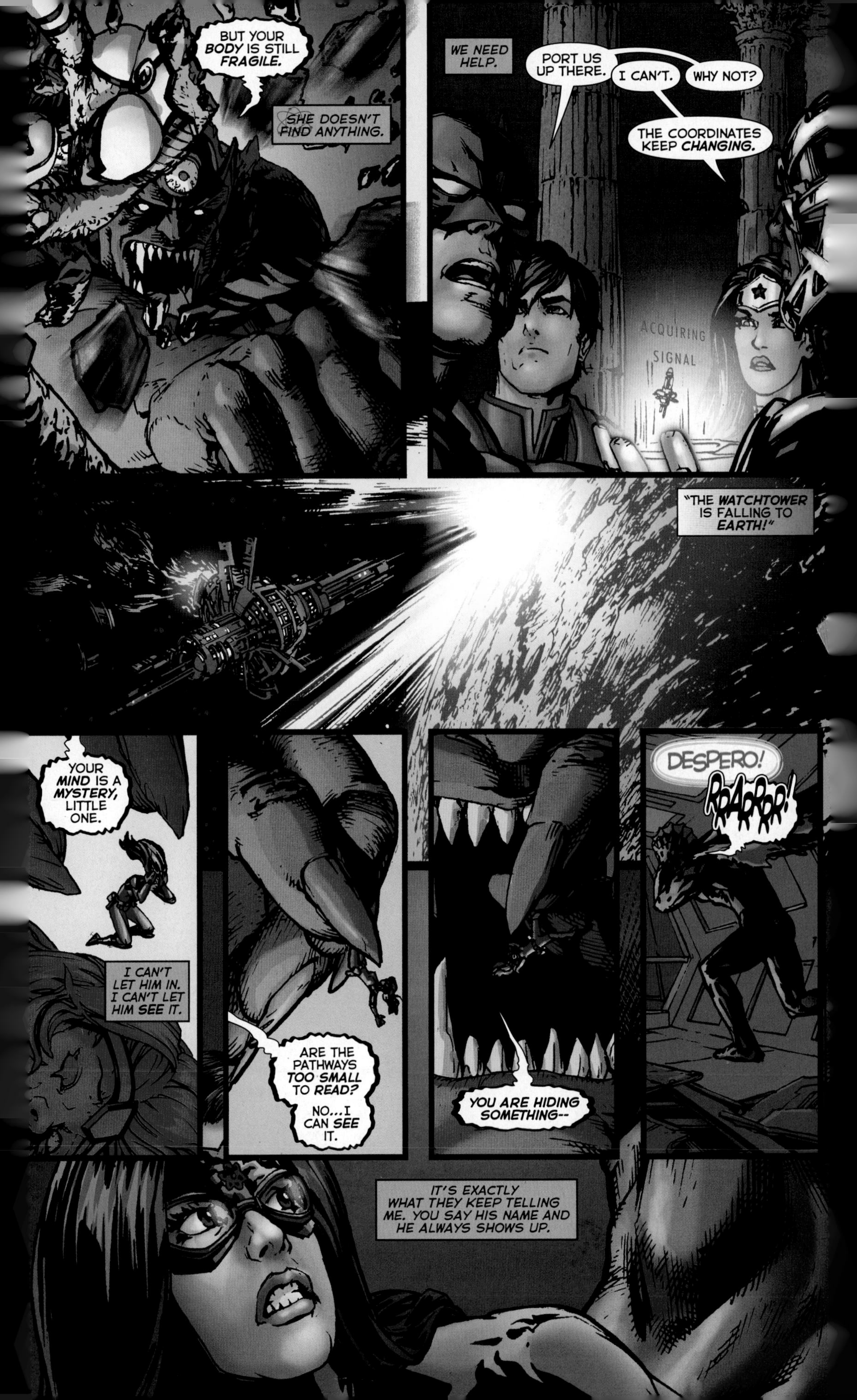
BUT YOUR BODY IS STILL FRAGILE.
SHE DOESN'T FIND ANYTHING.
WE NEED HELP.
PORT US UP THERE.
I CAN'T.
WHY NOT?
THE COORDINATES KEEP CHANGING.
ACQUIRING SIGNAL
"THE WATCHTOWER IS FALLING TO EARTH!"
YOUR MIND IS A MYSTERY, LITTLE ONE.
I CAN'T LET HIM IN. I CAN'T LET HIM SEE IT.
ARE THE PATHWAYS TOO SMALL TO READ?
NO...I CAN SEE IT.
YOU ARE HIDING SOMETHING--
DESPERO!
RRARRRR!
IT'S EXACTLY WHAT THEY KEEP TELLING ME. YOU SAY HIS NAME AND HE ALWAYS SHOWS UP.

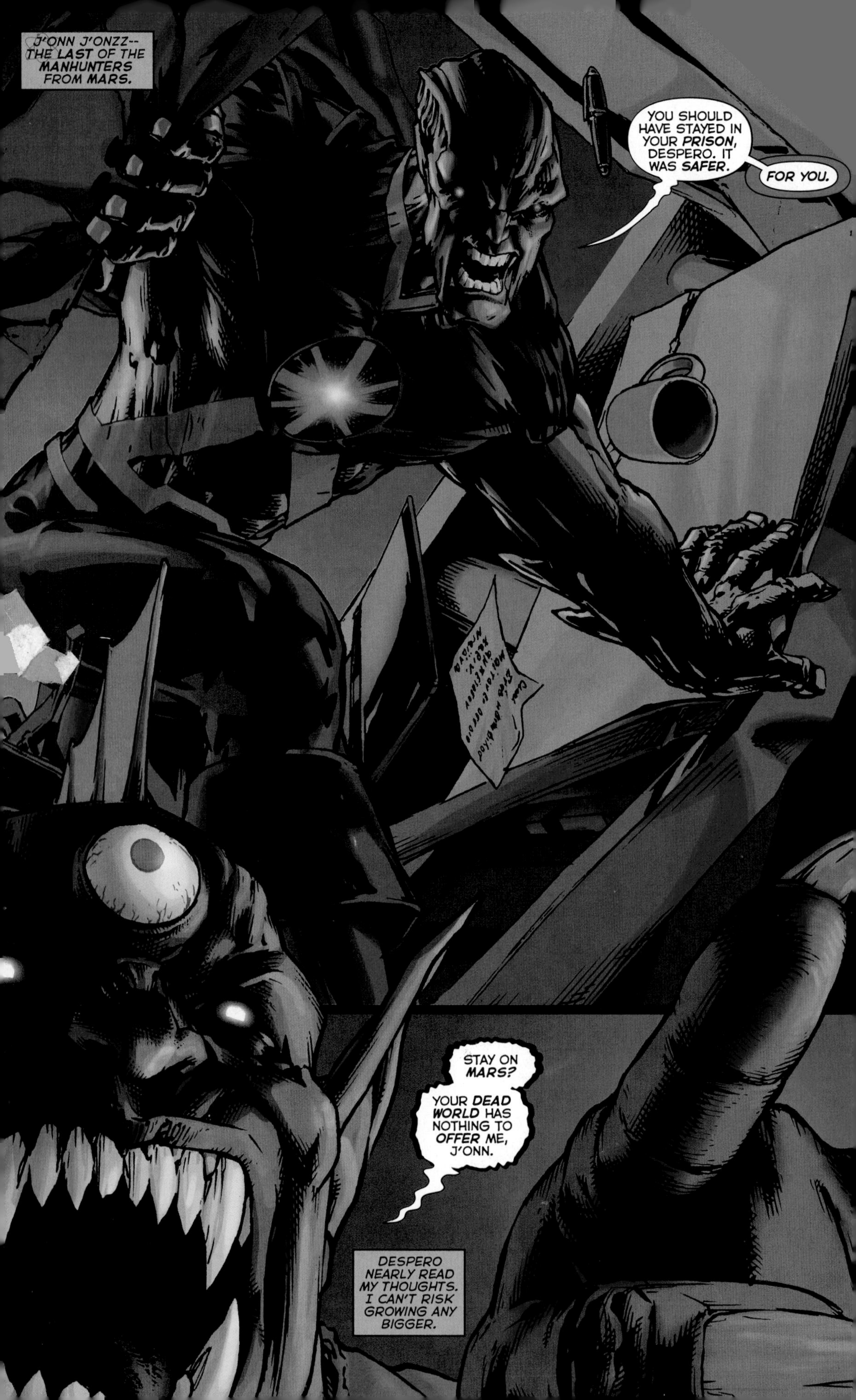
J'ONN J'ONZZ-- THE LAST OF THE MANHUNTERS FROM MARS.
YOU SHOULD HAVE STAYED IN YOUR PRISON, DESPERO. IT WAS SAFER.
FOR YOU.
STAY ON MARS?
YOUR DEAD WORLD HAS NOTHING TO OFFER ME, J'ONN.
DESPERO NEARLY READ MY THOUGHTS. I CAN'T RISK GROWING ANY BIGGER.

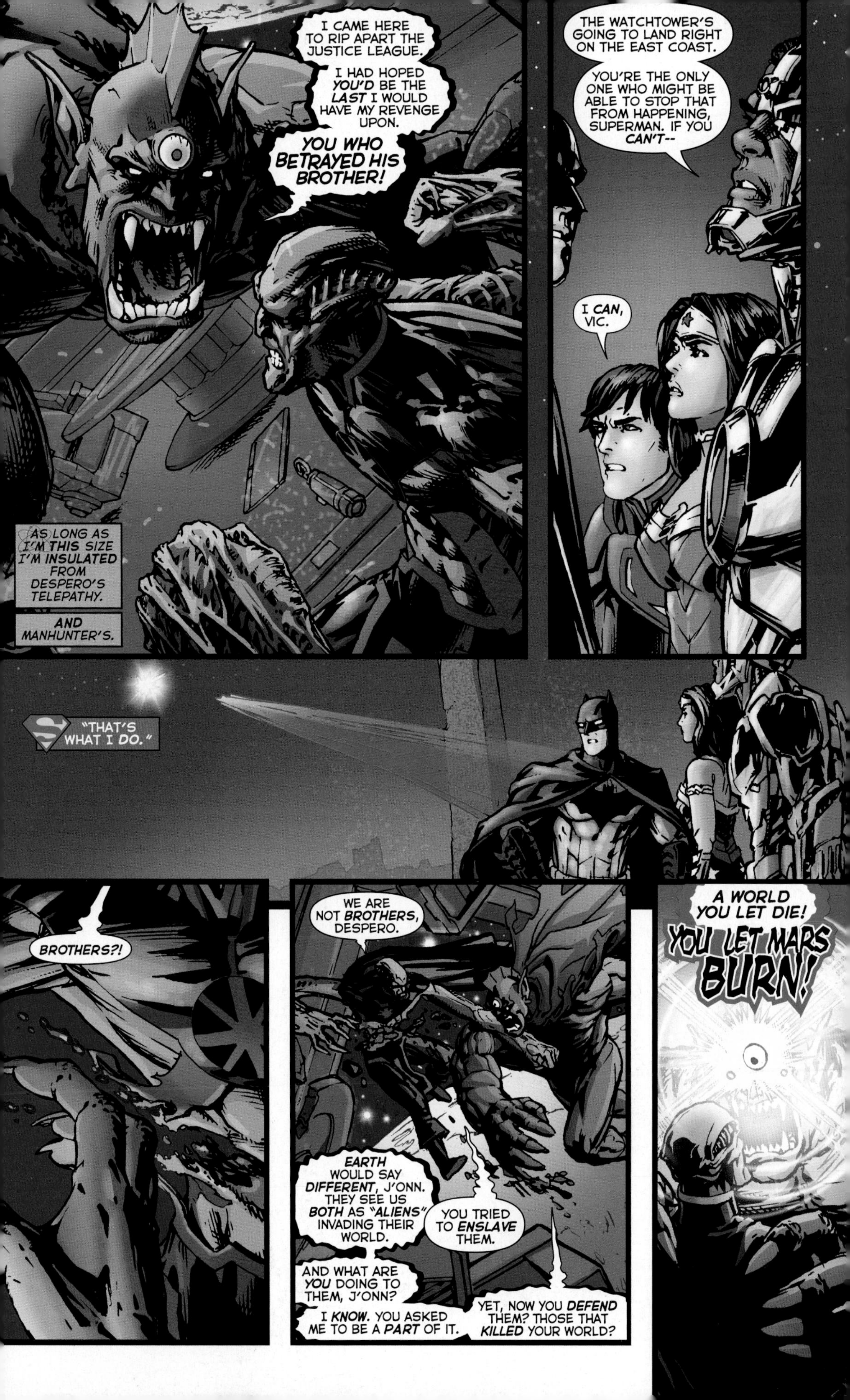
I CAME HERE TO RIP APART THE JUSTICE LEAGUE.
I HAD HOPED YOU'D BE THE LAST I WOULD HAVE MY REVENGE UPON.
YOU WHO BETRAYED HIS BROTHER!
AS LONG AS I'M THIS SIZE I'M INSULATED FROM DESPERO'S TELEPATHY.
AND MANHUNTER'S.
THE WATCHTOWER'S GOING TO LAND RIGHT ON THE EAST COAST.
YOU'RE THE ONLY ONE WHO MIGHT BE ABLE TO STOP THAT FROM HAPPENING, SUPERMAN. IF YOU CAN'T--
I CAN, VIC.
"THAT'S WHAT I DO."
BROTHERS?!
WE ARE NOT BROTHERS, DESPERO.
EARTH WOULD SAY DIFFERENT, J'ONN. THEY SEE US BOTH AS "ALIENS" INVADING THEIR WORLD.
YOU TRIED TO ENSLAVE THEM.
AND WHAT ARE YOU DOING TO THEM, J'ONN?
I KNOW. YOU ASKED ME TO BE A PART OF IT.
YET, NOW YOU DEFEND THEM? THOSE THAT KILLED YOUR WORLD?
A WORLD YOU LET DIE!
YOU LET MARS BURN!

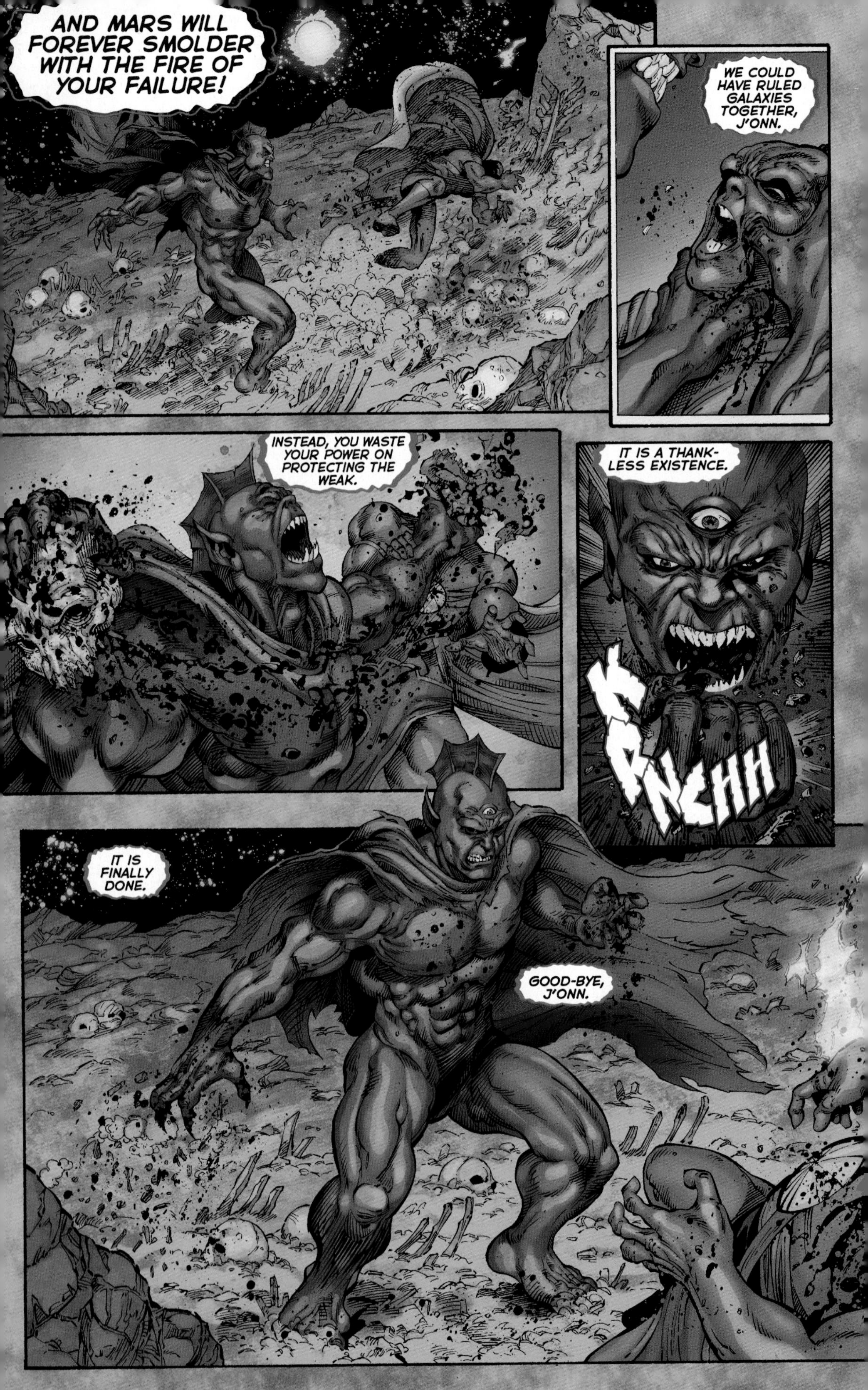
AND MARS WILL FOREVER SMOLDER WITH THE FIRE OF YOUR FAILURE!
WE COULD HAVE RULED GALAXIES TOGETHER, J'ONN.
INSTEAD, YOU WASTE YOUR POWER ON PROTECTING THE WEAK.
IT IS A THANK-LESS EXISTENCE.
KRNCHH
IT IS FINALLY DONE.
GOOD-BYE, J'ONN.

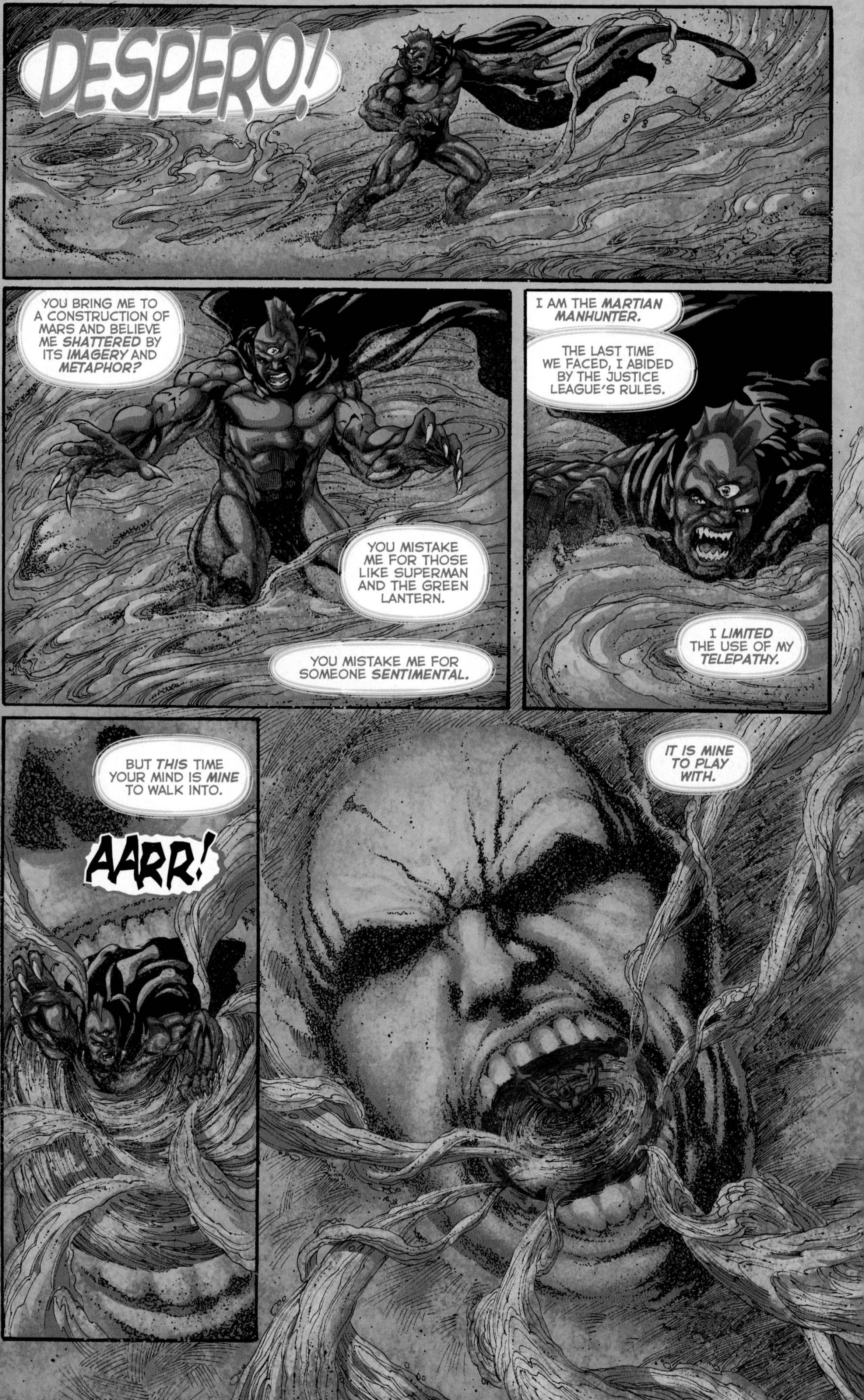
DESPERO!
YOU BRING ME TO A CONSTRUCTION OF MARS AND BELIEVE ME SHATTERED BY ITS IMAGERY AND METAPHOR?
YOU MISTAKE ME FOR THOSE LIKE SUPERMAN AND THE GREEN LANTERN.
YOU MISTAKE ME FOR SOMEONE SENTIMENTAL.
I AM THE MARTIAN MANHUNTER.
THE LAST TIME WE FACED, I ABIDED BY THE JUSTICE LEAGUE'S RULES.
I LIMITED THE USE OF MY TELEPATHY.
BUT THIS TIME YOUR MIND IS MINE TO WALK INTO.
AARR!
IT IS MINE TO PLAY WITH.

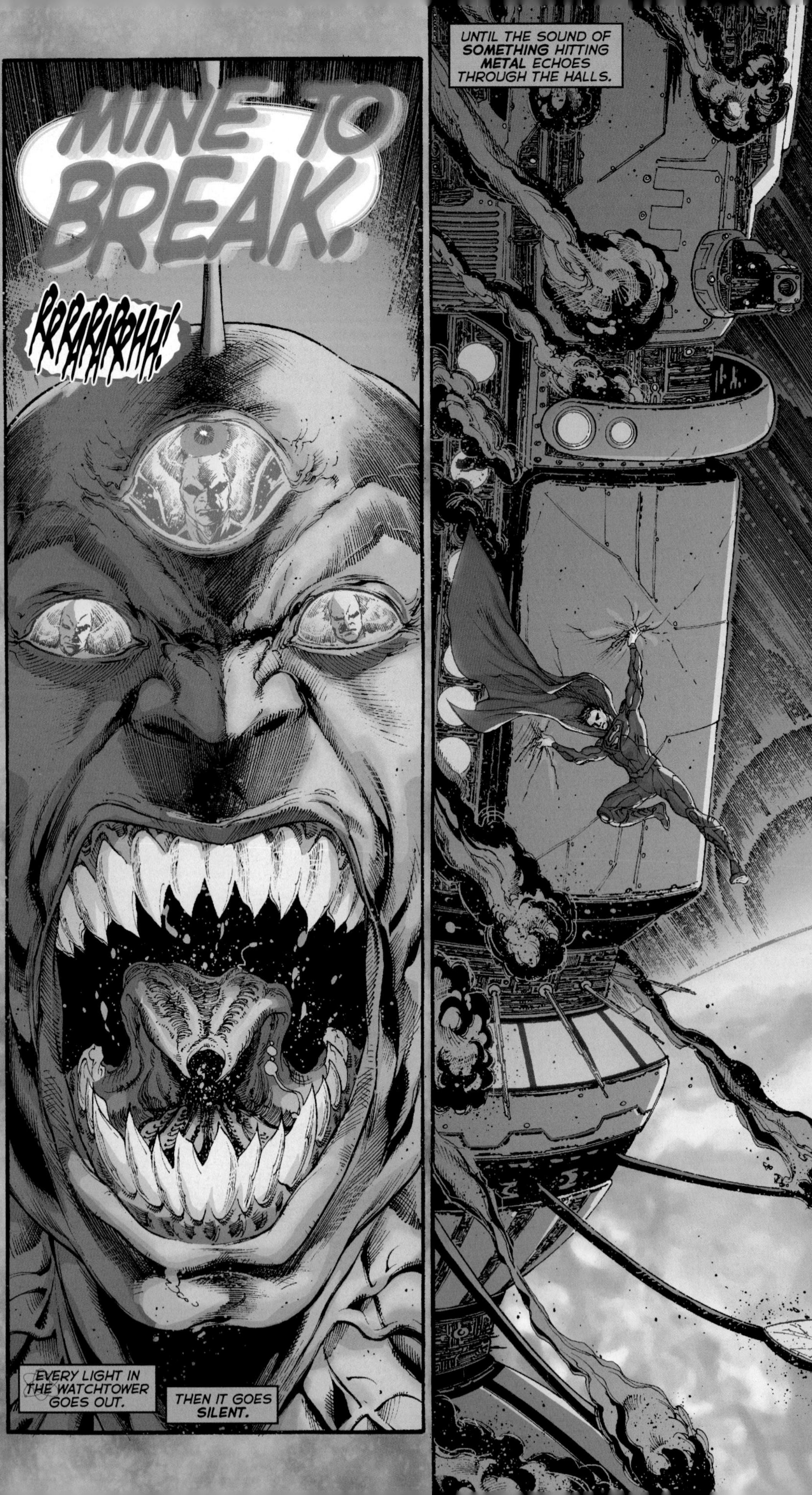
MINE TO BREAK.
RRRAAARRHH!
EVERY LIGHT IN THE WATCHTOWER GOES OUT.
THEN IT GOES SILENT.
UNTIL THE SOUND OF SOMETHING HITTING METAL ECHOES THROUGH THE HALLS.

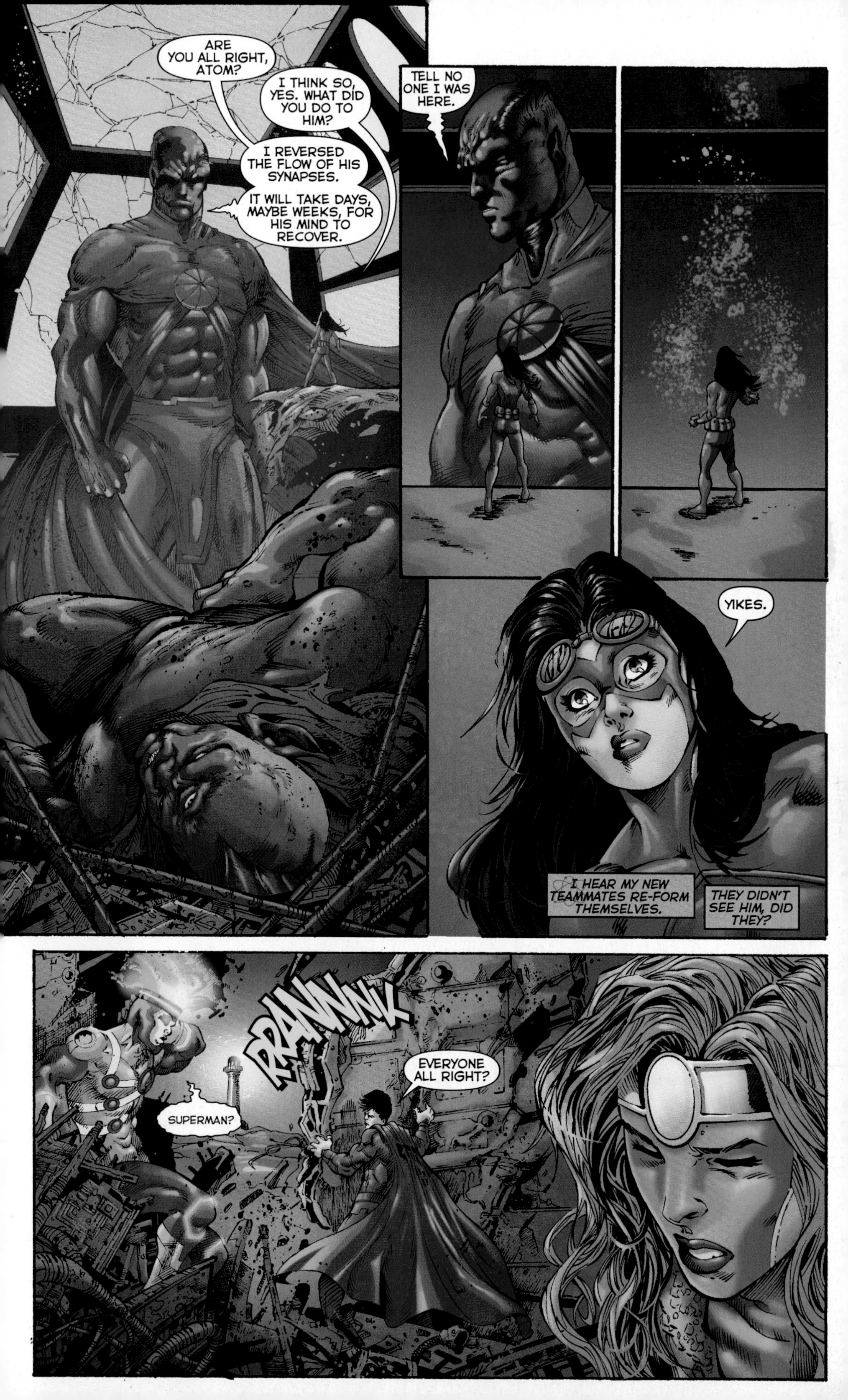
ARE YOU ALL RIGHT, ATOM?
I THINK SO, YES. WHAT DID YOU DO TO HIM?
I REVERSED THE FLOW OF HIS SYNAPSES.
IT WILL TAKE DAYS, MAYBE WEEKS, FOR HIS MIND TO RECOVER.
TELL NO ONE I WAS HERE.
YIKES.
I HEAR MY NEW TEAMMATES RE-FORM THEMSELVES.
THEY DIDN'T SEE HIM, DID THEY?
RRANNNNK
SUPERMAN?
EVERYONE ALL RIGHT?

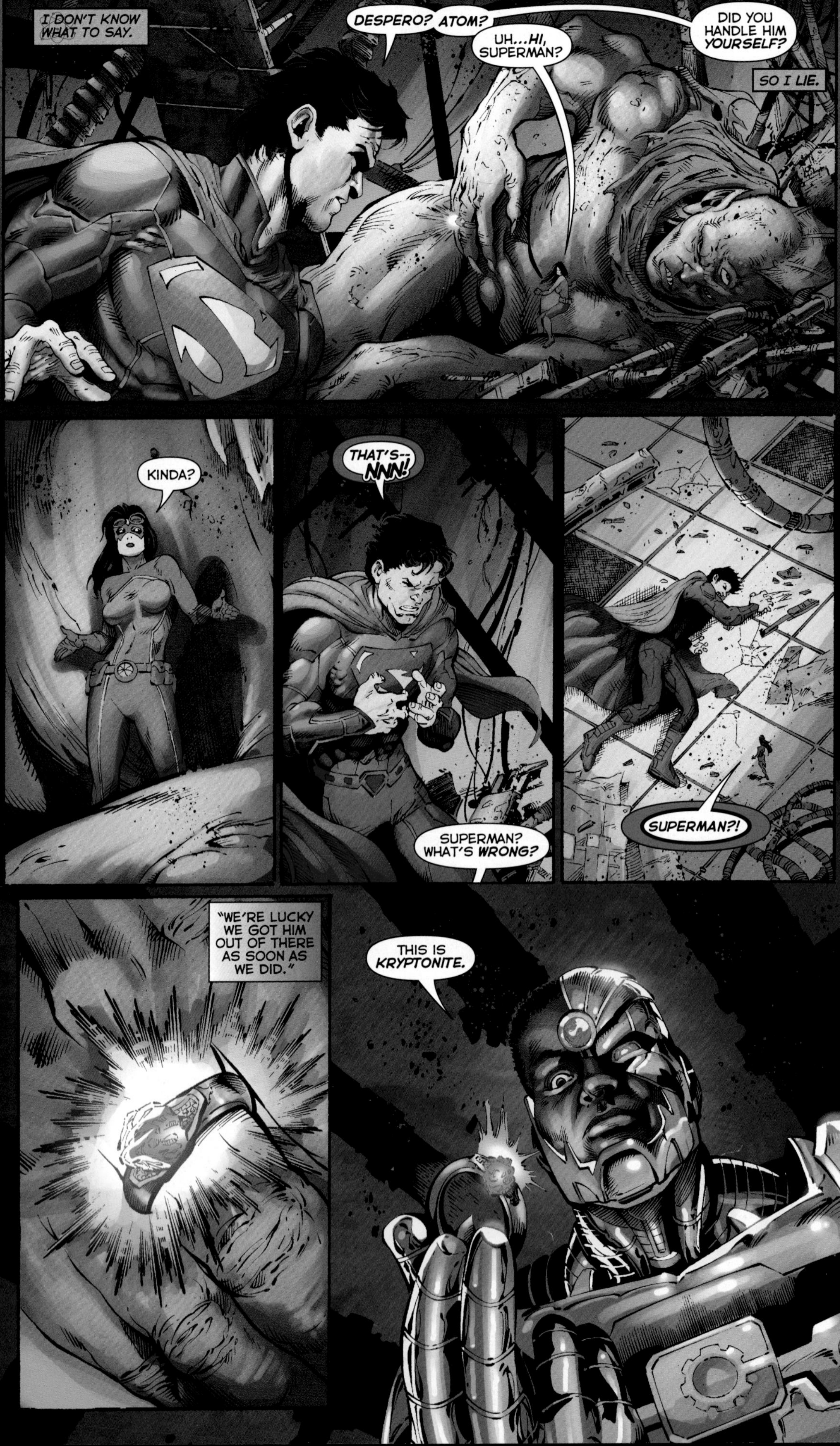
I DON'T KNOW WHAT TO SAY.
DESPERO? ATOM?
UH...HI, SUPERMAN?
DID YOU HANDLE HIM YOURSELF?
SO I LIE.
KINDA?
THAT'S--NNN!
SUPERMAN? WHAT'S WRONG?
SUPERMAN?!
"WE'RE LUCKY WE GOT HIM OUT OF THERE AS SOON AS WE DID."
THIS IS KRYPTONITE.

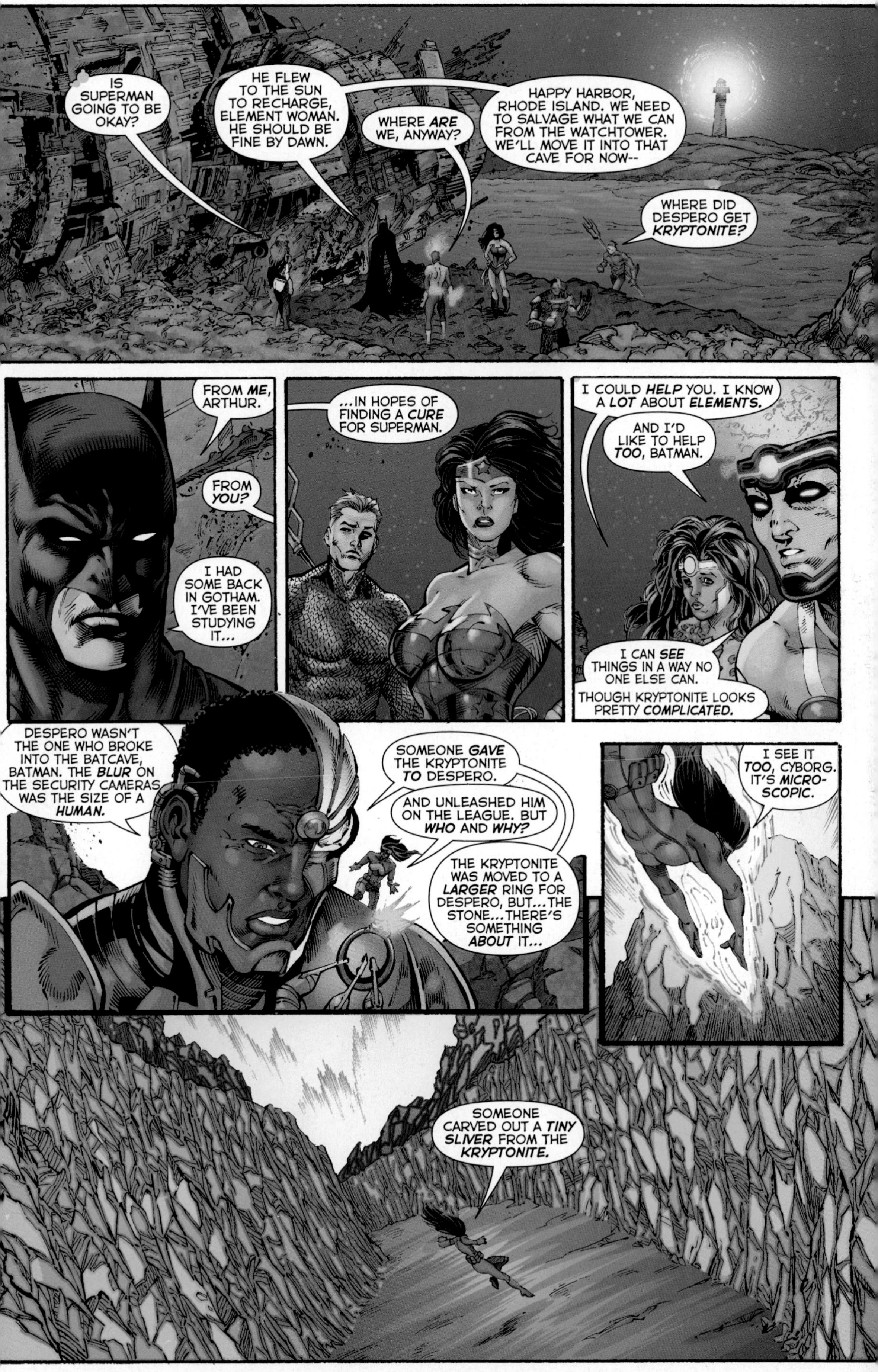
IS SUPERMAN GOING TO BE OKAY?
HE FLEW TO THE SUN TO RECHARGE, ELEMENT WOMAN. HE SHOULD BE FINE BY DAWN.
WHERE ARE WE, ANYWAY?
HAPPY HARBOR, RHODE ISLAND. WE NEED TO SALVAGE WHAT WE CAN FROM THE WATCHTOWER. WE'LL MOVE IT INTO THAT CAVE FOR NOW--
WHERE DID DESPERO GET KRYPTONITE?
FROM ME, ARTHUR.
FROM YOU?
I HAD SOME BACK IN GOTHAM. I'VE BEEN STUDYING IT...
...IN HOPES OF FINDING A CURE FOR SUPERMAN.
I COULD HELP YOU. I KNOW A LOT ABOUT ELEMENTS.
AND I'D LIKE TO HELP TOO, BATMAN.
I CAN SEE THINGS IN A WAY NO ONE ELSE CAN.
THOUGH KRYPTONITE LOOKS PRETTY COMPLICATED.
DESPERO WASN'T THE ONE WHO BROKE INTO THE BATCAVE, BATMAN. THE BLUR ON THE SECURITY CAMERAS WAS THE SIZE OF A HUMAN.
SOMEONE GAVE THE KRYPTONITE TO DESPERO.
AND UNLEASHED HIM ON THE LEAGUE. BUT WHO AND WHY?
THE KRYPTONITE WAS MOVED TO A LARGER RING FOR DESPERO, BUT...THE STONE...THERE'S SOMETHING ABOUT IT...
I SEE IT TOO, CYBORG. IT'S MICRO-SCOPIC.
SOMEONE CARVED OUT A TINY SLIVER FROM THE KRYPTONITE.

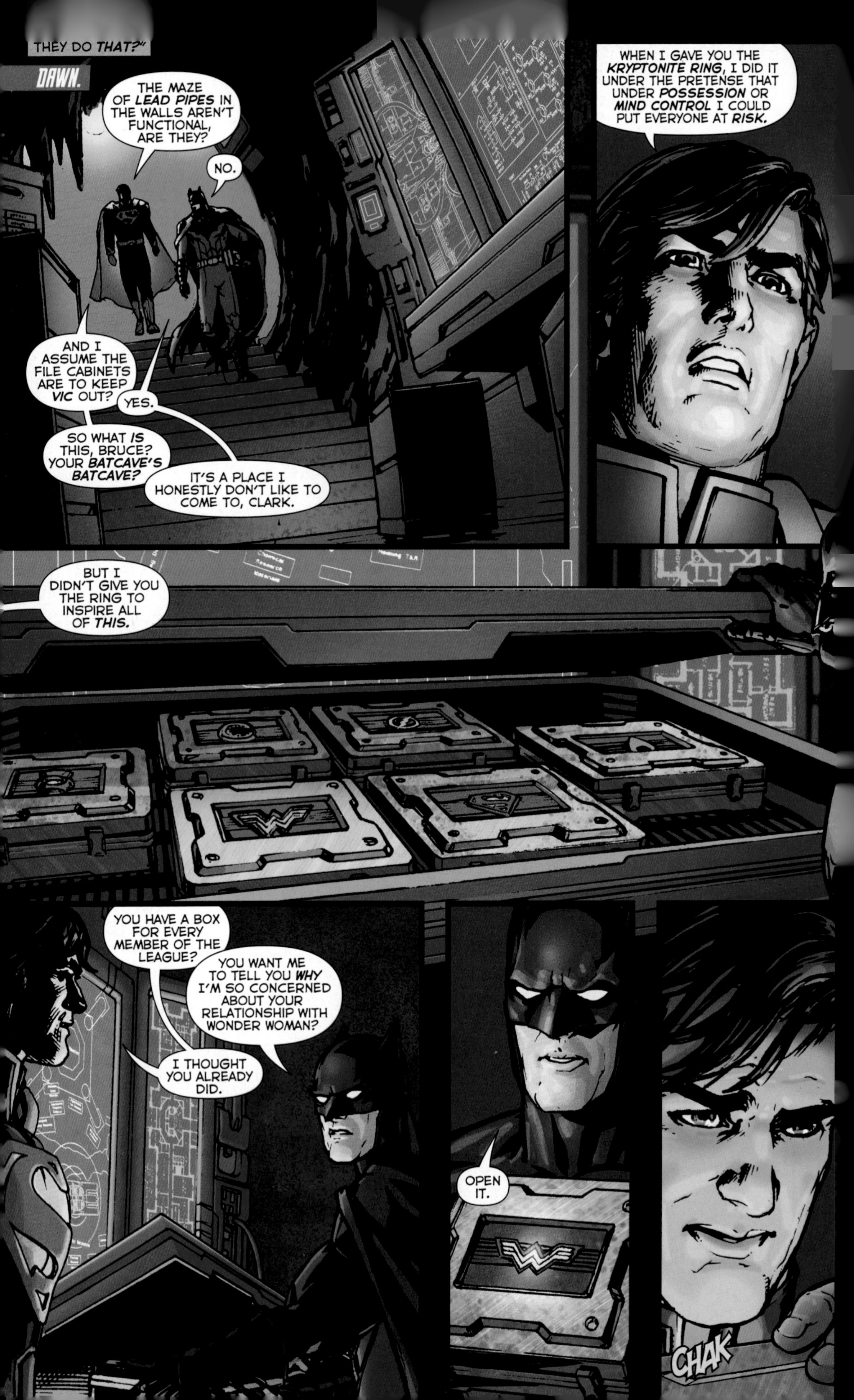
THEY DO THAT?"
DAWN.
THE MAZE OF LEAD PIPES IN THE WALLS AREN'T FUNCTIONAL, ARE THEY?
NO.
AND I ASSUME THE FILE CABINETS ARE TO KEEP VIC OUT?
YES.
SO WHAT IS THIS, BRUCE? YOUR BATCAVE'S BATCAVE?
IT'S A PLACE I HONESTLY DON'T LIKE TO COME TO, CLARK.
WHEN I GAVE YOU THE KRYPTONITE RING, I DID IT UNDER THE PRETENSE THAT UNDER POSSESSION OR MIND CONTROL I COULD PUT EVERYONE AT RISK.
BUT I DIDN'T GIVE YOU THE RING TO INSPIRE ALL OF THIS.
YOU HAVE A BOX FOR EVERY MEMBER OF THE LEAGUE?
I THOUGHT YOU ALREADY DID.
YOU WANT ME TO TELL YOU WHY I'M SO CONCERNED ABOUT YOUR RELATIONSHIP WITH WONDER WOMAN?
OPEN IT.
CHAK

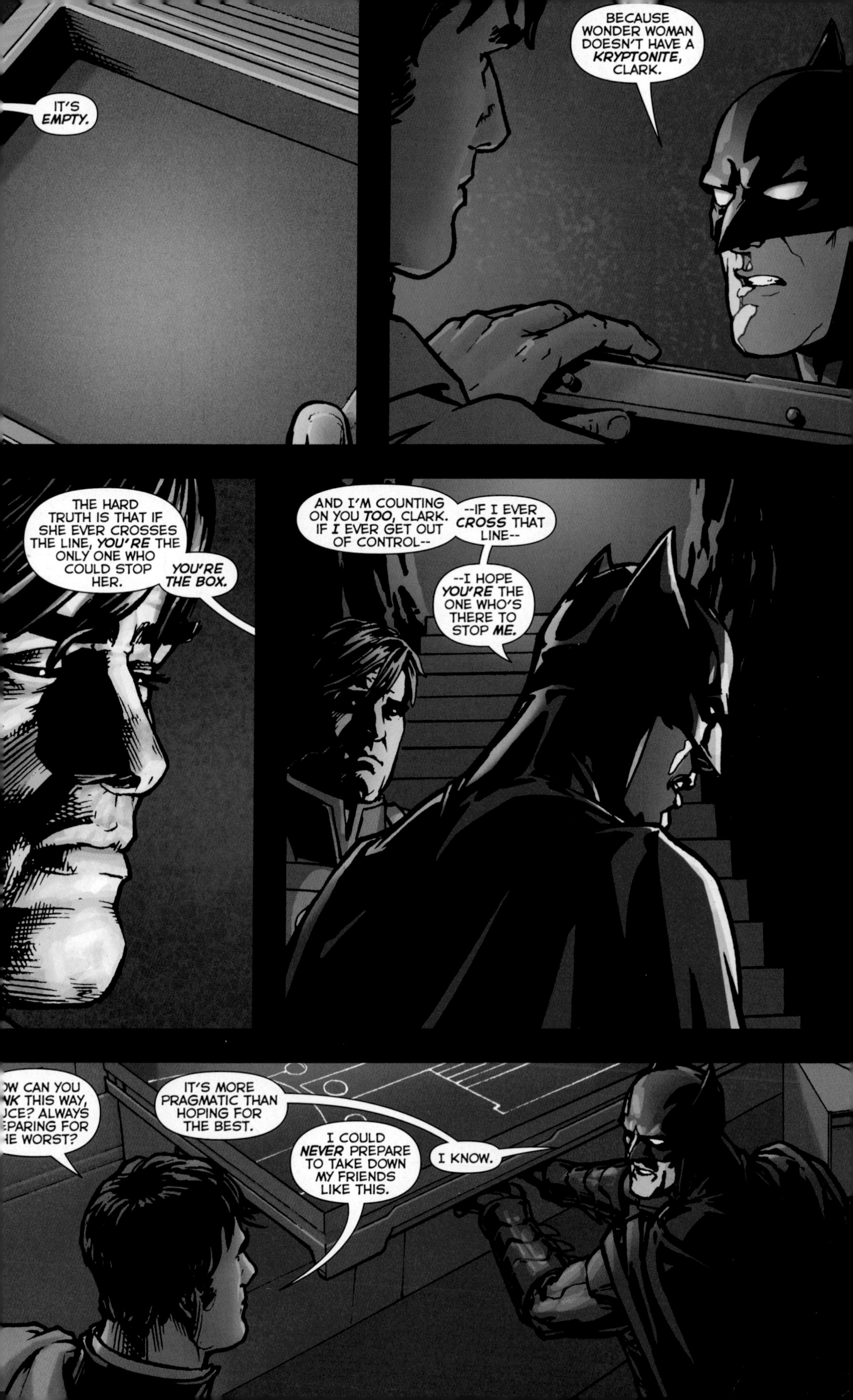
IT'S *EMPTY.*
BECAUSE WONDER WOMAN DOESN'T HAVE A *KRYPTONITE,* CLARK.
THE HARD TRUTH IS THAT IF SHE EVER CROSSES THE LINE, *YOU'RE* THE ONLY ONE WHO COULD STOP HER.
YOU'RE THE BOX.
AND I'M COUNTING ON YOU *TOO,* CLARK. IF *I* EVER GET OUT OF CONTROL--
--IF I EVER *CROSS* THAT LINE--
--I HOPE *YOU'RE* THE ONE WHO'S THERE TO STOP *ME.*
OW CAN YOU NK THIS WAY, UCE? ALWAYS EPARING FOR HE WORST?
IT'S MORE PRAGMATIC THAN HOPING FOR THE BEST.
I COULD *NEVER* PREPARE TO TAKE DOWN MY FRIENDS LIKE THIS.
I KNOW.

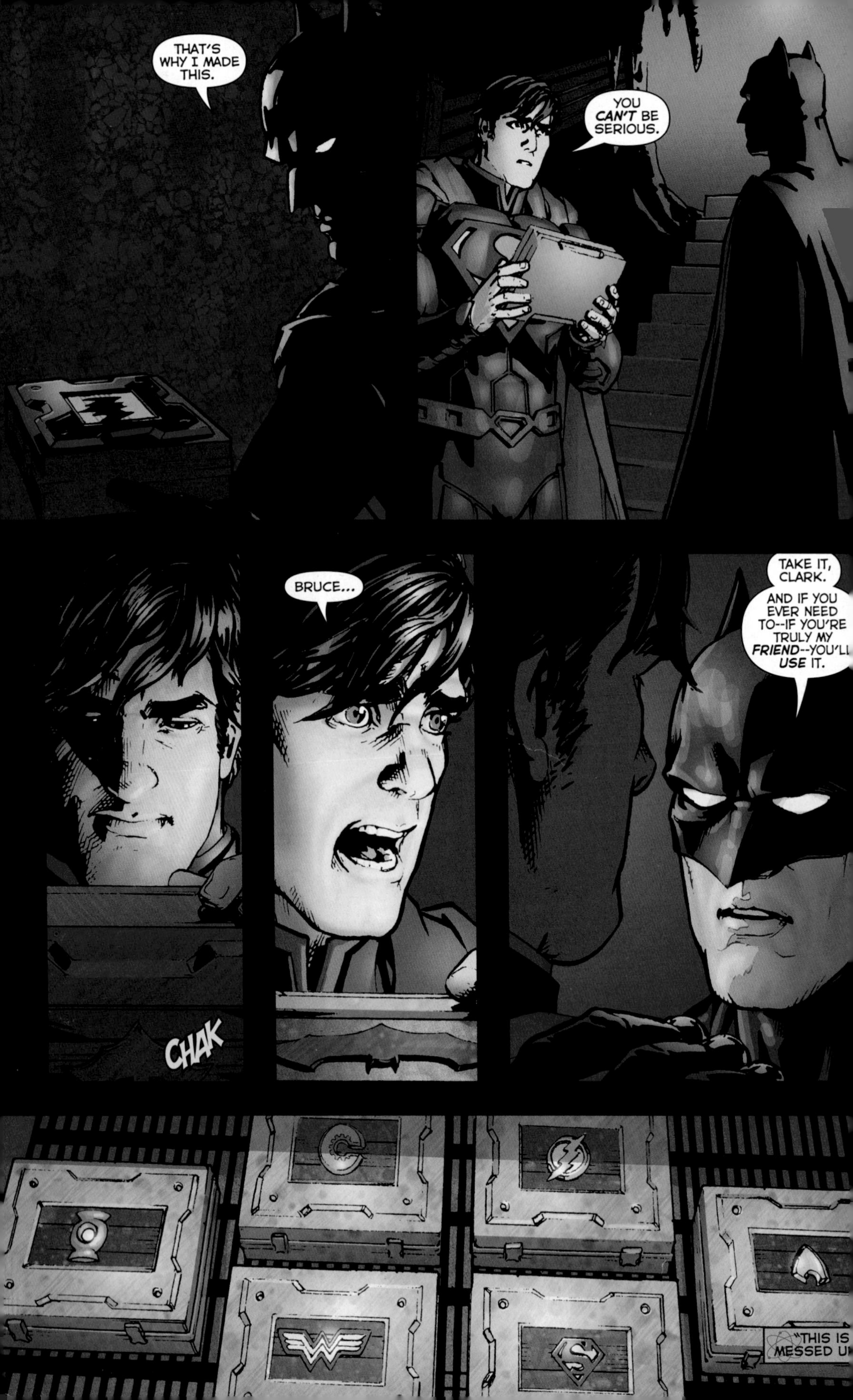
THAT'S WHY I MADE THIS.
YOU *CAN'T* BE SERIOUS.
CHAK
BRUCE...
TAKE IT, CLARK.
AND IF YOU EVER NEED TO--IF YOU'RE TRULY MY *FRIEND*--YOU'LL *USE* IT.
"THIS IS MESSED

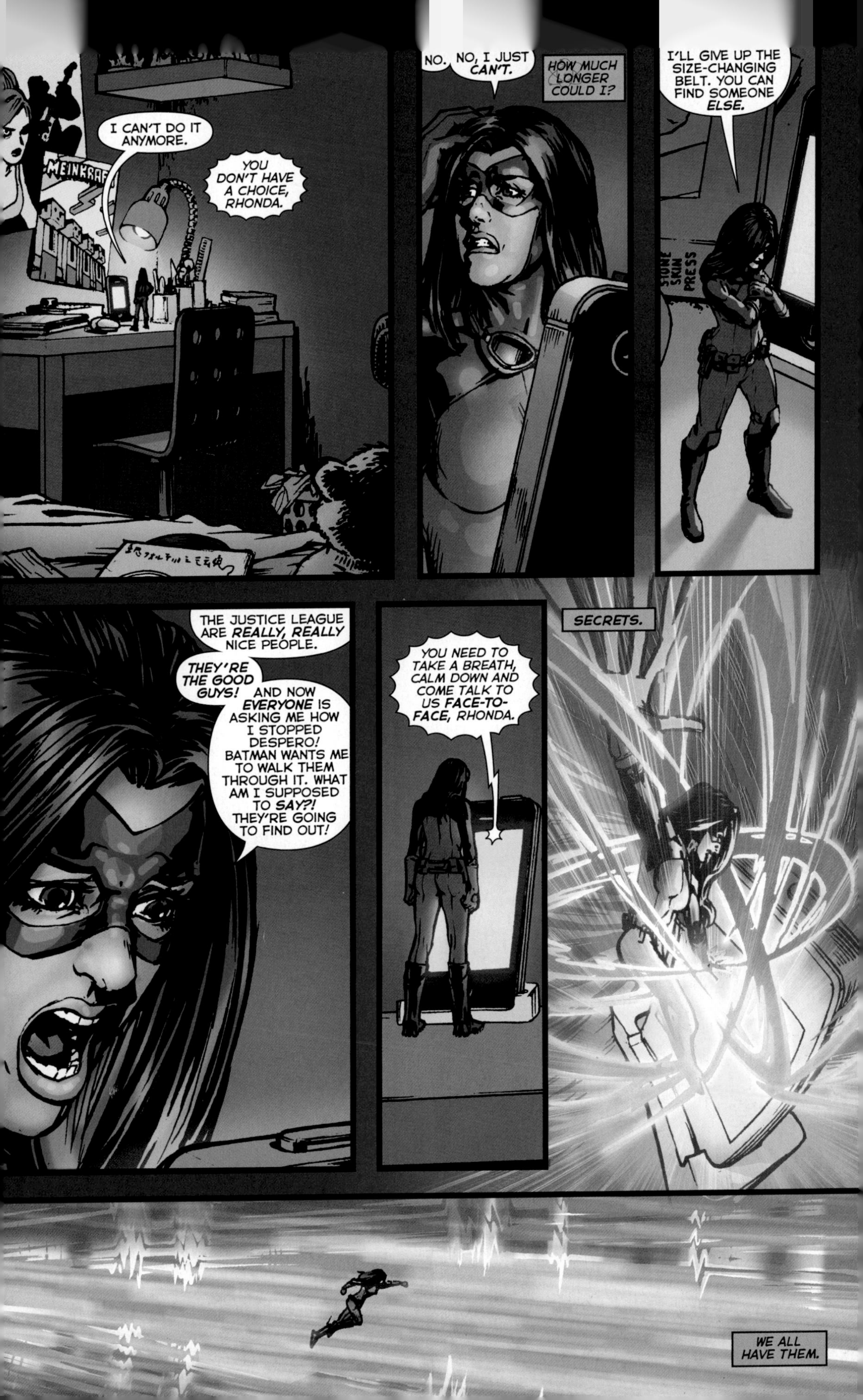

I CAN'T DO IT ANYMORE.
YOU DON'T HAVE A CHOICE, RHONDA.
NO.
NO, I JUST CAN'T.
HOW MUCH LONGER COULD I?
STONE SKIN PRESS
I'LL GIVE UP THE SIZE-CHANGING BELT. YOU CAN FIND SOMEONE ELSE.
THE JUSTICE LEAGUE ARE REALLY, REALLY NICE PEOPLE.
THEY'RE THE GOOD GUYS!
AND NOW EVERYONE IS ASKING ME HOW I STOPPED DESPERO! BATMAN WANTS ME TO WALK THEM THROUGH IT. WHAT AM I SUPPOSED TO SAY?! THEY'RE GOING TO FIND OUT!
YOU NEED TO TAKE A BREATH, CALM DOWN AND COME TALK TO US FACE-TO-FACE, RHONDA.
SECRETS.
WE ALL HAVE THEM.

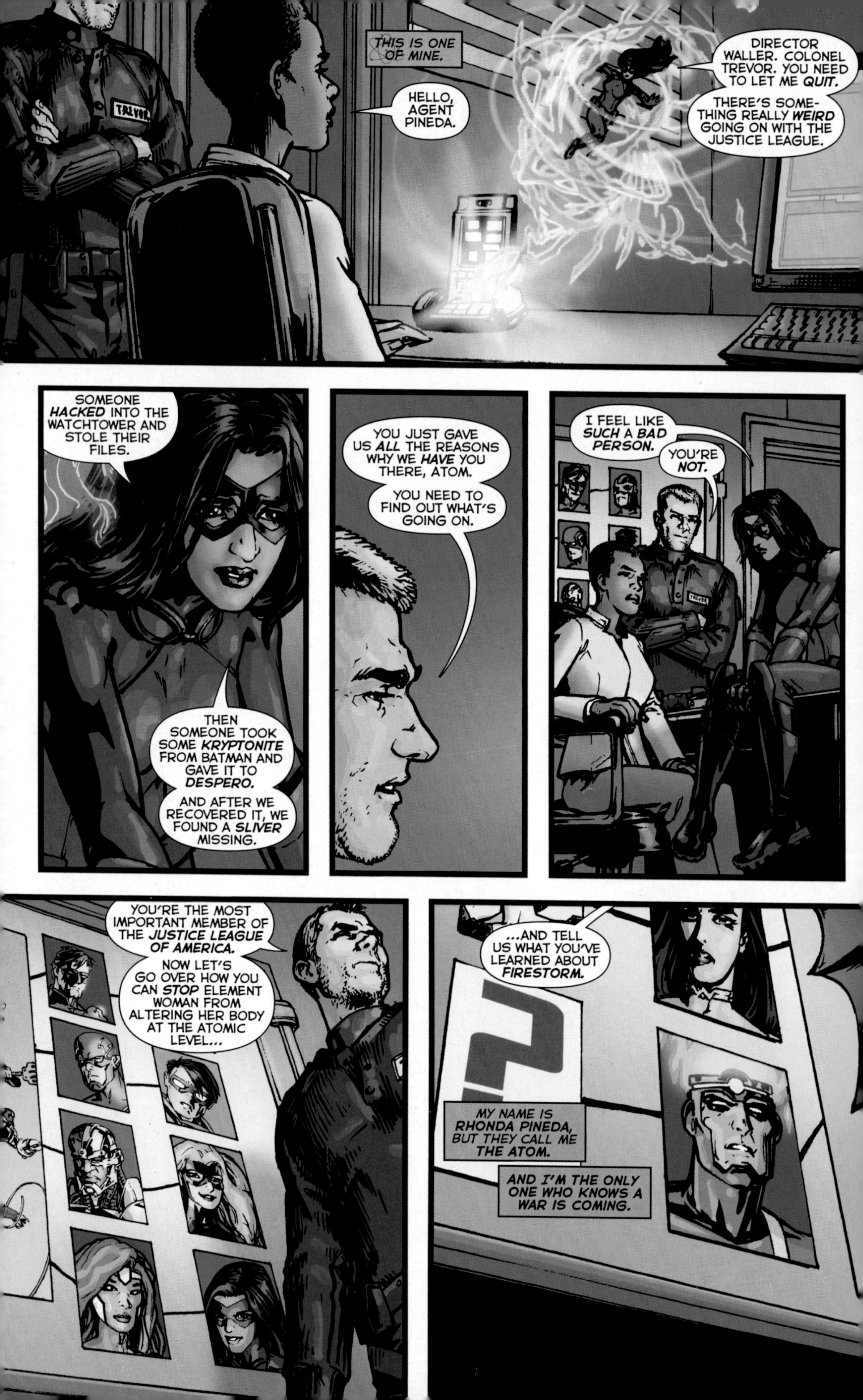
THIS IS ONE OF MINE.
HELLO, AGENT PINEDA.
DIRECTOR WALLER. COLONEL TREVOR. YOU NEED TO LET ME QUIT.
THERE'S SOMETHING REALLY WEIRD GOING ON WITH THE JUSTICE LEAGUE.
SOMEONE HACKED INTO THE WATCHTOWER AND STOLE THEIR FILES.
THEN SOMEONE TOOK SOME KRYPTONITE FROM BATMAN AND GAVE IT TO DESPERO.
AND AFTER WE RECOVERED IT, WE FOUND A SLIVER MISSING.
YOU JUST GAVE US ALL THE REASONS WHY WE HAVE YOU THERE, ATOM.
YOU NEED TO FIND OUT WHAT'S GOING ON.
I FEEL LIKE SUCH A BAD PERSON.
YOU'RE NOT.
YOU'RE THE MOST IMPORTANT MEMBER OF THE JUSTICE LEAGUE OF AMERICA.
NOW LET'S GO OVER HOW YOU CAN STOP ELEMENT WOMAN FROM ALTERING HER BODY AT THE ATOMIC LEVEL...
...AND TELL US WHAT YOU'VE LEARNED ABOUT FIRESTORM.
MY NAME IS RHONDA PINEDA, BUT THEY CALL ME THE ATOM.
AND I'M THE ONLY ONE WHO KNOWS A WAR IS COMING.

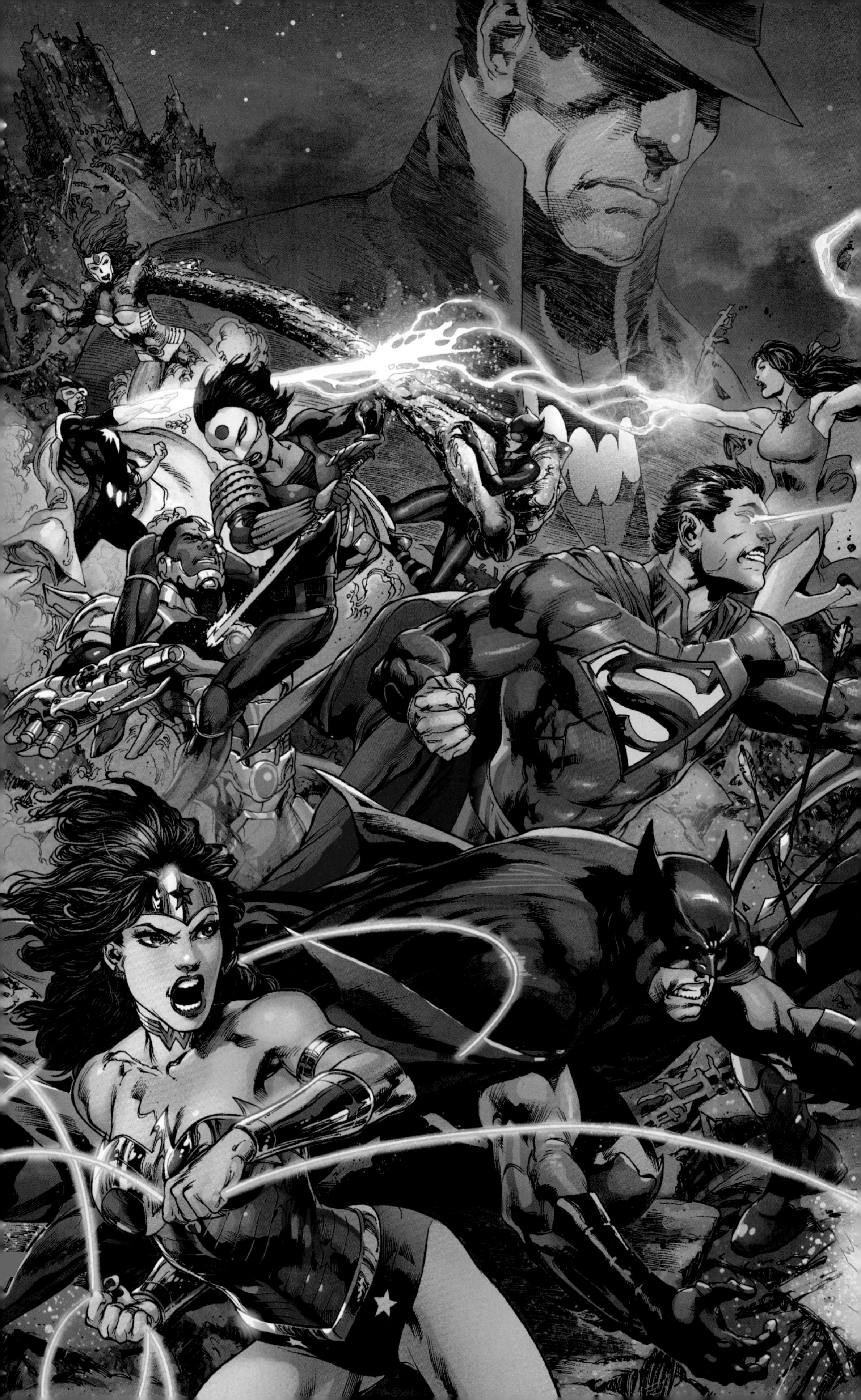

TRINITY WAR: THE DEATH CARD

GEOFF JOHNS writer **IVAN REIS** penciller **JOE PRADO** and **OCLAIR ALBERT** inkers **ROD REIS** colorist **IVAN REIS, JOE PRADO** and **ROD REIS** cover arists

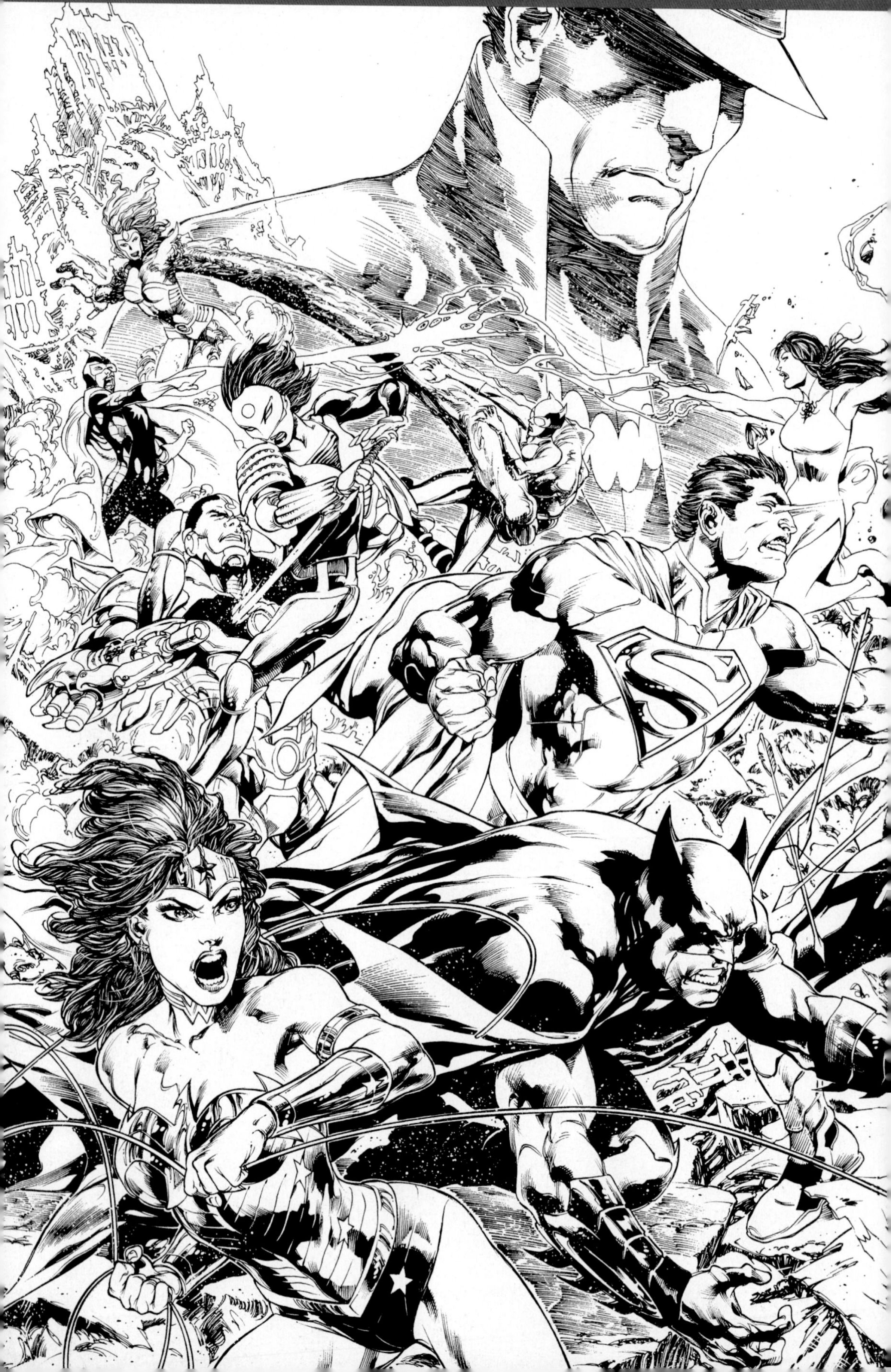

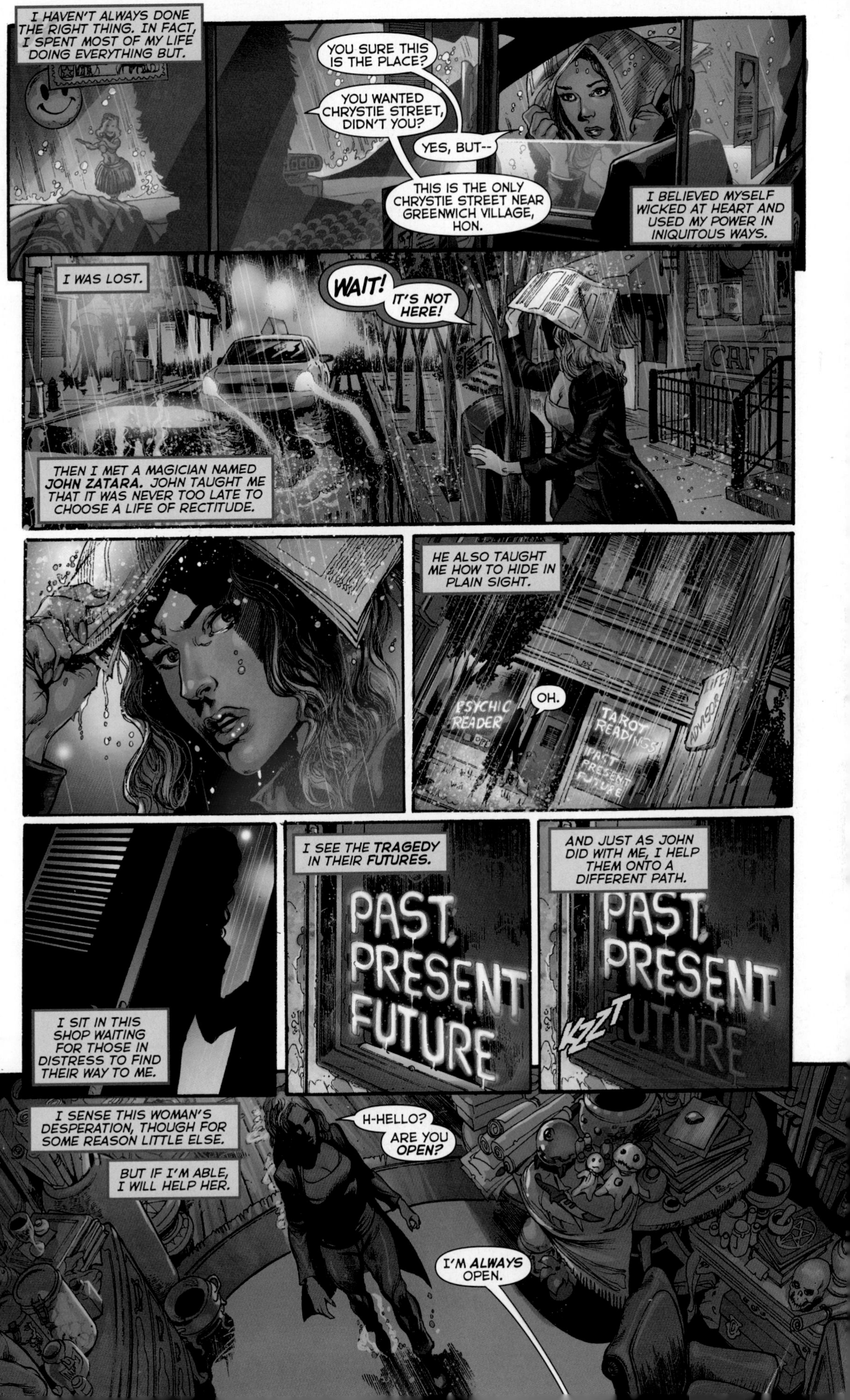
I HAVEN'T ALWAYS DONE THE RIGHT THING. IN FACT, I SPENT MOST OF MY LIFE DOING EVERYTHING BUT.
YOU SURE THIS IS THE PLACE?
YOU WANTED CHRYSTIE STREET, DIDN'T YOU?
YES, BUT--
THIS IS THE ONLY CHRYSTIE STREET NEAR GREENWICH VILLAGE, HON.
I BELIEVED MYSELF WICKED AT HEART AND USED MY POWER IN INIQUITOUS WAYS.
I WAS LOST.
WAIT! IT'S NOT HERE!
CAFE
THEN I MET A MAGICIAN NAMED JOHN ZATARA. JOHN TAUGHT ME THAT IT WAS NEVER TOO LATE TO CHOOSE A LIFE OF RECTITUDE.
HE ALSO TAUGHT ME HOW TO HIDE IN PLAIN SIGHT.
PSYCHIC READER
OH.
TAROT READINGS!
PAST PRESENT FUTURE
LIFE ADVISOR
I SIT IN THIS SHOP WAITING FOR THOSE IN DISTRESS TO FIND THEIR WAY TO ME.
I SEE THE TRAGEDY IN THEIR FUTURES.
PAST, PRESENT FUTURE
AND JUST AS JOHN DID WITH ME, I HELP THEM ONTO A DIFFERENT PATH.
PAST, PRESENT FUTURE
KZZT
I SENSE THIS WOMAN'S DESPERATION, THOUGH FOR SOME REASON LITTLE ELSE.
BUT IF I'M ABLE, I WILL HELP HER.
H-HELLO? ARE YOU OPEN?
I'M ALWAYS OPEN.

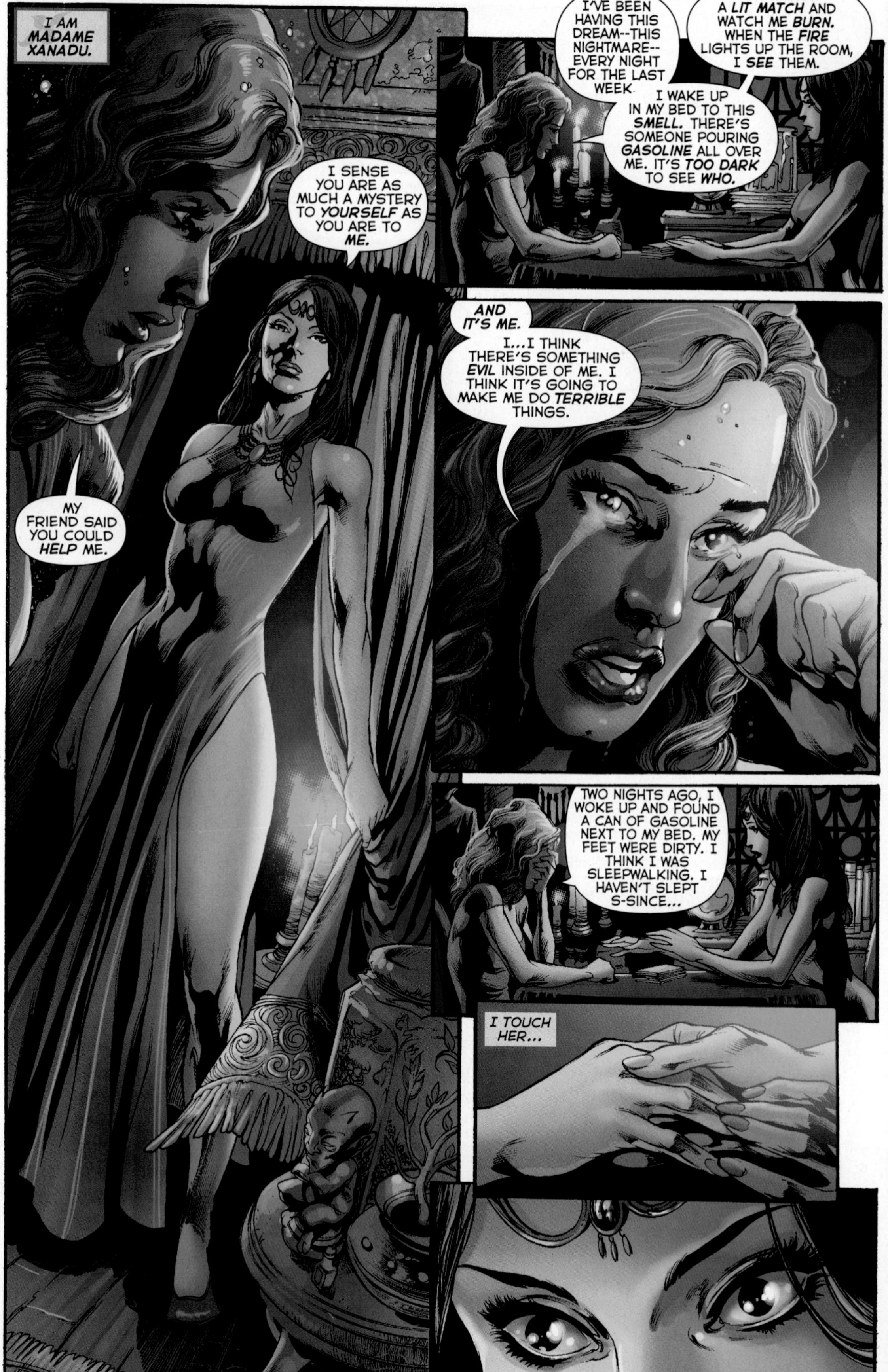
I AM MADAME XANADU.
I SENSE YOU ARE AS MUCH A MYSTERY TO YOURSELF AS YOU ARE TO ME.
MY FRIEND SAID YOU COULD HELP ME.
I'VE BEEN HAVING THIS DREAM--THIS NIGHTMARE--EVERY NIGHT FOR THE LAST WEEK.
I WAKE UP IN MY BED TO THIS SMELL. THERE'S SOMEONE POURING GASOLINE ALL OVER ME. IT'S TOO DARK TO SEE WHO.
THEY THROW A LIT MATCH AND WATCH ME BURN. WHEN THE FIRE LIGHTS UP THE ROOM, I SEE THEM.
AND IT'S ME.
I...I THINK THERE'S SOMETHING EVIL INSIDE OF ME. I THINK IT'S GOING TO MAKE ME DO TERRIBLE THINGS.
TWO NIGHTS AGO, I WOKE UP AND FOUND A CAN OF GASOLINE NEXT TO MY BED. MY FEET WERE DIRTY. I THINK I WAS SLEEPWALKING. I HAVEN'T SLEPT S-SINCE...
I TOUCH HER...
...AND I SEE THE FUTURE.

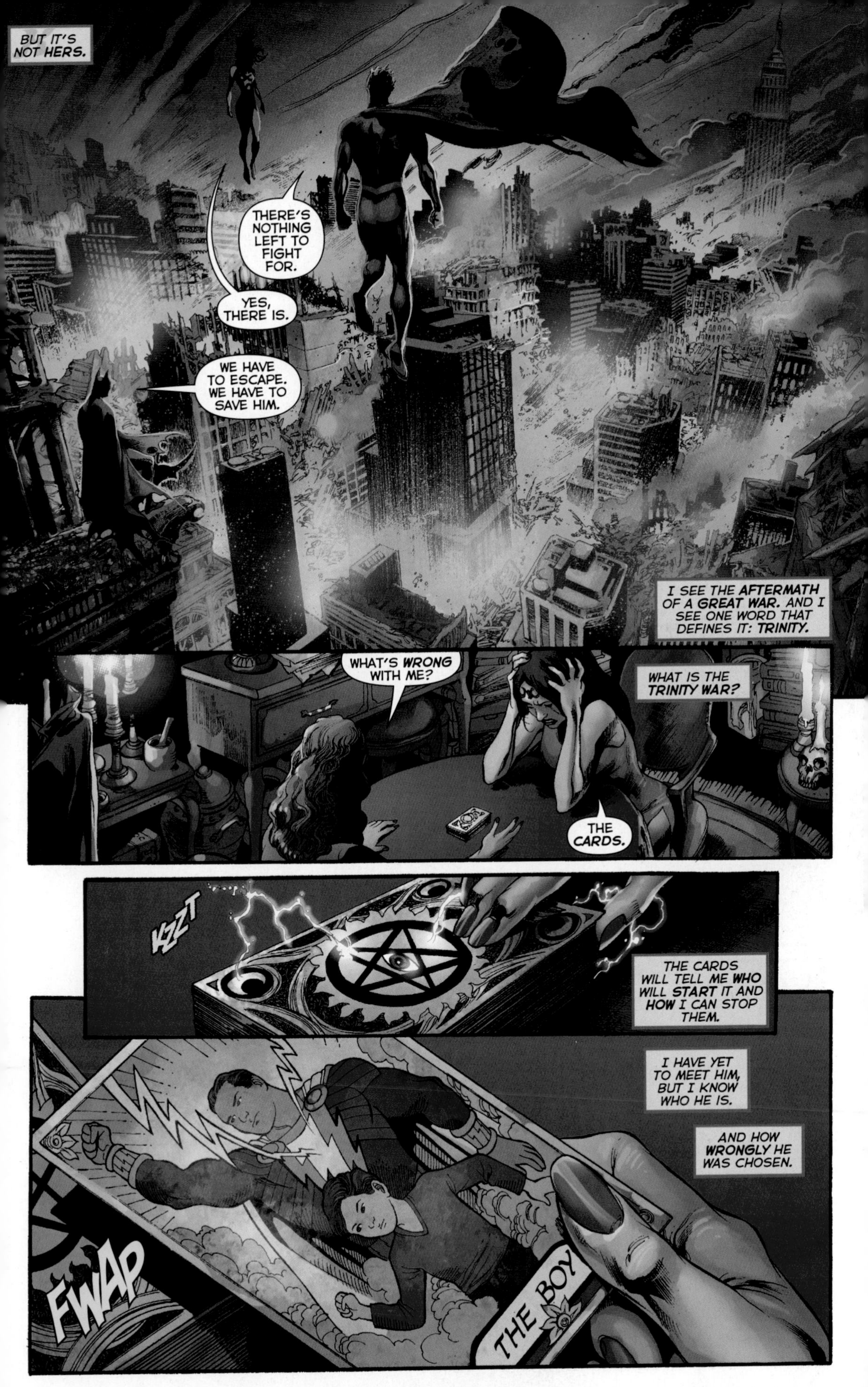
BUT IT'S NOT HERS.
THERE'S NOTHING LEFT TO FIGHT FOR.
YES, THERE IS.
WE HAVE TO ESCAPE. WE HAVE TO SAVE HIM.
I SEE THE AFTERMATH OF A GREAT WAR. AND I SEE ONE WORD THAT DEFINES IT: TRINITY.
WHAT'S WRONG WITH ME?
WHAT IS THE TRINITY WAR?
THE CARDS.
KZZT
THE CARDS WILL TELL ME WHO WILL START IT AND HOW I CAN STOP THEM.
I HAVE YET TO MEET HIM, BUT I KNOW WHO HE IS.
AND HOW WRONGLY HE WAS CHOSEN.
FWAP
THE BOY

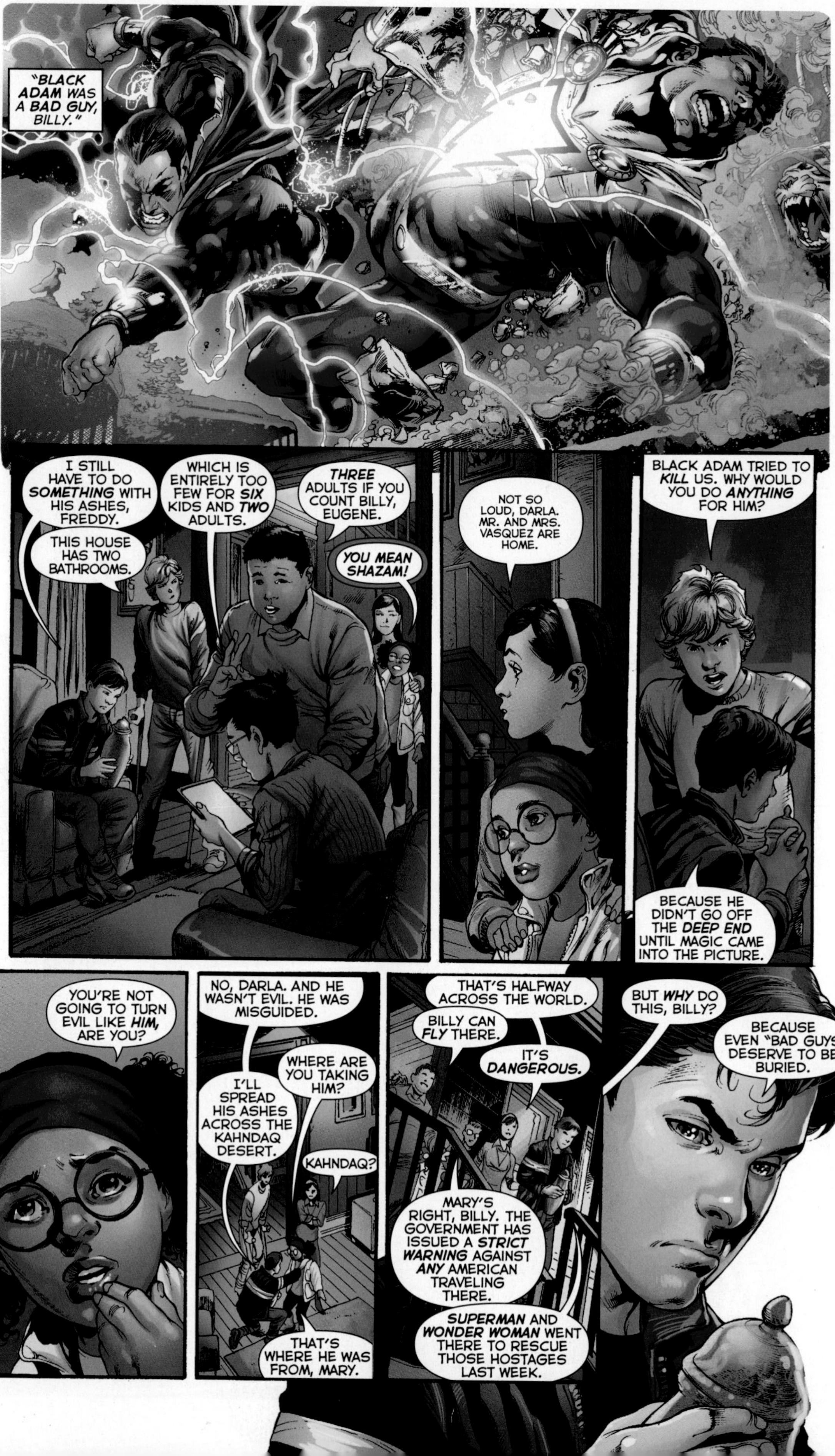
"BLACK ADAM WAS A BAD GUY, BILLY."
I STILL HAVE TO DO SOMETHING WITH HIS ASHES, FREDDY.
THIS HOUSE HAS TWO BATHROOMS.
WHICH IS ENTIRELY TOO FEW FOR SIX KIDS AND TWO ADULTS.
THREE ADULTS IF YOU COUNT BILLY, EUGENE.
YOU MEAN SHAZAM!
NOT SO LOUD, DARLA. MR. AND MRS. VASQUEZ ARE HOME.
BLACK ADAM TRIED TO KILL US. WHY WOULD YOU DO ANYTHING FOR HIM?
BECAUSE HE DIDN'T GO OFF THE DEEP END UNTIL MAGIC CAME INTO THE PICTURE.
YOU'RE NOT GOING TO TURN EVIL LIKE HIM, ARE YOU?
NO, DARLA. AND HE WASN'T EVIL. HE WAS MISGUIDED.
I'LL SPREAD HIS ASHES ACROSS THE KAHNDAQ DESERT.
WHERE ARE YOU TAKING HIM?
KAHNDAQ?
THAT'S WHERE HE WAS FROM, MARY.
THAT'S HALFWAY ACROSS THE WORLD.
BILLY CAN FLY THERE.
IT'S DANGEROUS.
MARY'S RIGHT, BILLY. THE GOVERNMENT HAS ISSUED A STRICT WARNING AGAINST ANY AMERICAN TRAVELING THERE.
SUPERMAN AND WONDER WOMAN WENT THERE TO RESCUE THOSE HOSTAGES LAST WEEK.
BUT WHY DO THIS, BILLY?
BECAUSE EVEN "BAD GUYS" DESERVE TO BE BURIED.

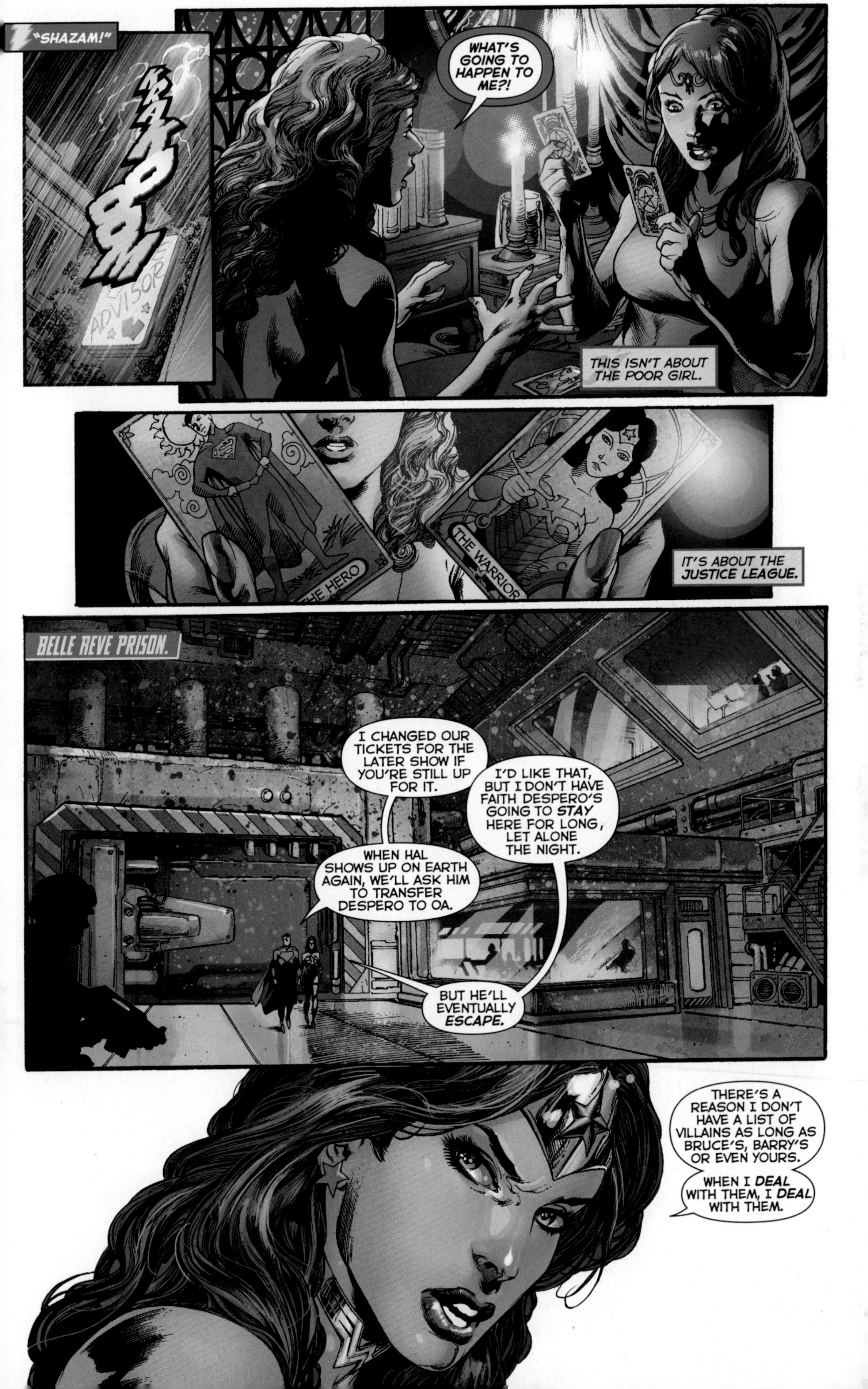
"SHAZAM!"
KRAKOOM
ADVISOR
WHAT'S GOING TO HAPPEN TO ME?!
THIS ISN'T ABOUT THE POOR GIRL.
THE HERO
THE WARRIOR
IT'S ABOUT THE *JUSTICE LEAGUE.*
BELLE REVE PRISON.
I CHANGED OUR TICKETS FOR THE LATER SHOW IF YOU'RE STILL UP FOR IT.
I'D LIKE THAT, BUT I DON'T HAVE FAITH DESPERO'S GOING TO *STAY* HERE FOR LONG, LET ALONE THE NIGHT.
WHEN HAL SHOWS UP ON EARTH AGAIN, WE'LL ASK HIM TO TRANSFER DESPERO TO OA.
BUT HE'LL EVENTUALLY *ESCAPE.*
THERE'S A REASON I DON'T HAVE A LIST OF VILLAINS AS LONG AS BRUCE'S, BARRY'S OR EVEN YOURS.
WHEN I *DEAL* WITH THEM, I *DEAL* WITH THEM.

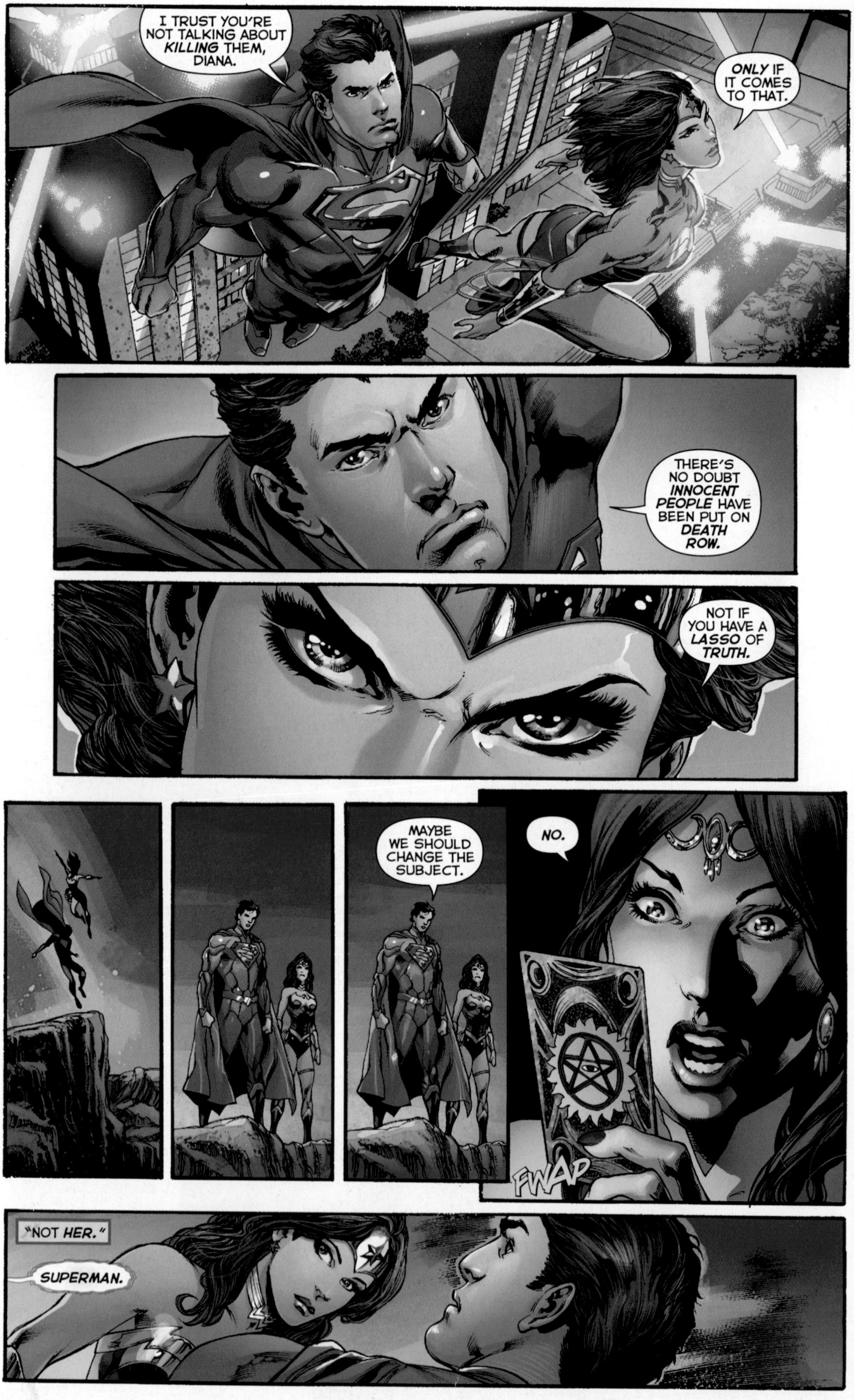
I TRUST YOU'RE NOT TALKING ABOUT *KILLING* THEM, DIANA.
ONLY IF IT COMES TO THAT.
THERE'S NO DOUBT *INNOCENT PEOPLE* HAVE BEEN PUT ON *DEATH ROW.*
NOT IF YOU HAVE A *LASSO* OF *TRUTH.*
MAYBE WE SHOULD CHANGE THE SUBJECT.
NO.
FWAP
"NOT *HER.*"
SUPERMAN.

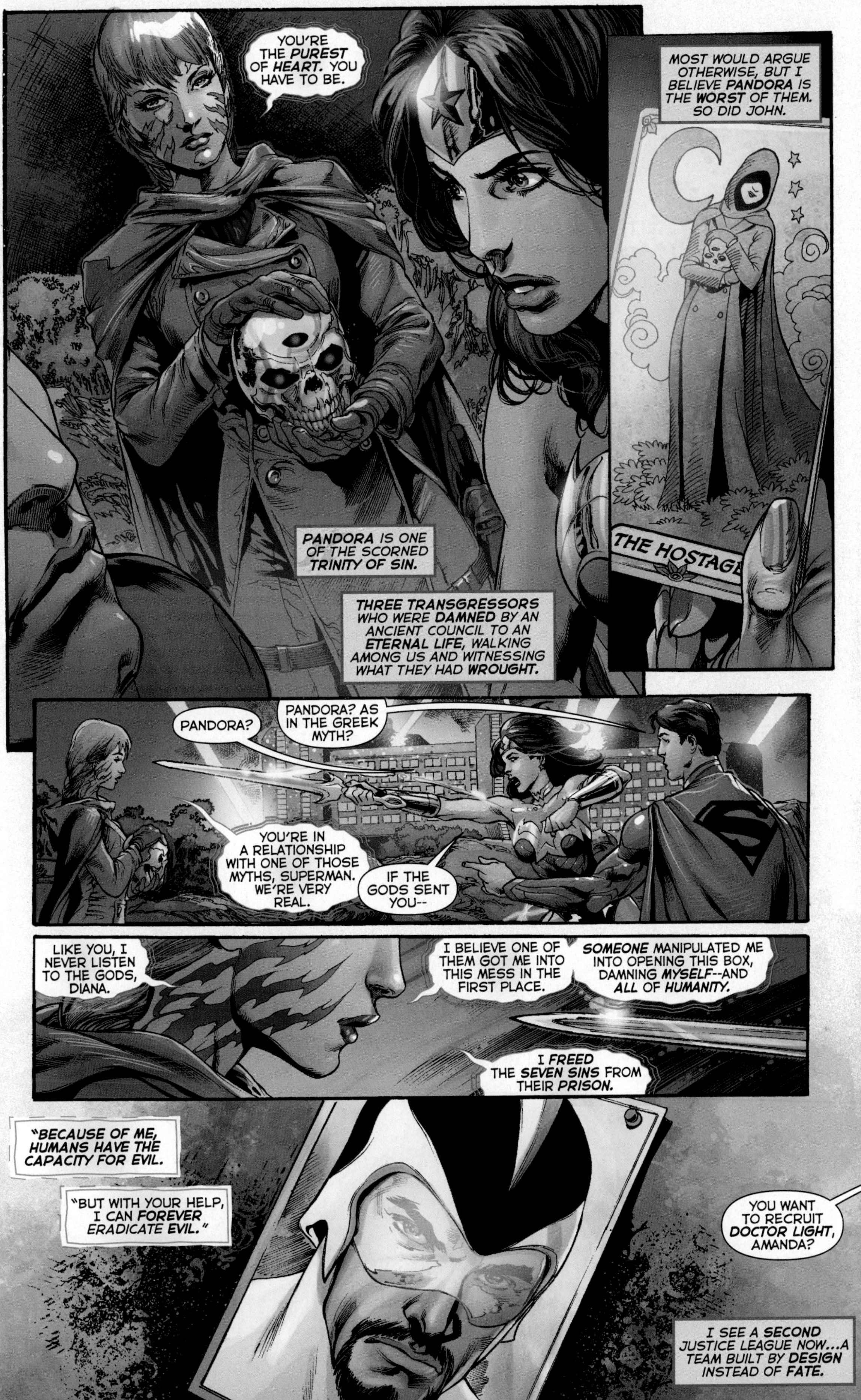
YOU'RE THE PUREST OF HEART. YOU HAVE TO BE.
PANDORA IS ONE OF THE SCORNED TRINITY OF SIN.
THREE TRANSGRESSORS WHO WERE DAMNED BY AN ANCIENT COUNCIL TO AN ETERNAL LIFE, WALKING AMONG US AND WITNESSING WHAT THEY HAD WROUGHT.
MOST WOULD ARGUE OTHERWISE, BUT I BELIEVE PANDORA IS THE WORST OF THEM. SO DID JOHN.
THE HOSTAGE
PANDORA?
PANDORA? AS IN THE GREEK MYTH?
YOU'RE IN A RELATIONSHIP WITH ONE OF THOSE MYTHS, SUPERMAN. WE'RE VERY REAL.
IF THE GODS SENT YOU--
LIKE YOU, I NEVER LISTEN TO THE GODS, DIANA.
I BELIEVE ONE OF THEM GOT ME INTO THIS MESS IN THE FIRST PLACE.
SOMEONE MANIPULATED ME INTO OPENING THIS BOX, DAMNING MYSELF--AND ALL OF HUMANITY.
I FREED THE SEVEN SINS FROM THEIR PRISON.
"BECAUSE OF ME, HUMANS HAVE THE CAPACITY FOR EVIL.
"BUT WITH YOUR HELP, I CAN FOREVER ERADICATE EVIL."
YOU WANT TO RECRUIT DOCTOR LIGHT, AMANDA?
I SEE A SECOND JUSTICE LEAGUE NOW...A TEAM BUILT BY DESIGN INSTEAD OF FATE.

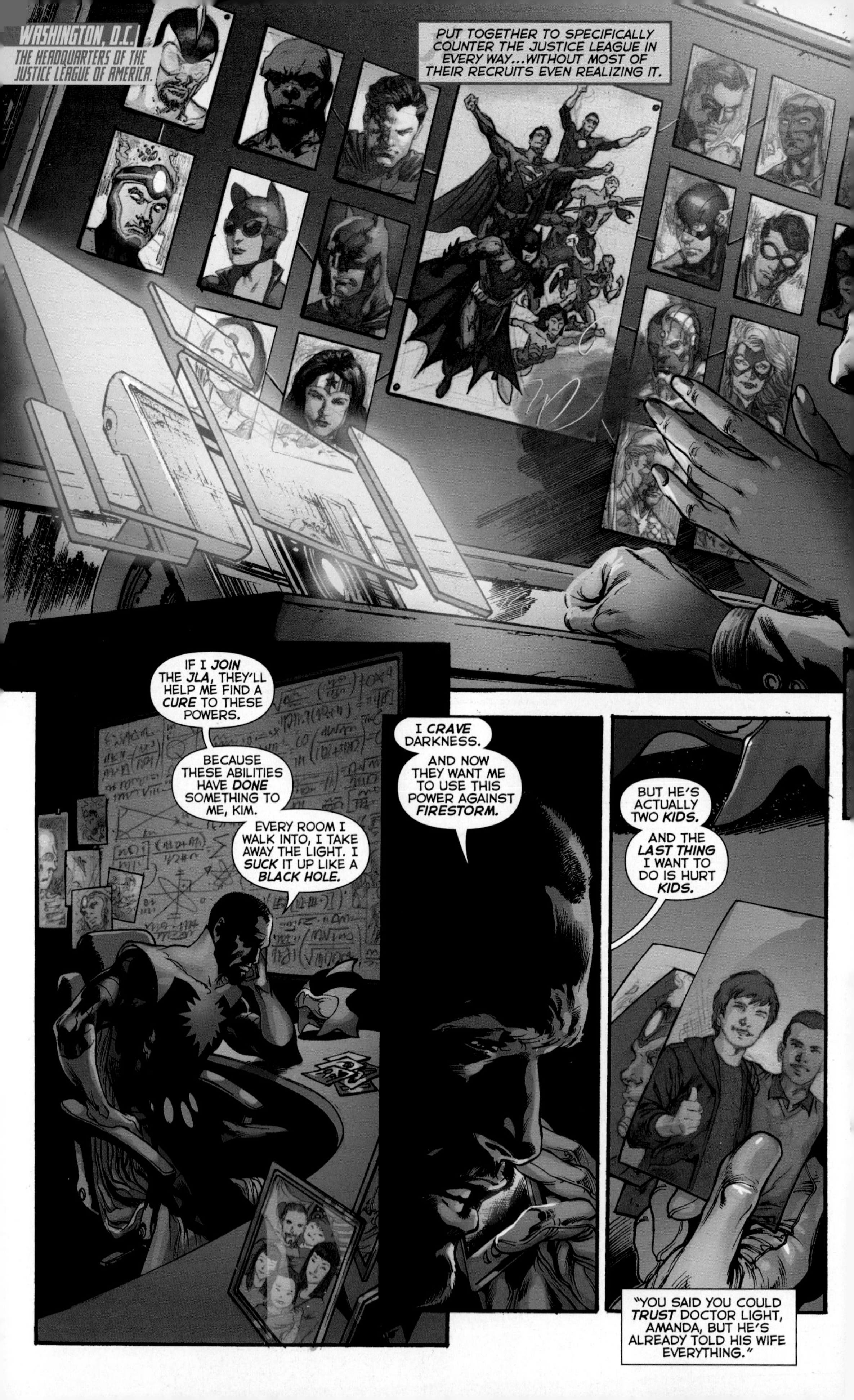
WASHINGTON, D.C.
THE HEADQUARTERS OF THE JUSTICE LEAGUE OF AMERICA.
PUT TOGETHER TO SPECIFICALLY COUNTER THE JUSTICE LEAGUE IN EVERY WAY...WITHOUT MOST OF THEIR RECRUITS EVEN REALIZING IT.
IF I JOIN THE JLA, THEY'LL HELP ME FIND A CURE TO THESE POWERS.
BECAUSE THESE ABILITIES HAVE DONE SOMETHING TO ME, KIM.
EVERY ROOM I WALK INTO, I TAKE AWAY THE LIGHT. I SUCK IT UP LIKE A BLACK HOLE.
I CRAVE DARKNESS.
AND NOW THEY WANT ME TO USE THIS POWER AGAINST FIRESTORM.
BUT HE'S ACTUALLY TWO KIDS.
AND THE LAST THING I WANT TO DO IS HURT KIDS.
"YOU SAID YOU COULD TRUST DOCTOR LIGHT, AMANDA, BUT HE'S ALREADY TOLD HIS WIFE EVERYTHING."

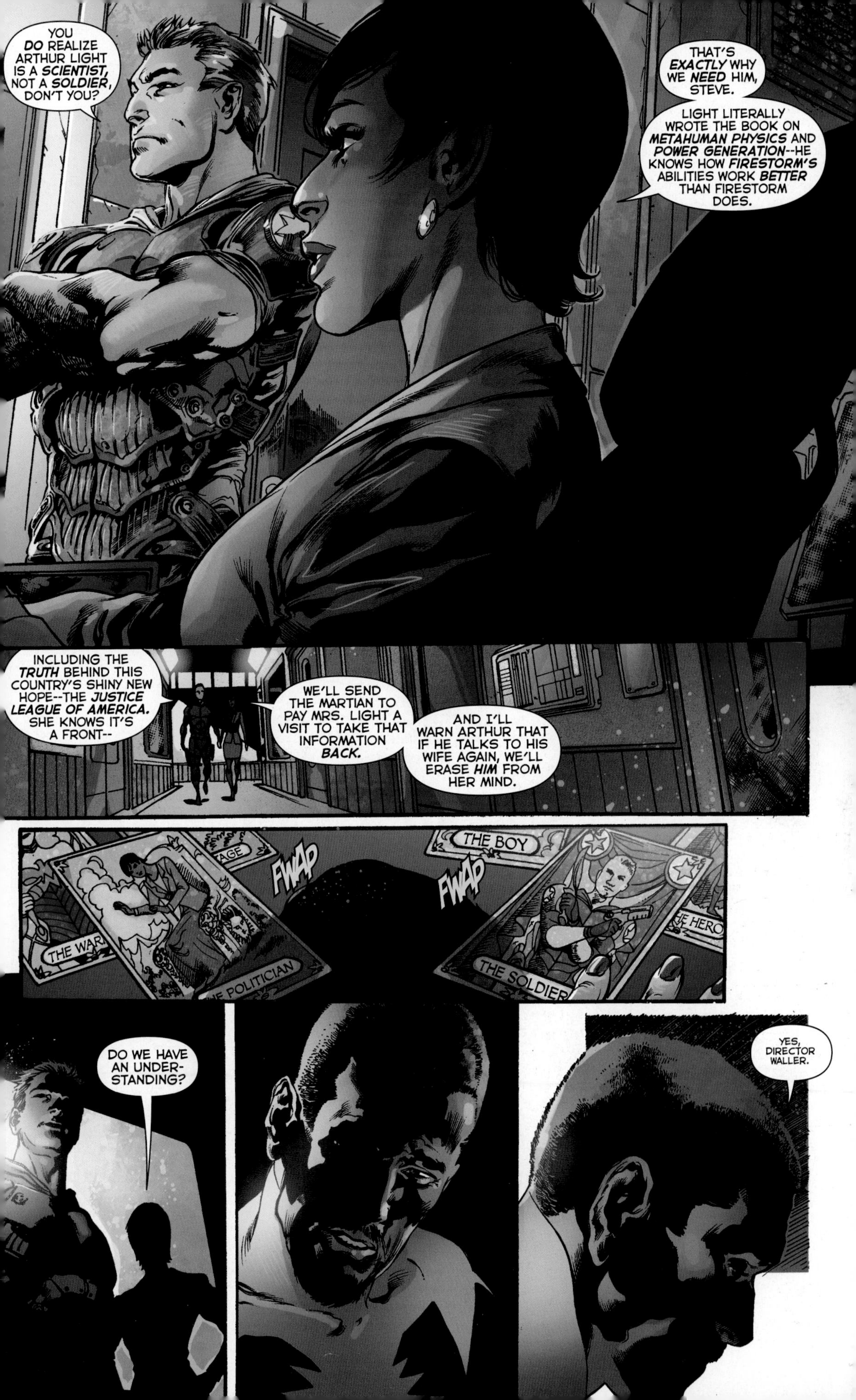
YOU DO REALIZE ARTHUR LIGHT IS A SCIENTIST, NOT A SOLDIER, DON'T YOU?
THAT'S EXACTLY WHY WE NEED HIM, STEVE.
LIGHT LITERALLY WROTE THE BOOK ON METAHUMAN PHYSICS AND POWER GENERATION--HE KNOWS HOW FIRESTORM'S ABILITIES WORK BETTER THAN FIRESTORM DOES.
INCLUDING THE TRUTH BEHIND THIS COUNTRY'S SHINY NEW HOPE--THE JUSTICE LEAGUE OF AMERICA. SHE KNOWS IT'S A FRONT--
WE'LL SEND THE MARTIAN TO PAY MRS. LIGHT A VISIT TO TAKE THAT INFORMATION BACK.
AND I'LL WARN ARTHUR THAT IF HE TALKS TO HIS WIFE AGAIN, WE'LL ERASE HIM FROM HER MIND.
THE WAR
THE POLITICIAN
FWAP
FWAP
THE BOY
THE HERO
THE SOLDIER
DO WE HAVE AN UNDER-STANDING?
YES, DIRECTOR WALLER.

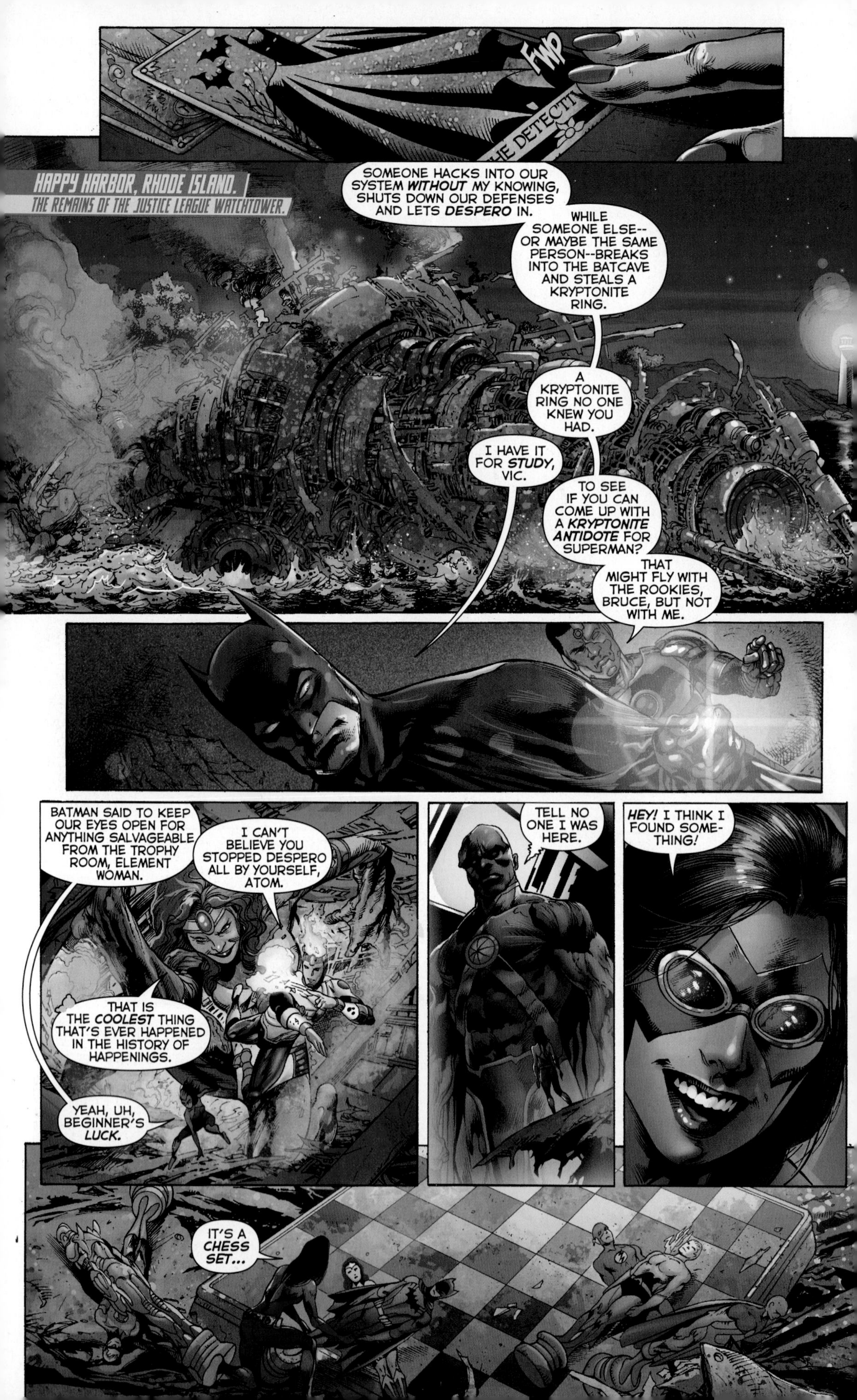
FWP
THE DETECTI
HAPPY HARBOR, RHODE ISLAND.
THE REMAINS OF THE JUSTICE LEAGUE WATCHTOWER.
SOMEONE HACKS INTO OUR SYSTEM WITHOUT MY KNOWING, SHUTS DOWN OUR DEFENSES AND LETS DESPERO IN.
WHILE SOMEONE ELSE-- OR MAYBE THE SAME PERSON--BREAKS INTO THE BATCAVE AND STEALS A KRYPTONITE RING.
A KRYPTONITE RING NO ONE KNEW YOU HAD.
I HAVE IT FOR STUDY, VIC.
TO SEE IF YOU CAN COME UP WITH A KRYPTONITE ANTIDOTE FOR SUPERMAN?
THAT MIGHT FLY WITH THE ROOKIES, BRUCE, BUT NOT WITH ME.
BATMAN SAID TO KEEP OUR EYES OPEN FOR ANYTHING SALVAGEABLE FROM THE TROPHY ROOM, ELEMENT WOMAN.
I CAN'T BELIEVE YOU STOPPED DESPERO ALL BY YOURSELF, ATOM.
THAT IS THE COOLEST THING THAT'S EVER HAPPENED IN THE HISTORY OF HAPPENINGS.
YEAH, UH, BEGINNER'S LUCK.
TELL NO ONE I WAS HERE.
HEY! I THINK I FOUND SOME-THING!
IT'S A CHESS SET...

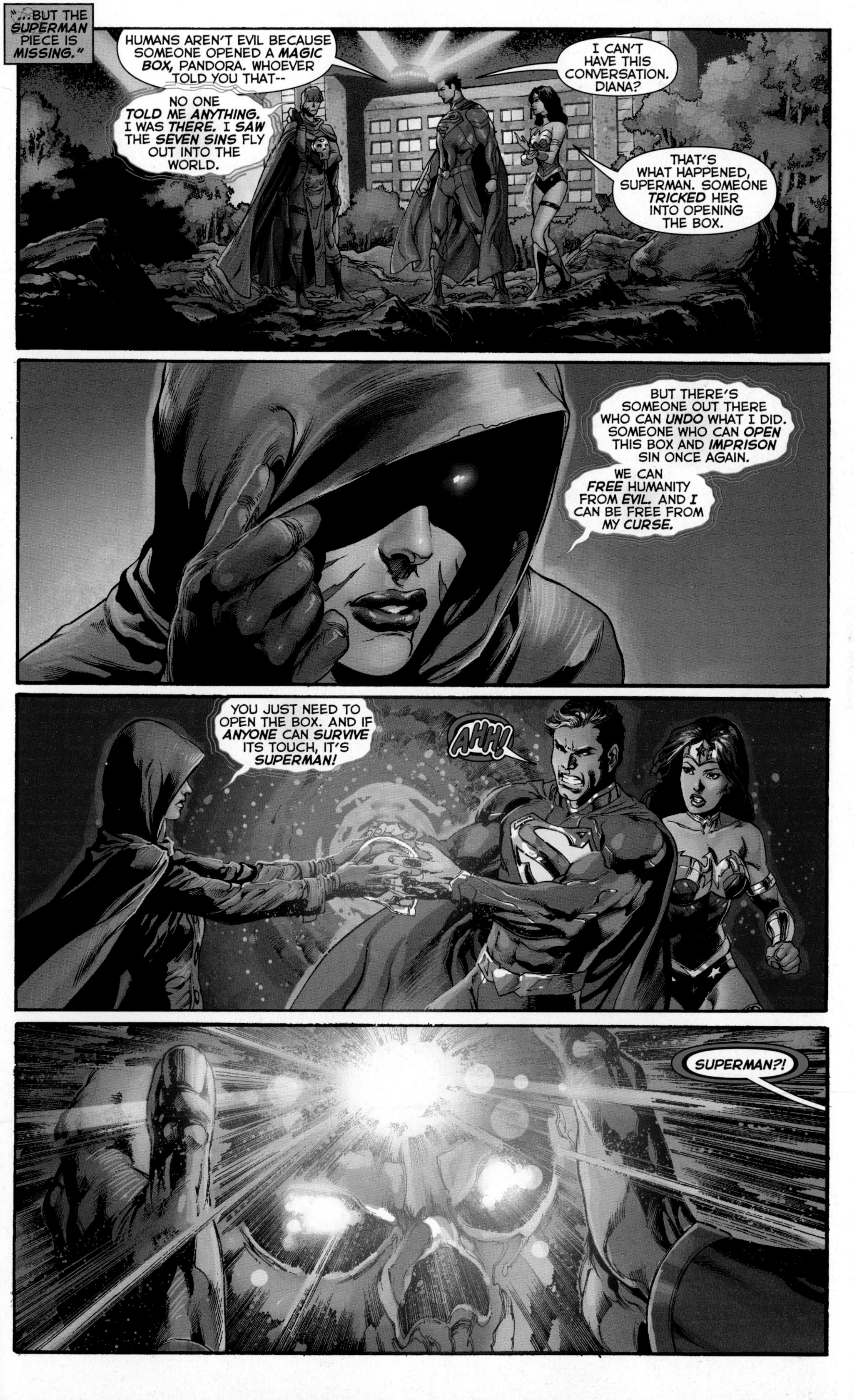
"...BUT THE SUPERMAN PIECE IS MISSING."
HUMANS AREN'T EVIL BECAUSE SOMEONE OPENED A MAGIC BOX, PANDORA. WHOEVER TOLD YOU THAT--
NO ONE TOLD ME ANYTHING. I WAS THERE. I SAW THE SEVEN SINS FLY OUT INTO THE WORLD.
I CAN'T HAVE THIS CONVERSATION. DIANA?
THAT'S WHAT HAPPENED, SUPERMAN. SOMEONE TRICKED HER INTO OPENING THE BOX.
BUT THERE'S SOMEONE OUT THERE WHO CAN UNDO WHAT I DID. SOMEONE WHO CAN OPEN THIS BOX AND IMPRISON SIN ONCE AGAIN.
WE CAN FREE HUMANITY FROM EVIL. AND I CAN BE FREE FROM MY CURSE.
YOU JUST NEED TO OPEN THE BOX. AND IF ANYONE CAN SURVIVE ITS TOUCH, IT'S SUPERMAN!
AHH!
SUPERMAN?!

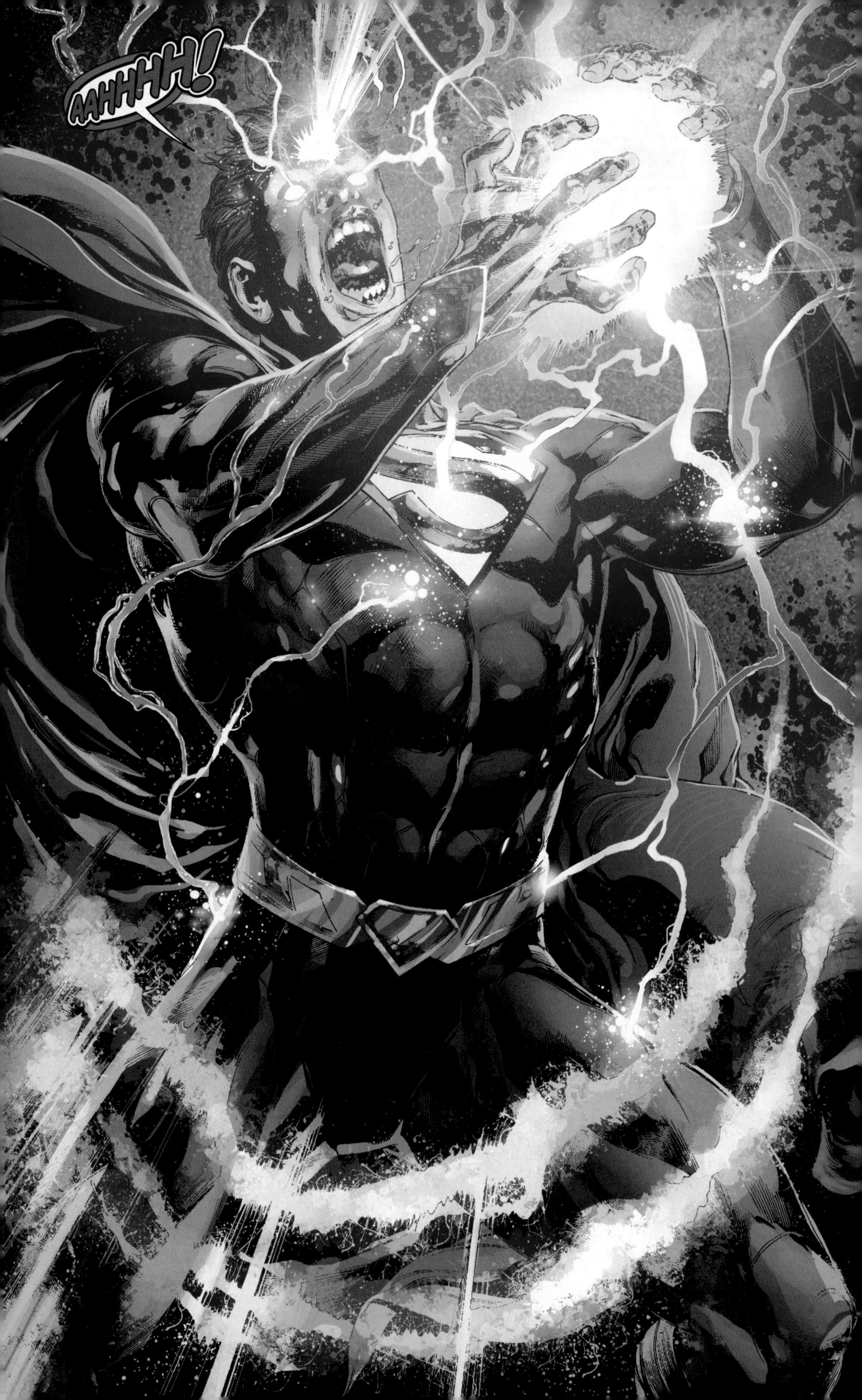
AAHHHH!

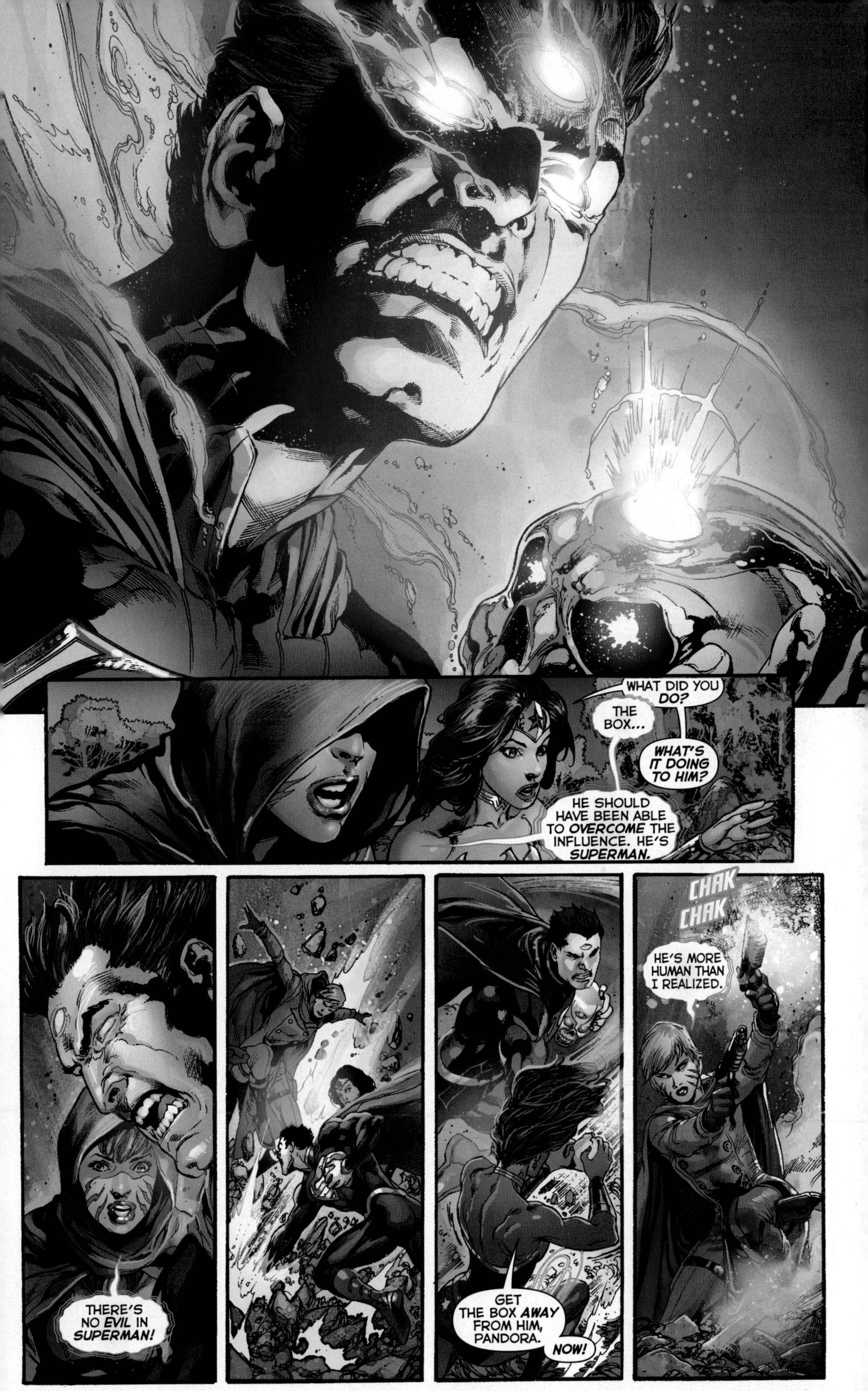
WHAT DID YOU DO?
THE BOX...
WHAT'S IT DOING TO HIM?
HE SHOULD HAVE BEEN ABLE TO OVERCOME THE INFLUENCE. HE'S SUPERMAN.
THERE'S NO EVIL IN SUPERMAN!
GET THE BOX AWAY FROM HIM, PANDORA.
NOW!
CHAK
CHAK
HE'S MORE HUMAN THAN I REALIZED.

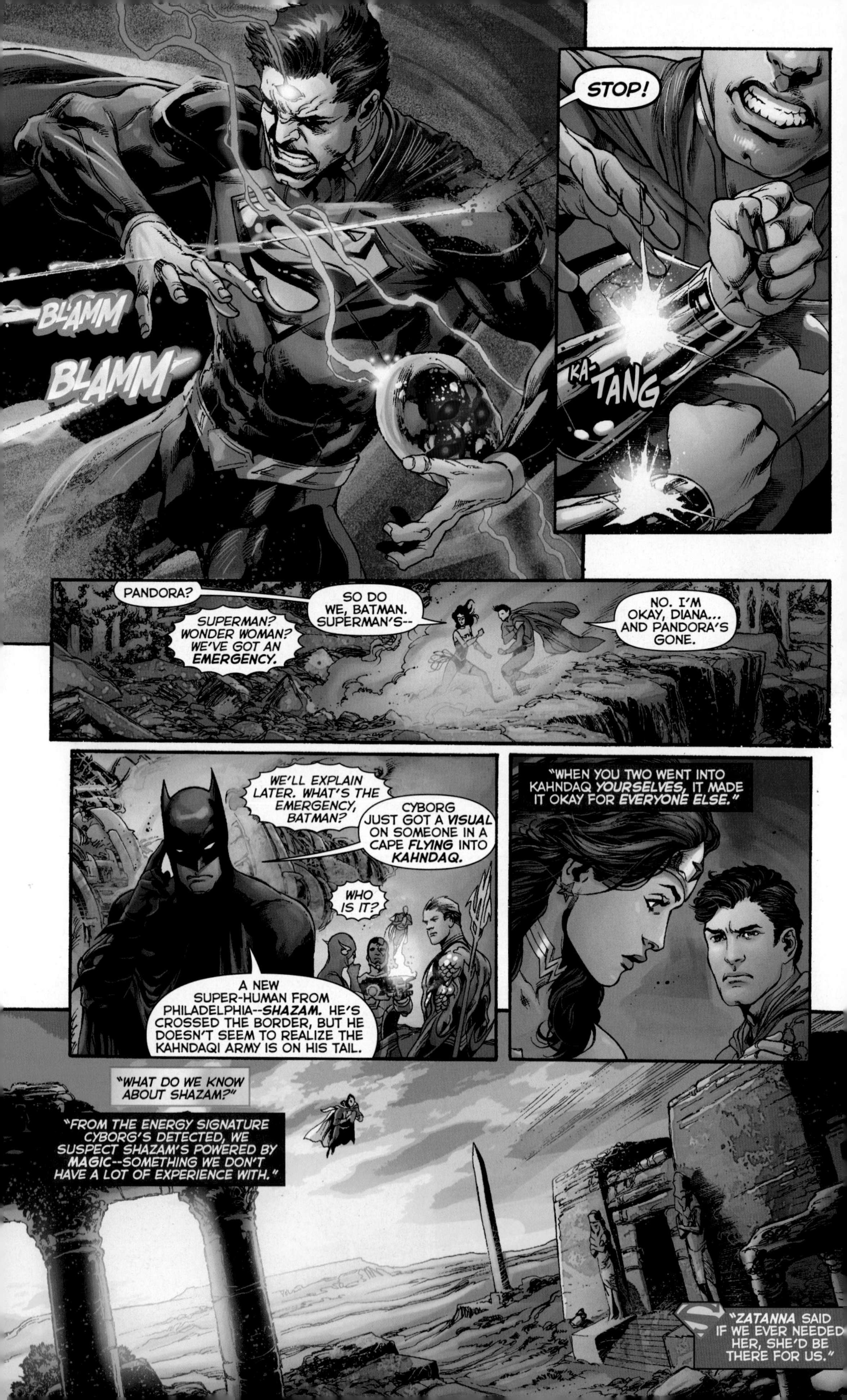
BLAMM
BLAMM
STOP!
KA-TANG
PANDORA?
SUPERMAN? WONDER WOMAN? WE'VE GOT AN EMERGENCY.
SO DO WE, BATMAN. SUPERMAN'S--
NO. I'M OKAY, DIANA... AND PANDORA'S GONE.
WE'LL EXPLAIN LATER. WHAT'S THE EMERGENCY, BATMAN?
CYBORG JUST GOT A VISUAL ON SOMEONE IN A CAPE FLYING INTO KAHNDAQ.
WHO IS IT?
A NEW SUPER-HUMAN FROM PHILADELPHIA--SHAZAM. HE'S CROSSED THE BORDER, BUT HE DOESN'T SEEM TO REALIZE THE KAHNDAQI ARMY IS ON HIS TAIL.
"WHEN YOU TWO WENT INTO KAHNDAQ YOURSELVES, IT MADE IT OKAY FOR EVERYONE ELSE."
"WHAT DO WE KNOW ABOUT SHAZAM?"
"FROM THE ENERGY SIGNATURE CYBORG'S DETECTED, WE SUSPECT SHAZAM'S POWERED BY MAGIC--SOMETHING WE DON'T HAVE A LOT OF EXPERIENCE WITH."
"ZATANNA SAID IF WE EVER NEEDED HER, SHE'D BE THERE FOR US."

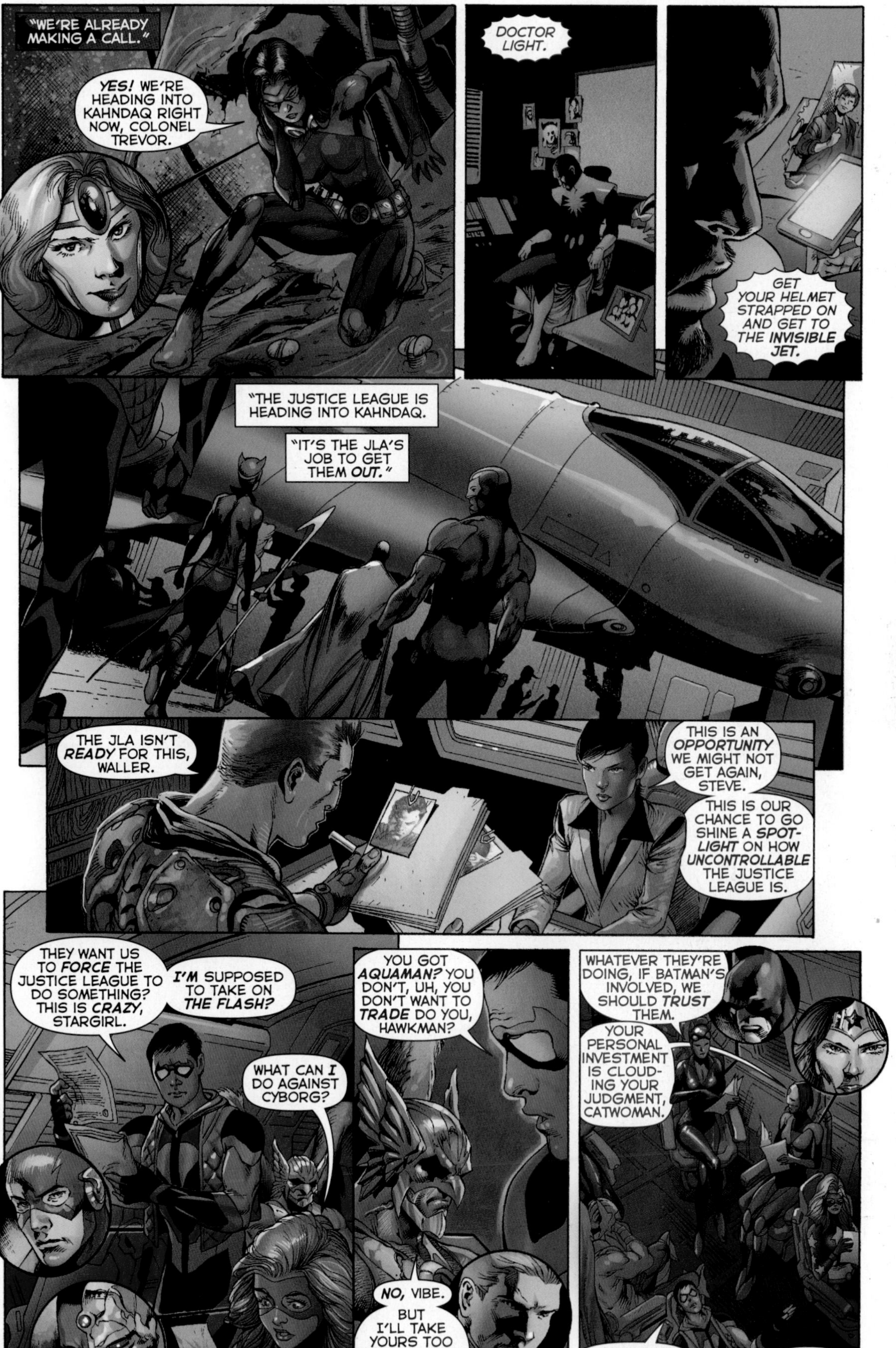
"WE'RE ALREADY MAKING A CALL."
YES! WE'RE HEADING INTO KAHNDAQ RIGHT NOW, COLONEL TREVOR.
DOCTOR LIGHT.
GET YOUR HELMET STRAPPED ON AND GET TO THE INVISIBLE JET.
"THE JUSTICE LEAGUE IS HEADING INTO KAHNDAQ.
"IT'S THE JLA'S JOB TO GET THEM OUT."
THE JLA ISN'T READY FOR THIS, WALLER.
THIS IS AN OPPORTUNITY WE MIGHT NOT GET AGAIN, STEVE.
THIS IS OUR CHANCE TO GO SHINE A SPOT-LIGHT ON HOW UNCONTROLLABLE THE JUSTICE LEAGUE IS.
THEY WANT US TO FORCE THE JUSTICE LEAGUE TO DO SOMETHING? THIS IS CRAZY, STARGIRL.
I'M SUPPOSED TO TAKE ON THE FLASH?
WHAT CAN I DO AGAINST CYBORG?
YOU GOT AQUAMAN? YOU DON'T, UH, YOU DON'T WANT TO TRADE DO YOU, HAWKMAN?
NO, VIBE.
BUT I'LL TAKE YOURS TOO IF YOU DON'T THINK YOU CAN HANDLE IT.
WHATEVER THEY'RE DOING, IF BATMAN'S INVOLVED, WE SHOULD TRUST THEM.
YOUR PERSONAL INVESTMENT IS CLOUD-ING YOUR JUDGMENT, CATWOMAN.
WHY'S IT GETTING DARK IN HERE?
THIS IS WRONG.

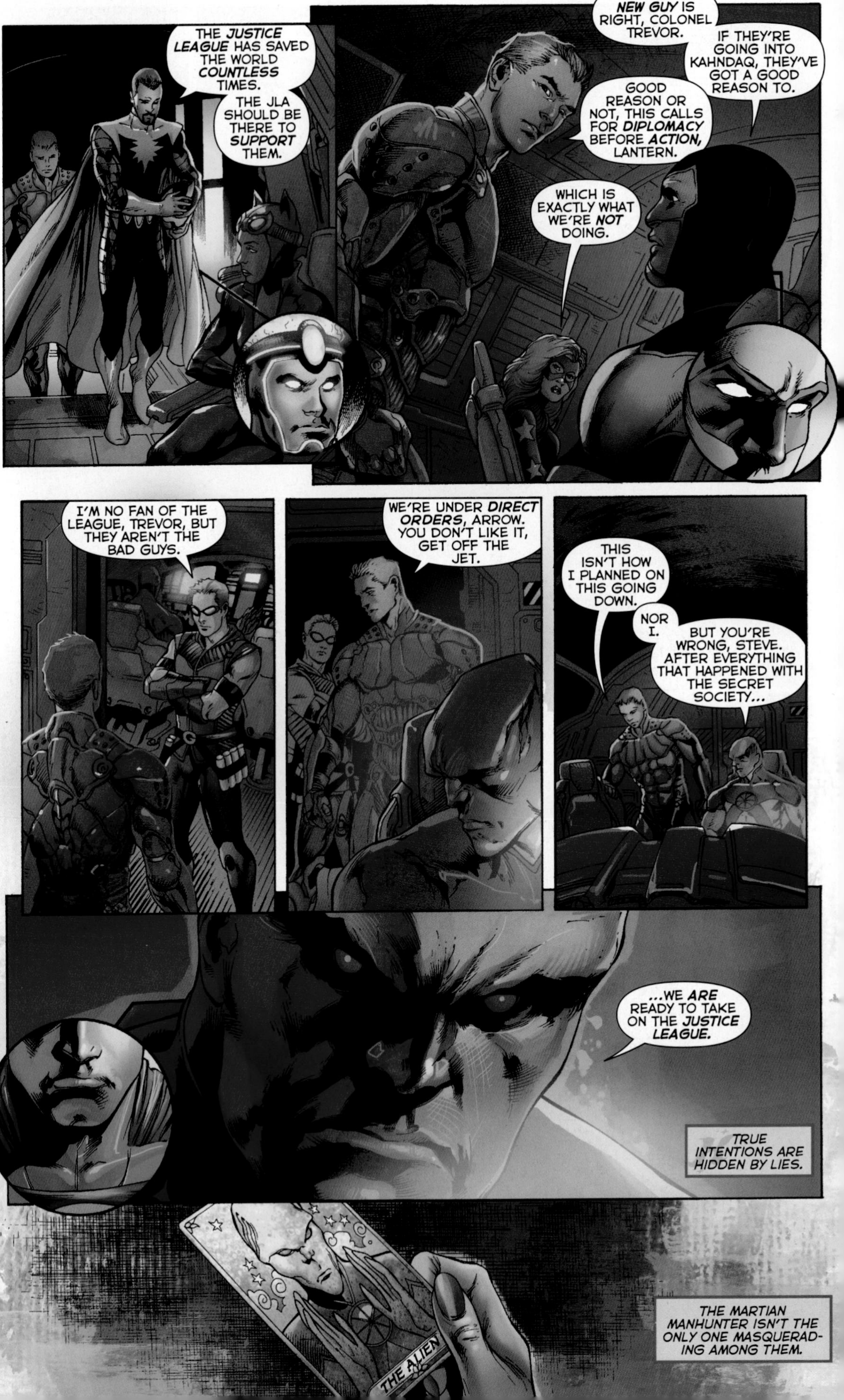
THE JUSTICE LEAGUE HAS SAVED THE WORLD COUNTLESS TIMES.
THE JLA SHOULD BE THERE TO SUPPORT THEM.
THE NEW GUY IS RIGHT, COLONEL TREVOR.
IF THEY'RE GOING INTO KAHNDAQ, THEY'VE GOT A GOOD REASON TO.
GOOD REASON OR NOT, THIS CALLS FOR DIPLOMACY BEFORE ACTION, LANTERN.
WHICH IS EXACTLY WHAT WE'RE NOT DOING.
I'M NO FAN OF THE LEAGUE, TREVOR, BUT THEY AREN'T THE BAD GUYS.
WE'RE UNDER DIRECT ORDERS, ARROW. YOU DON'T LIKE IT, GET OFF THE JET.
THIS ISN'T HOW I PLANNED ON THIS GOING DOWN.
NOR I.
BUT YOU'RE WRONG, STEVE. AFTER EVERYTHING THAT HAPPENED WITH THE SECRET SOCIETY...
...WE ARE READY TO TAKE ON THE JUSTICE LEAGUE.
TRUE INTENTIONS ARE HIDDEN BY LIES.
THE ALIEN
THE MARTIAN MANHUNTER ISN'T THE ONLY ONE MASQUERADING AMONG THEM.

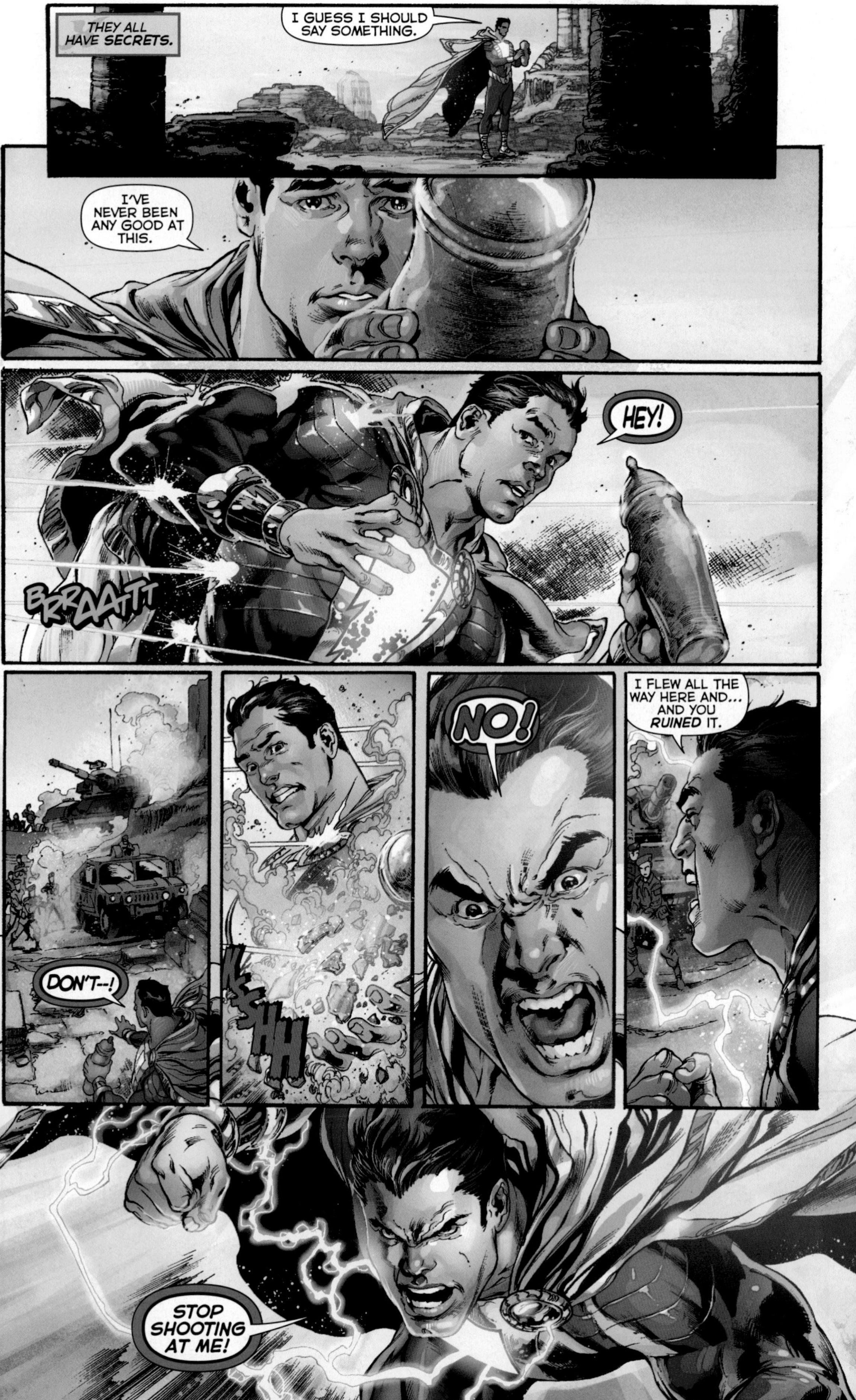
THEY ALL HAVE SECRETS.
I GUESS I SHOULD SAY SOMETHING.
I'VE NEVER BEEN ANY GOOD AT THIS.
BRRAATTT
HEY!
DON'T--!
KRASHH
NO!
I FLEW ALL THE WAY HERE AND... AND YOU RUINED IT.
STOP SHOOTING AT ME!

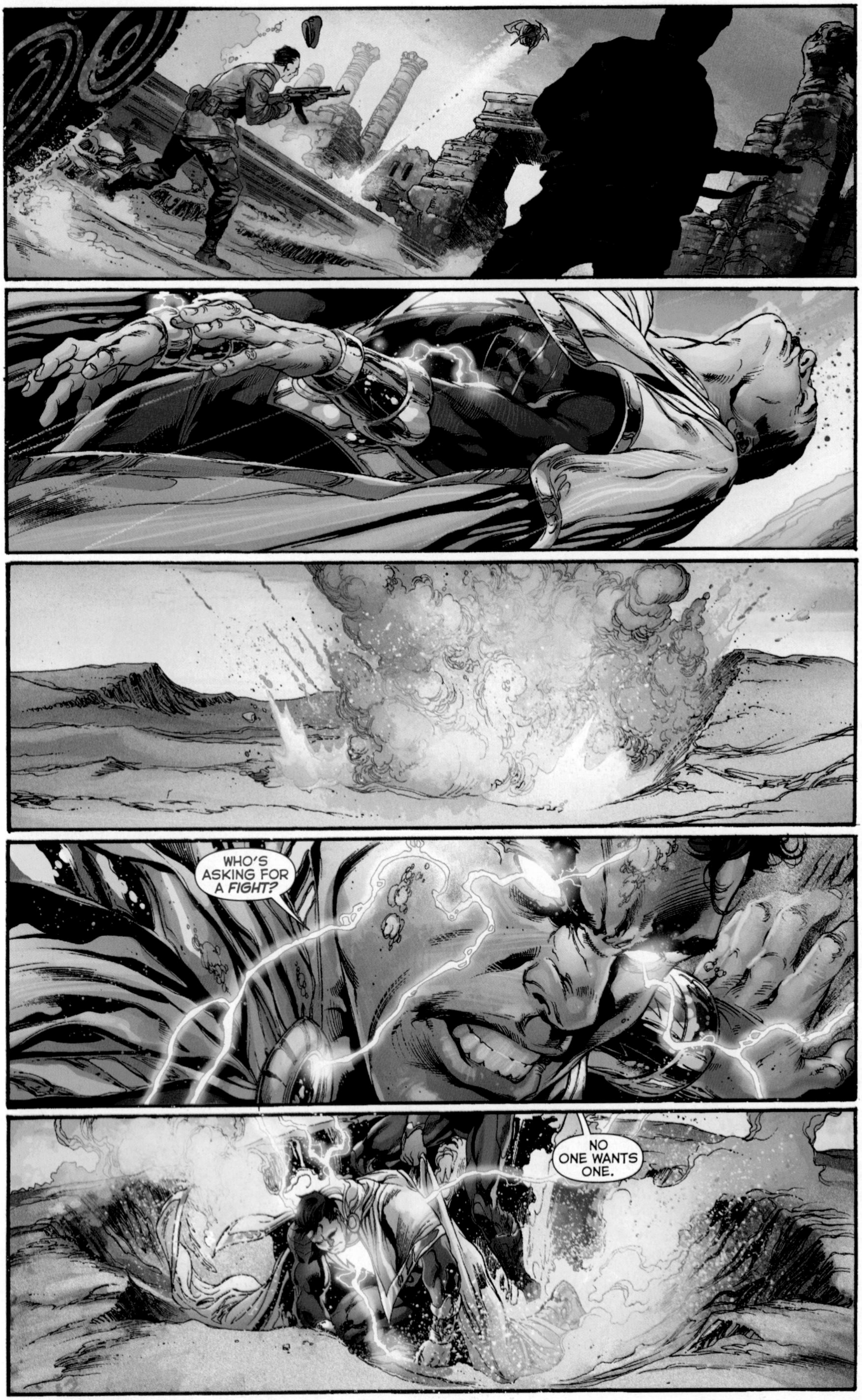
WHO'S ASKING FOR A *FIGHT?*
NO ONE WANTS ONE.

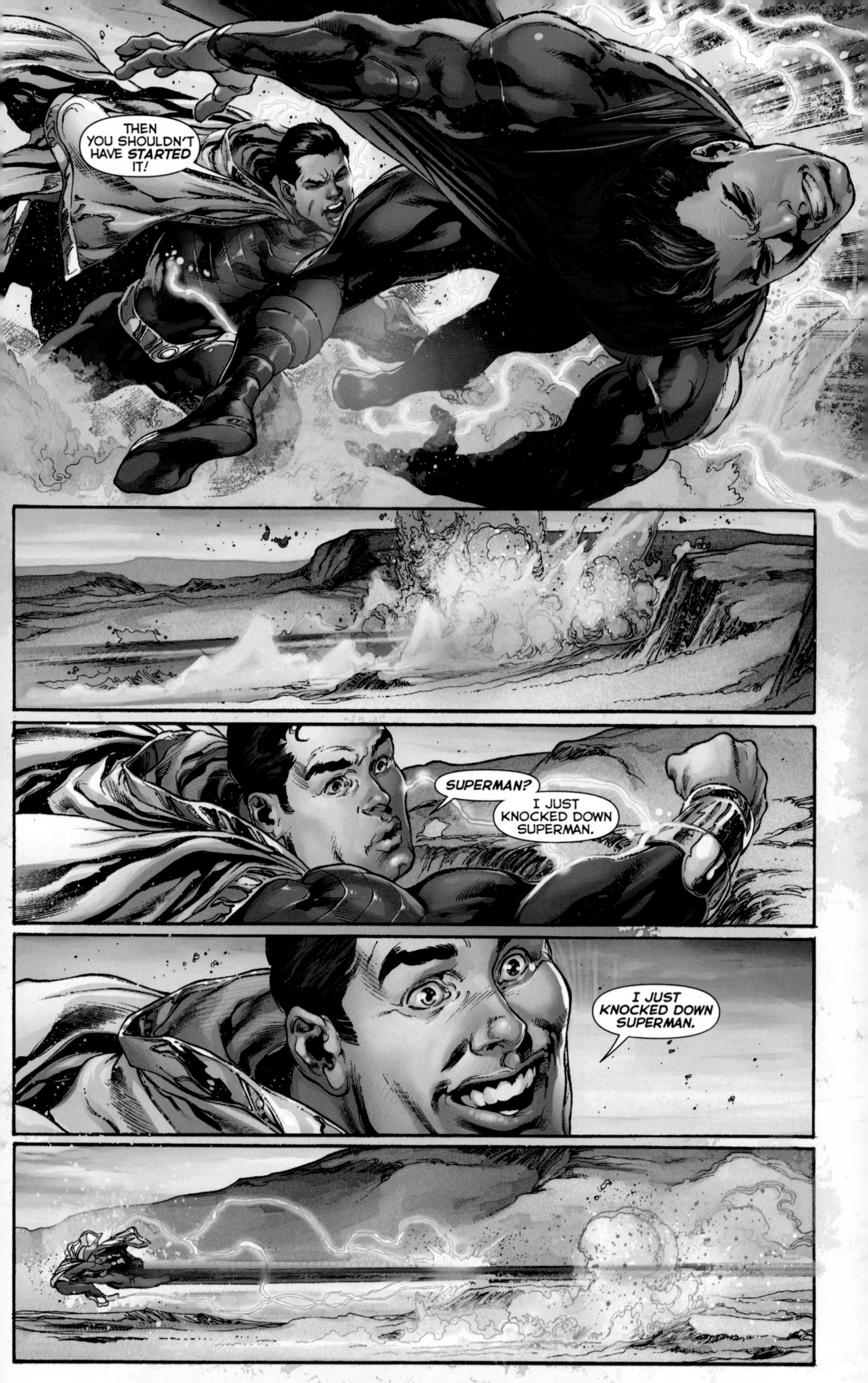
THEN YOU SHOULDN'T HAVE STARTED IT!
SUPERMAN?
I JUST KNOCKED DOWN SUPERMAN.
I JUST KNOCKED DOWN SUPERMAN.

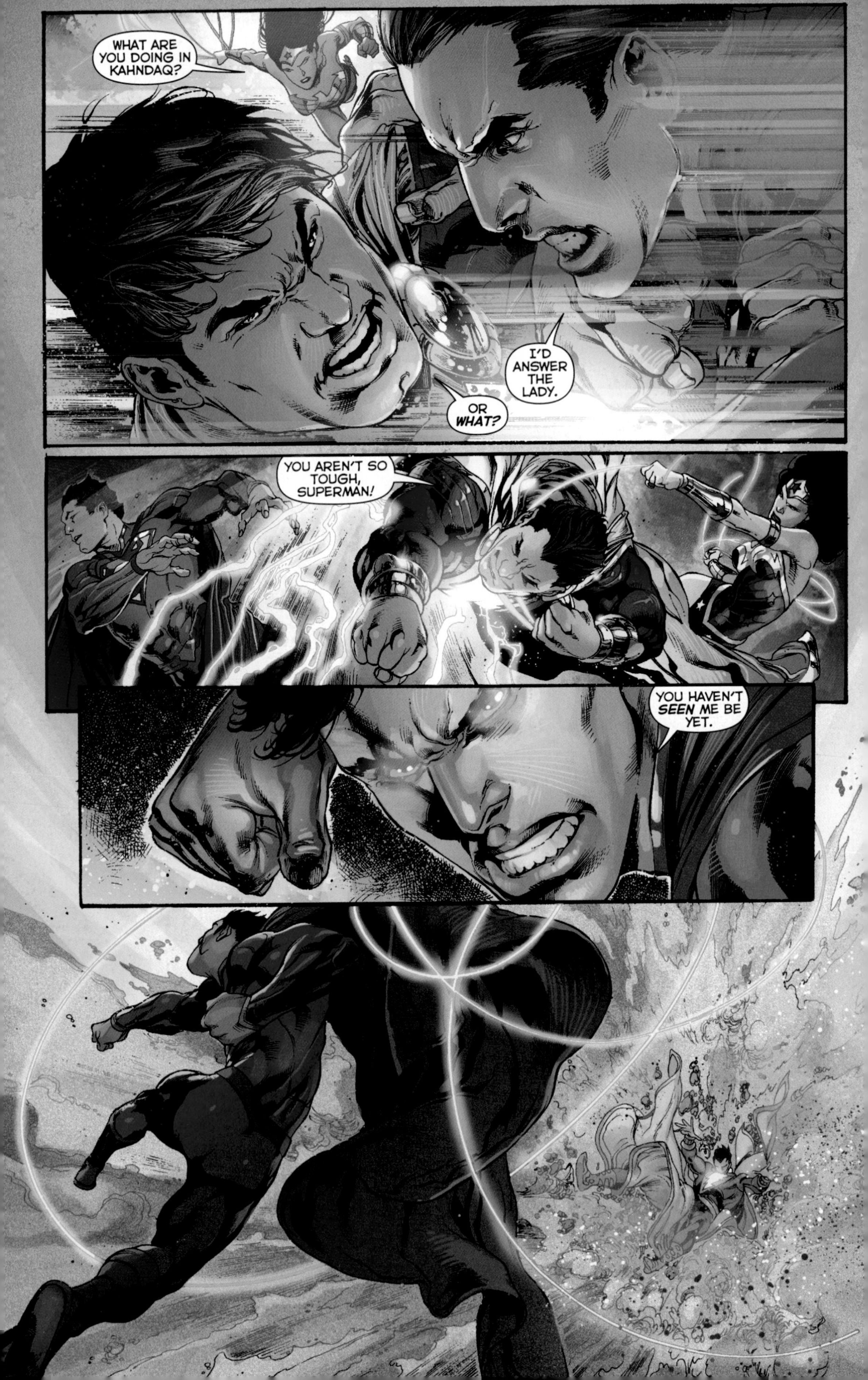
WHAT ARE YOU DOING IN KAHNDAQ?
I'D ANSWER THE LADY.
OR *WHAT?*
YOU AREN'T SO TOUGH, SUPERMAN!
YOU HAVEN'T *SEEN* ME BE YET.

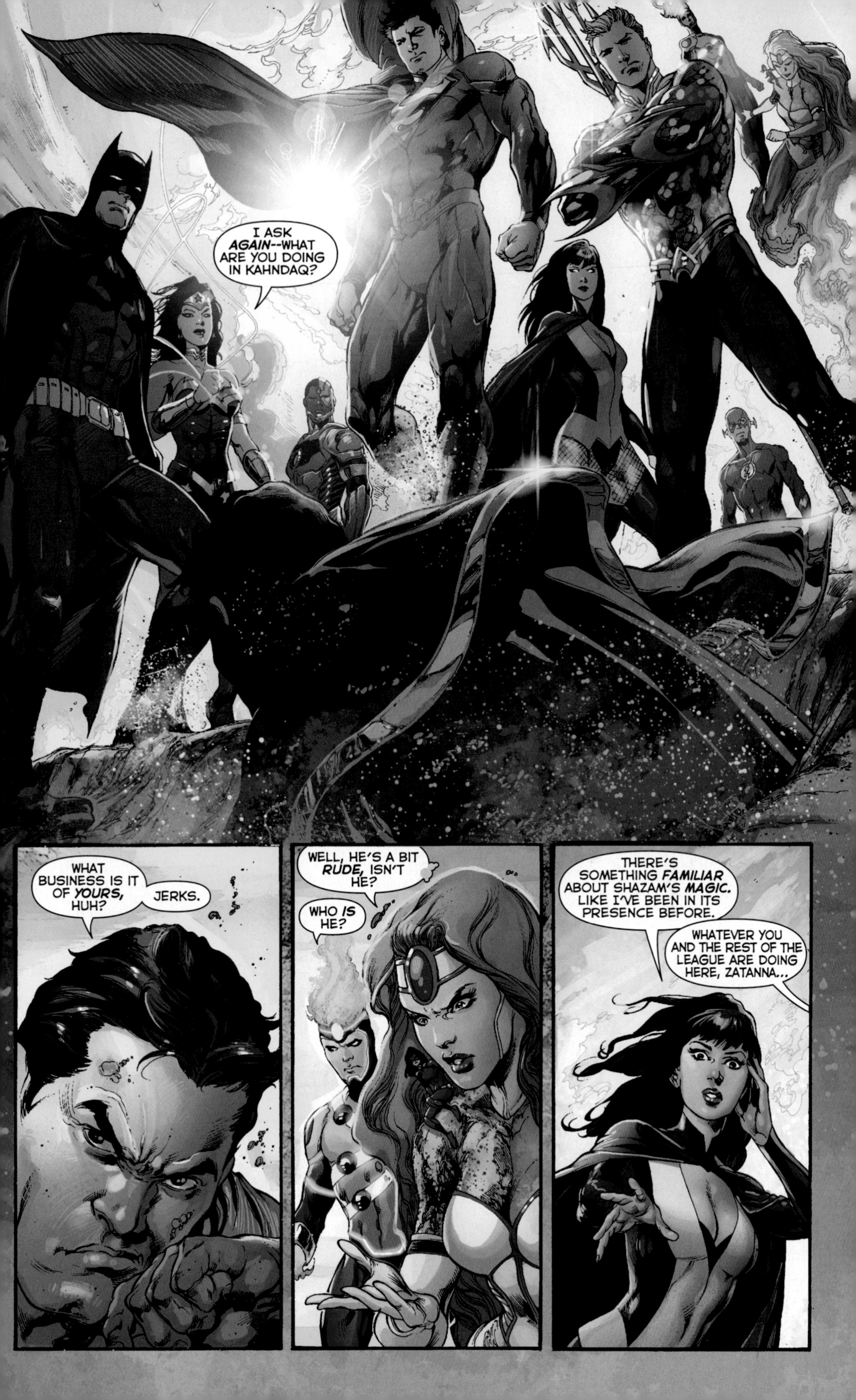
I ASK AGAIN--WHAT ARE YOU DOING IN KAHNDAQ?
WHAT BUSINESS IS IT OF YOURS, HUH?
JERKS.
WELL, HE'S A BIT RUDE, ISN'T HE?
WHO IS HE?
THERE'S SOMETHING FAMILIAR ABOUT SHAZAM'S MAGIC. LIKE I'VE BEEN IN ITS PRESENCE BEFORE.
WHATEVER YOU AND THE REST OF THE LEAGUE ARE DOING HERE, ZATANNA...

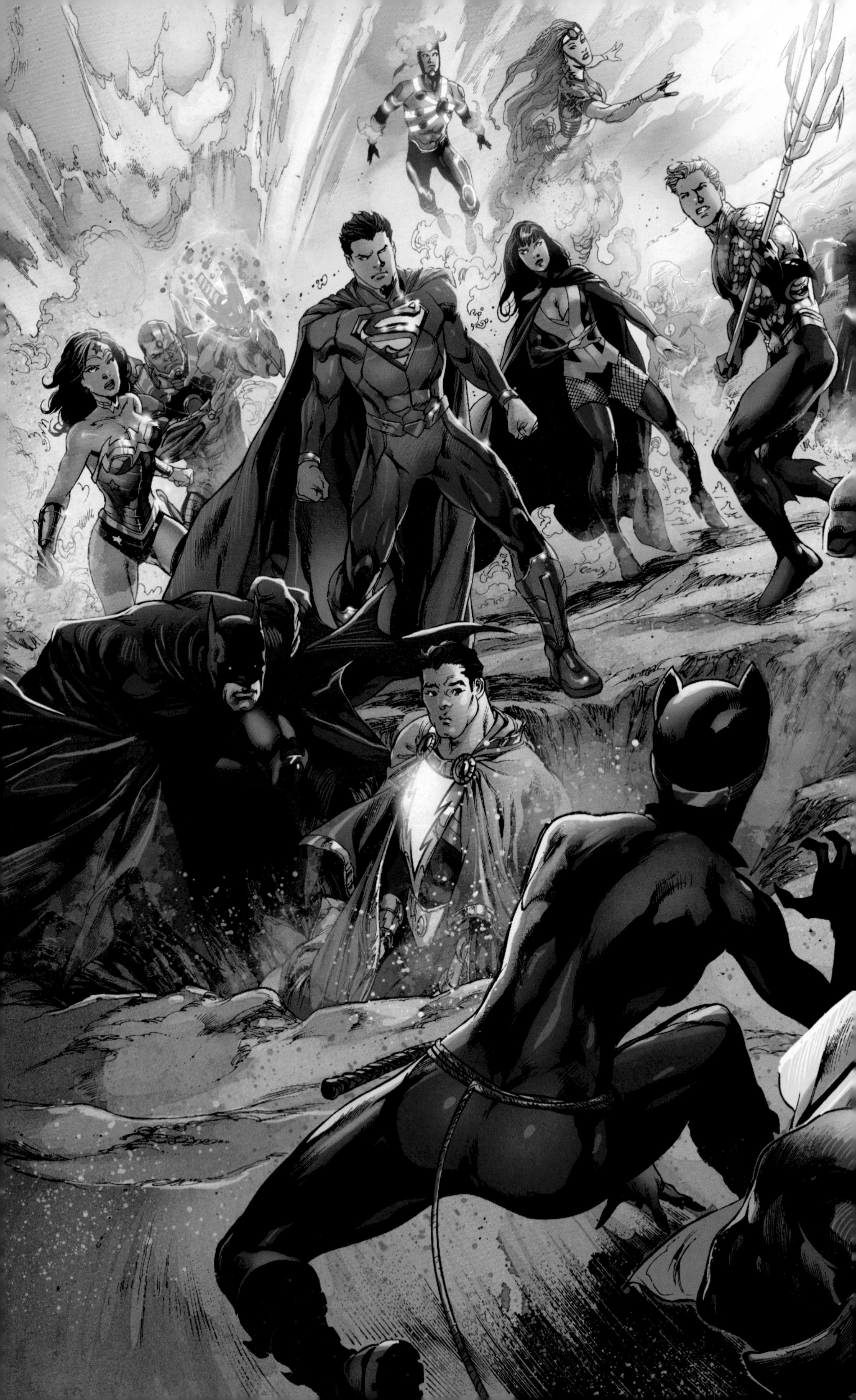

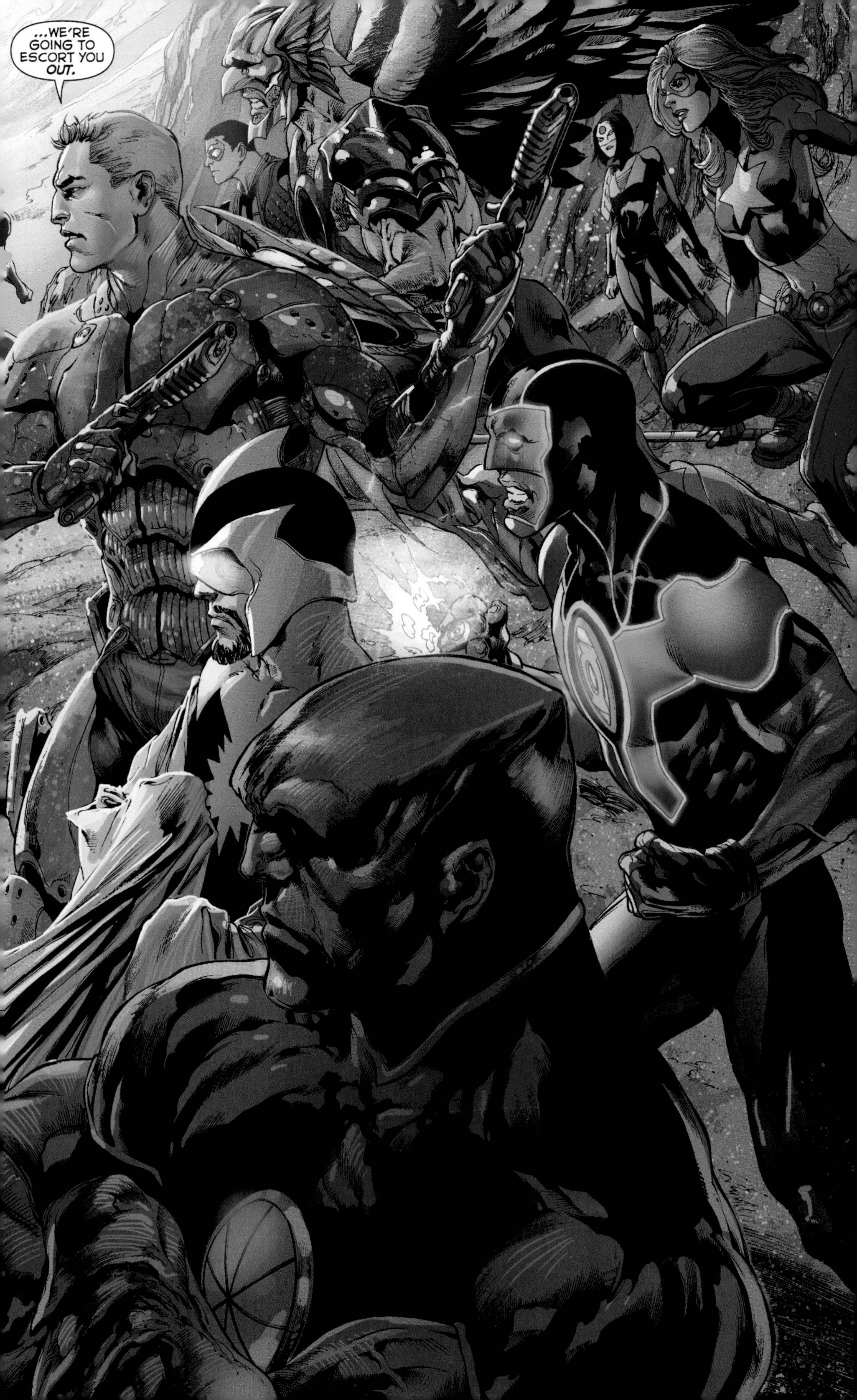
...WE'RE GOING TO ESCORT YOU OUT.

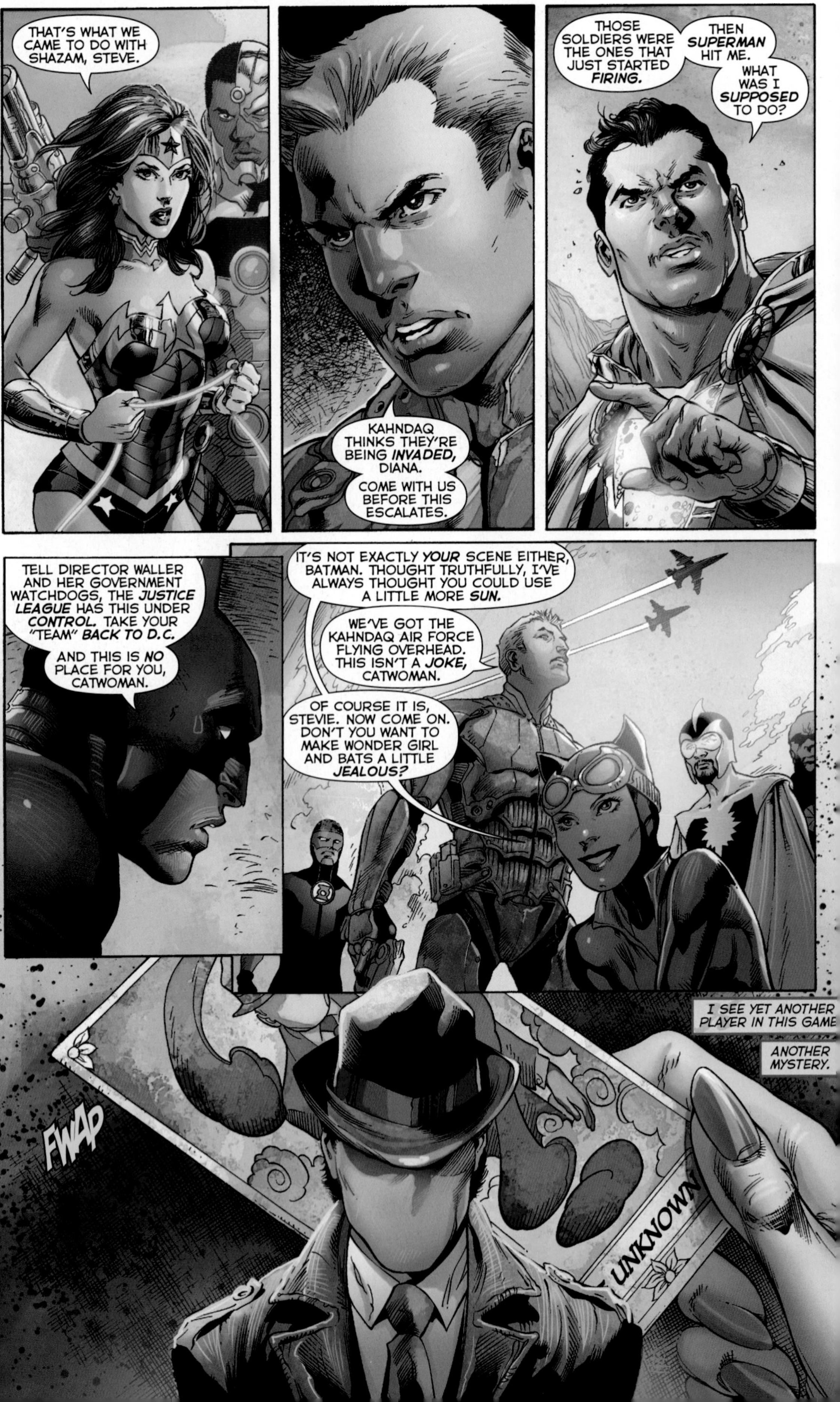
THAT'S WHAT WE CAME TO DO WITH SHAZAM, STEVE.
KAHNDAQ THINKS THEY'RE BEING INVADED, DIANA.
COME WITH US BEFORE THIS ESCALATES.
THOSE SOLDIERS WERE THE ONES THAT JUST STARTED FIRING.
THEN SUPERMAN HIT ME.
WHAT WAS I SUPPOSED TO DO?
TELL DIRECTOR WALLER AND HER GOVERNMENT WATCHDOGS, THE JUSTICE LEAGUE HAS THIS UNDER CONTROL. TAKE YOUR "TEAM" BACK TO D.C.
AND THIS IS NO PLACE FOR YOU, CATWOMAN.
IT'S NOT EXACTLY YOUR SCENE EITHER, BATMAN. THOUGHT TRUTHFULLY, I'VE ALWAYS THOUGHT YOU COULD USE A LITTLE MORE SUN.
WE'VE GOT THE KAHNDAQ AIR FORCE FLYING OVERHEAD. THIS ISN'T A JOKE, CATWOMAN.
OF COURSE IT IS, STEVIE. NOW COME ON. DON'T YOU WANT TO MAKE WONDER GIRL AND BATS A LITTLE JEALOUS?
I SEE YET ANOTHER PLAYER IN THIS GAME.
ANOTHER MYSTERY.
FWAP
UNKNOWN

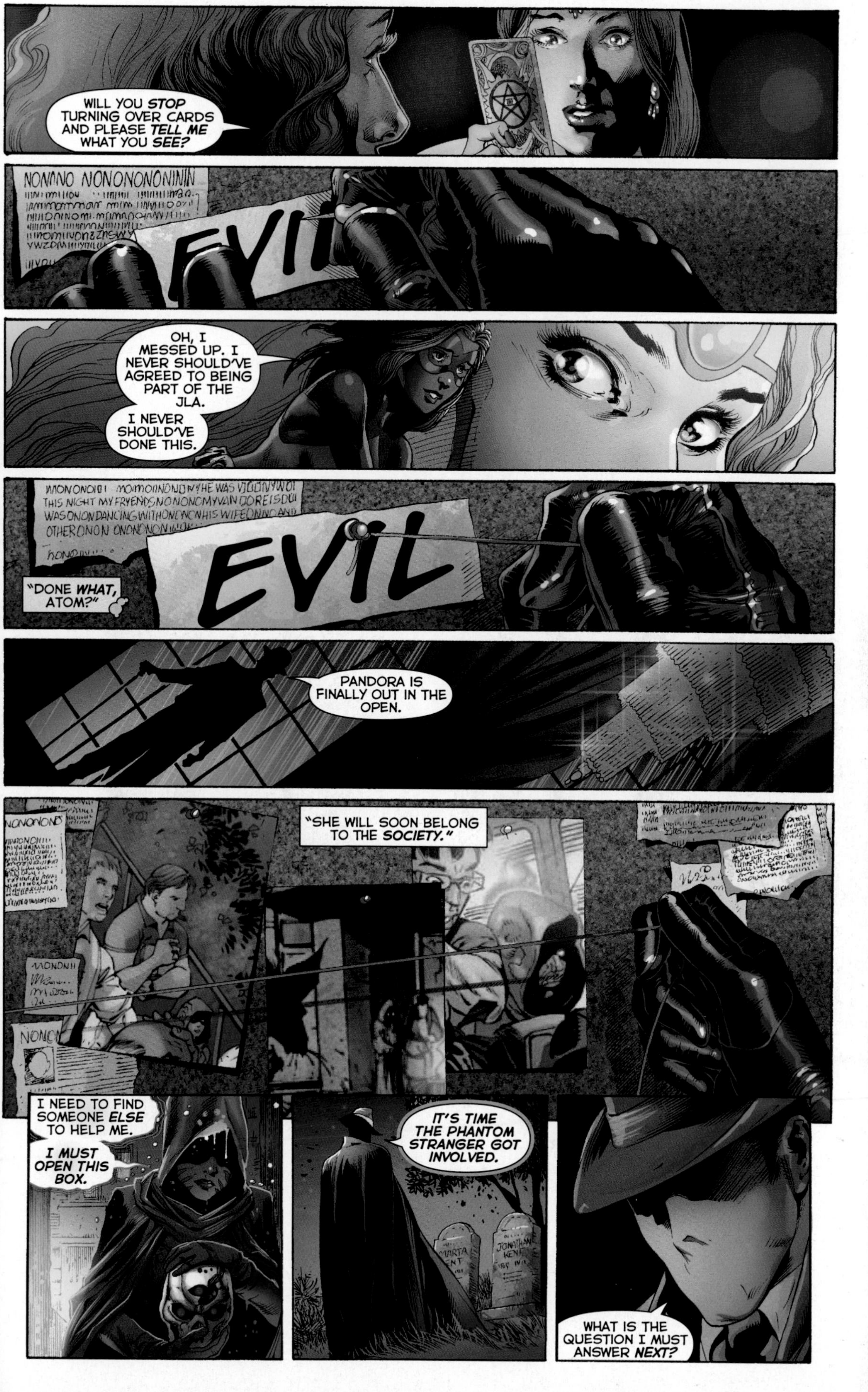

WILL YOU STOP TURNING OVER CARDS AND PLEASE TELL ME WHAT YOU SEE?
EVIL
OH, I MESSED UP. I NEVER SHOULD'VE AGREED TO BEING PART OF THE JLA.
I NEVER SHOULD'VE DONE THIS.
"DONE WHAT, ATOM?"
EVIL
PANDORA IS FINALLY OUT IN THE OPEN.
"SHE WILL SOON BELONG TO THE SOCIETY."
I NEED TO FIND SOMEONE ELSE TO HELP ME.
I MUST OPEN THIS BOX.
IT'S TIME THE PHANTOM STRANGER GOT INVOLVED.
WHAT IS THE QUESTION I MUST ANSWER NEXT?

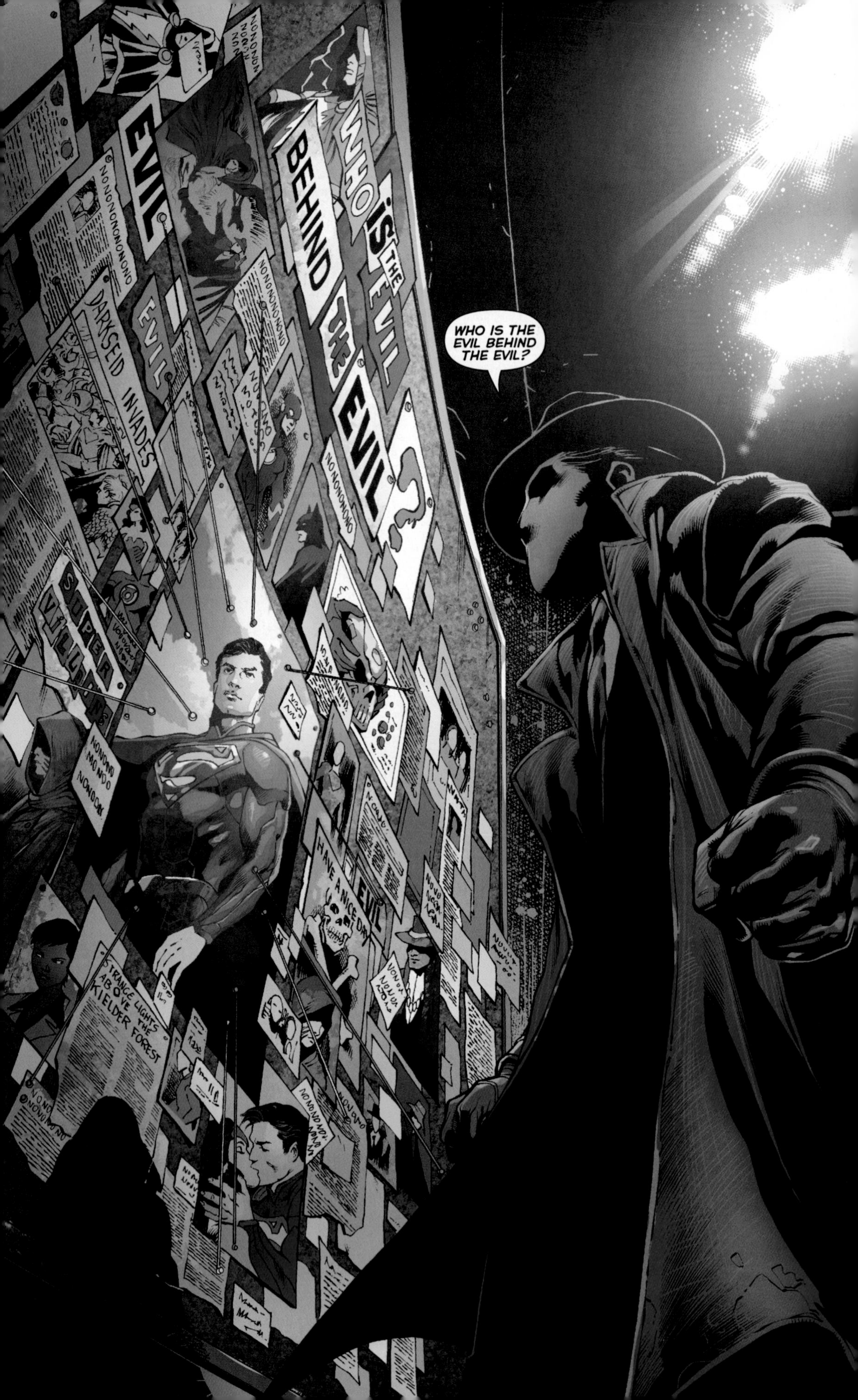
EVIL
WHO IS THE EVIL BEHIND THE EVIL
DARKSEID INVADES
EVIL
SUPER VILLAINS
HAVE A NICE DAY
EVIL
STRANGE LIGHTS ABOVE THE KIELDER FOREST
WHO IS THE EVIL BEHIND THE EVIL?

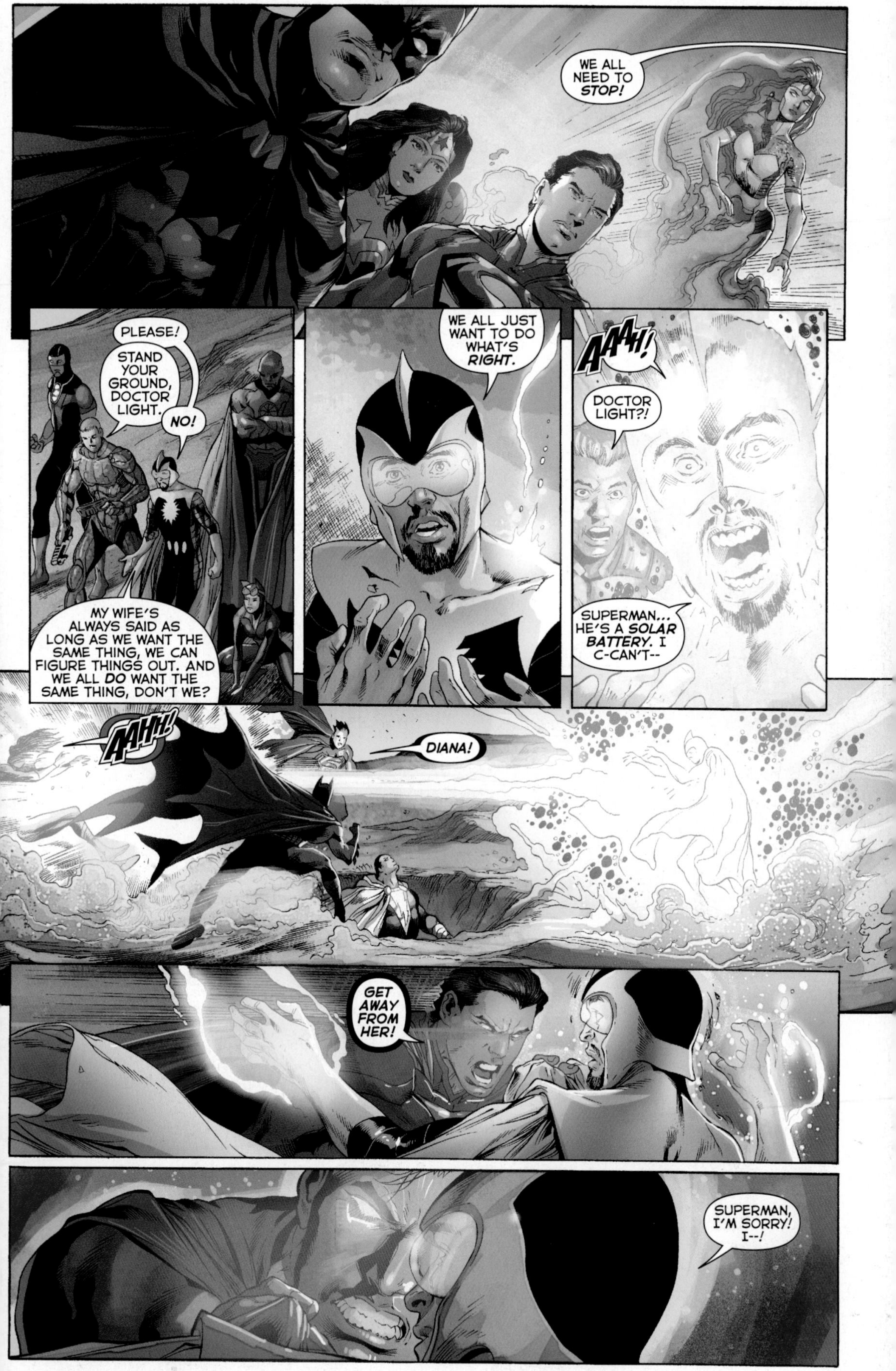
WE ALL NEED TO STOP!
PLEASE!
STAND YOUR GROUND, DOCTOR LIGHT.
NO!
MY WIFE'S ALWAYS SAID AS LONG AS WE WANT THE SAME THING, WE CAN FIGURE THINGS OUT. AND WE ALL DO WANT THE SAME THING, DON'T WE?
WE ALL JUST WANT TO DO WHAT'S RIGHT.
AAAH!
DOCTOR LIGHT?!
SUPERMAN... HE'S A SOLAR BATTERY. I C-CAN'T--
AAHH!
DIANA!
GET AWAY FROM HER!
SUPERMAN, I'M SORRY! I--!

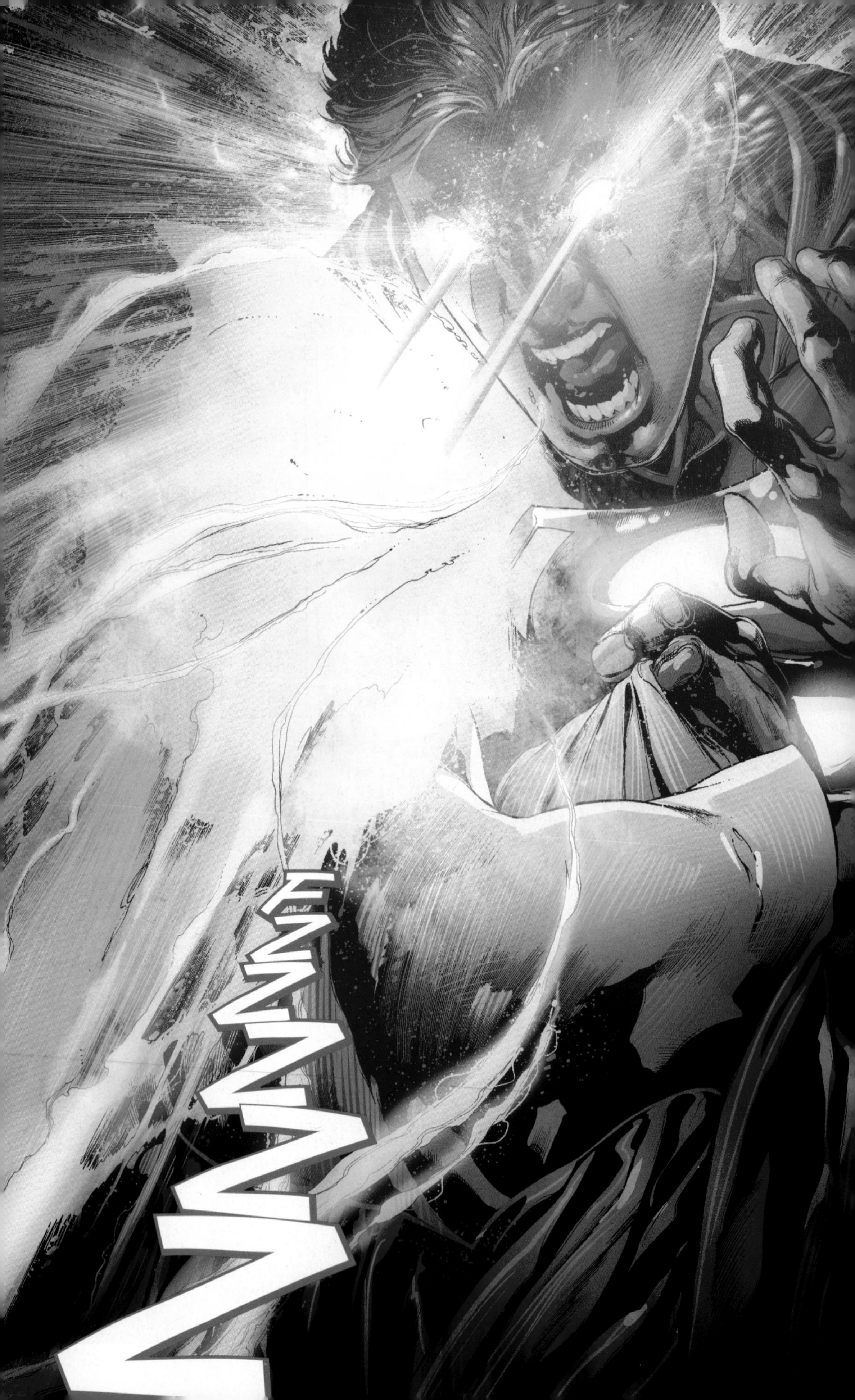
ZZZZZZT

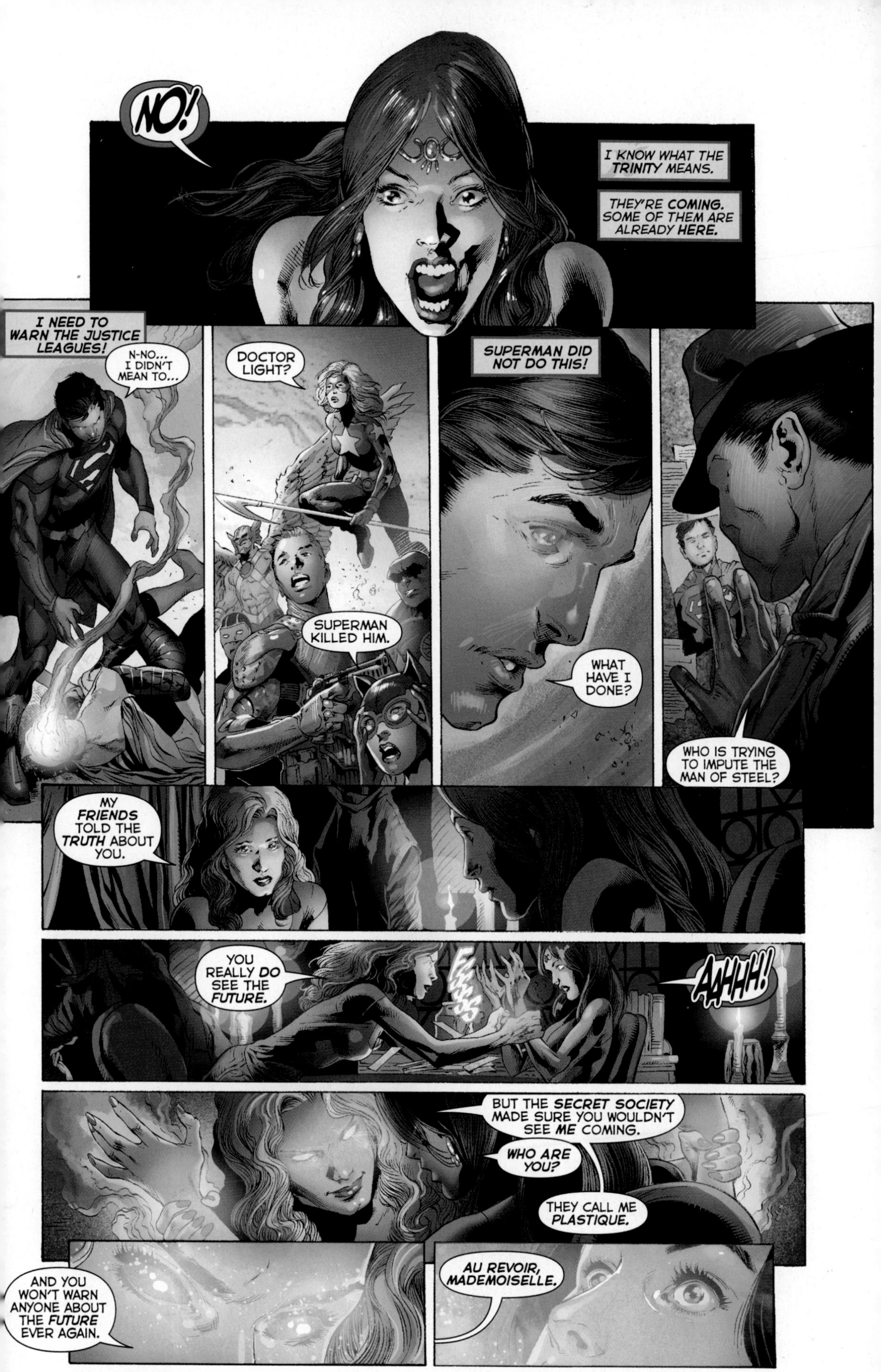
NO!
I KNOW WHAT THE TRINITY MEANS.
THEY'RE COMING. SOME OF THEM ARE ALREADY HERE.
I NEED TO WARN THE JUSTICE LEAGUES!
N-NO... I DIDN'T MEAN TO...
DOCTOR LIGHT?
SUPERMAN KILLED HIM.
SUPERMAN DID NOT DO THIS!
WHAT HAVE I DONE?
WHO IS TRYING TO IMPUTE THE MAN OF STEEL?
MY FRIENDS TOLD THE TRUTH ABOUT YOU.
YOU REALLY DO SEE THE FUTURE.
AAHHH!
BUT THE SECRET SOCIETY MADE SURE YOU WOULDN'T SEE ME COMING.
WHO ARE YOU?
THEY CALL ME PLASTIQUE.
AND YOU WON'T WARN ANYONE ABOUT THE FUTURE EVER AGAIN.
AU REVOIR, MADEMOISELLE.

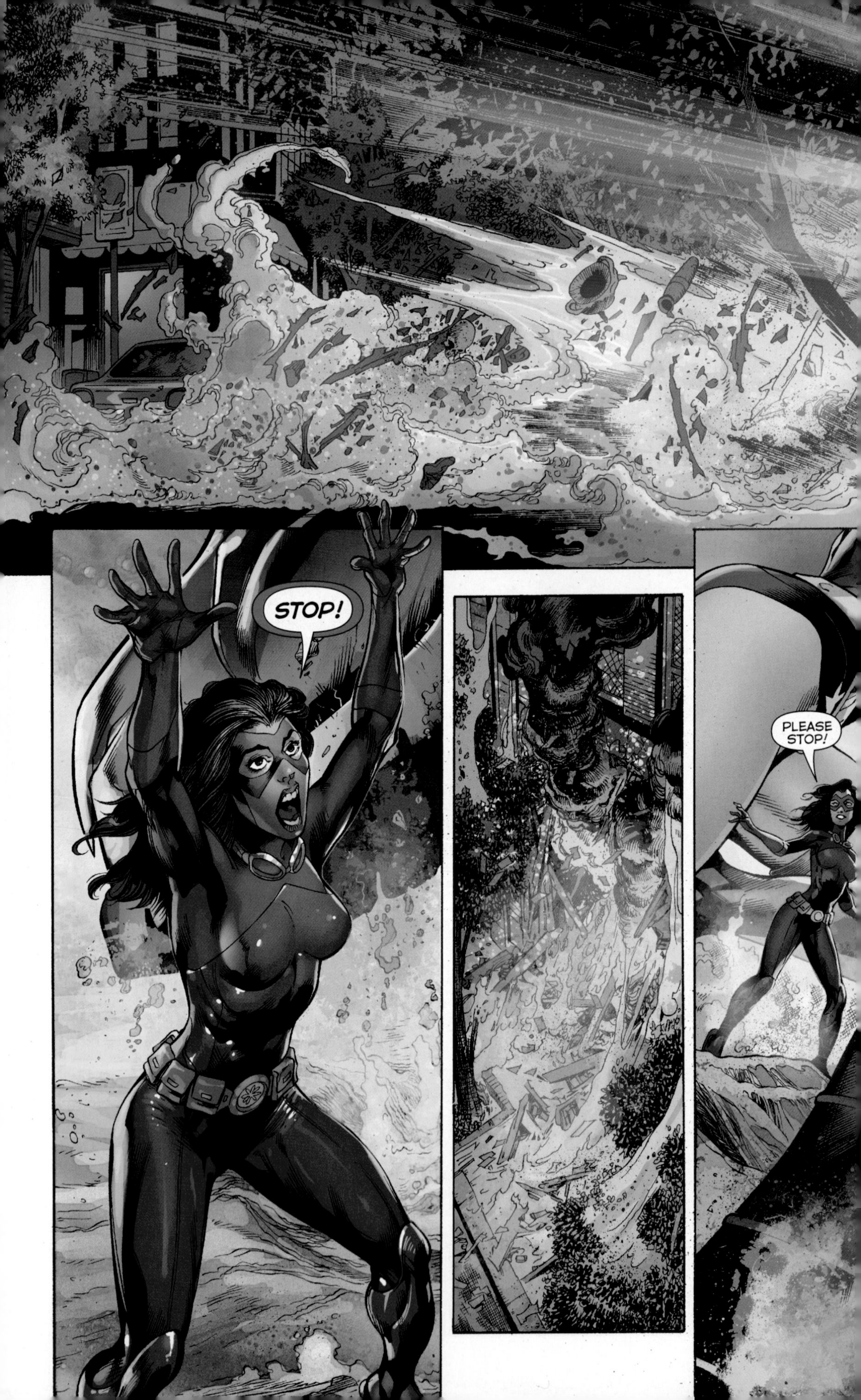
STOP!
PLEASE STOP!

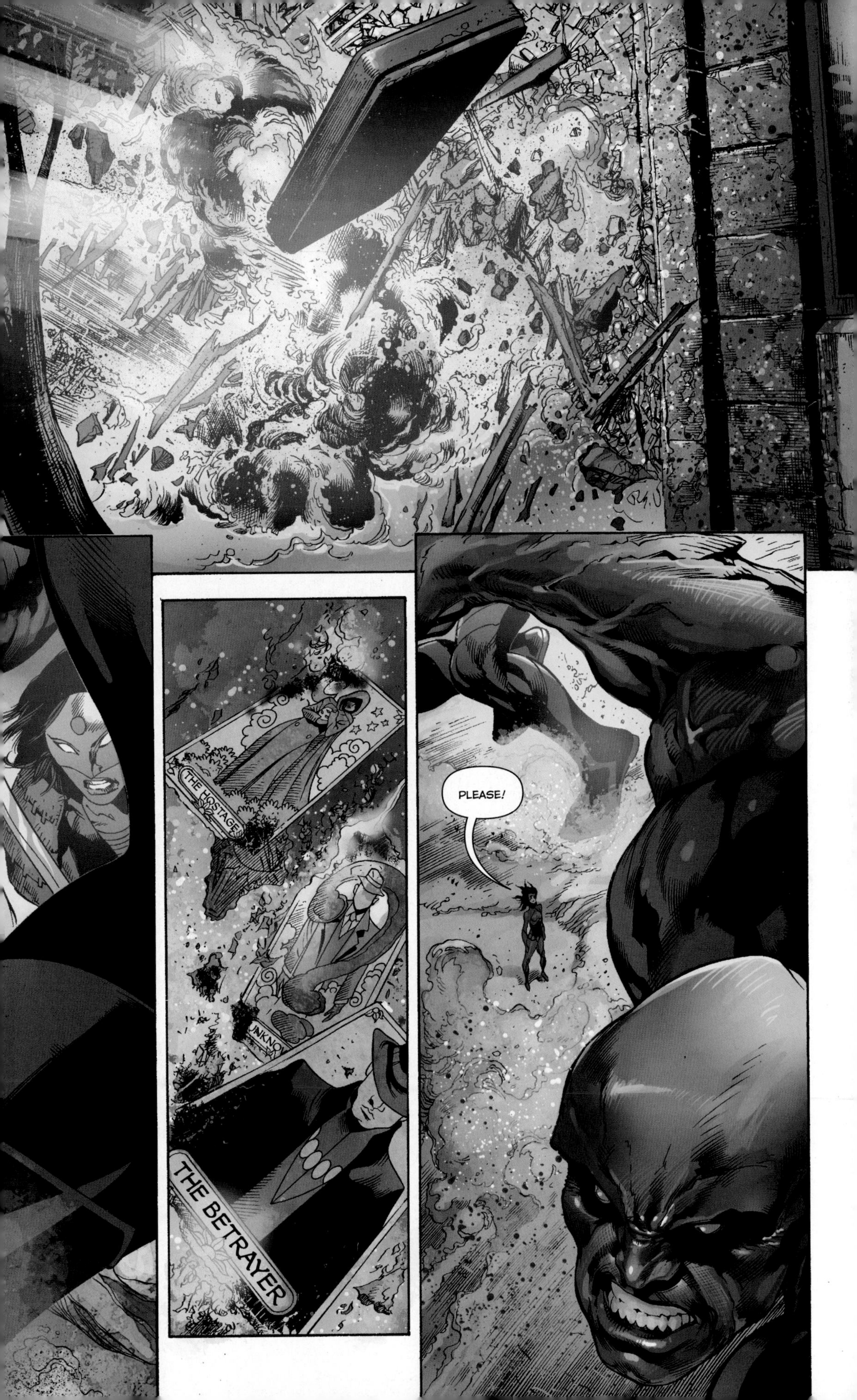
THE HOSTAGE
THE BETRAYER
PLEASE!

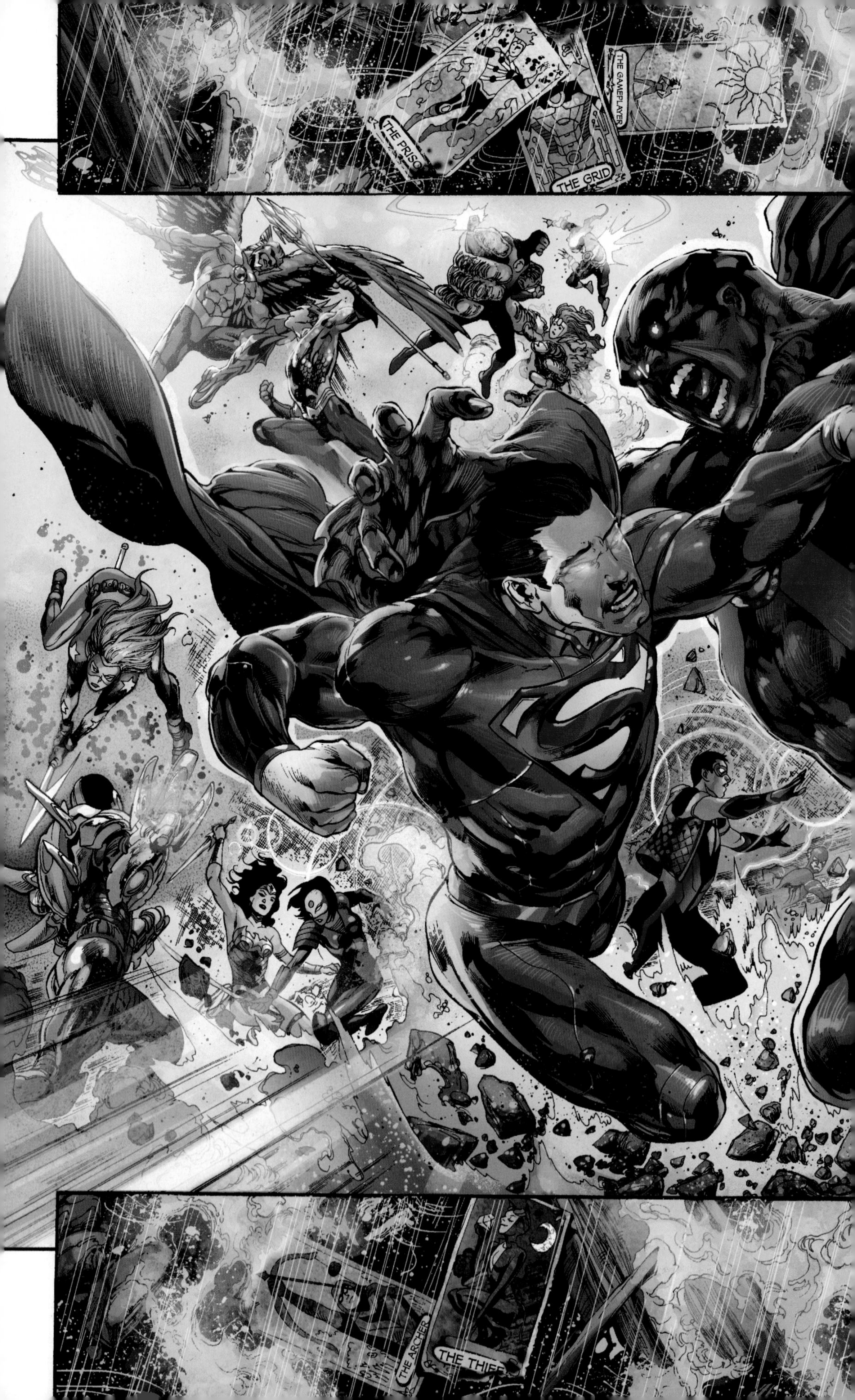
THE PRISO
THE GAMEPLAYER
THE GRID
THE ARCHER
THE THIEF

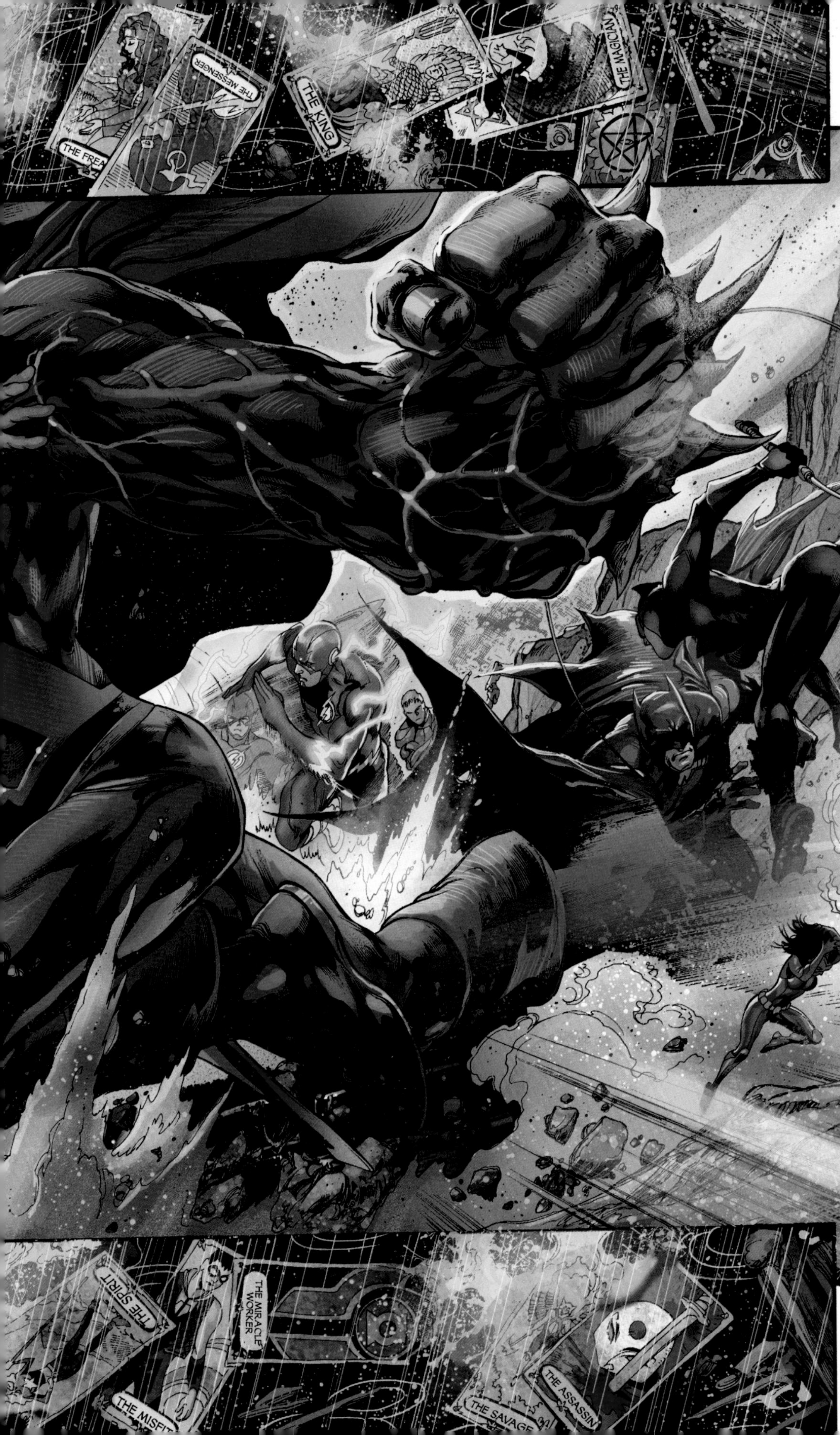
THE MESSENGER
THE KING
THE MAGICIAN
THE SPIRIT
THE MIRACLE WORKER
THE MISFIT
THE SAVAGE
THE ASSASSIN

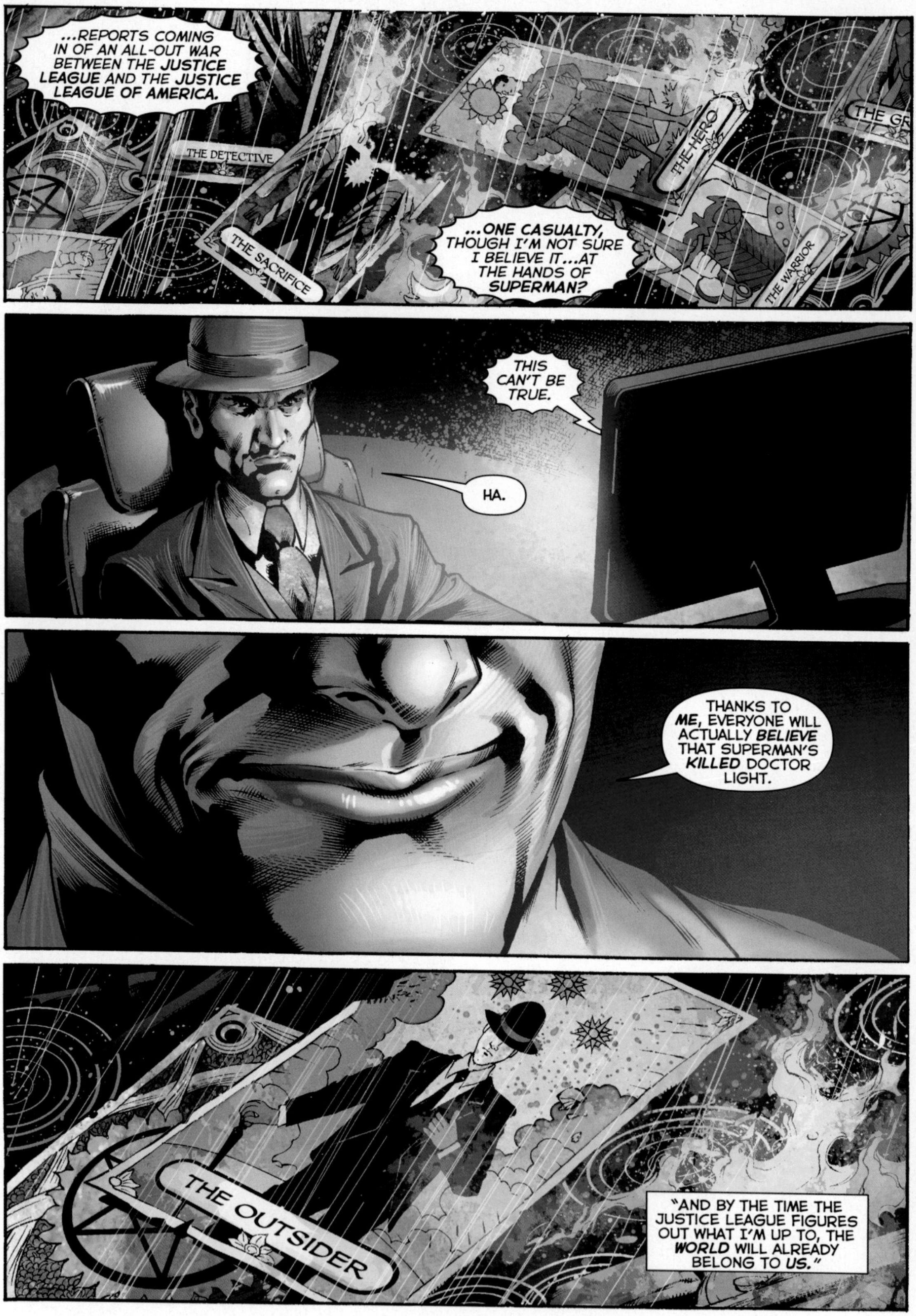
...REPORTS COMING IN OF AN ALL-OUT WAR BETWEEN THE JUSTICE LEAGUE AND THE JUSTICE LEAGUE OF AMERICA.
THE DETECTIVE
THE SACRIFICE
THE HERO
THE WARRIOR
...ONE CASUALTY, THOUGH I'M NOT SURE I BELIEVE IT...AT THE HANDS OF SUPERMAN?
THIS CAN'T BE TRUE.
HA.
THANKS TO ME, EVERYONE WILL ACTUALLY BELIEVE THAT SUPERMAN'S KILLED DOCTOR LIGHT.
THE OUTSIDER
"AND BY THE TIME THE JUSTICE LEAGUE FIGURES OUT WHAT I'M UP TO, THE WORLD WILL ALREADY BELONG TO US."

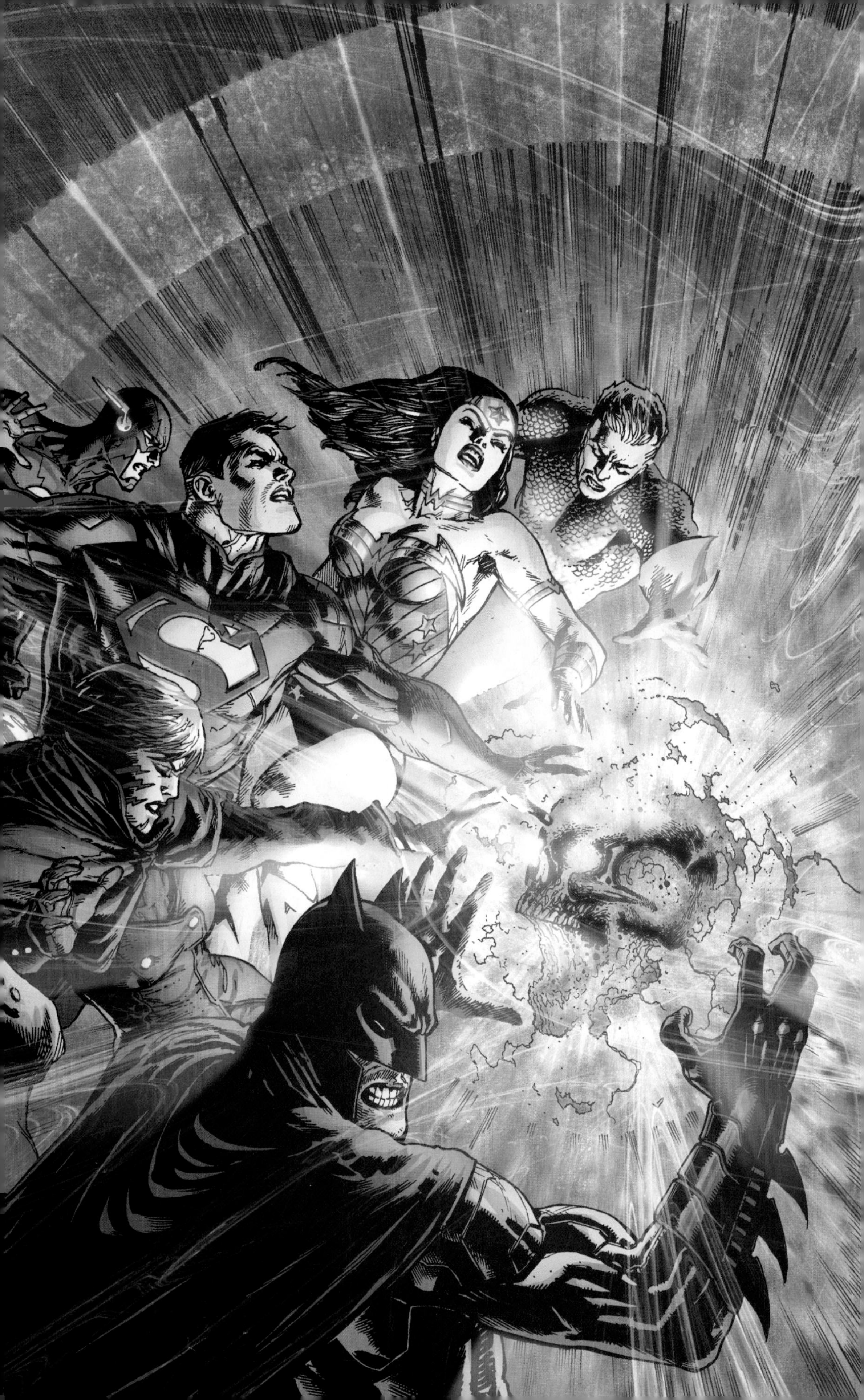

TRINITY WAR: CONCLUSION

GEOFF JOHNS writer **IVAN REIS** penciller **JOE PRADO, OCLAIR ALBERT** and **EBER FERREIRA** inkers
ROD REIS colorist **DOUG MAHNKE** and **ALEX SINCLAIR** cover artists

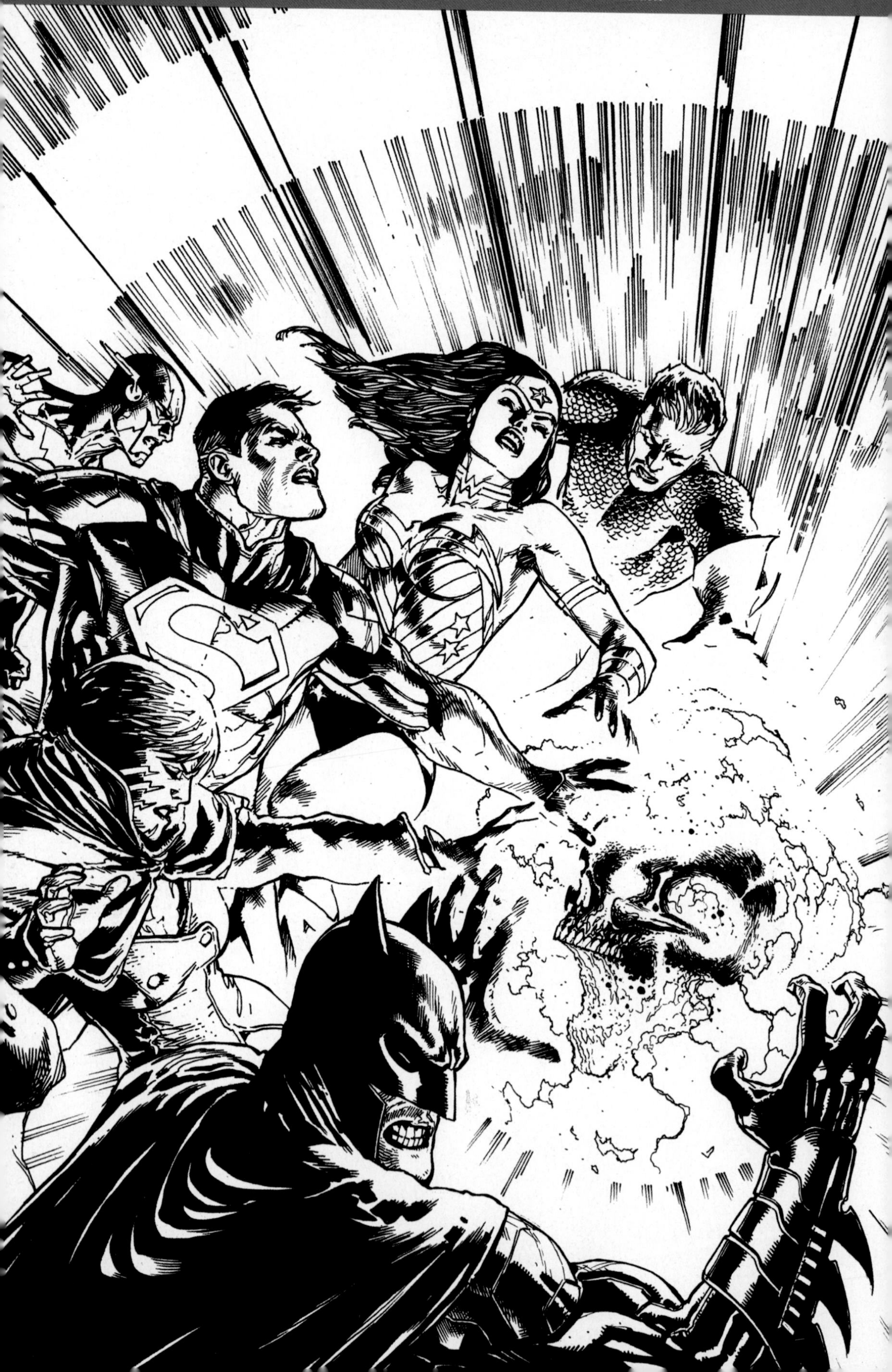

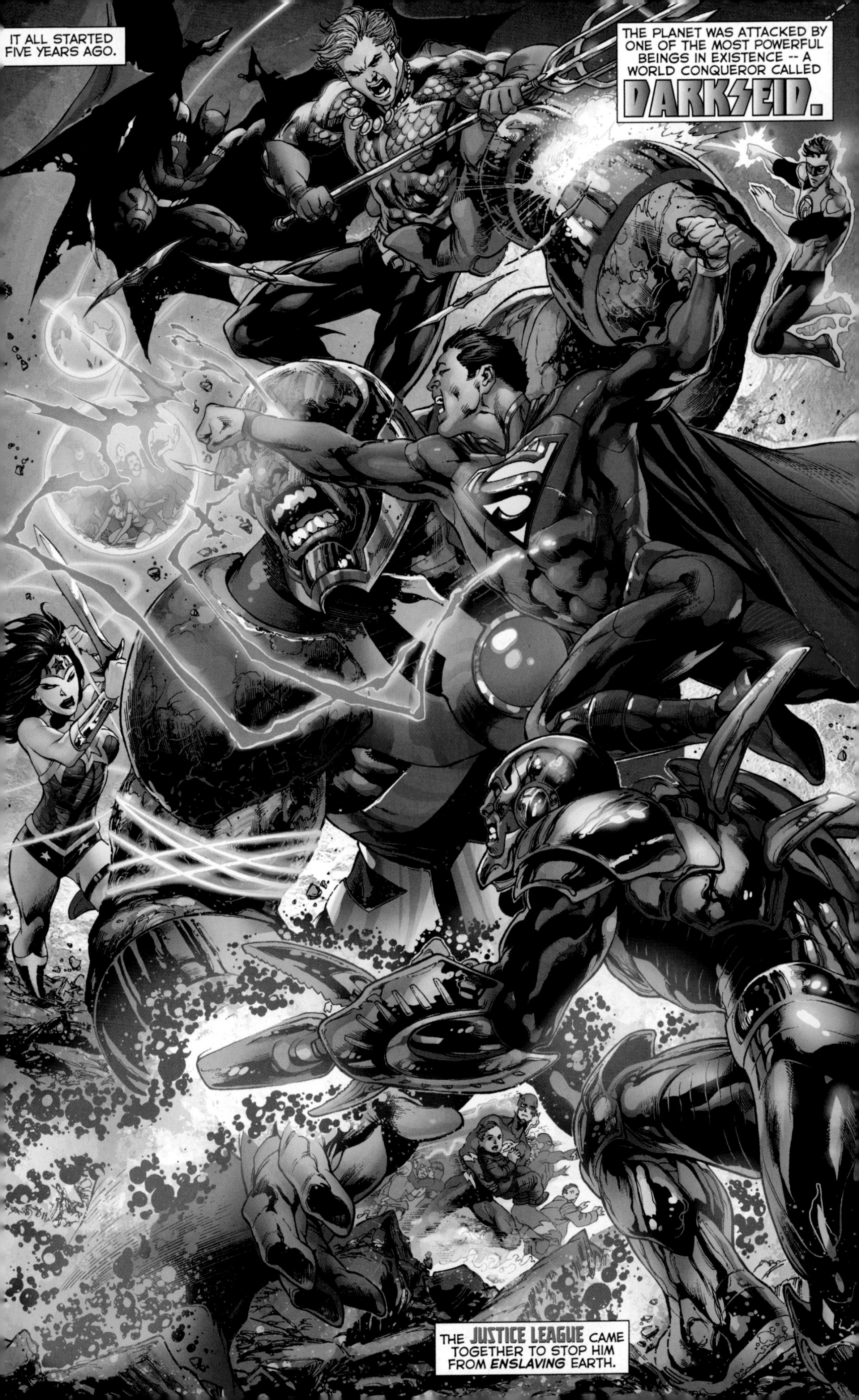
IT ALL STARTED FIVE YEARS AGO.
THE PLANET WAS ATTACKED BY ONE OF THE MOST POWERFUL BEINGS IN EXISTENCE -- A WORLD CONQUEROR CALLED
DARKSEID.
THE JUSTICE LEAGUE CAME TOGETHER TO STOP HIM FROM ENSLAVING EARTH.

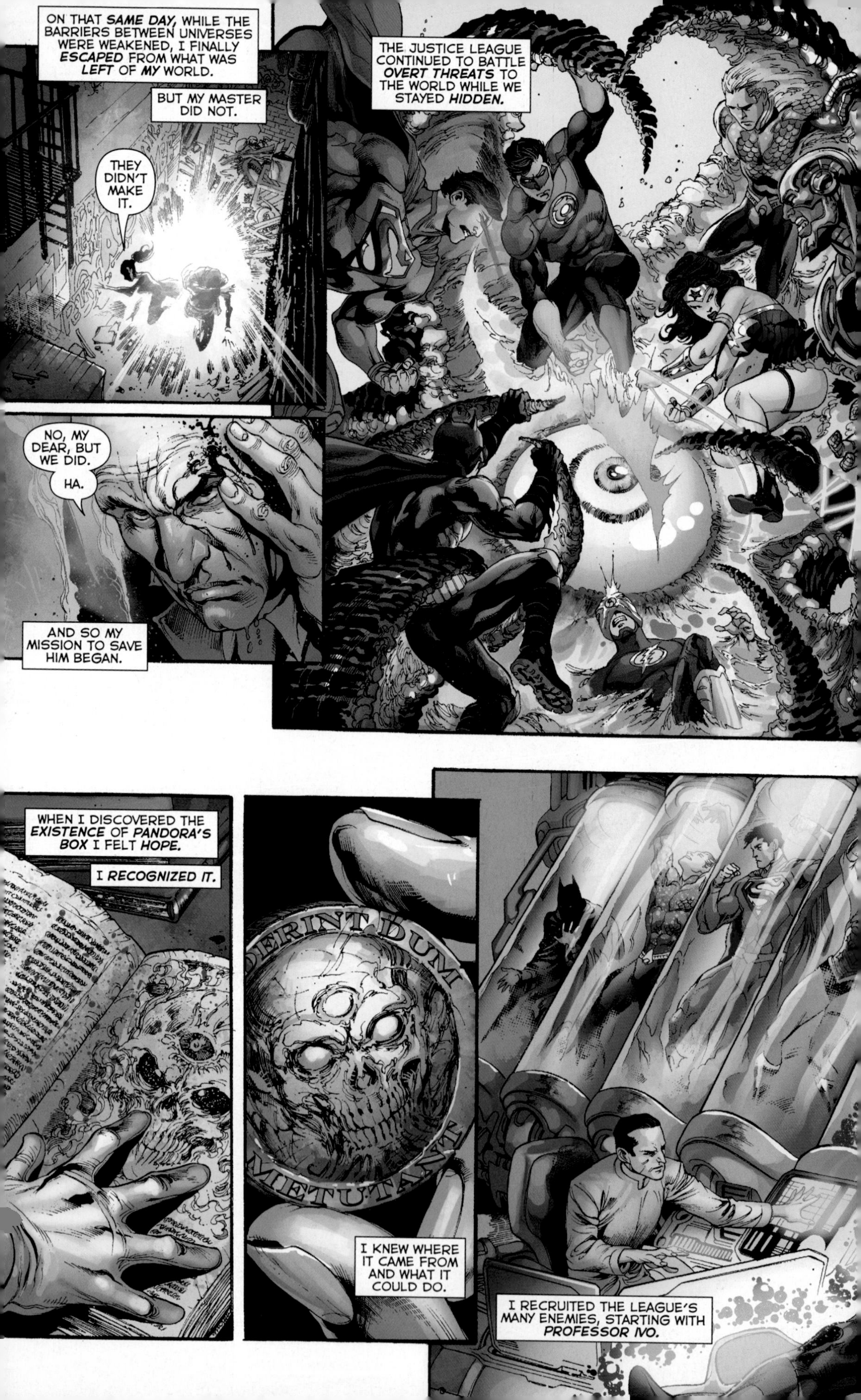
ON THAT SAME DAY, WHILE THE BARRIERS BETWEEN UNIVERSES WERE WEAKENED, I FINALLY ESCAPED FROM WHAT WAS LEFT OF MY WORLD.
BUT MY MASTER DID NOT.
THEY DIDN'T MAKE IT.
NO, MY DEAR, BUT WE DID.
HA.
AND SO MY MISSION TO SAVE HIM BEGAN.
THE JUSTICE LEAGUE CONTINUED TO BATTLE OVERT THREATS TO THE WORLD WHILE WE STAYED HIDDEN.
WHEN I DISCOVERED THE EXISTENCE OF PANDORA'S BOX I FELT HOPE.
I RECOGNIZED IT.
I KNEW WHERE IT CAME FROM AND WHAT IT COULD DO.
I RECRUITED THE LEAGUE'S MANY ENEMIES, STARTING WITH PROFESSOR IVO.

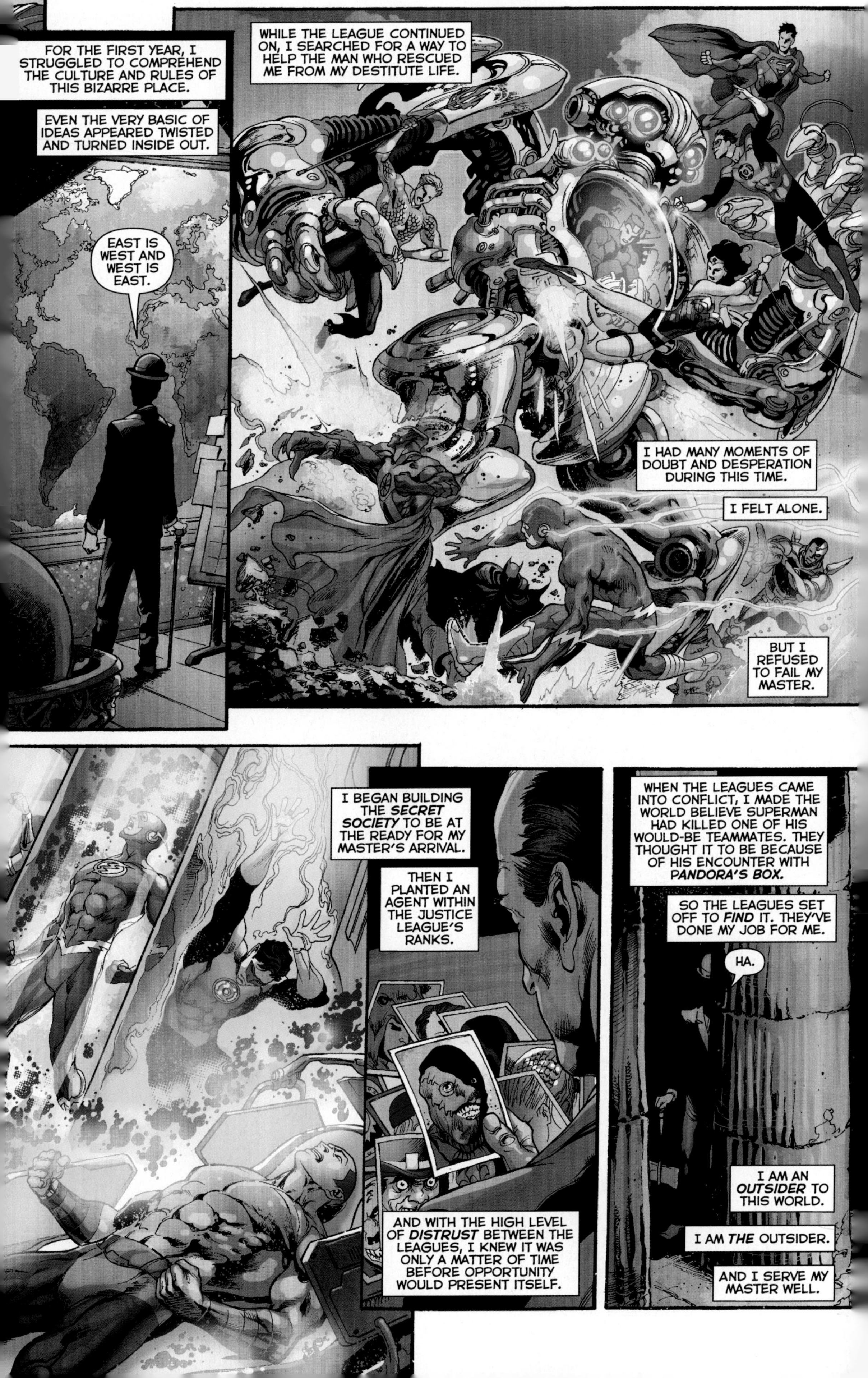
FOR THE FIRST YEAR, I STRUGGLED TO COMPREHEND THE CULTURE AND RULES OF THIS BIZARRE PLACE.
EVEN THE VERY BASIC OF IDEAS APPEARED TWISTED AND TURNED INSIDE OUT.
EAST IS WEST AND WEST IS EAST.
WHILE THE LEAGUE CONTINUED ON, I SEARCHED FOR A WAY TO HELP THE MAN WHO RESCUED ME FROM MY DESTITUTE LIFE.
I HAD MANY MOMENTS OF DOUBT AND DESPERATION DURING THIS TIME.
I FELT ALONE.
BUT I REFUSED TO FAIL MY MASTER.
I BEGAN BUILDING THE *SECRET SOCIETY* TO BE AT THE READY FOR MY MASTER'S ARRIVAL.
THEN I PLANTED AN AGENT WITHIN THE JUSTICE LEAGUE'S RANKS.
AND WITH THE HIGH LEVEL OF *DISTRUST* BETWEEN THE LEAGUES, I KNEW IT WAS ONLY A MATTER OF TIME BEFORE OPPORTUNITY WOULD PRESENT ITSELF.
WHEN THE LEAGUES CAME INTO CONFLICT, I MADE THE WORLD BELIEVE SUPERMAN HAD KILLED ONE OF HIS WOULD-BE TEAMMATES. THEY THOUGHT IT TO BE BECAUSE OF HIS ENCOUNTER WITH *PANDORA'S BOX.*
SO THE LEAGUES SET OFF TO *FIND* IT. THEY'VE DONE MY JOB FOR ME.
HA.
I AM AN *OUTSIDER* TO THIS WORLD.
I AM *THE* OUTSIDER.
AND I SERVE MY MASTER WELL.

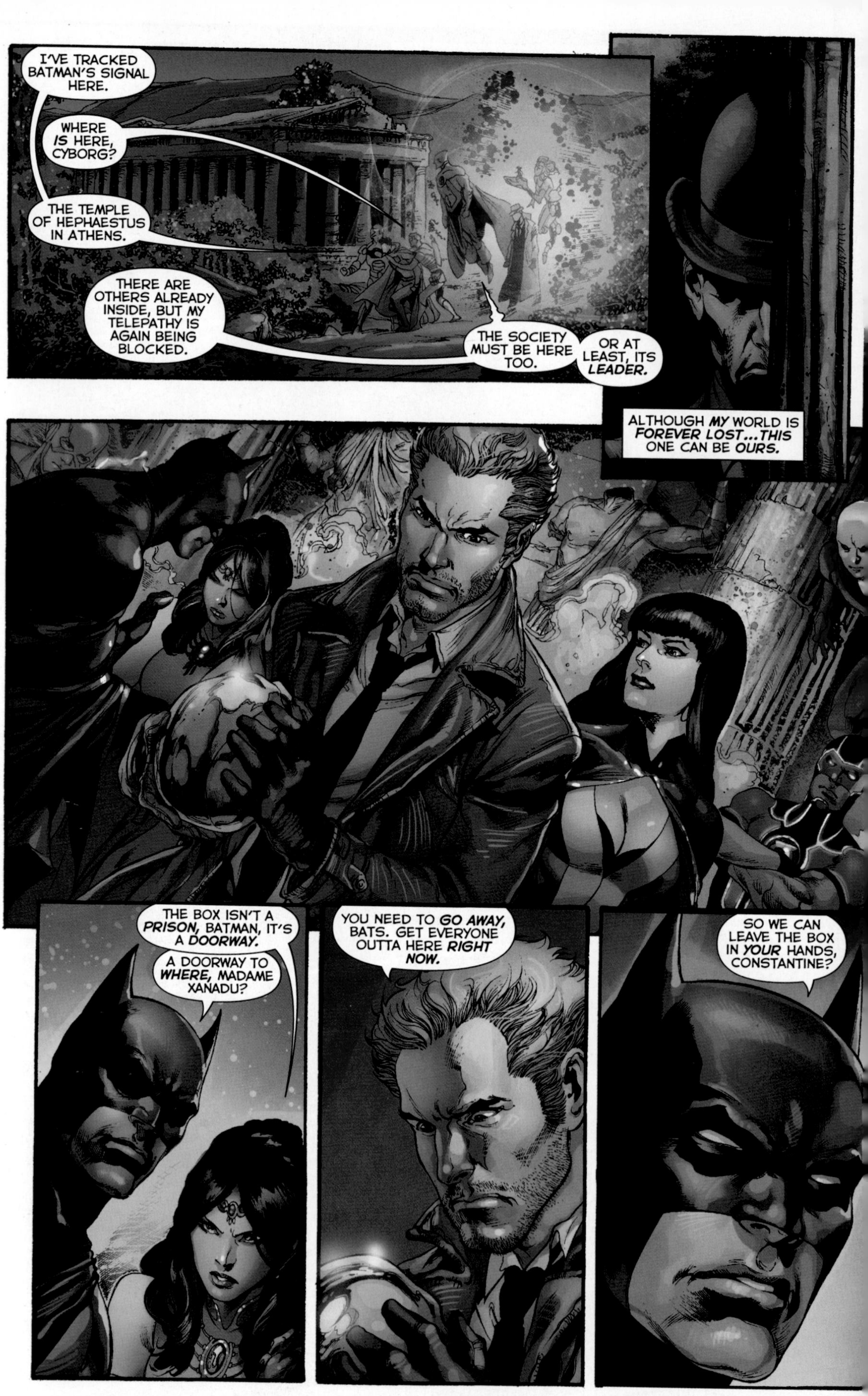
I'VE TRACKED BATMAN'S SIGNAL HERE.
WHERE IS HERE, CYBORG?
THE TEMPLE OF HEPHAESTUS IN ATHENS.
THERE ARE OTHERS ALREADY INSIDE, BUT MY TELEPATHY IS AGAIN BEING BLOCKED.
THE SOCIETY MUST BE HERE TOO.
OR AT LEAST, ITS LEADER.
ALTHOUGH MY WORLD IS FOREVER LOST...THIS ONE CAN BE OURS.
THE BOX ISN'T A PRISON, BATMAN, IT'S A DOORWAY.
A DOORWAY TO WHERE, MADAME XANADU?
YOU NEED TO GO AWAY, BATS. GET EVERYONE OUTTA HERE RIGHT NOW.
SO WE CAN LEAVE THE BOX IN YOUR HANDS, CONSTANTINE?

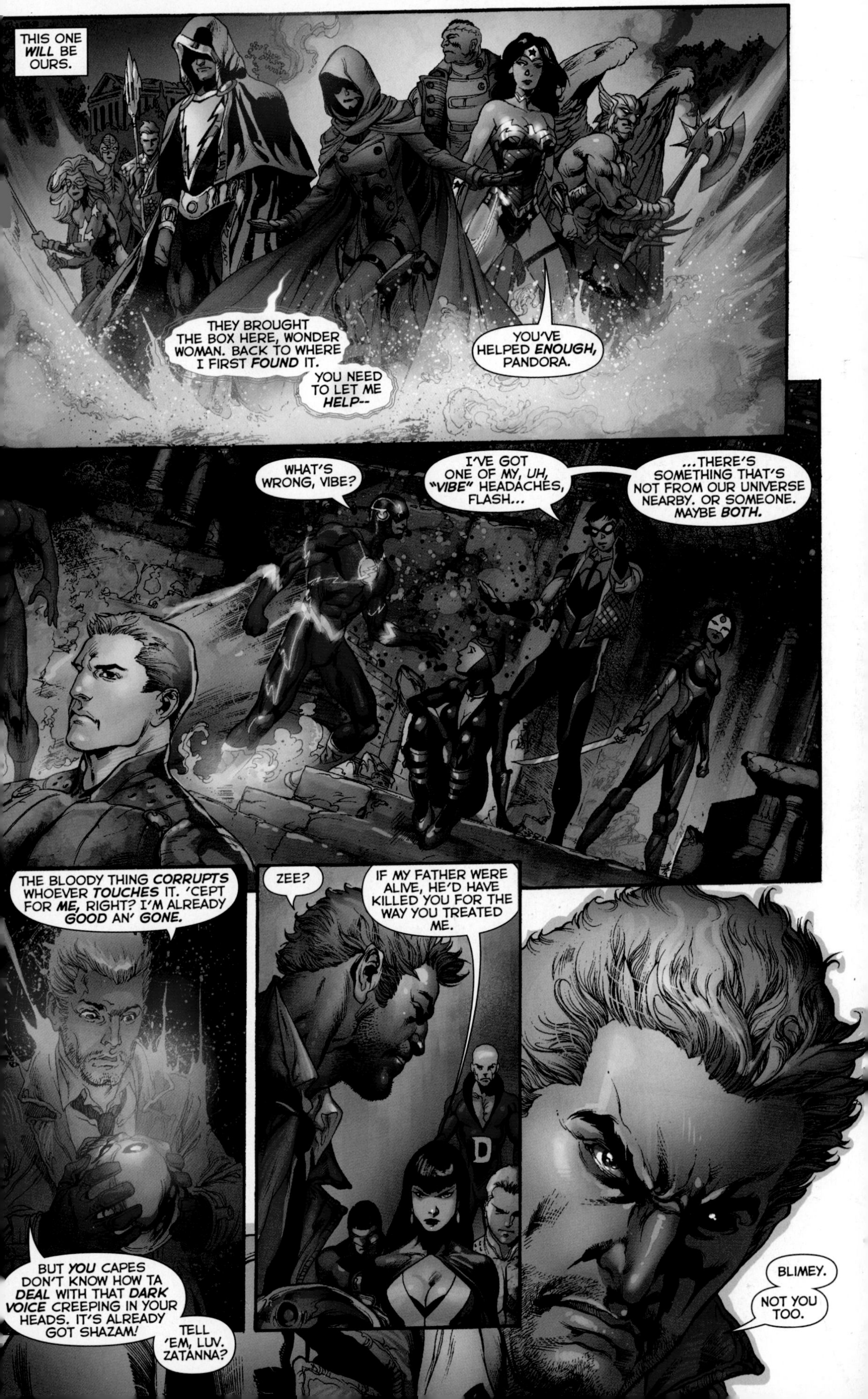
THIS ONE WILL BE OURS.
THEY BROUGHT THE BOX HERE, WONDER WOMAN. BACK TO WHERE I FIRST FOUND IT.
YOU NEED TO LET ME HELP--
YOU'VE HELPED ENOUGH, PANDORA.
WHAT'S WRONG, VIBE?
I'VE GOT ONE OF MY, UH, "VIBE" HEADACHES, FLASH...
...THERE'S SOMETHING THAT'S NOT FROM OUR UNIVERSE NEARBY. OR SOMEONE. MAYBE BOTH.
THE BLOODY THING CORRUPTS WHOEVER TOUCHES IT. 'CEPT FOR ME, RIGHT? I'M ALREADY GOOD AN' GONE.
BUT YOU CAPES DON'T KNOW HOW TA DEAL WITH THAT DARK VOICE CREEPING IN YOUR HEADS. IT'S ALREADY GOT SHAZAM!
TELL 'EM, LUV. ZATANNA?
ZEE?
IF MY FATHER WERE ALIVE, HE'D HAVE KILLED YOU FOR THE WAY YOU TREATED ME.
BLIMEY.
NOT YOU TOO.

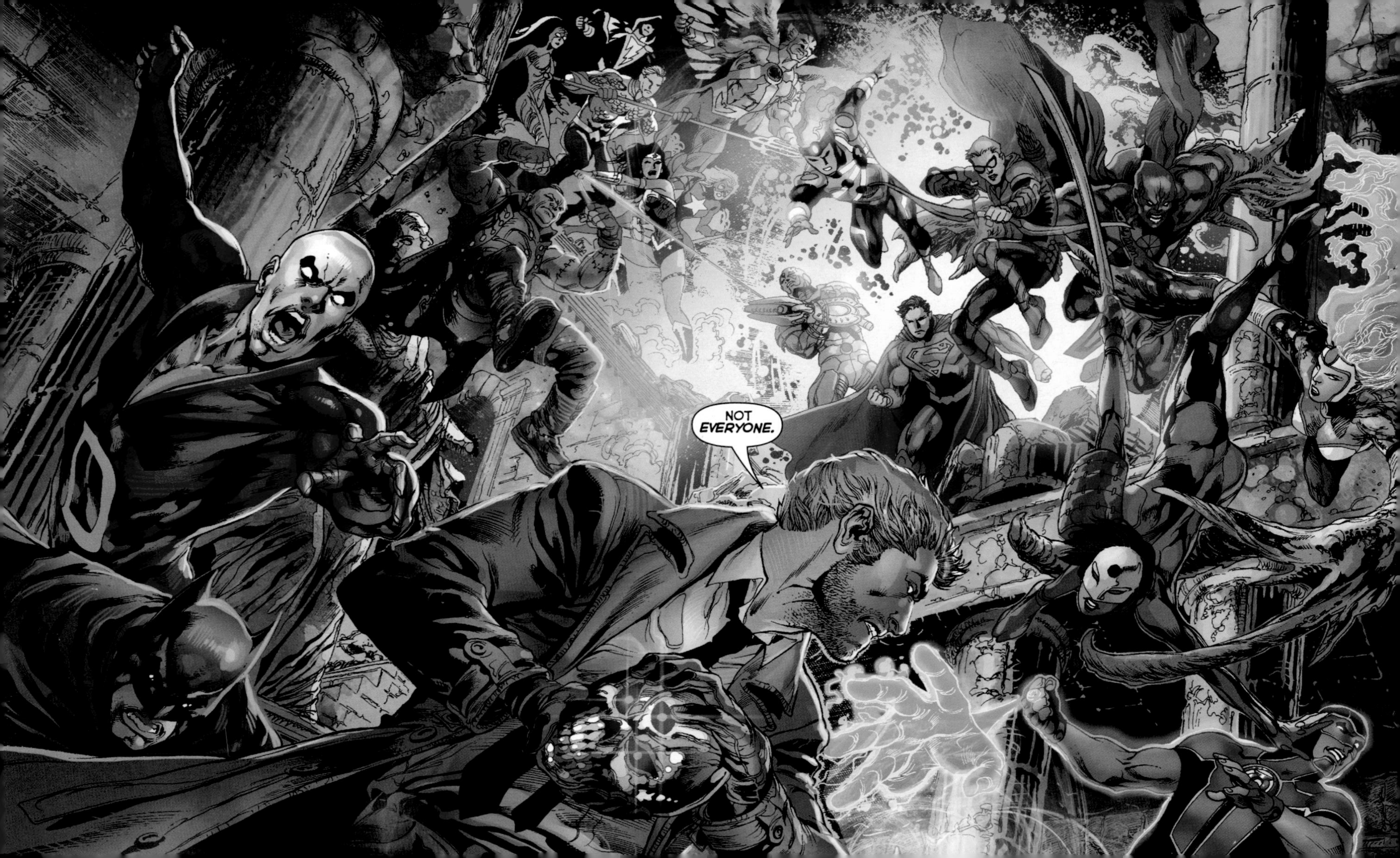
NOT EVERYONE.

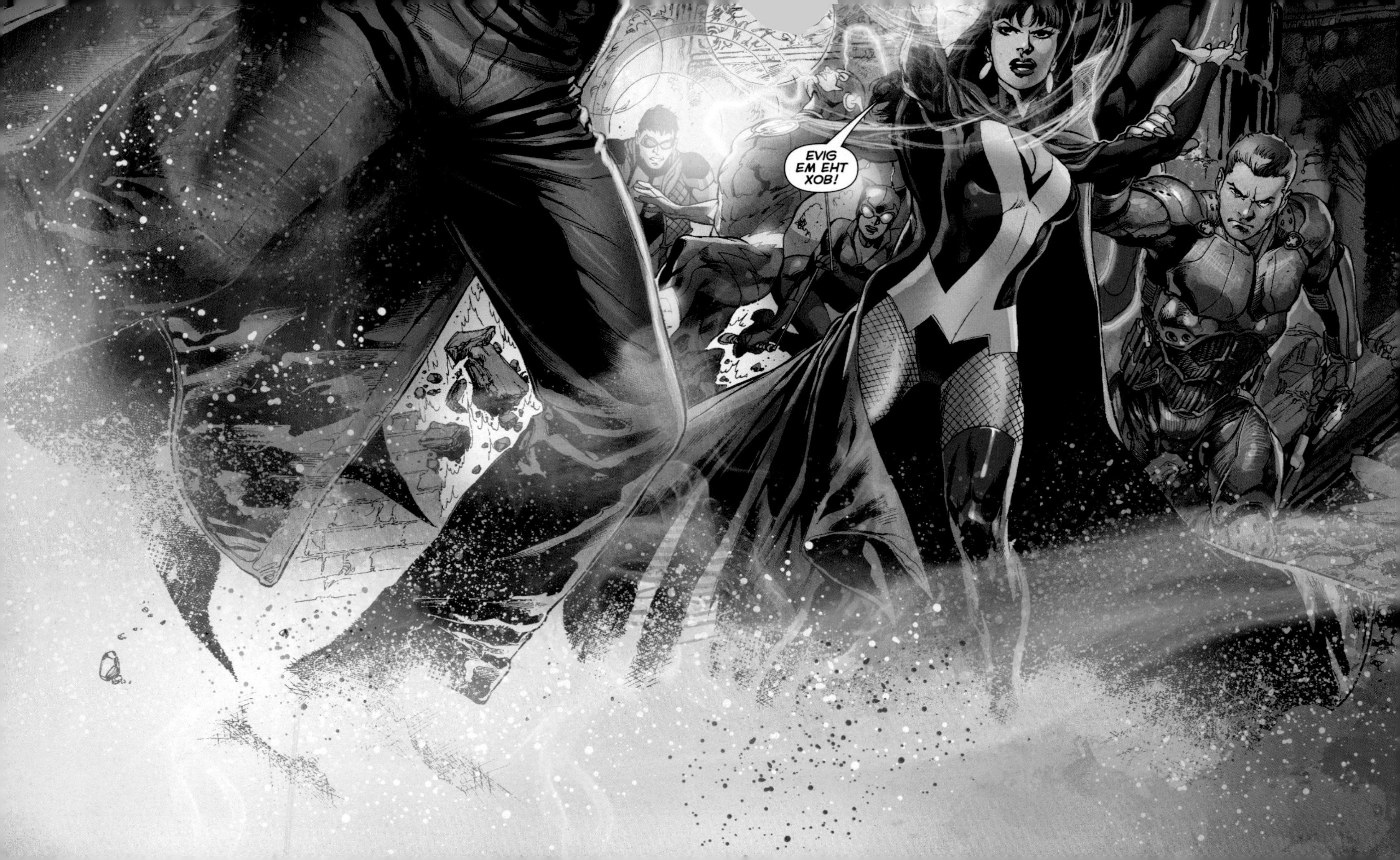
EVIG EM EHT XOB!

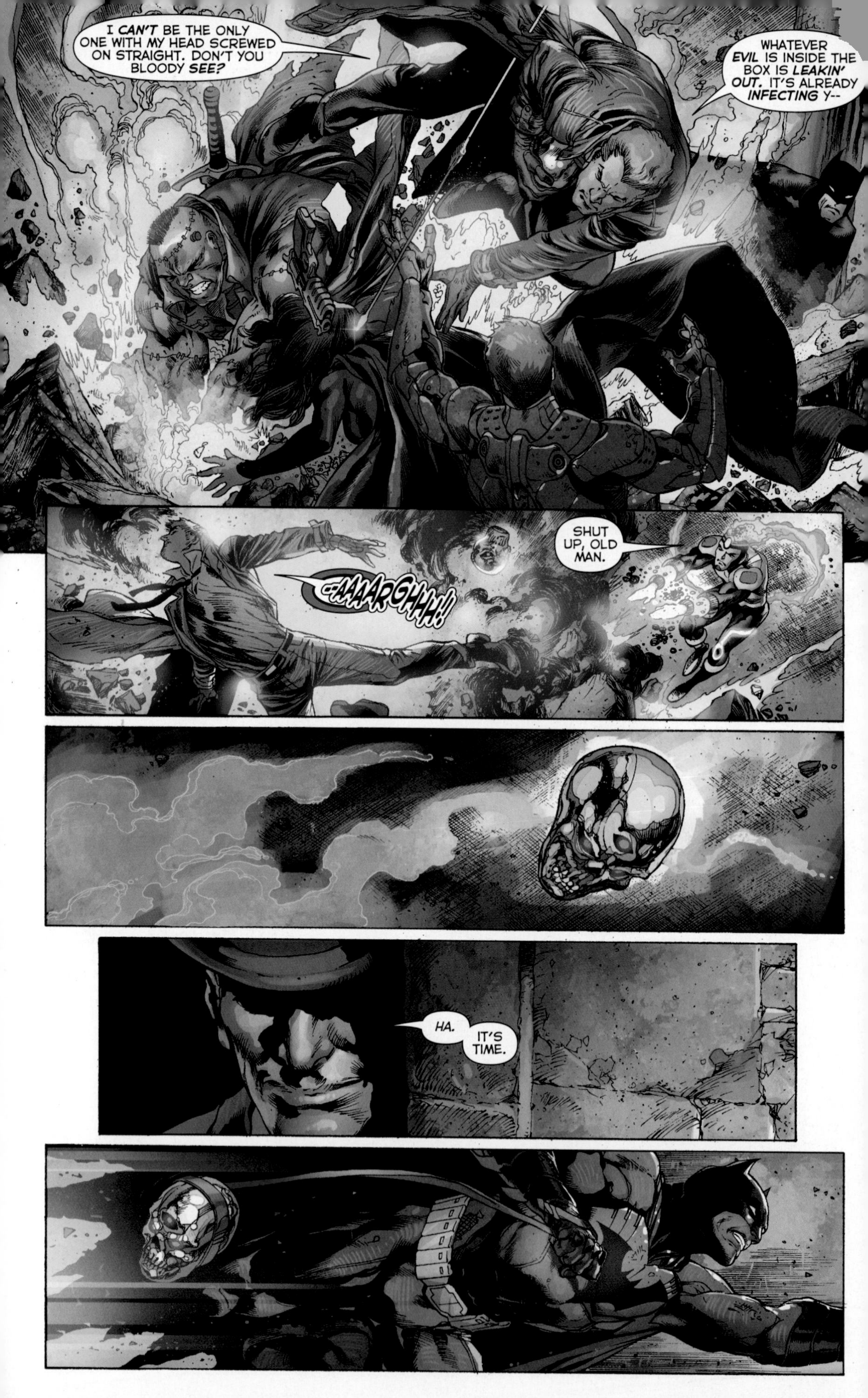
I CAN'T BE THE ONLY ONE WITH MY HEAD SCREWED ON STRAIGHT. DON'T YOU BLOODY SEE?
WHATEVER EVIL IS INSIDE THE BOX IS LEAKIN' OUT. IT'S ALREADY INFECTING Y--
--AAAARGHHH!!
SHUT UP, OLD MAN.
HA.
IT'S TIME.

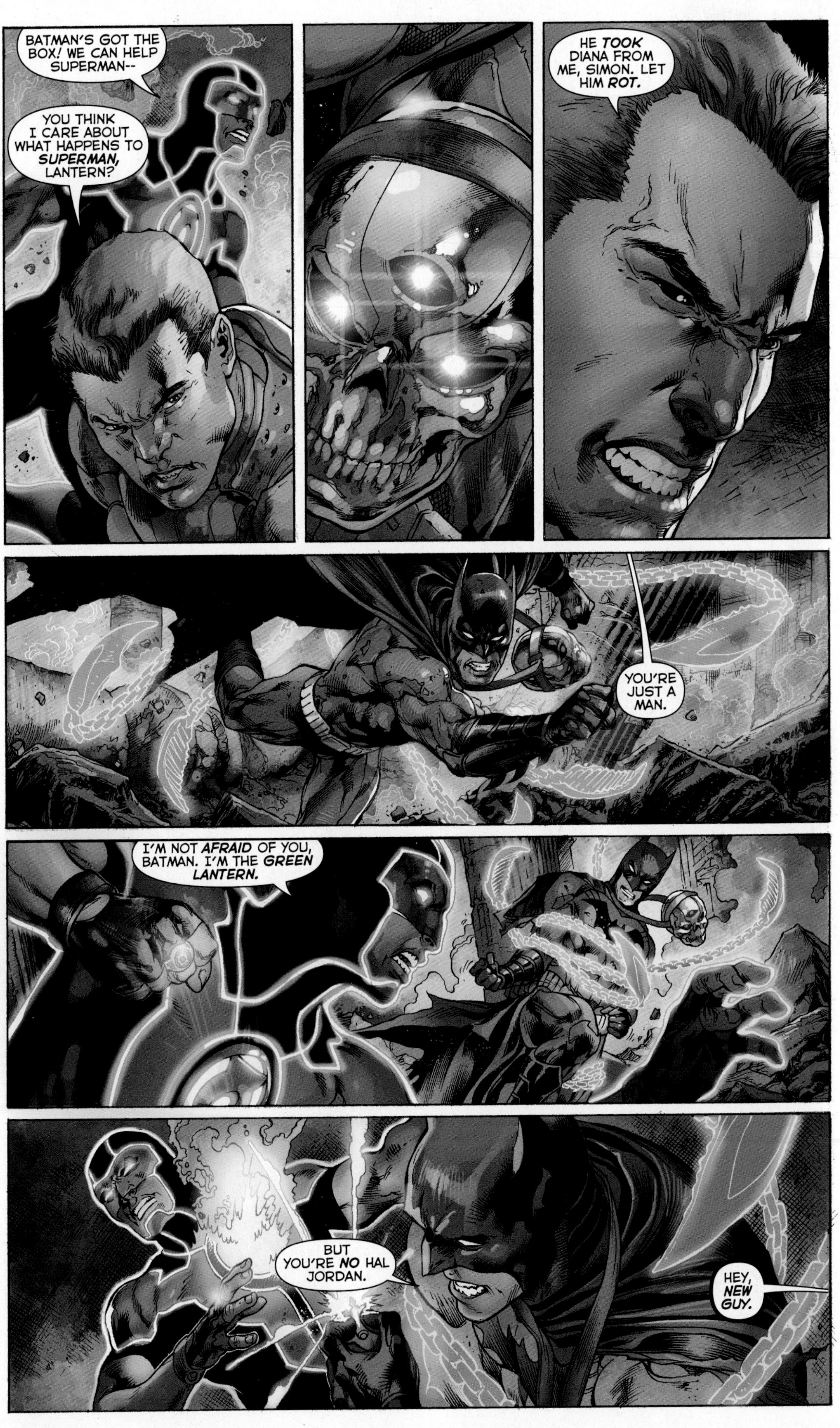
BATMAN'S GOT THE BOX! WE CAN HELP SUPERMAN--
YOU THINK I CARE ABOUT WHAT HAPPENS TO SUPERMAN, LANTERN?
HE TOOK DIANA FROM ME, SIMON. LET HIM ROT.
YOU'RE JUST A MAN.
I'M NOT AFRAID OF YOU, BATMAN. I'M THE GREEN LANTERN.
BUT YOU'RE NO HAL JORDAN.
HEY, NEW GUY.

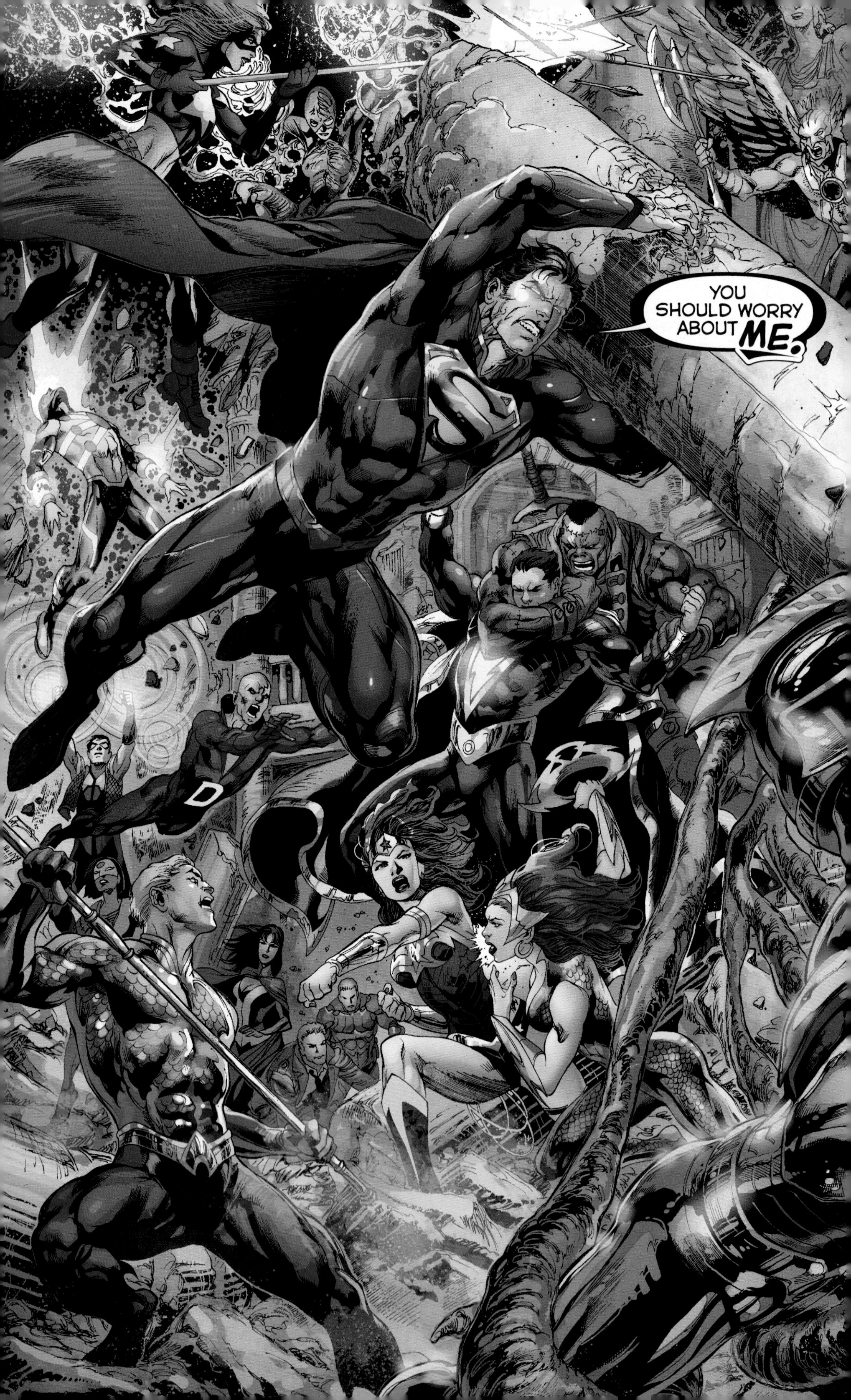
YOU SHOULD WORRY ABOUT ME.

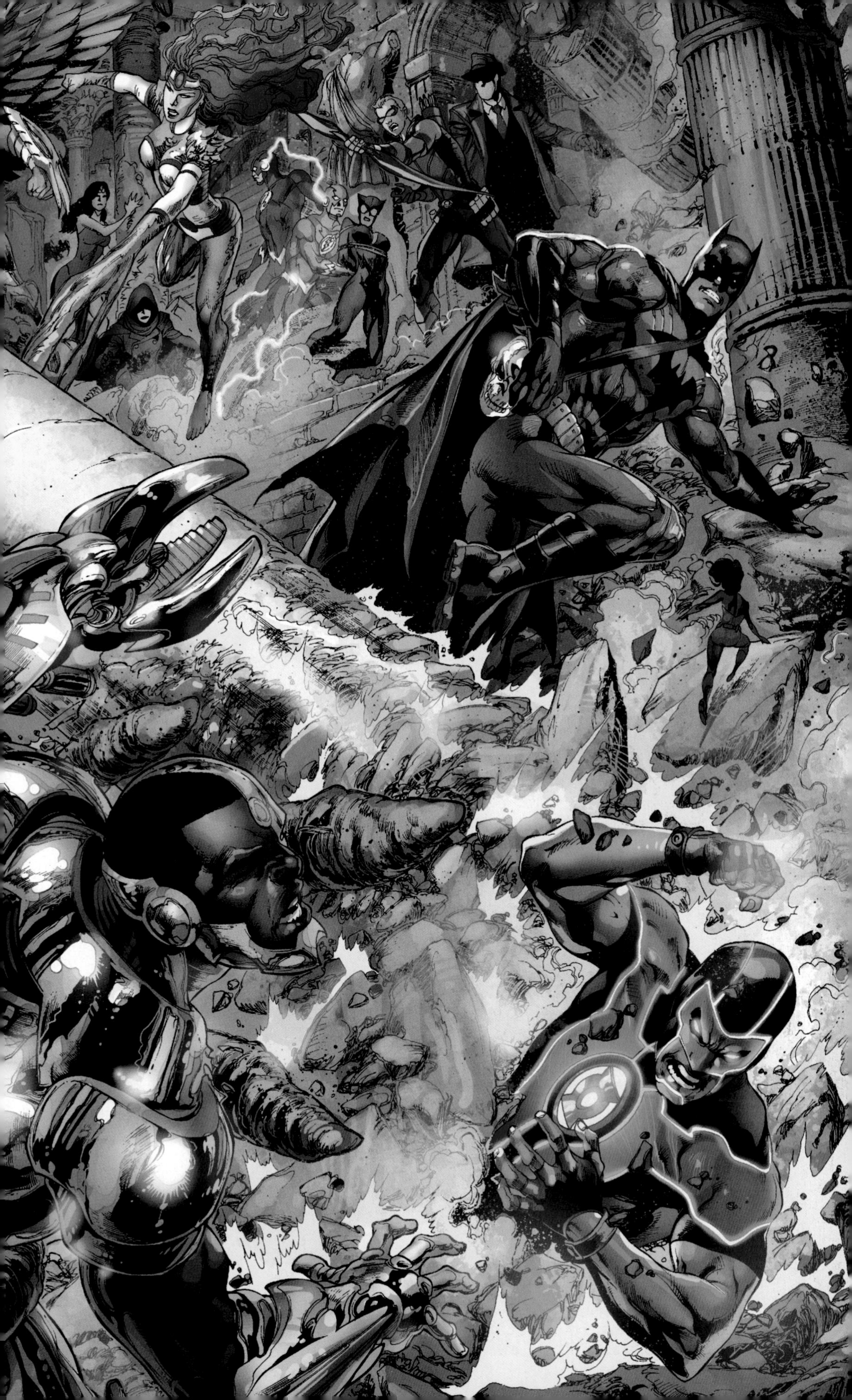

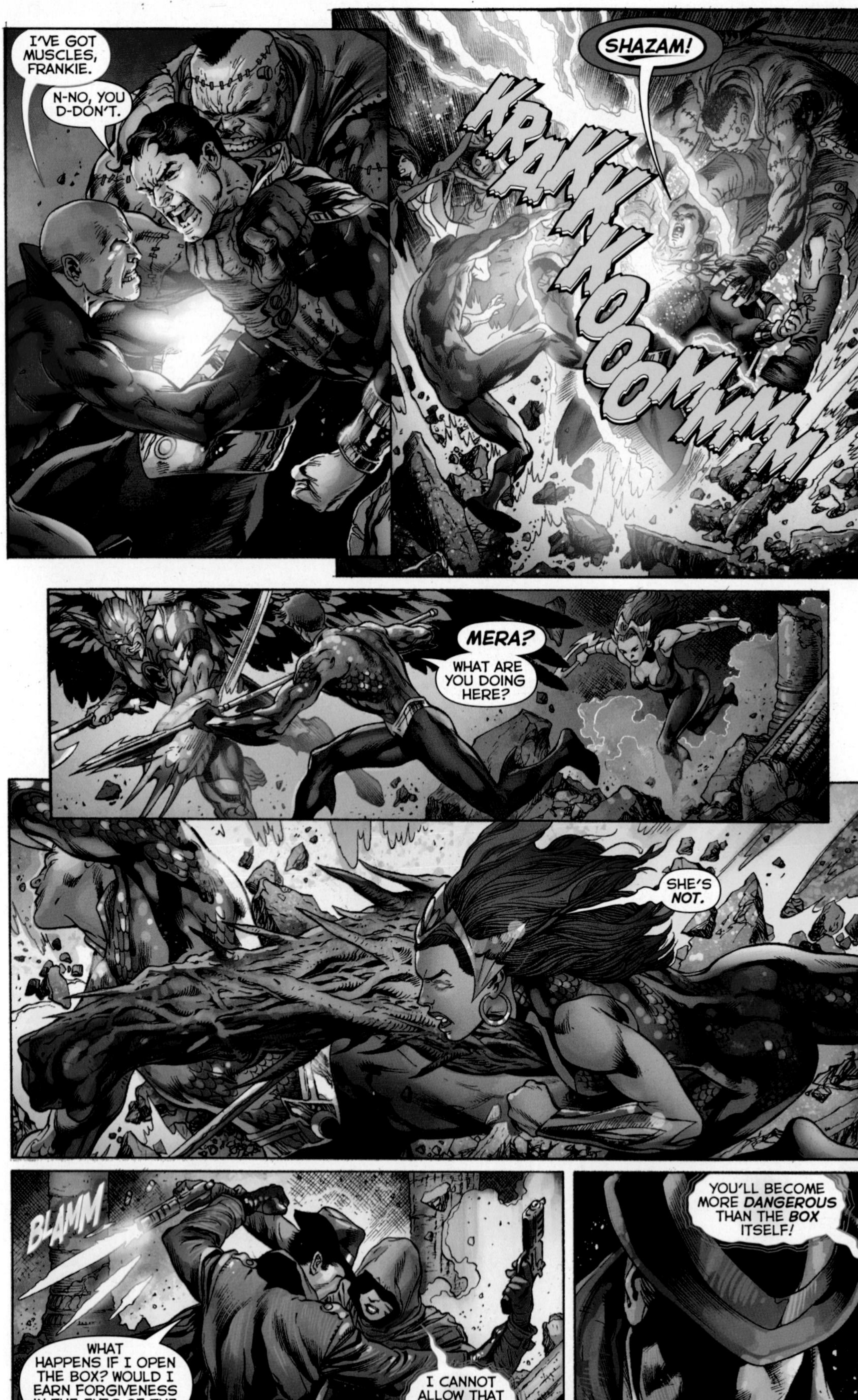
I'VE GOT MUSCLES, FRANKIE.
N-NO, YOU D-DON'T.
SHAZAM!
KRAKKKOOOMMMM
MERA?
WHAT ARE YOU DOING HERE?
SHE'S NOT.
BLAMM
WHAT HAPPENS IF I OPEN THE BOX? WOULD I EARN FORGIVENESS IN THE EYES OF THE GODS?
WOULD I FINALLY GET THE ANSWER TO: WHO AM I?
I CANNOT ALLOW THAT TO HAPPEN, QUESTION!
YOU'LL BECOME MORE DANGEROUS THAN THE BOX ITSELF!

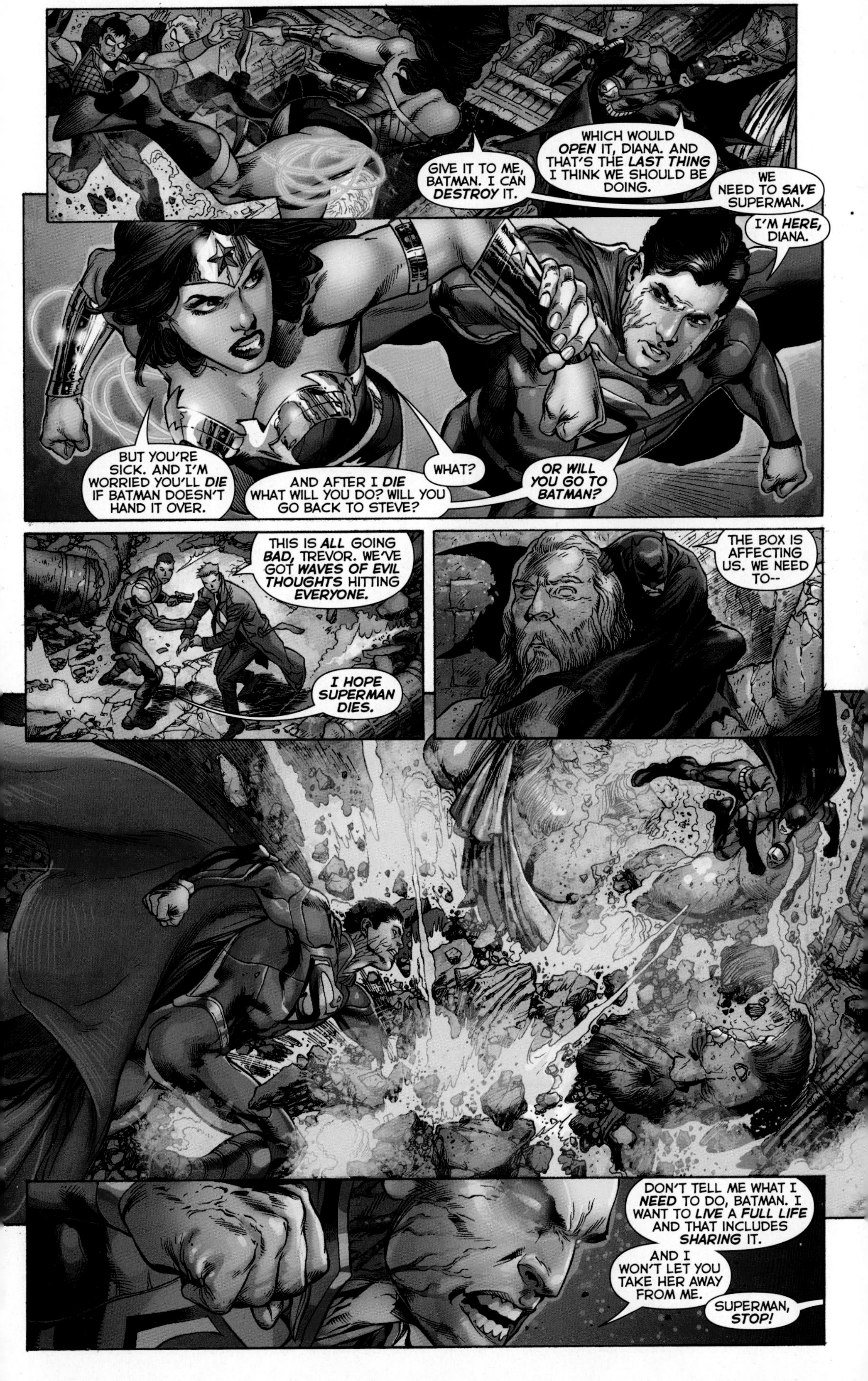

GIVE IT TO ME, BATMAN. I CAN DESTROY IT.
WHICH WOULD OPEN IT, DIANA. AND THAT'S THE LAST THING I THINK WE SHOULD BE DOING.
WE NEED TO SAVE SUPERMAN.
I'M HERE, DIANA.
BUT YOU'RE SICK. AND I'M WORRIED YOU'LL DIE IF BATMAN DOESN'T HAND IT OVER.
WHAT?
AND AFTER I DIE WHAT WILL YOU DO? WILL YOU GO BACK TO STEVE?
OR WILL YOU GO TO BATMAN?
THIS IS ALL GOING BAD, TREVOR. WE'VE GOT WAVES OF EVIL THOUGHTS HITTING EVERYONE.
I HOPE SUPERMAN DIES.
THE BOX IS AFFECTING US. WE NEED TO--
DON'T TELL ME WHAT I NEED TO DO, BATMAN. I WANT TO LIVE A FULL LIFE AND THAT INCLUDES SHARING IT.
AND I WON'T LET YOU TAKE HER AWAY FROM ME.
SUPERMAN, STOP!

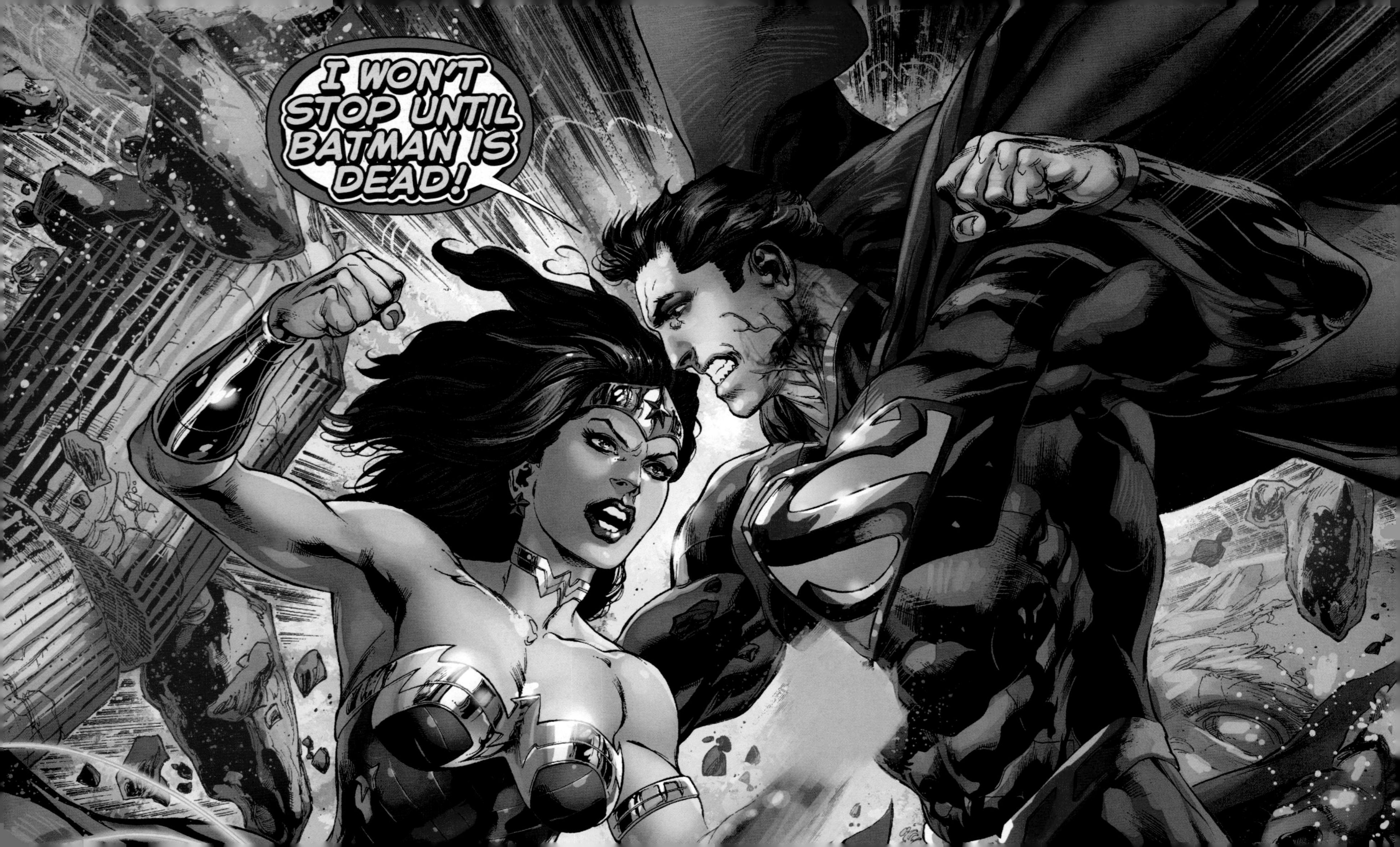
I WON'T STOP UNTIL BATMAN IS DEAD!

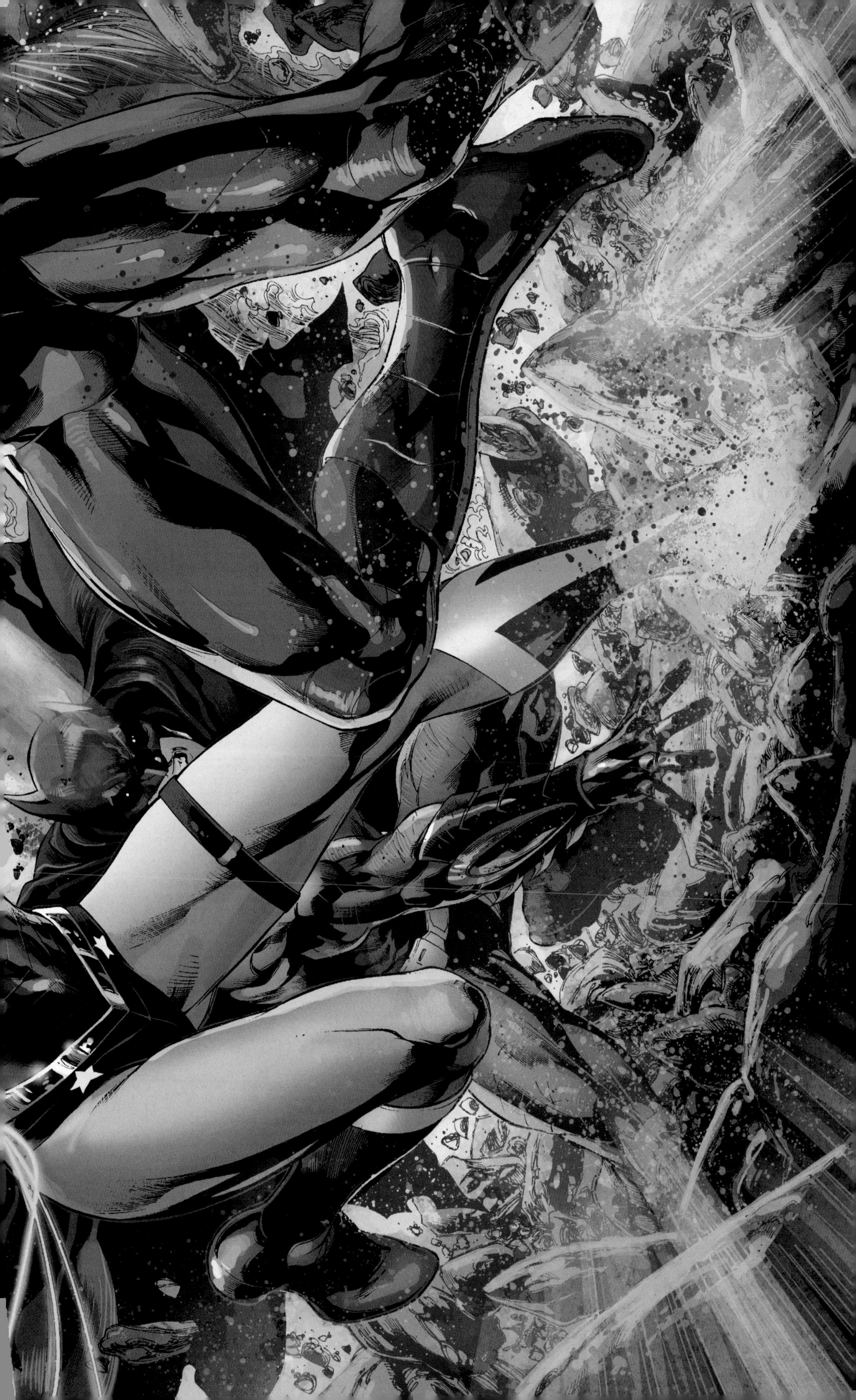

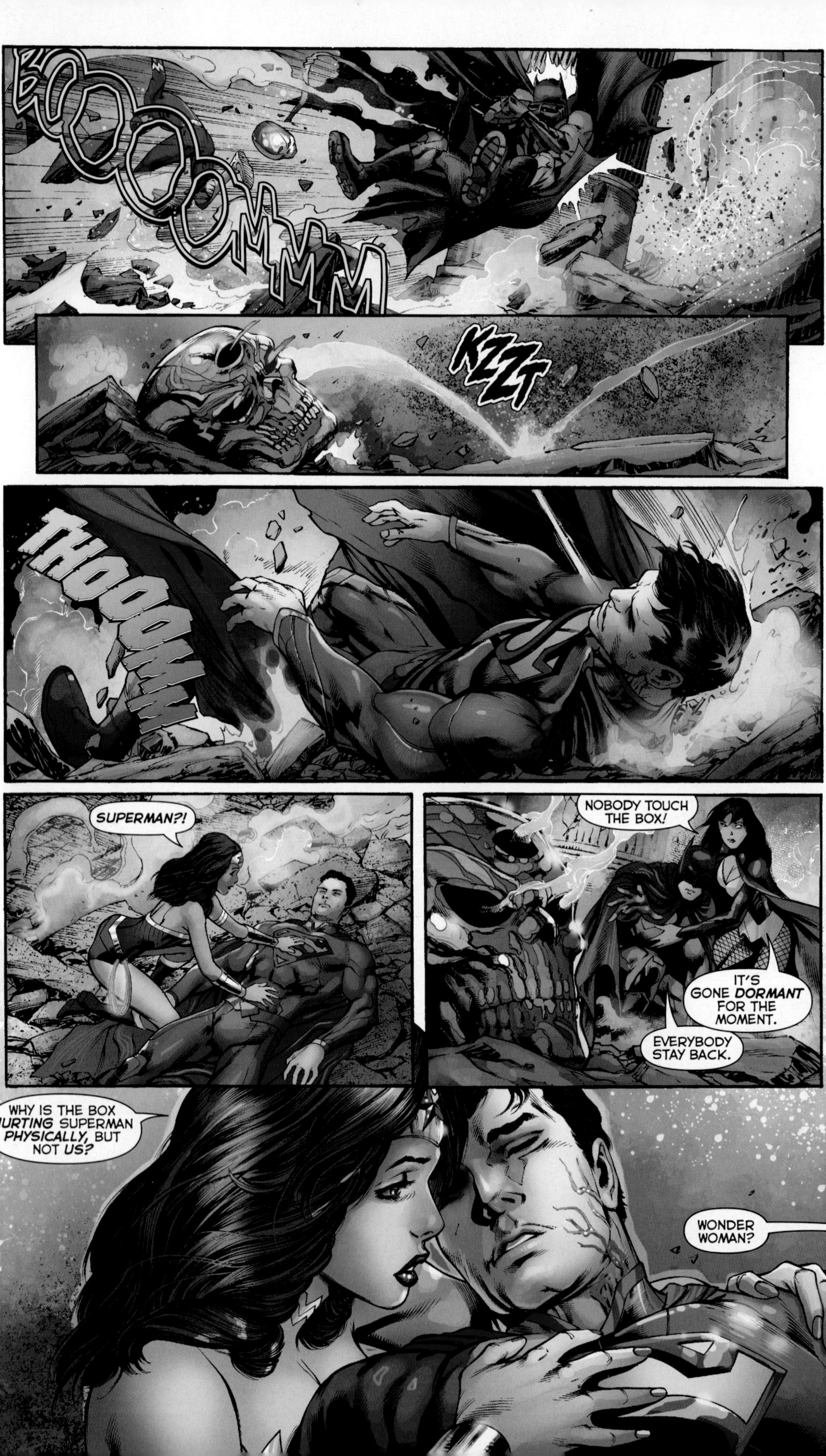
BOOOOOMMMM
KZZT
THOOOMM
SUPERMAN?!
NOBODY TOUCH THE BOX!
IT'S GONE DORMANT FOR THE MOMENT.
EVERYBODY STAY BACK.
WHY IS THE BOX HURTING SUPERMAN PHYSICALLY, BUT NOT US?
WONDER WOMAN?

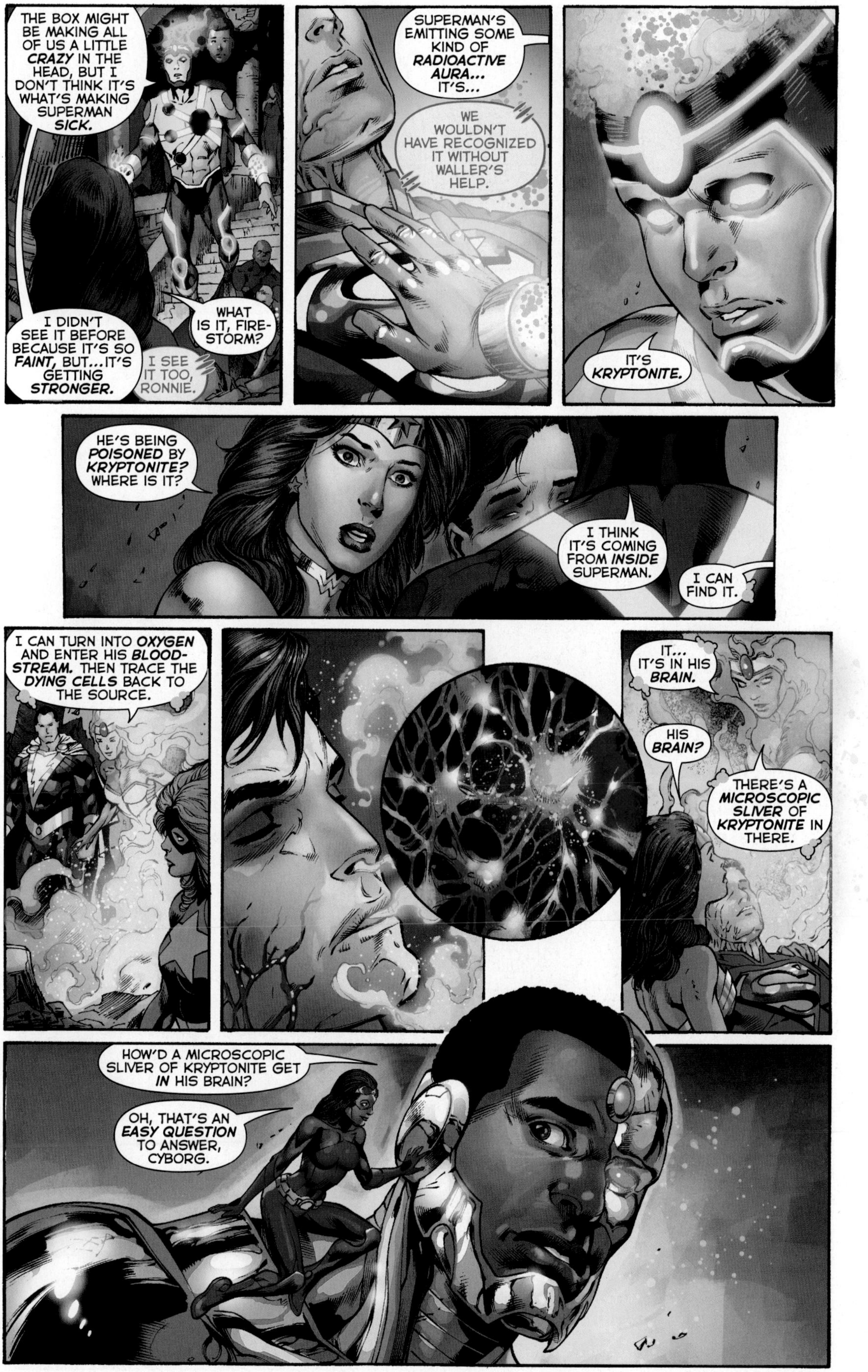
THE BOX MIGHT BE MAKING ALL OF US A LITTLE CRAZY IN THE HEAD, BUT I DON'T THINK IT'S WHAT'S MAKING SUPERMAN SICK.
I DIDN'T SEE IT BEFORE BECAUSE IT'S SO FAINT, BUT...IT'S GETTING STRONGER.
WHAT IS IT, FIRE-STORM?
I SEE IT TOO, RONNIE.
SUPERMAN'S EMITTING SOME KIND OF RADIOACTIVE AURA... IT'S...
WE WOULDN'T HAVE RECOGNIZED IT WITHOUT WALLER'S HELP.
IT'S KRYPTONITE.
HE'S BEING POISONED BY KRYPTONITE? WHERE IS IT?
I THINK IT'S COMING FROM INSIDE SUPERMAN.
I CAN FIND IT.
I CAN TURN INTO OXYGEN AND ENTER HIS BLOOD-STREAM. THEN TRACE THE DYING CELLS BACK TO THE SOURCE.
IT... IT'S IN HIS BRAIN.
HIS BRAIN?
THERE'S A MICROSCOPIC SLIVER OF KRYPTONITE IN THERE.
HOW'D A MICROSCOPIC SLIVER OF KRYPTONITE GET IN HIS BRAIN?
OH, THAT'S AN EASY QUESTION TO ANSWER, CYBORG.

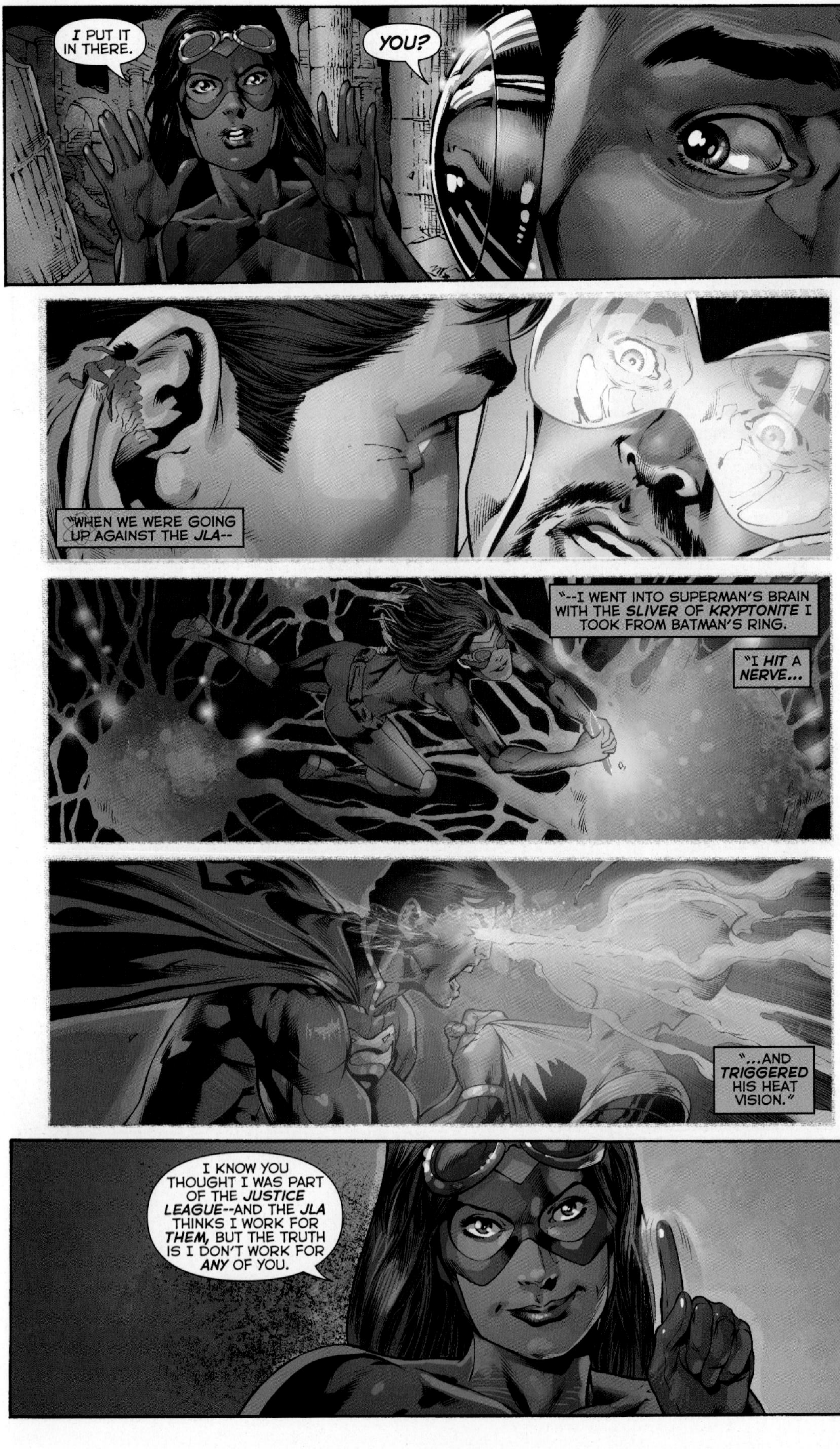
I PUT IT IN THERE.
YOU?
"WHEN WE WERE GOING UP AGAINST THE JLA--
"--I WENT INTO SUPERMAN'S BRAIN WITH THE SLIVER OF KRYPTONITE I TOOK FROM BATMAN'S RING.
"I HIT A NERVE...
"...AND TRIGGERED HIS HEAT VISION."
I KNOW YOU THOUGHT I WAS PART OF THE JUSTICE LEAGUE--AND THE JLA THINKS I WORK FOR THEM, BUT THE TRUTH IS I DON'T WORK FOR ANY OF YOU.

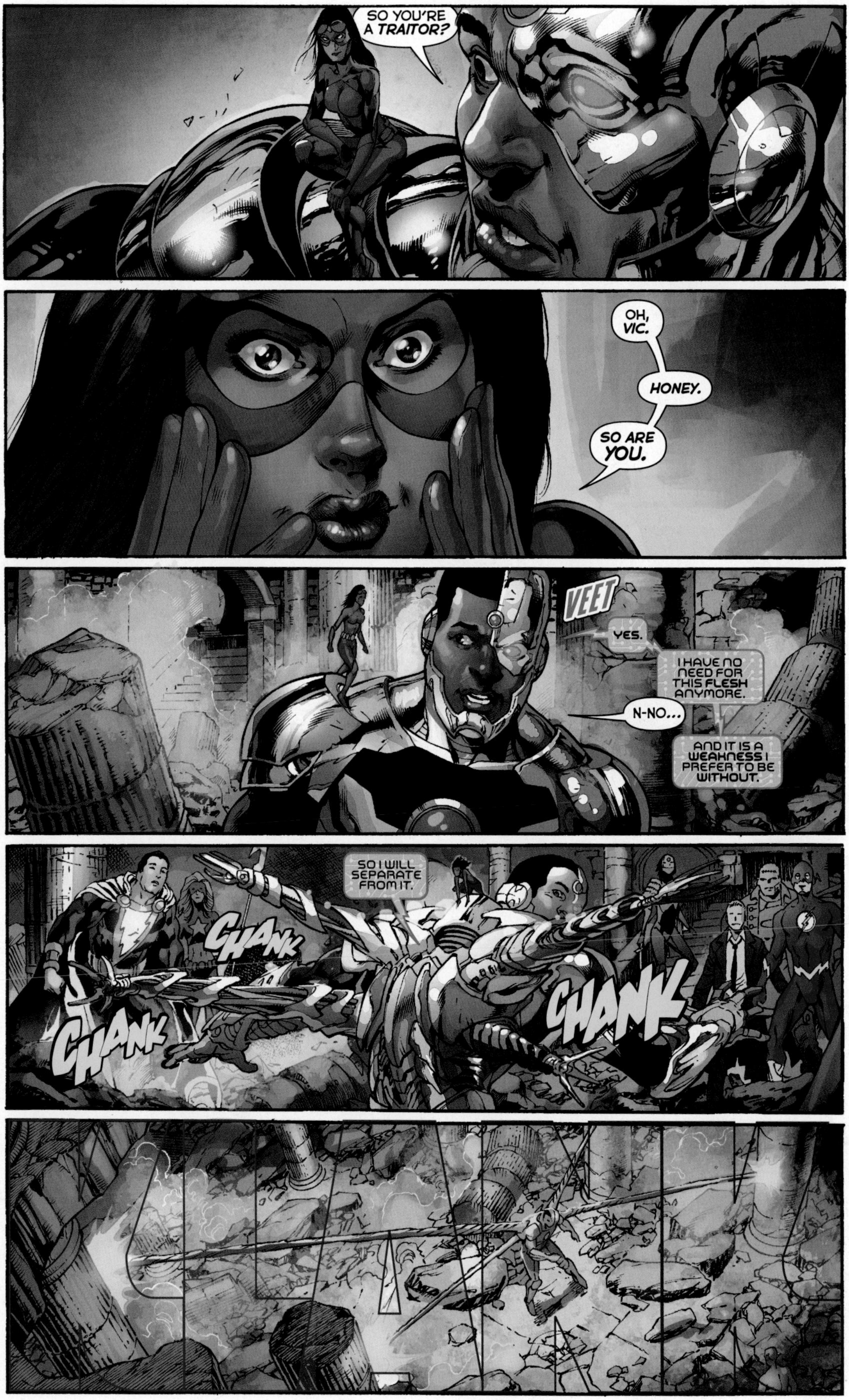
SO YOU'RE A TRAITOR?
OH, VIC.
HONEY.
SO ARE YOU.
VEET
YES.
I HAVE NO NEED FOR THIS FLESH ANYMORE.
N-NO...
AND IT IS A WEAKNESS I PREFER TO BE WITHOUT.
SO I WILL SEPARATE FROM IT.
CHANK
CHANK
CHANK

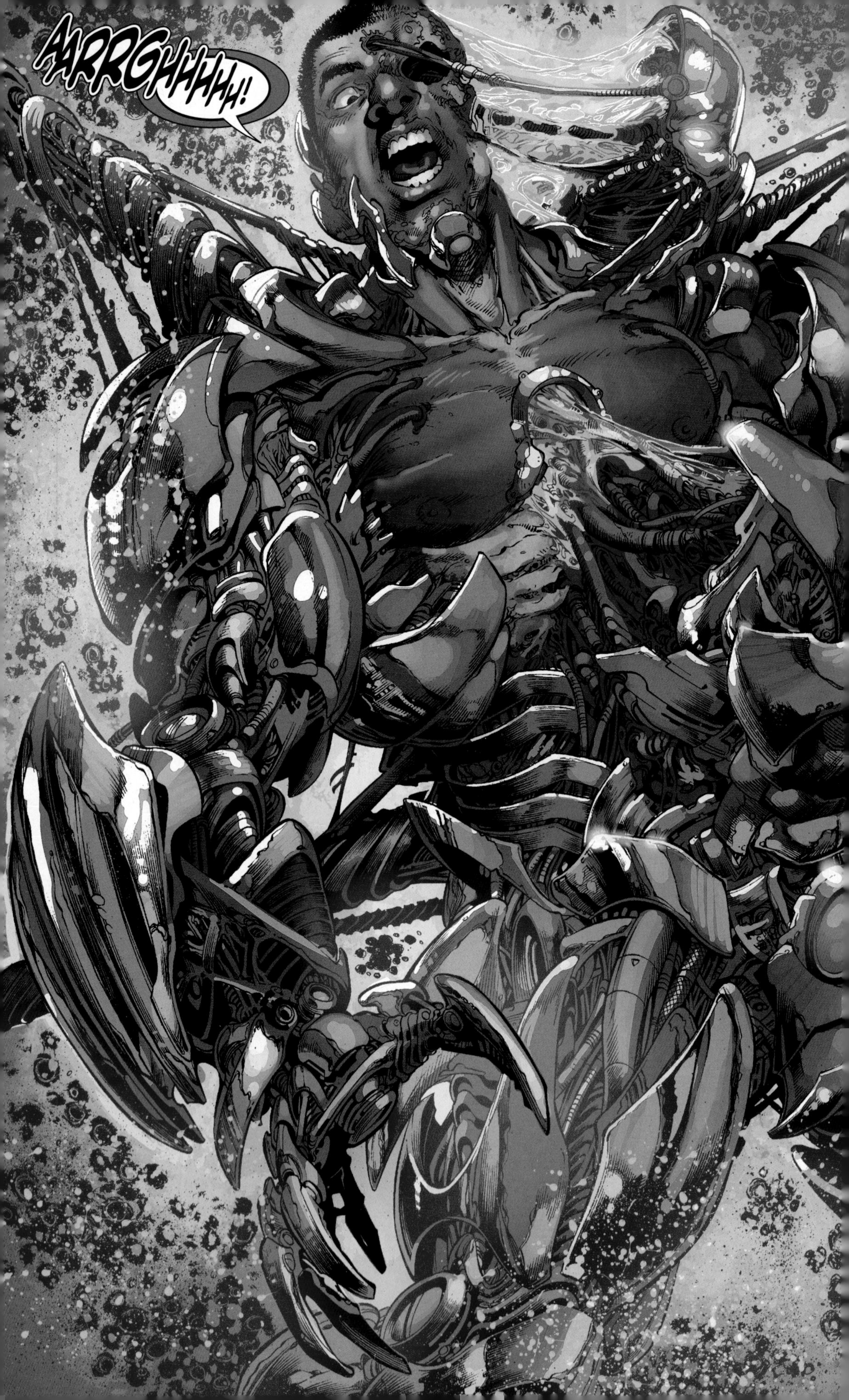
AARRGHHHHH!

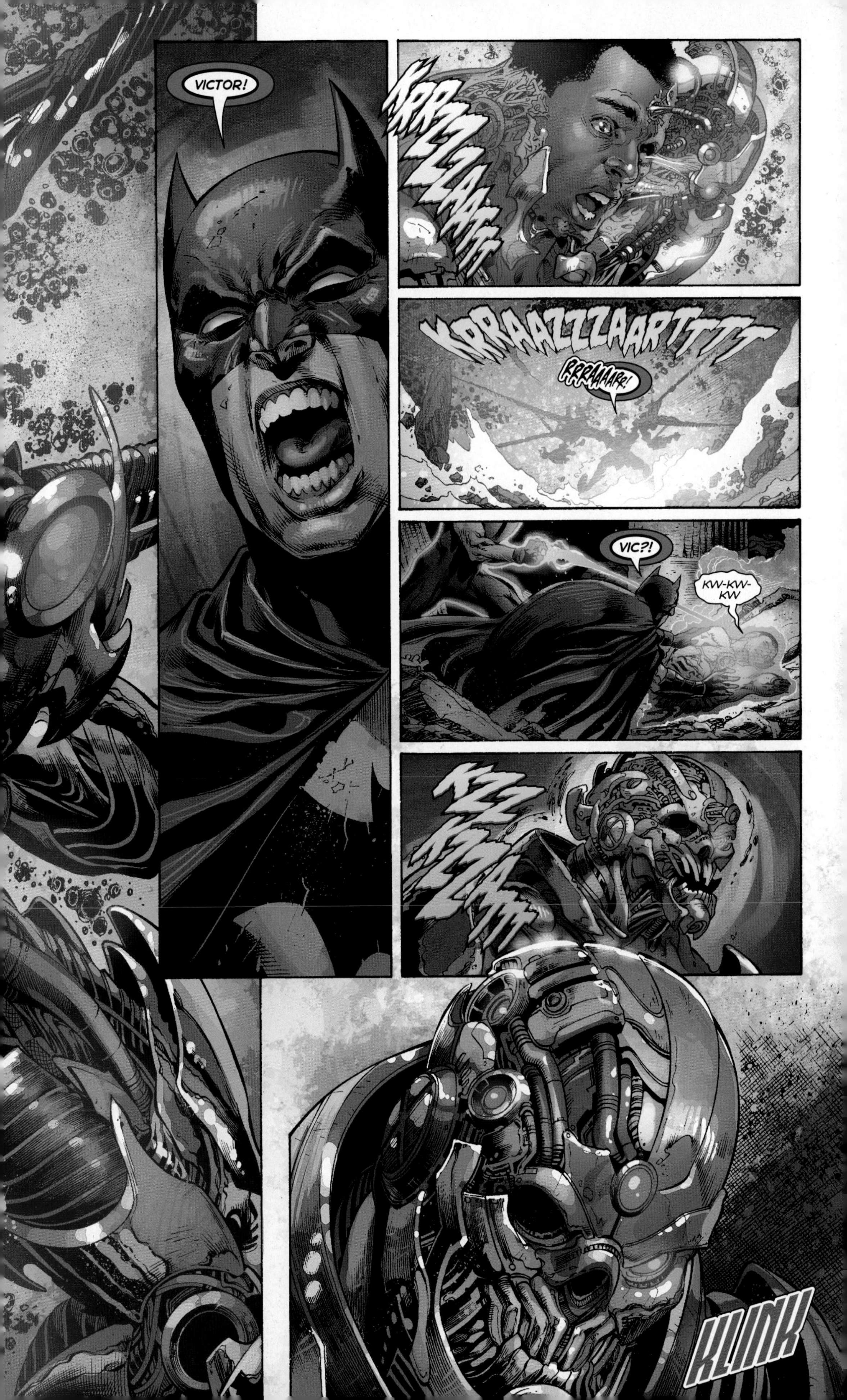
VICTOR!
KRRZZZAATTT
KRRAAZZZAARTTTT
RRRAAAAR!
VIC?!
KW-KW-KW
KZZ KZZAMM
KLINK

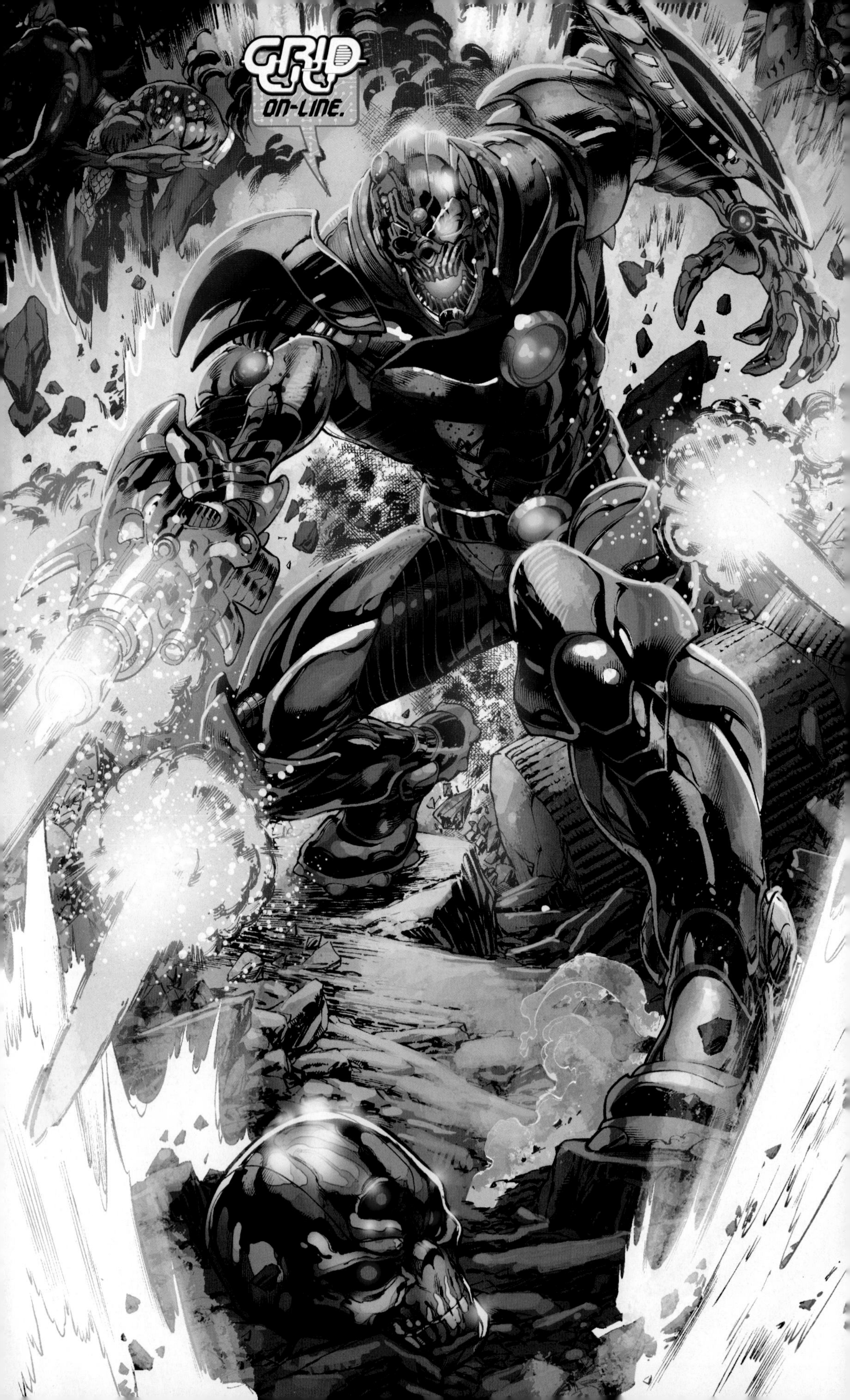
GRID
ON-LINE.

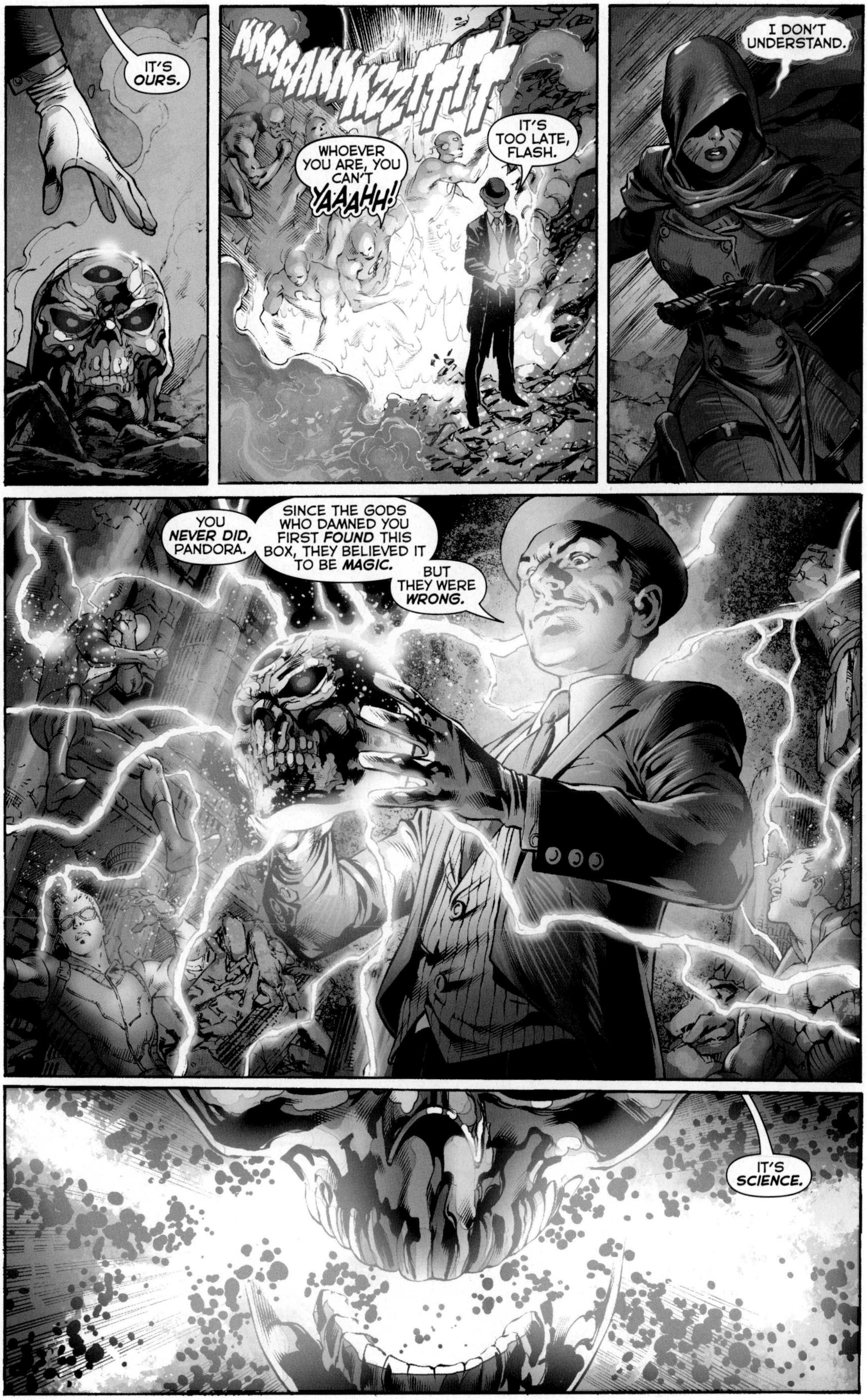
IT'S OURS.
KKKRAKKKZZTTTT
WHOEVER YOU ARE, YOU CAN'T YAAAHH!
IT'S TOO LATE, FLASH.
I DON'T UNDERSTAND.
YOU NEVER DID, PANDORA.
SINCE THE GODS WHO DAMNED YOU FIRST FOUND THIS BOX, THEY BELIEVED IT TO BE MAGIC.
BUT THEY WERE WRONG.
IT'S SCIENCE.

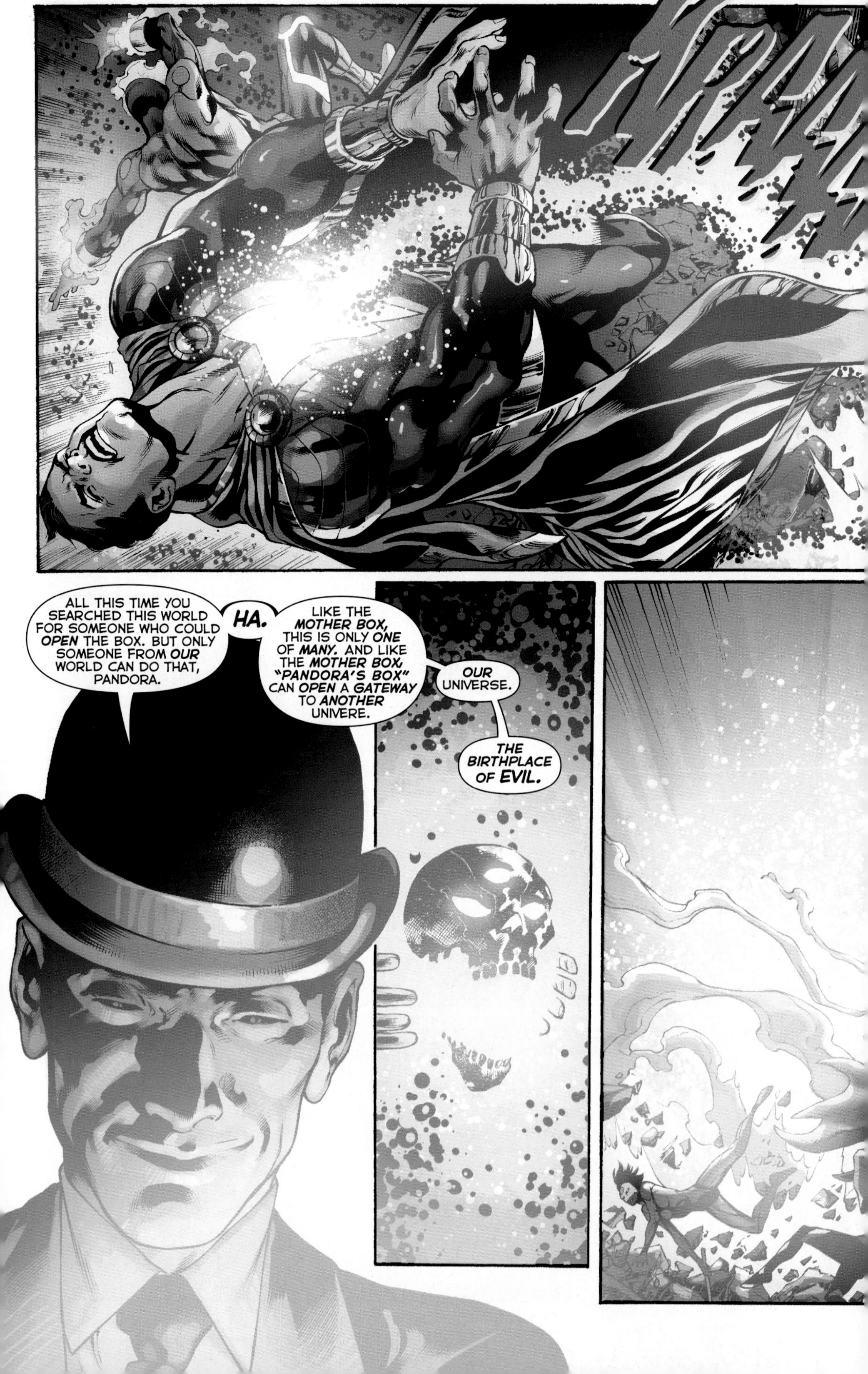
ALL THIS TIME YOU SEARCHED THIS WORLD FOR SOMEONE WHO COULD OPEN THE BOX. BUT ONLY SOMEONE FROM OUR WORLD CAN DO THAT, PANDORA.
HA.
LIKE THE MOTHER BOX, THIS IS ONLY ONE OF MANY. AND LIKE THE MOTHER BOX, "PANDORA'S BOX" CAN OPEN A GATEWAY TO ANOTHER UNIVERE.
OUR UNIVERSE.
THE BIRTHPLACE OF EVIL.

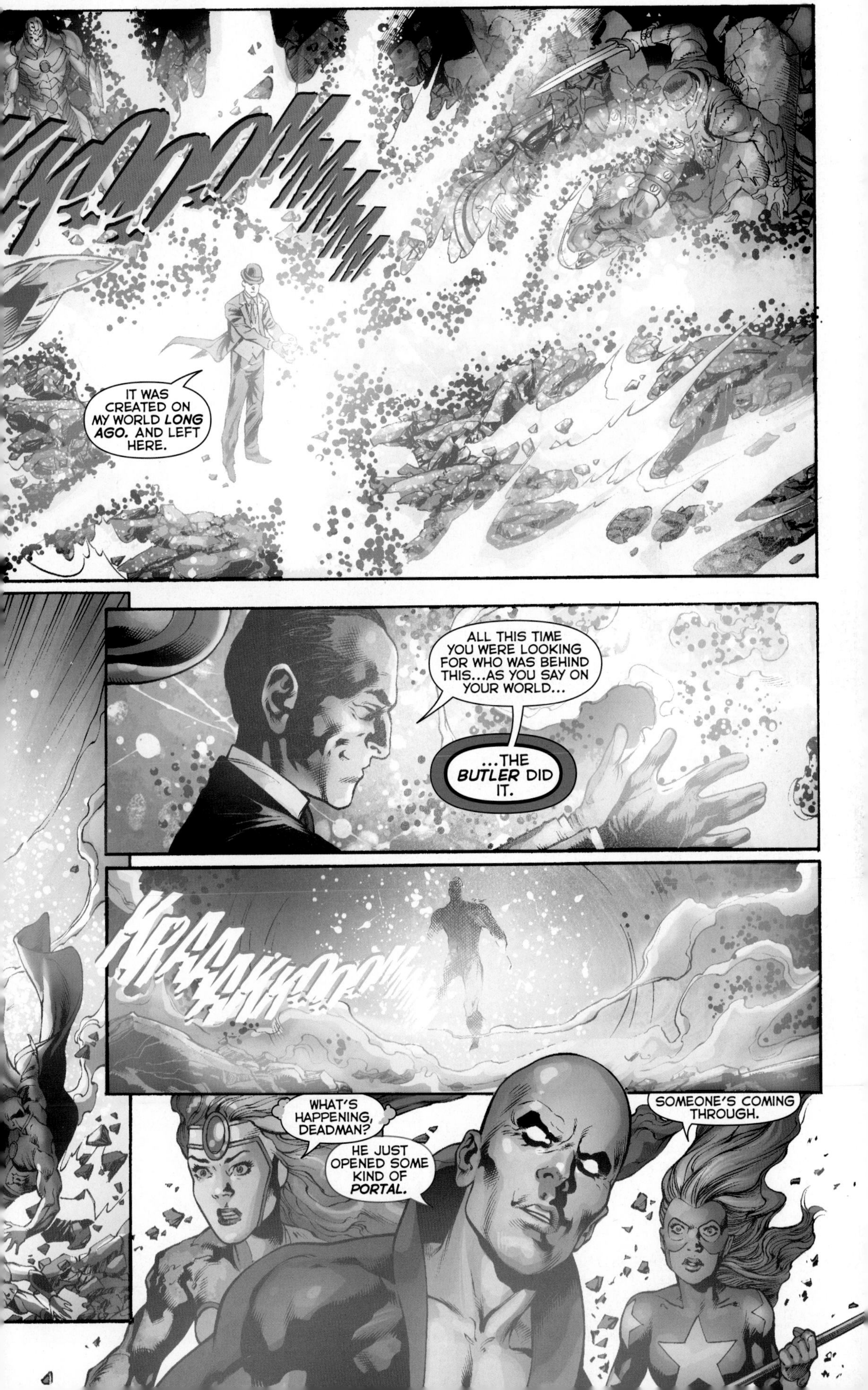
IT WAS CREATED ON MY WORLD LONG AGO. AND LEFT HERE.
ALL THIS TIME YOU WERE LOOKING FOR WHO WAS BEHIND THIS...AS YOU SAY ON YOUR WORLD...
...THE BUTLER DID IT.
WHAT'S HAPPENING, DEADMAN?
HE JUST OPENED SOME KIND OF PORTAL.
SOMEONE'S COMING THROUGH.

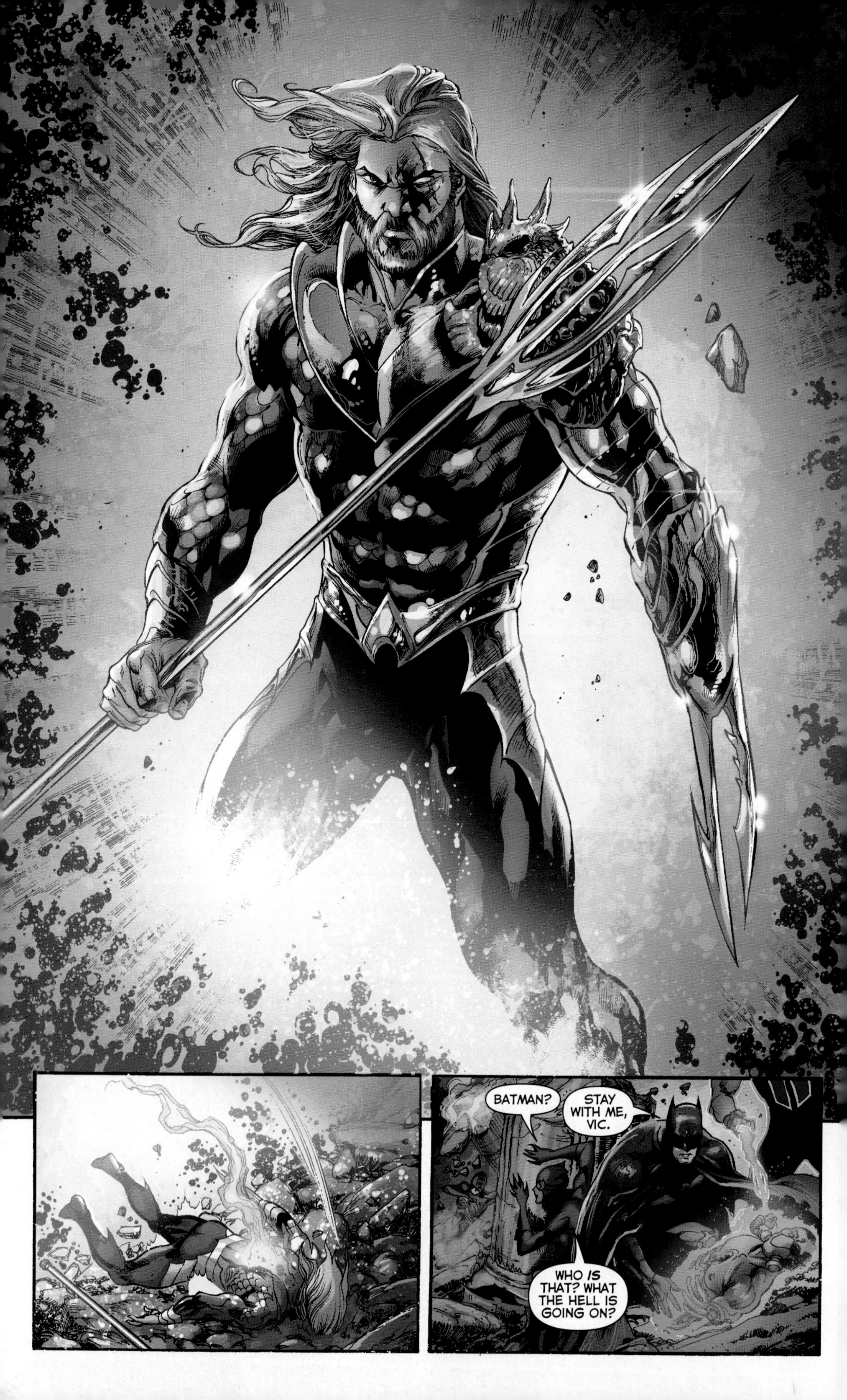
BATMAN?
STAY WITH ME, VIC.
WHO IS THAT? WHAT THE HELL IS GOING ON?

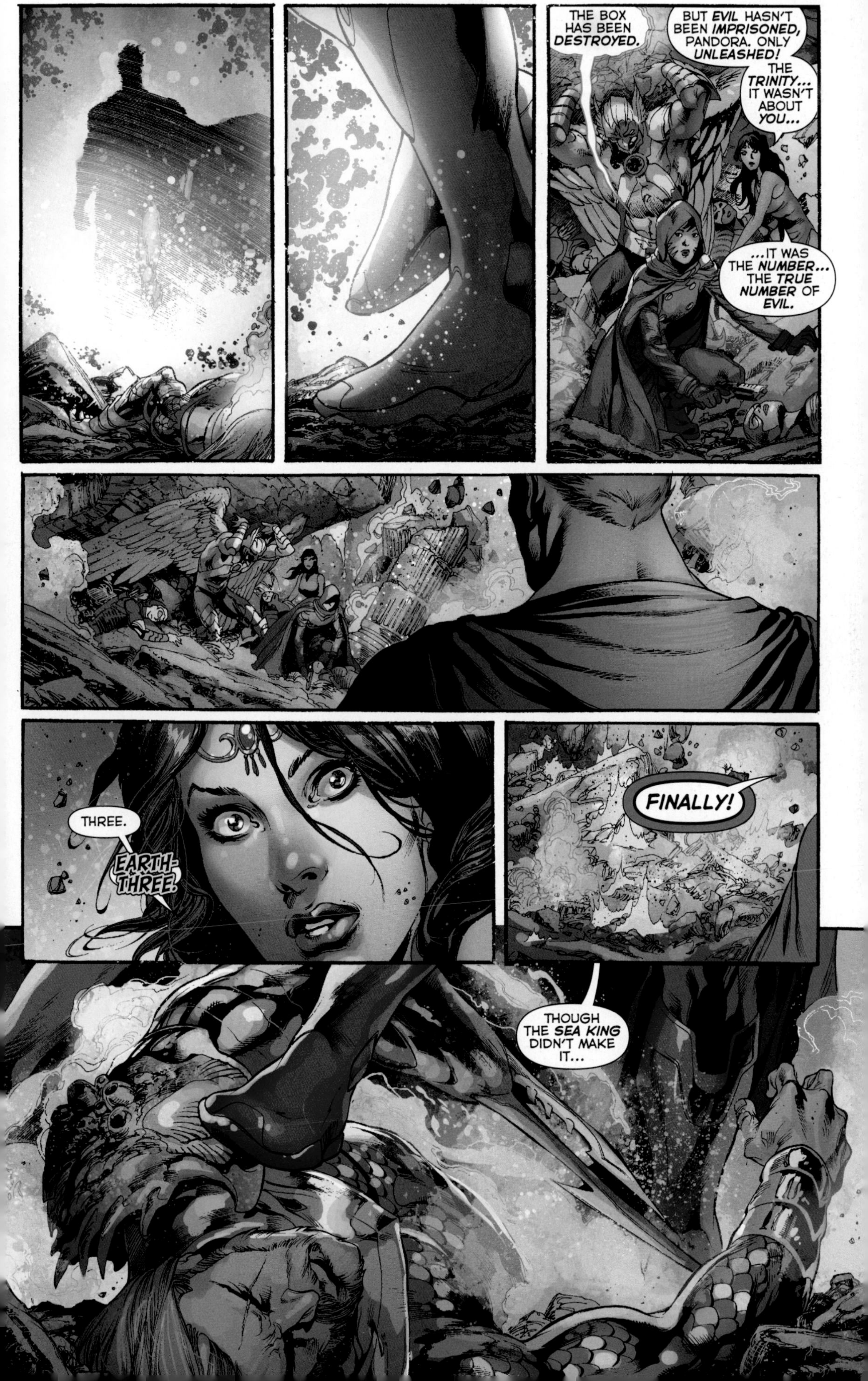
THE BOX HAS BEEN DESTROYED.
BUT EVIL HASN'T BEEN IMPRISONED, PANDORA. ONLY UNLEASHED!
THE TRINITY... IT WASN'T ABOUT YOU...
...IT WAS THE NUMBER... THE TRUE NUMBER OF EVIL.
THREE.
EARTH-THREE.
FINALLY!
THOUGH THE SEA KING DIDN'T MAKE IT...

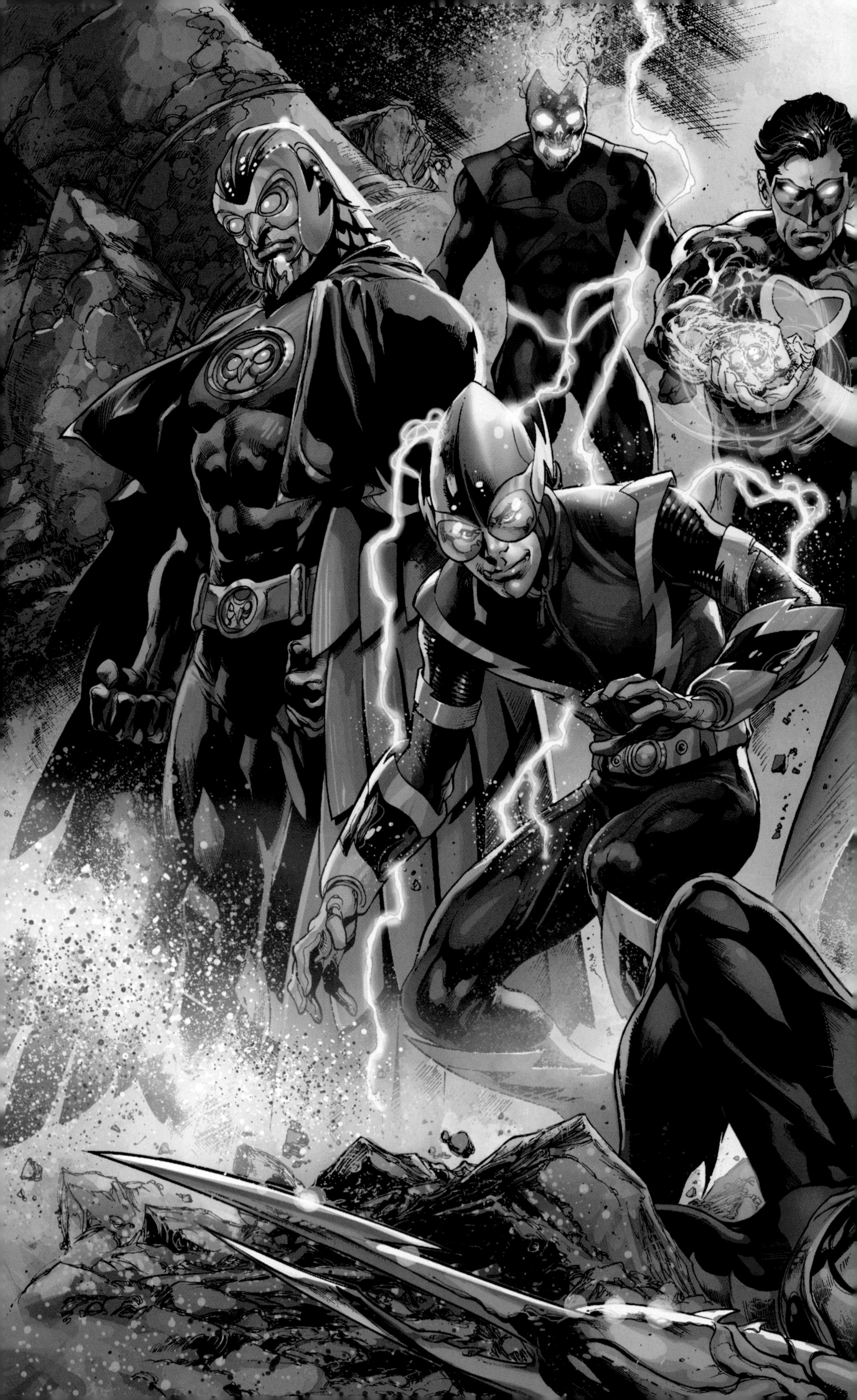

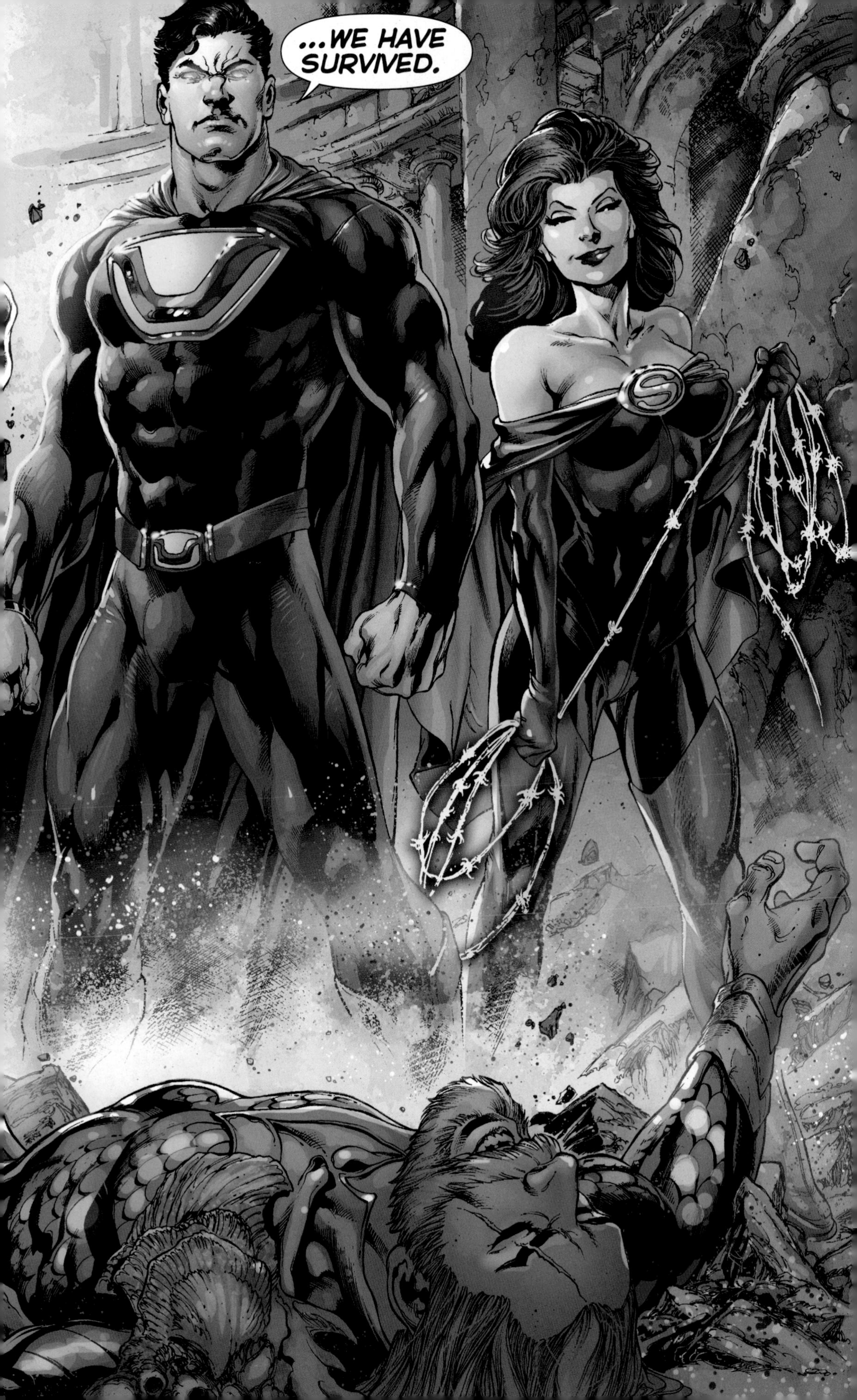
...WE HAVE SURVIVED.

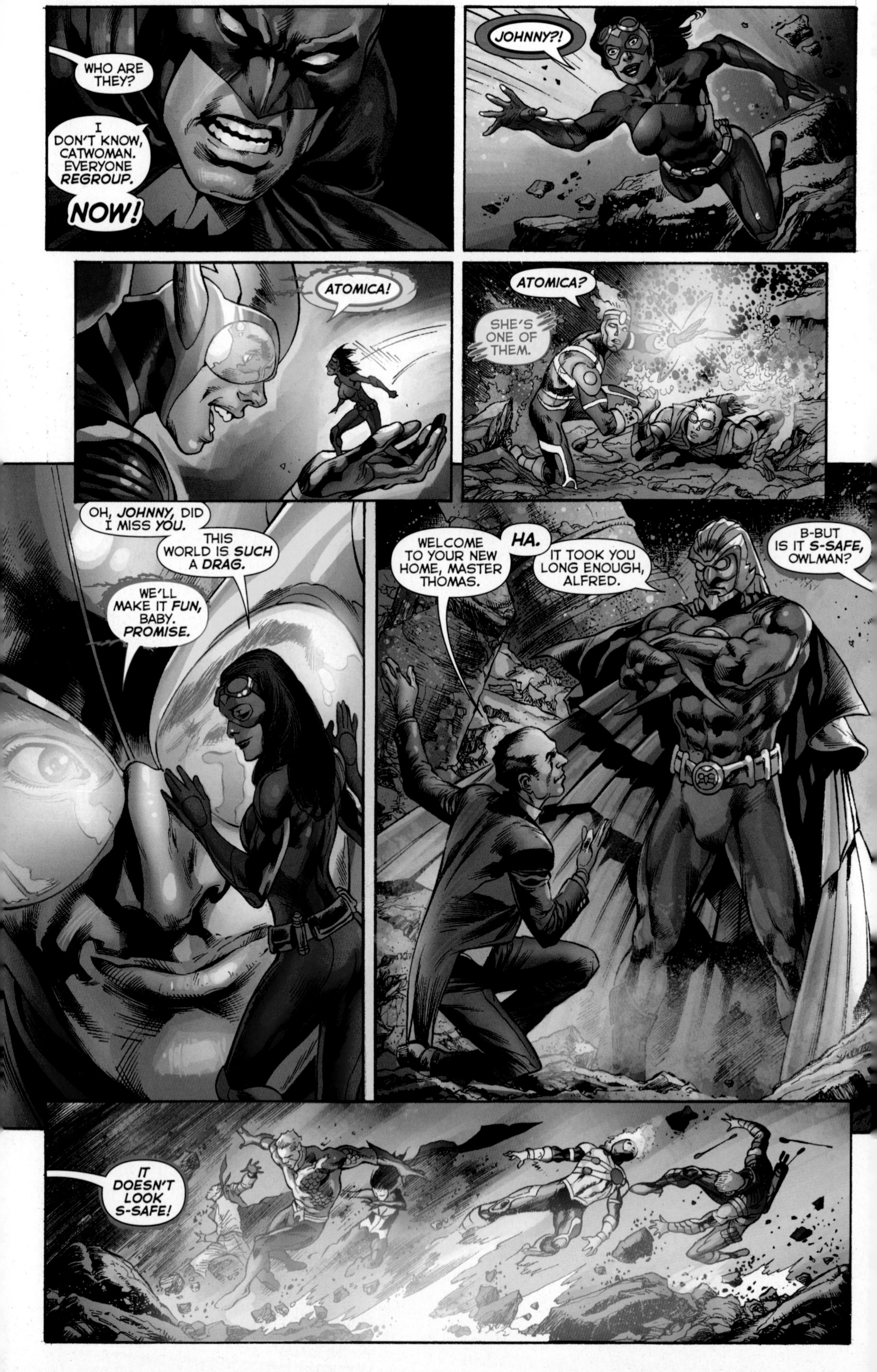
WHO ARE THEY?
I DON'T KNOW, CATWOMAN. EVERYONE REGROUP.
NOW!
JOHNNY?!
ATOMICA!
ATOMICA?
SHE'S ONE OF THEM.
OH, JOHNNY, DID I MISS YOU.
THIS WORLD IS SUCH A DRAG.
WE'LL MAKE IT FUN, BABY. PROMISE.
WELCOME TO YOUR NEW HOME, MASTER THOMAS.
HA.
IT TOOK YOU LONG ENOUGH, ALFRED.
B-BUT IS IT S-SAFE, OWLMAN?
IT DOESN'T LOOK S-SAFE!

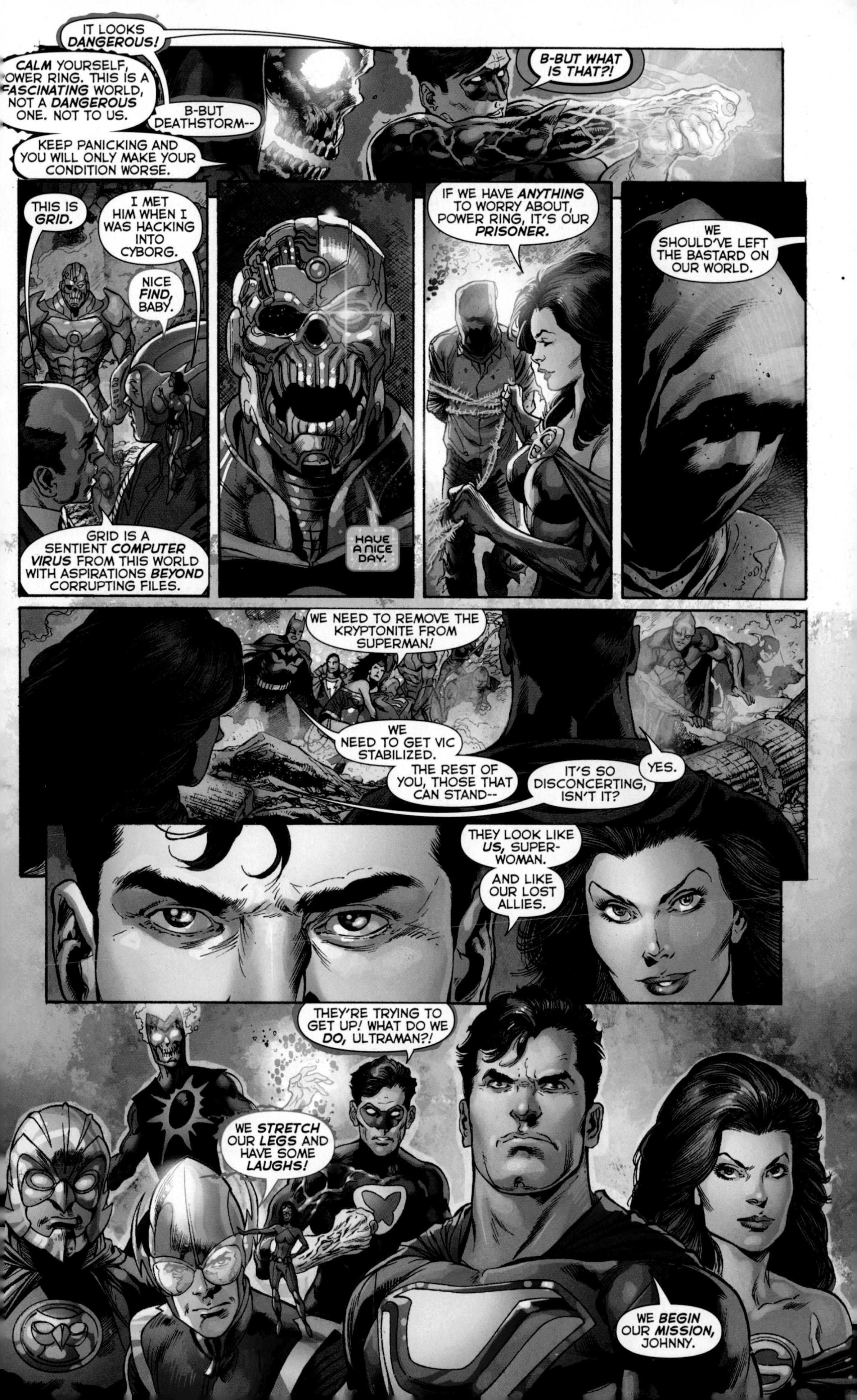
IT LOOKS DANGEROUS!
CALM YOURSELF, POWER RING. THIS IS A FASCINATING WORLD, NOT A DANGEROUS ONE. NOT TO US.
B-BUT DEATHSTORM--
KEEP PANICKING AND YOU WILL ONLY MAKE YOUR CONDITION WORSE.
B-BUT WHAT IS THAT?!
THIS IS GRID.
I MET HIM WHEN I WAS HACKING INTO CYBORG.
NICE FIND, BABY.
GRID IS A SENTIENT COMPUTER VIRUS FROM THIS WORLD WITH ASPIRATIONS BEYOND CORRUPTING FILES.
HAVE A NICE DAY.
IF WE HAVE ANYTHING TO WORRY ABOUT, POWER RING, IT'S OUR PRISONER.
WE SHOULD'VE LEFT THE BASTARD ON OUR WORLD.
WE NEED TO REMOVE THE KRYPTONITE FROM SUPERMAN!
WE NEED TO GET VIC STABILIZED.
THE REST OF YOU, THOSE THAT CAN STAND--
IT'S SO DISCONCERTING, ISN'T IT?
YES.
THEY LOOK LIKE US, SUPER-WOMAN.
AND LIKE OUR LOST ALLIES.
THEY'RE TRYING TO GET UP! WHAT DO WE DO, ULTRAMAN?!
WE STRETCH OUR LEGS AND HAVE SOME LAUGHS!
WE BEGIN OUR MISSION, JOHNNY.

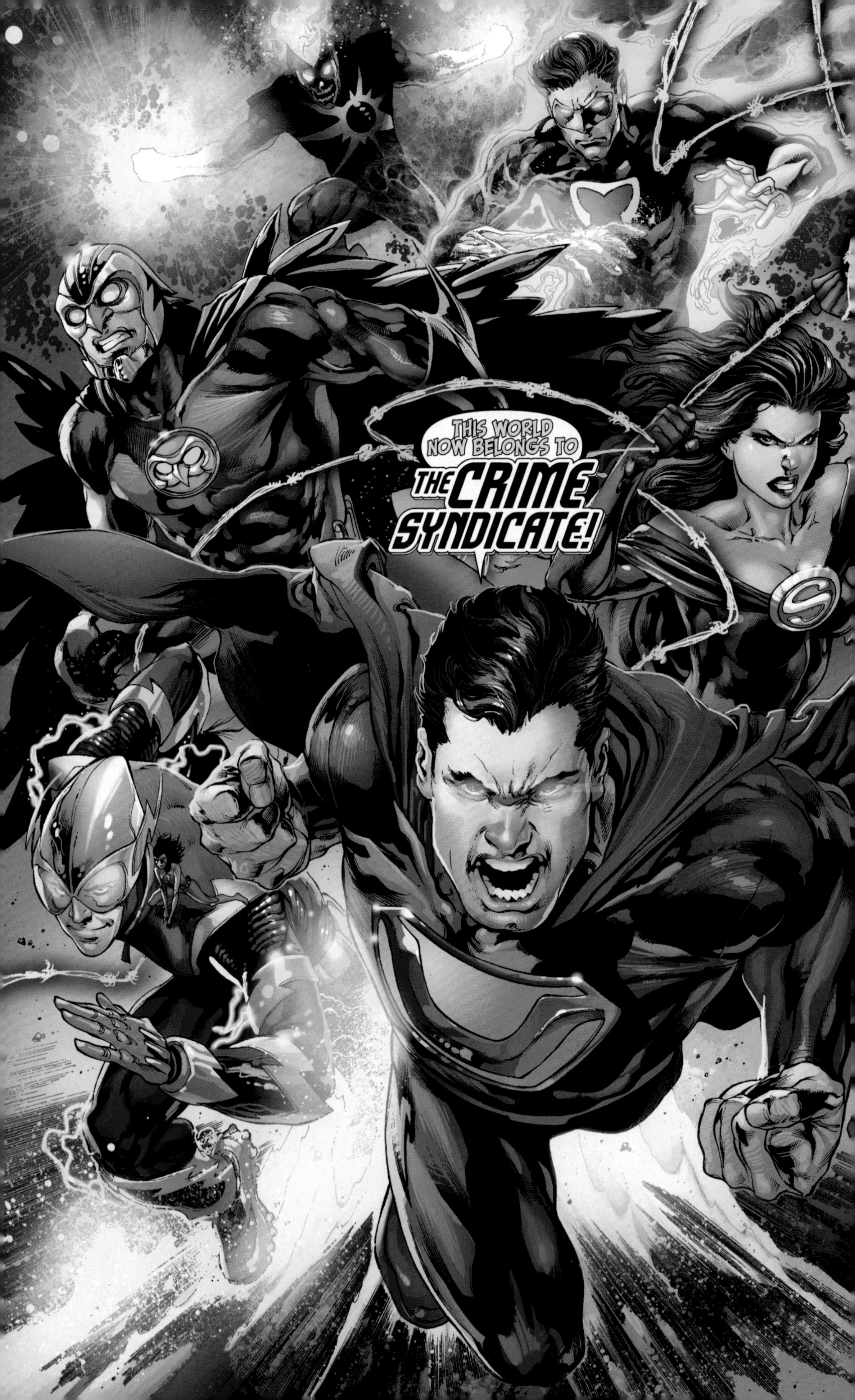
THIS WORLD NOW BELONGS TO THE CRIME SYNDICATE!

VARIANT COVER GALLERY

JUSTICE LEAGUE 18
Variant cover by Kenneth Rocafort & Blond

JUSTICE LEAGUE 19
Variant cover by Sergio Aragonés & Tom Luth

JUSTICE LEAGUE 19
Fold-out cover by Ivan Reis, Joe Prado & Rod Reis

JUSTICE LEAGUE 20
Variant cover by Tyler Kirkham, Sandra Hope Archer & Alex Sinclair

JUSTICE LEAGUE 23
Variant cover triptych by Mikel Janin, Vicente Cifuentes & Tomeu Morey

JUSTICE LEAGUE 22
Cover triptych by Ivan Reis, Joe Prado & Rod Reis

JUSTICE LEAGUE 22
Variant cover triptych by Brett Booth, Norm Rapmund & Andrew Dalhouse

JUSTICE LEAGUE 23
Cover triptych by Doug Mahnke & Alex Sinclair

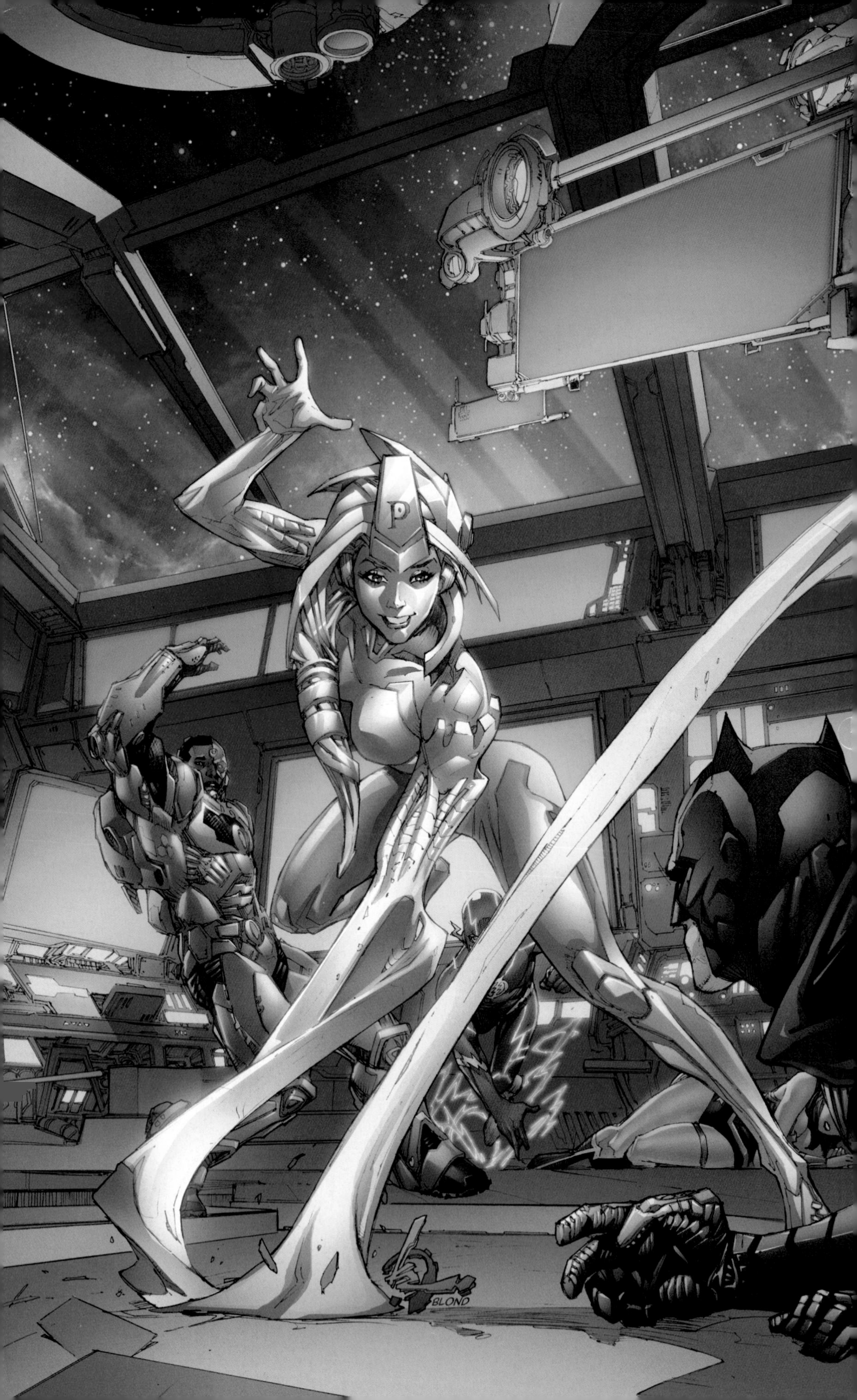
BLOND

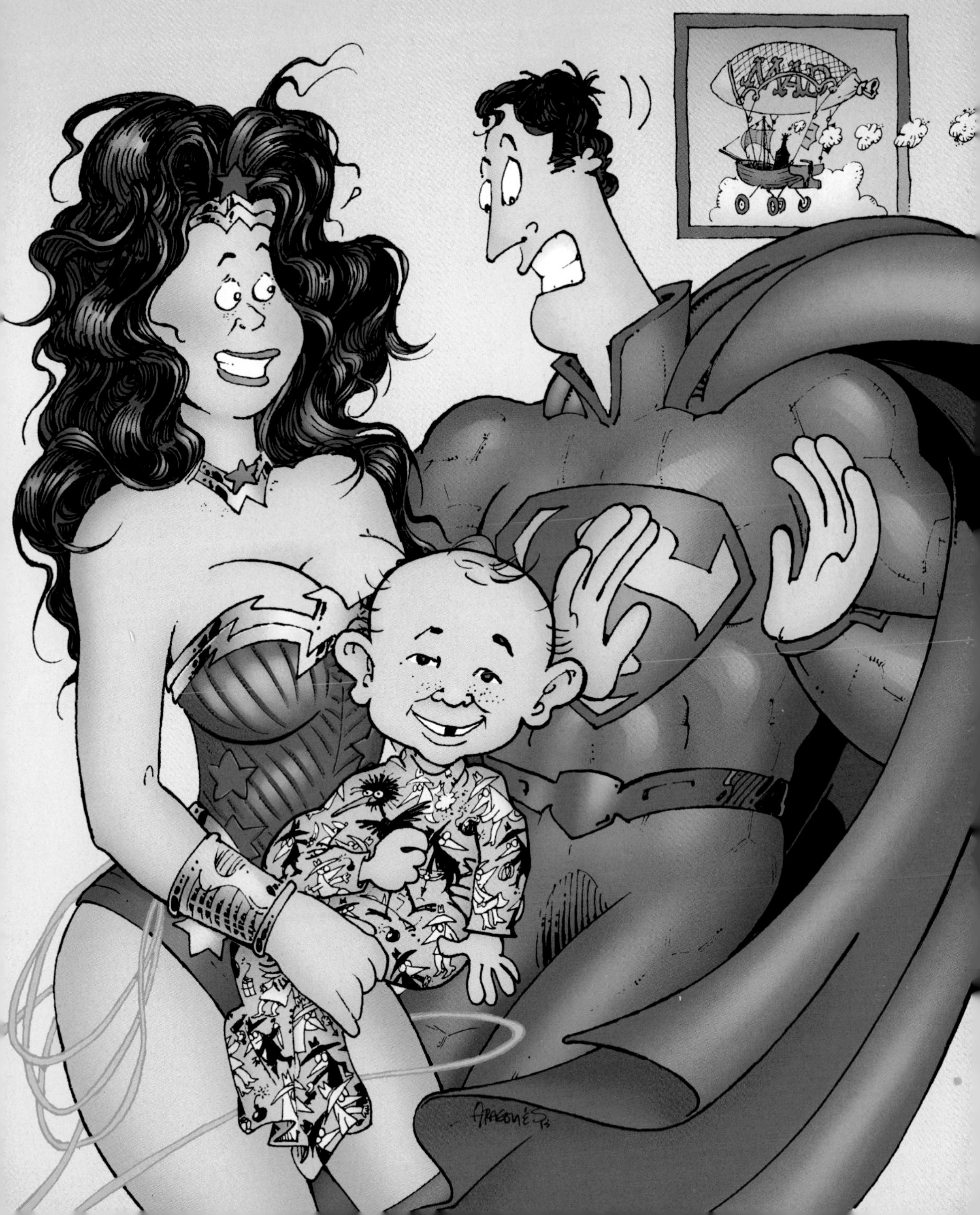

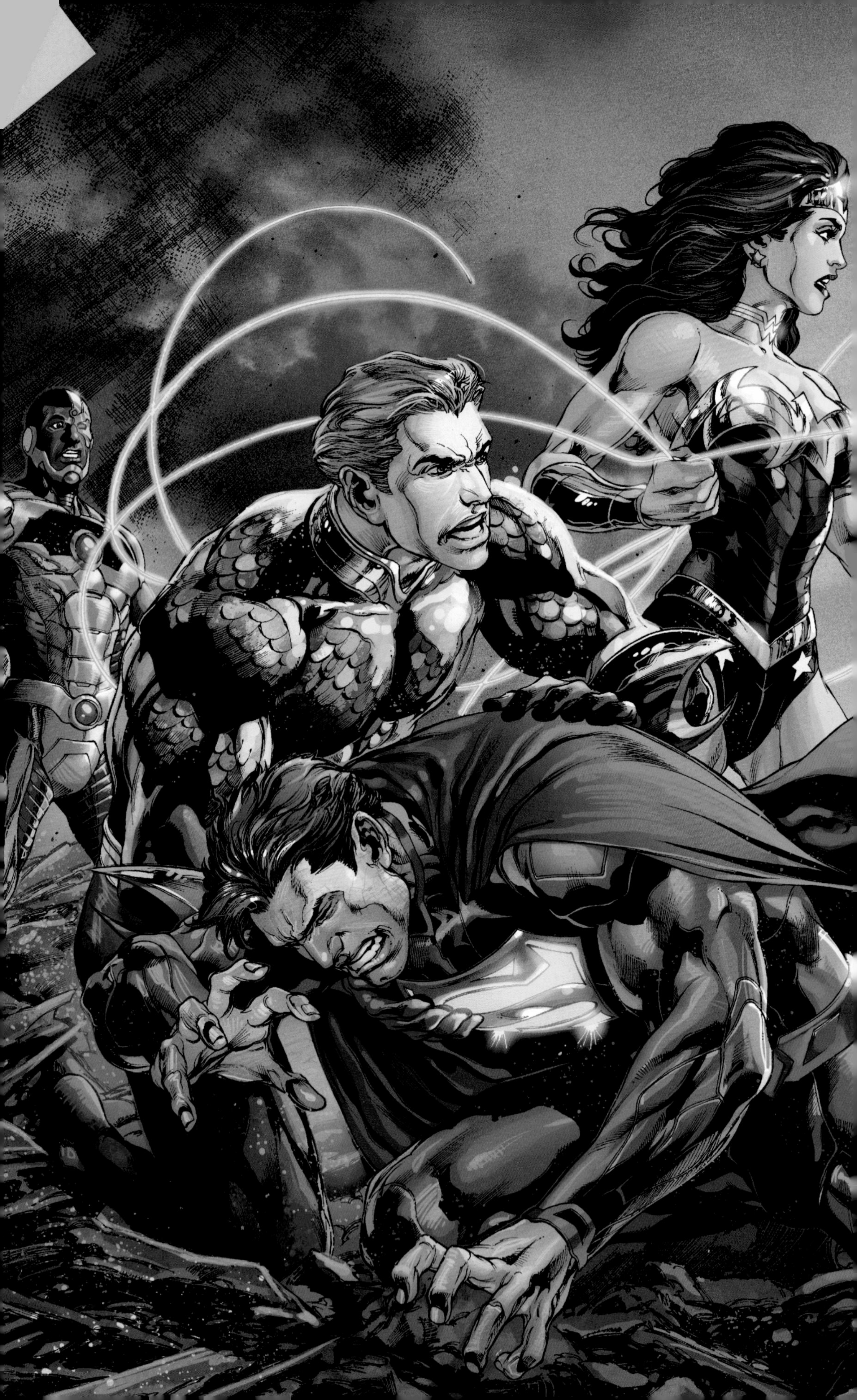

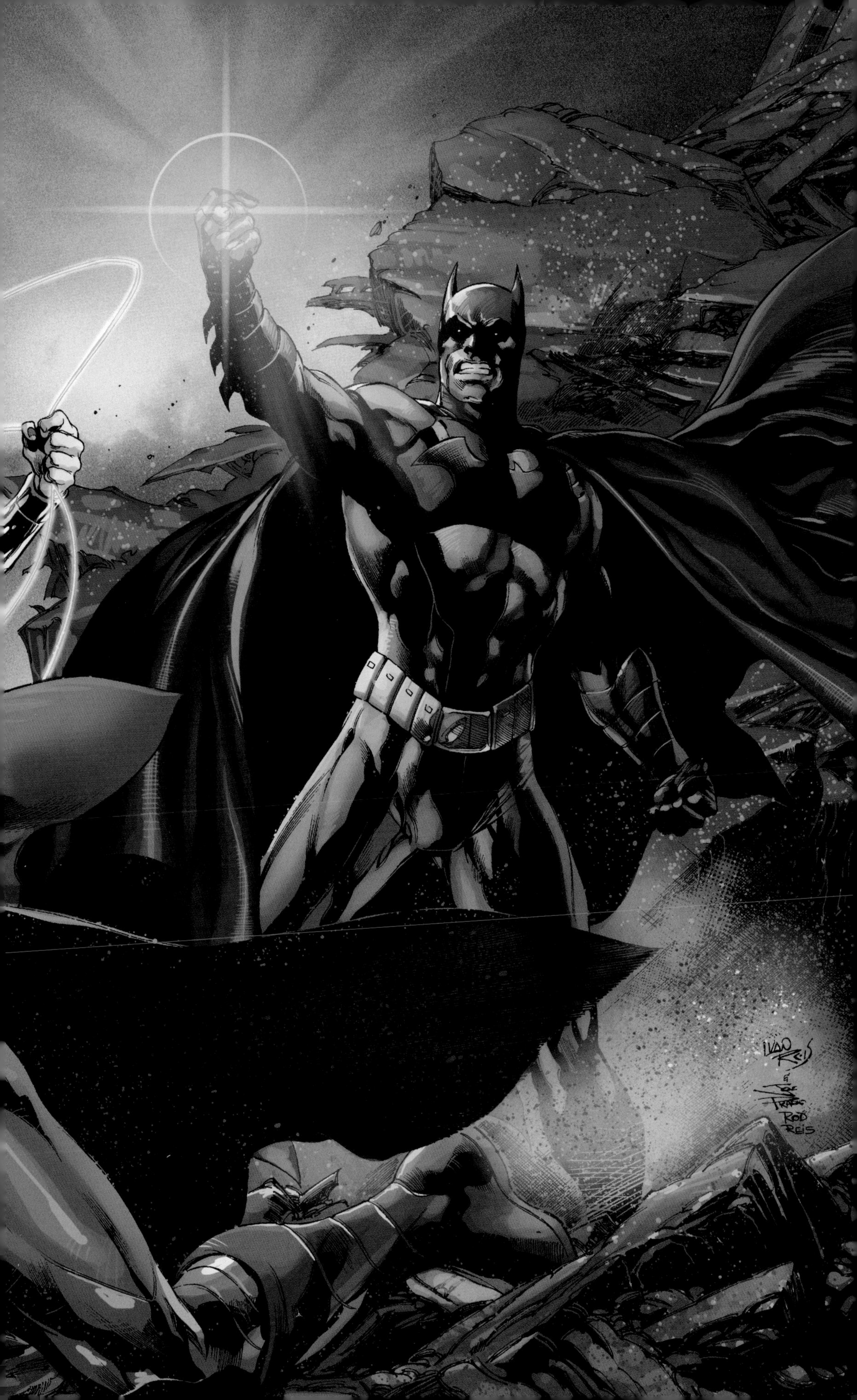

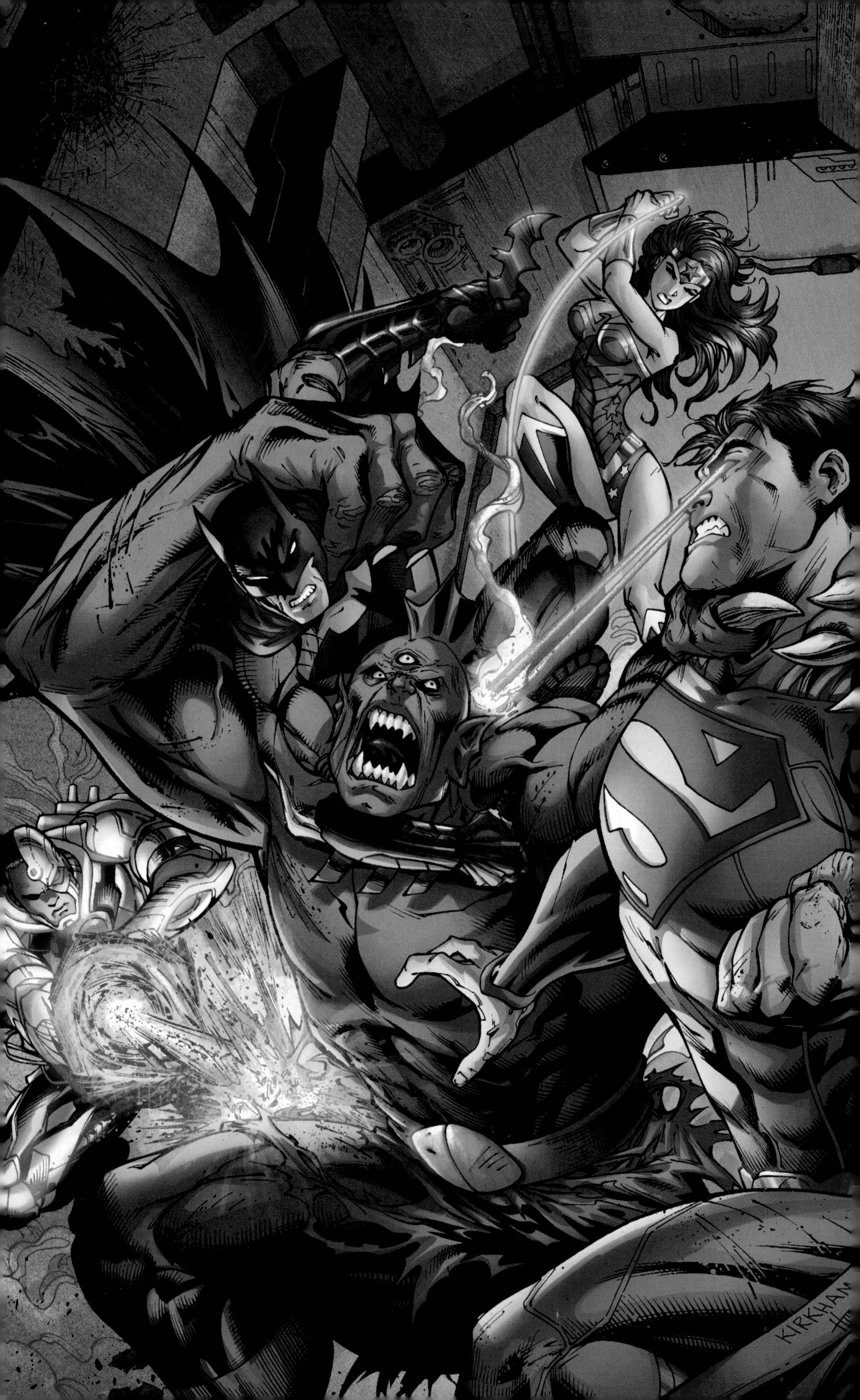
KIRKHAM

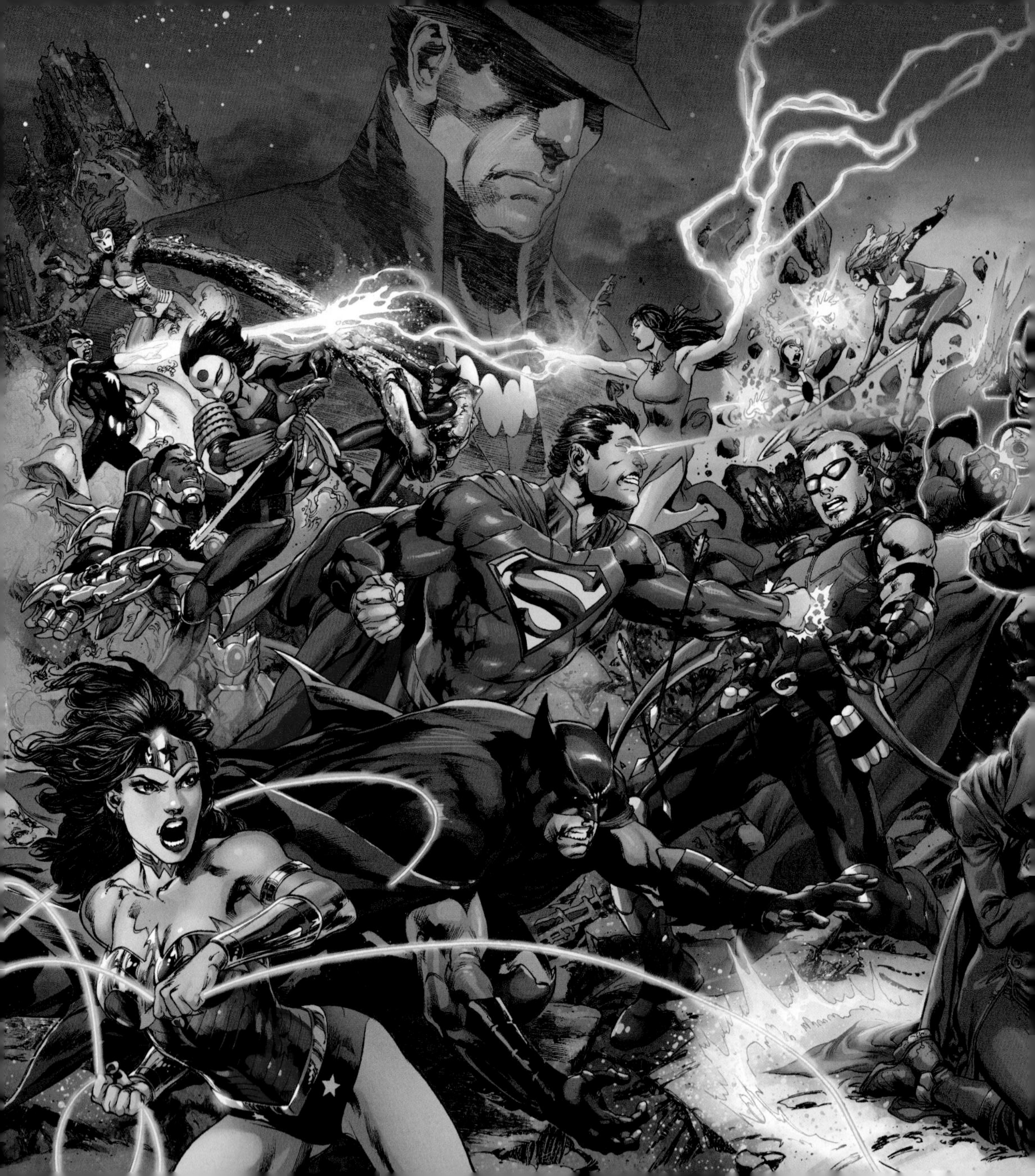

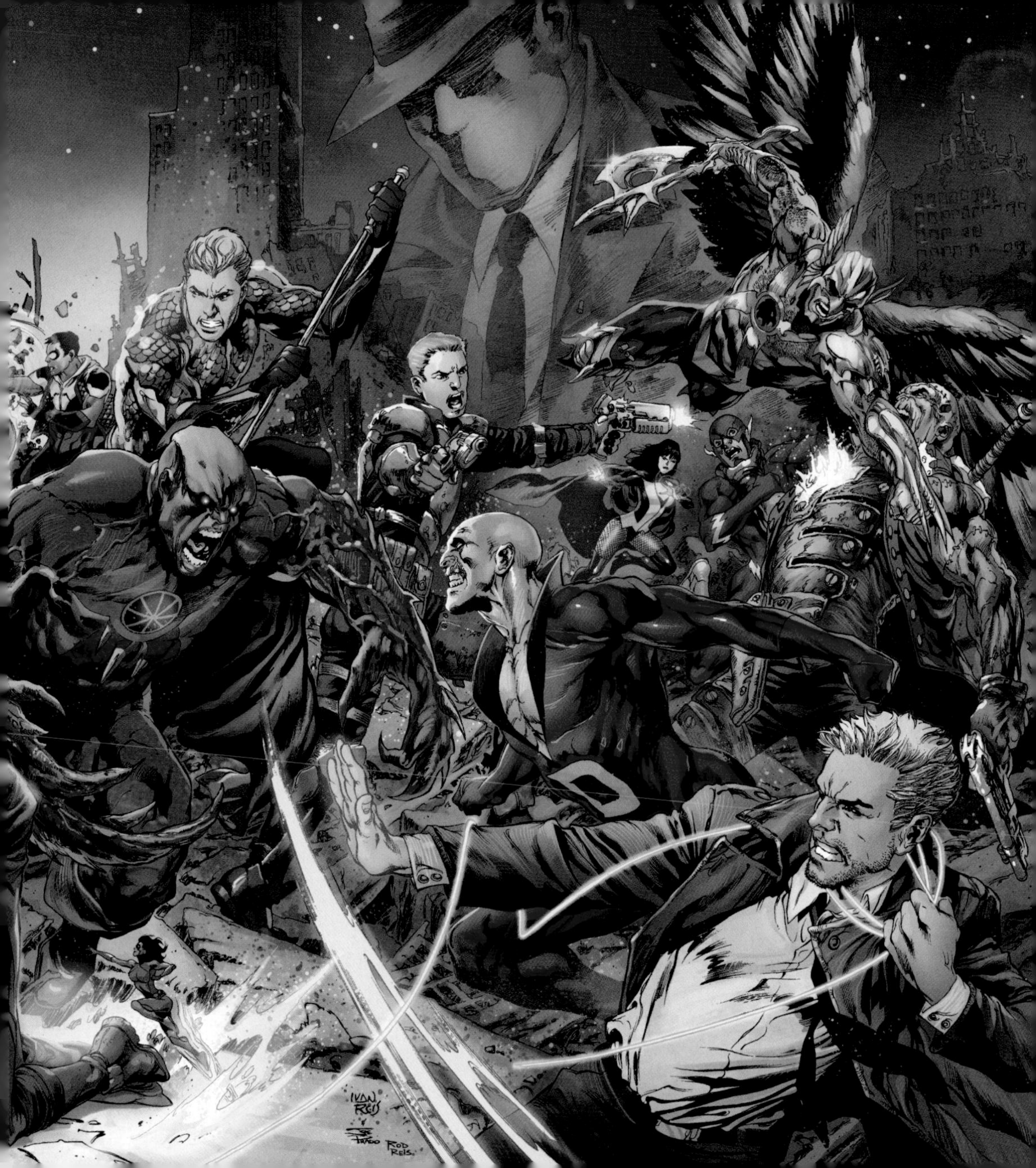
IVAN REIS
ROD REIS

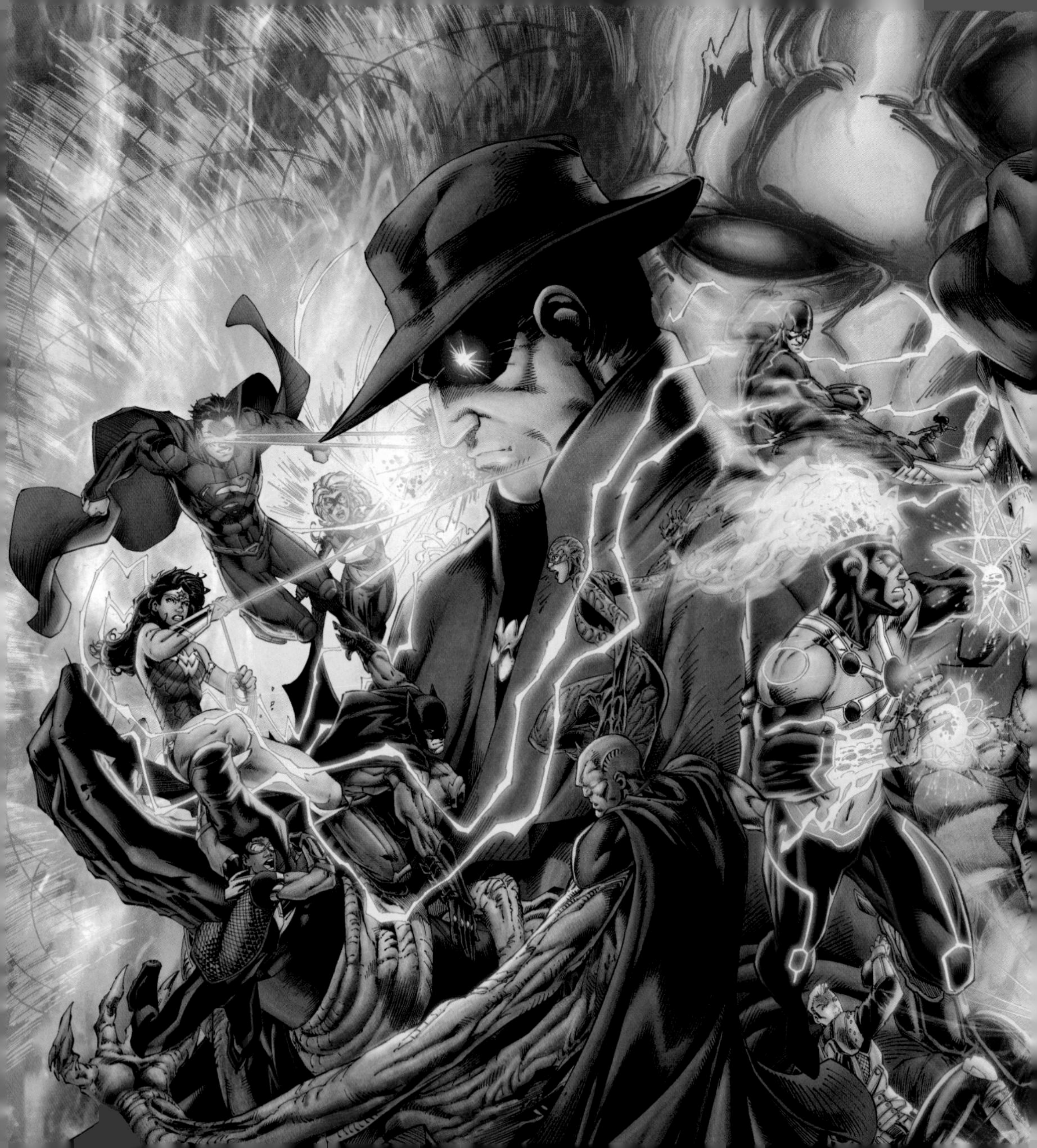

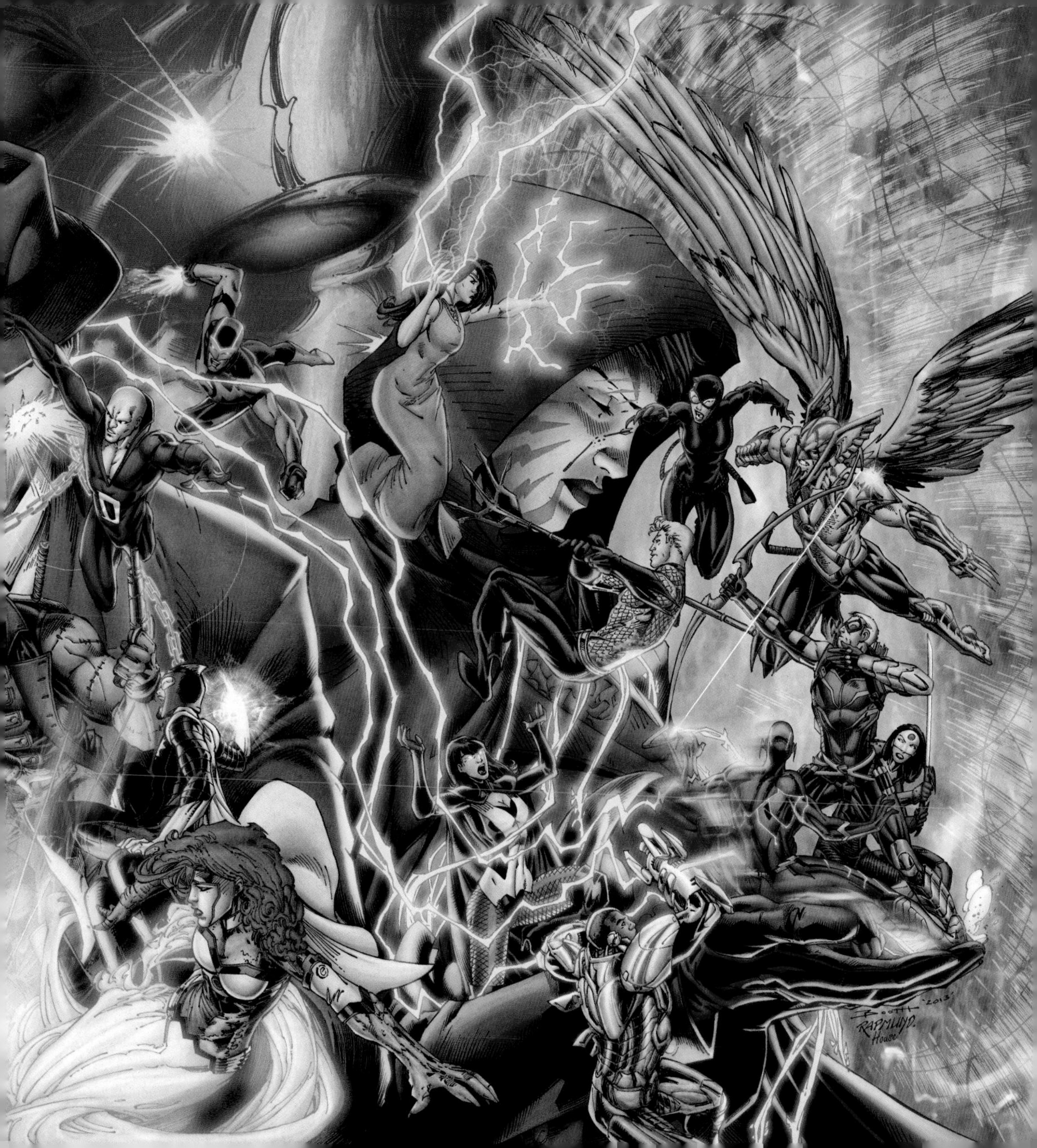
Booth '2013'
RAPMUND.
House

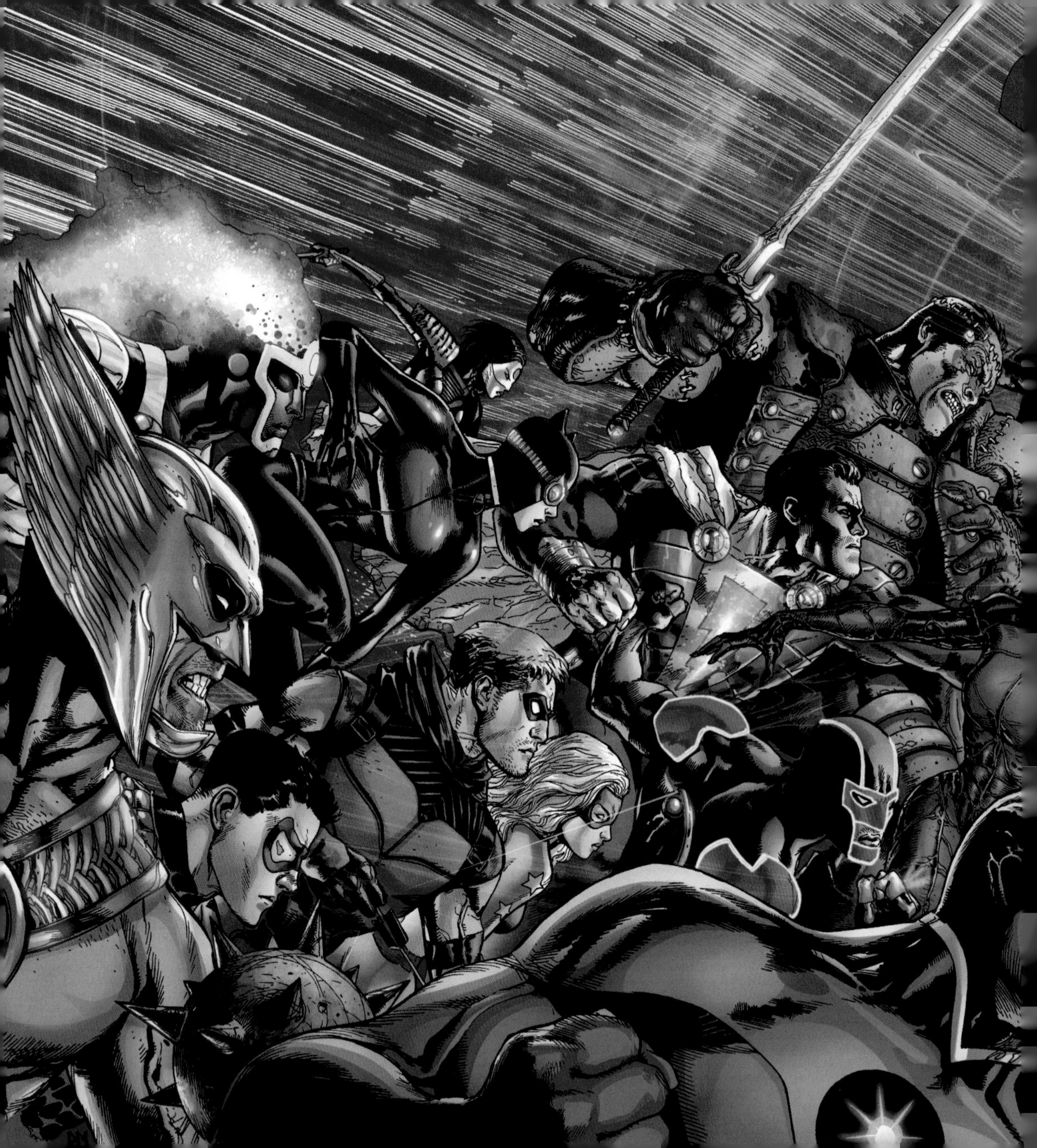

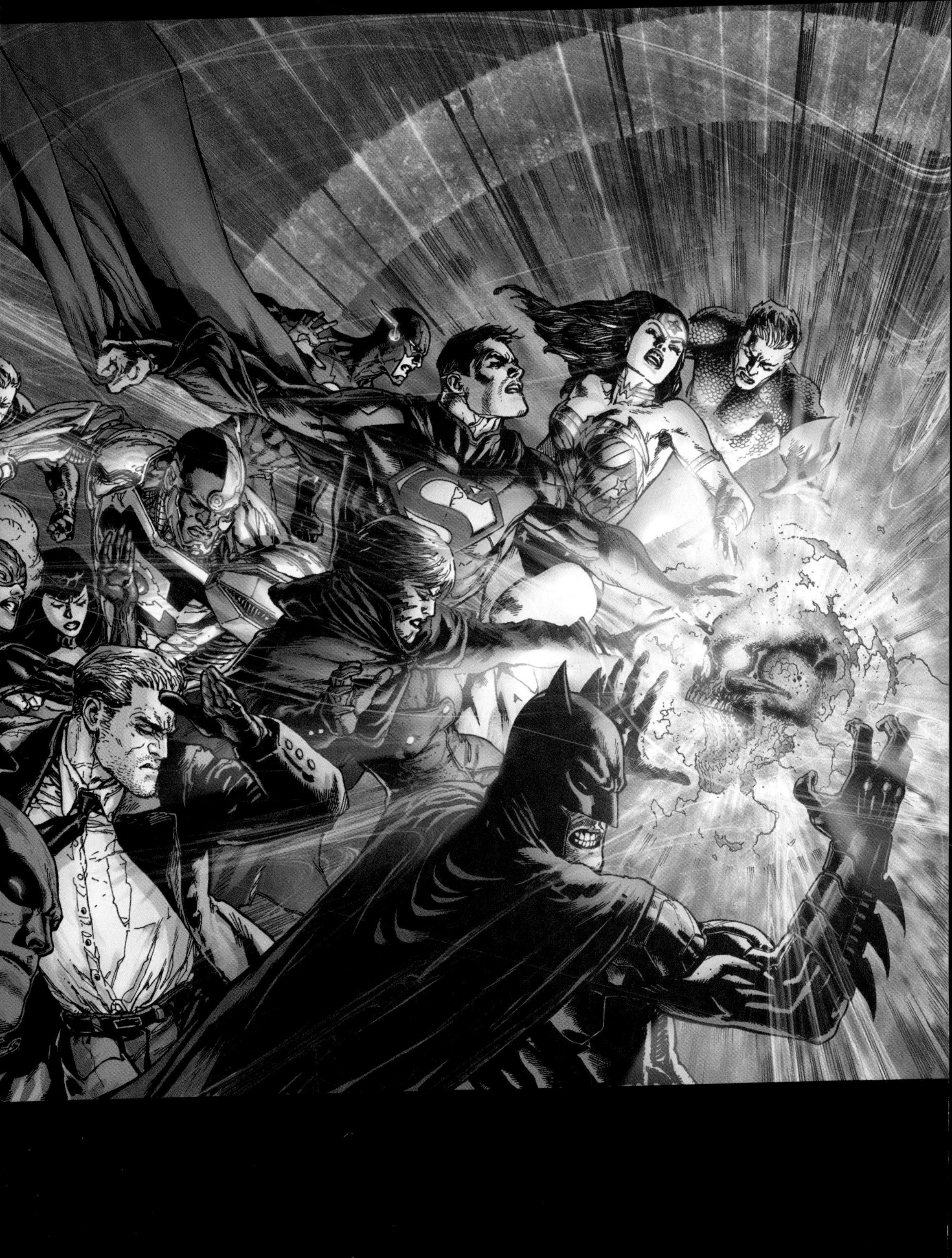

JUSTICE LEAGUE #22
TRINITY WAR CHAPTER ONE

PAGE ONE.
PANEL ONE.

A WIDESCREEN PANEL ACROSS THE TOP OF THE PAGE

An establishing shot of "Chrystie Street" in Greenwich Village at night. It's raining hard. Few people are on the street – an old man with an umbrella walking his dog in the rain and now a YELLOW TAXI that's pulled up, from right to left, with its lights on – a nondescript white female with red hair, we'll call her BETH, in her 20s, is getting out of the cab, holding an open newspaper over her head as an umbrella. She ducks down and calls out to the driver.

1. CAPTION (XANADU): I haven't always done the right thing. In fact, I spent most of my life doing everything but.

2. BETH (DOUBLE BALLOON): You sure this is the place?

3. TAXI (DOUBLE BALLOON): You wanted Chrystie Street, didn't you?

4. BETH (DOUBLE BALLOON): Yes, but --

5. TAXI (DOUBLE BALLOON): This is the only Chrystie Street in Greenwich Village, hon.

6. CAPTION (XANADU): I believed myself wicked at heart and used my power in iniquitous ways.

PANEL TWO.
A longshot of Beth standing there alone in the rain as the cab drives off. Beth looks over at it, the red lights the only real lights on the street. Beth is still holding the newspaper over her head.

7. CAPTION (XANADU): I was lost.

8. BETH (DOUBLE BALLOON): WAIT!

9. BETH (DOUBLE BALLOON): It's not here!

10. CAPTION (XANADU): Then I met a magician named John Zatara. John taught me that it was never too late to choose a life of rectitude.

PANEL THREE.
CLOSE ON Beth, turning and looking up – seeing something she hadn't seen a second ago – as if it wasn't there. A soft light shines on her – as if it just turned on – the glow of NEON SIGNS.

PANEL FOUR.
The newspaper down at her side now, as if she were stunned, Beth stands very small in the foreground, her back to us – she's looking over to a storefront – in the window a neon sign reads: PSYCHIC READER – and another neon sign reads TAROT READINGS (under that) PAST, PRESENT and FUTURE. Another sign reads LIFE ADVISOR (Ivan, check out the reference we'll provide on MADAME XANADU'S PARLOR and update the storefront however you see fit – it should look mysterious and OPEN – beckoning this young woman to come inside.)

11. CAPTION (XANADU): He also taught me how to hide in plain sight.

12. BETH: Oh.

PANEL FIVE.
SMALL PANEL. VERY CLOSE ON Beth's hand opening the door to go inside – a bell on it rings.

13. CAPTION (XANADU): I sit in this shop waiting for those in distress to find their way to me.

PANEL SIX.
SMALL PANEL. VERY CLOSE ON the PAST, PRESENT and FUTURE neon sign.

14. CAPTION (XANADU): I see the tragedy in their futures.

PANEL SEVEN.
SMALL PANEL. The "FUTURE" word goes dark.

15. CAPTION (XANADU): And just as John did with me, I help them onto a different path.

SFX: kzzt

PANEL EIGHT.
CUT TO the interior of the shop. Beth walks in cautiously... there's all sorts of stereotypical psychic items there – Madame Xanadu hides in plain sight as an everyday "cheap" psychic, just like Zatanna hides as a stage magician.

16. CAPTION (XANADU): I sense this woman's desperation, though for some reason little else.

17. CAPTION (XANADU): But if I'm able I will help her.

18. BETH: H-hello?

19. BETH: Are you OPEN?

20. MADAME XANADU (O/P): I'm ALWAYS open.

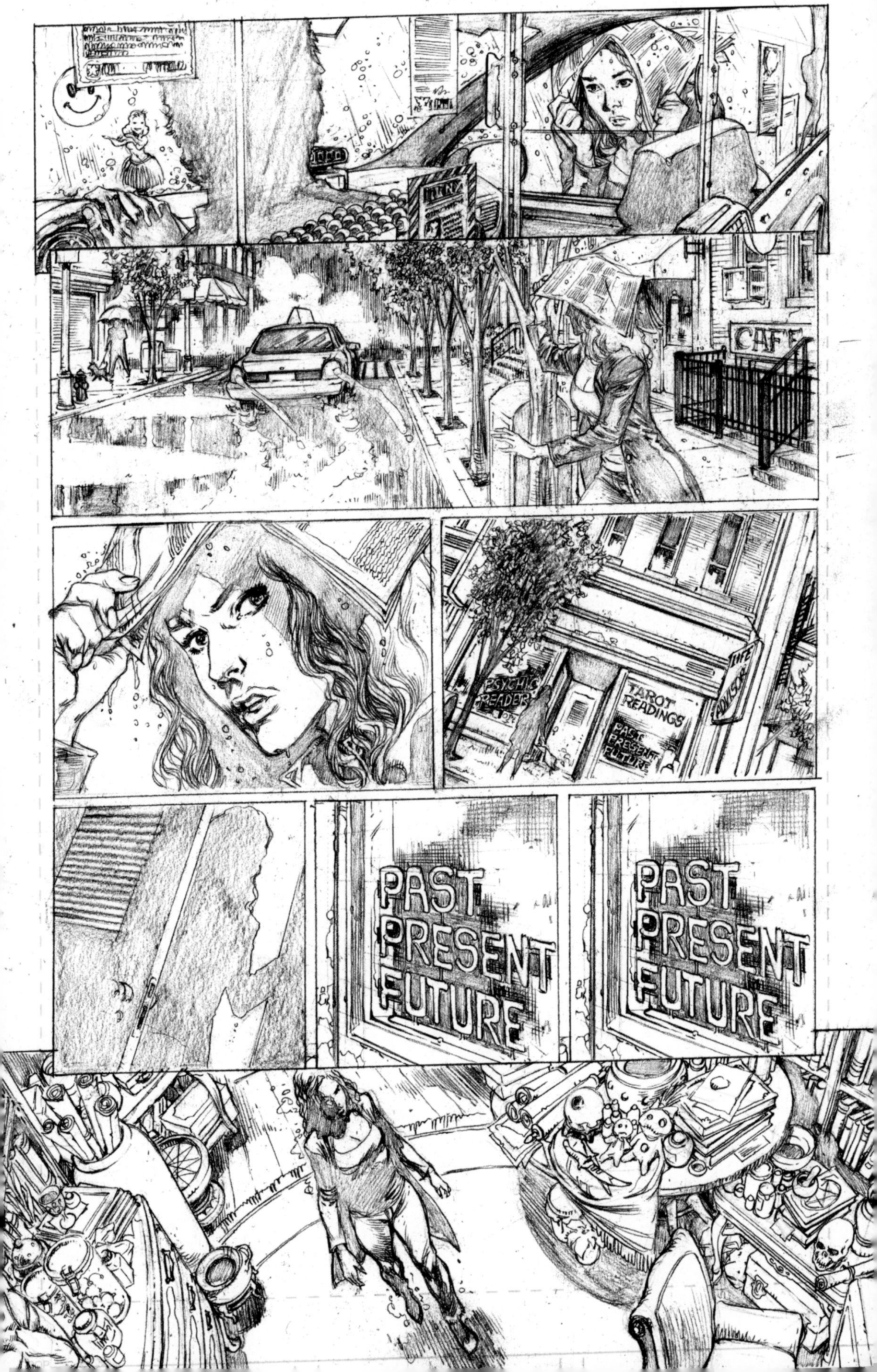
CAFE
PSYCHIC READER
TAROT READINGS
PAST PRESENT FUTURE
LIFE ADVISOR
PAST PRESENT FUTURE
PAST PRESENT FUTURE

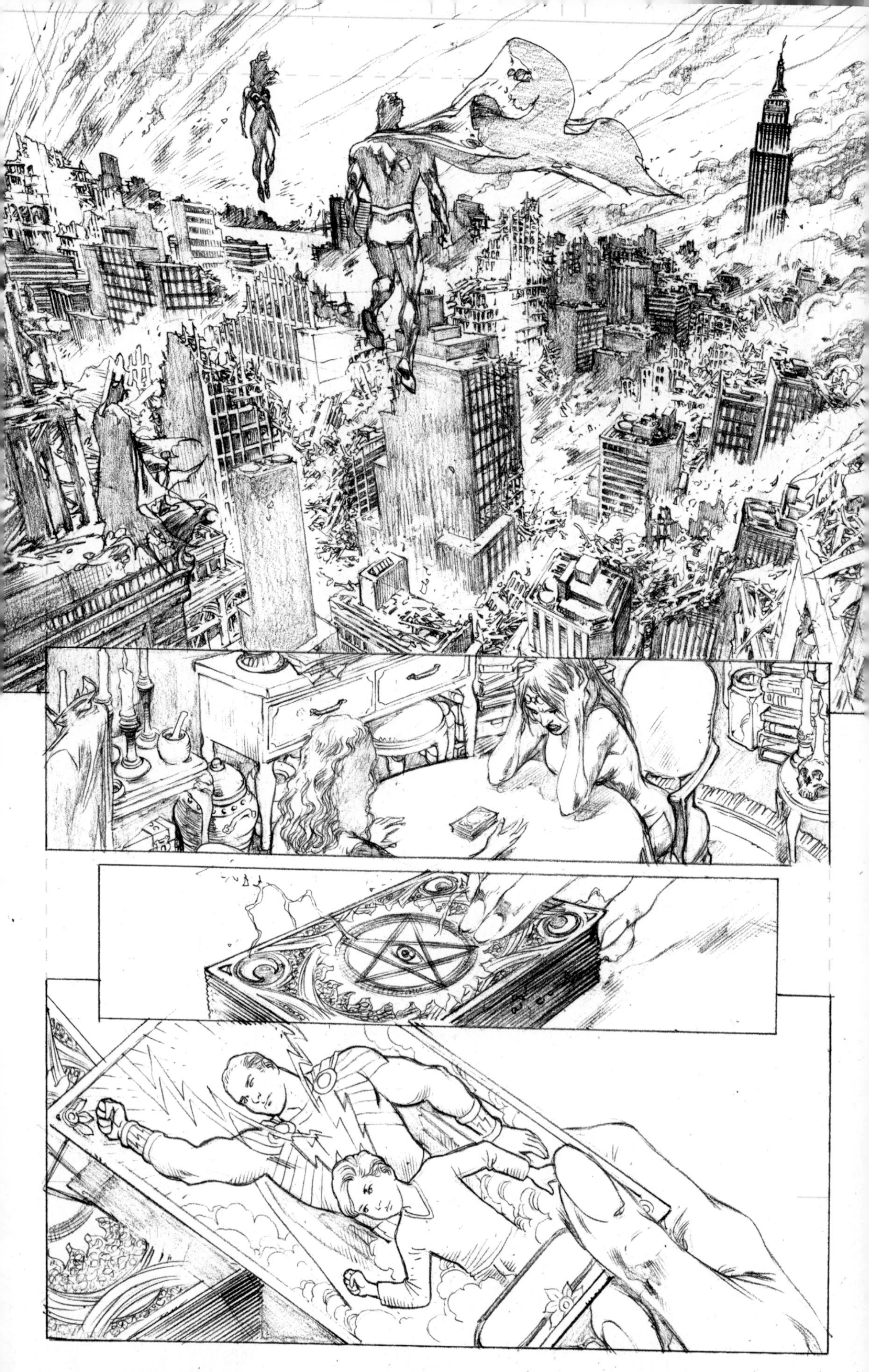

PAGE THREE.
PANEL ONE.

A WIDESCREEN PANEL ACROSS THE TOP OF THE PAGE

A VISION OF MANHATTAN BURNING AND CRUMBLED – the harbor filled with the DEAD. The sky is ON FIRE – AS RED AS THE WATER. There is no sign of the Statue of Liberty. Ivan, this should appear to be a vision of our world after a horrific attack...

In the FOREGROUND are silhouettes of SUPERMAN, WONDER WOMAN and BATMAN looking at the wreckage.

1. CAPTION (XANADU): But it's not HERS.

2. SUPERMAN-LIKE FIGURE: There's nothing left to fight for.

3. WONDER WOMAN-LIKE FIGURE: Yes, there is.

4. BATMAN-LIKE FIGURE: We have to escape. We have to save him.

5. CAPTION (XANADU): I see the AFTERMATH of a GREAT WAR. And I see one word that defines it: TRINITY.

PANEL TWO.
CUT BACK TO Beth and Madame Xanadu. Xanadu holds her head, a massive headache hits her. Beth is worried, scared.

6. BETH: What's WRONG with me?

7. CAPTION (XANADU): What is the TRINITY WAR?

8. MADAME XANADU: The CARDS.

PANEL THREE.
Madame Xanadu turns to one of her cards. There seems to be some kind of magical crackle as she turns the cards – a faint hint of electrical magic. SFX: kzzt

9. MADAME XANADU: The cards will tell me WHO will START it and HOW I can stop them.

PANEL FOUR.
CLOSE ON the first Tarot Card turned over -- it's of BILLY BATSON SHOUTING AND SHAZAM BEHIND HIM with a LIGHTNING BOLT icon in the background. But it doesn't say Shazam at the bottom, it just says – THE BOY.

Ivan, the cards should look like old-fashioned Tarot Cards – almost like flat woodprint versions of our characters when we see them.

SFX: fwap

10. CAPTION (XANADU): I have yet to meet him, but I know who he is.

11. CAPTION (XANADU): And how WRONGLY he was chosen.

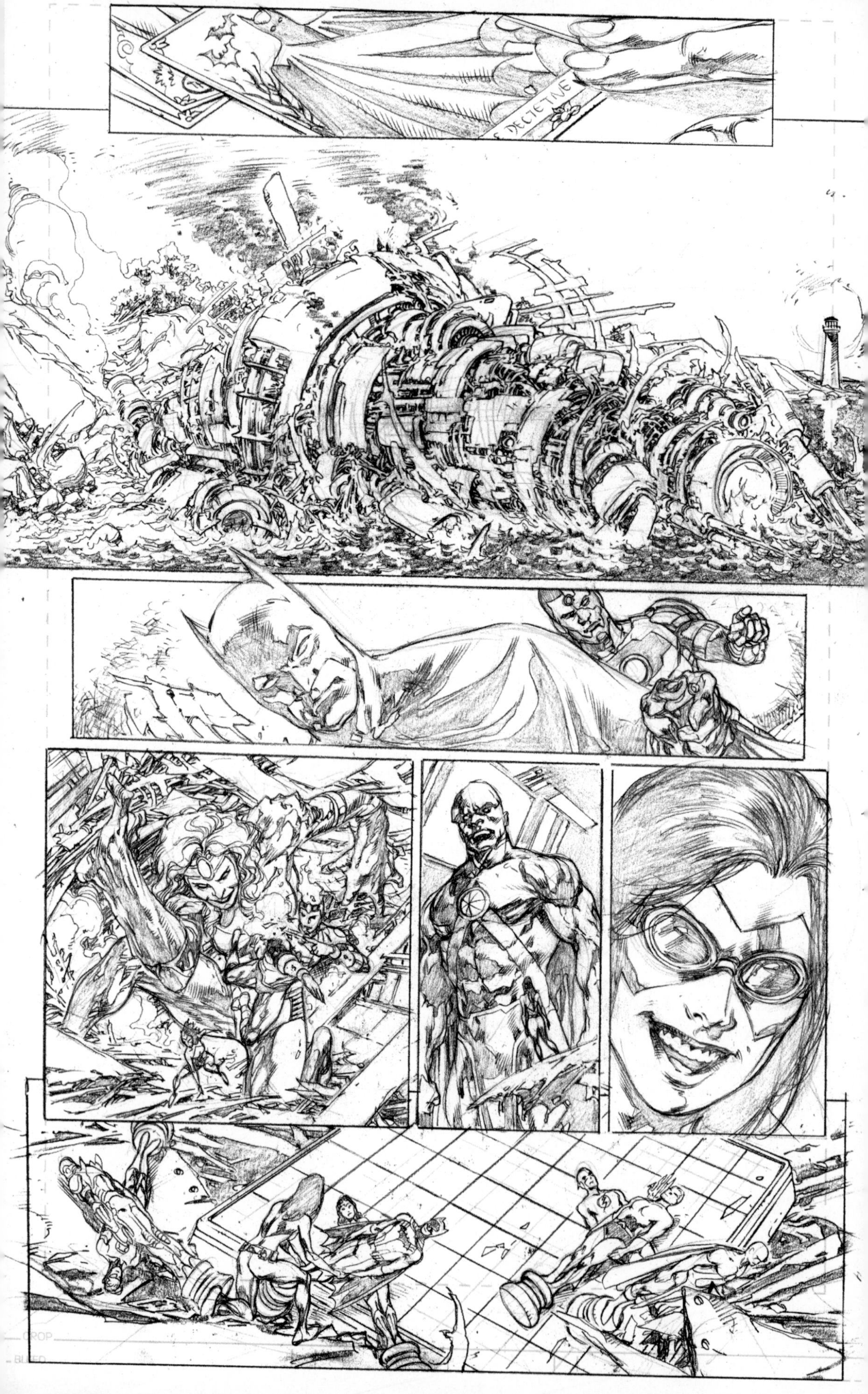

PAGE TEN.

PANEL ONE.
CUT BACK TO Madame Xanadu, her hands putting down the BATMAN Tarot Card – labeled THE DETECTIVE.

SFX: fwap

PANEL TWO.
CUT TO the Watchtower – but it's lying battered on the coast of Rhode Island (where it was set down/crashed at the end of JUSTICE LEAGUE #20). It's on a rocky coast in the city of Happy Harbor, Rhode Island (which was the original location of the Justice League cave in their first BRAVE & THE BOLD appearances). It's night.

BATMAN and CYBORG are examining the wreckage. The satellite is HUGE, Ivan – as wide as a building, partially in the water. The waves crashing up against it.

1. BANNER: Happy Harbor, Rhode Island.

2. The remains of the Justice League Watchtower.

3. CYBORG: So someone hacks into our system WITHOUT my knowing, shuts down our defenses and lets DESPERO in.

4. CYBORG: While someone else -- or maybe the same person -- breaks into the Batcave and steals a Kryptonite ring.

5. CYBORG: A Kryptonite ring no one knew you had.

PANEL THREE.
CLOSER ON Cyborg and Batman. Cyborg looks over at Batman, who has a FLASHLIGHT in his hand as he looks through the wreckage.

6. BATMAN: I have it for STUDY, Vic.

7. CYBORG: To see if you can come up with a KRYPTONITE ANTIDOTE for Superman?

8. CYBORG: That might fly with the rookies, Bruce, but not with me.

PANEL FOUR.
We move to another area of the satellite – Element Woman has turned herself into a giant JACK to lift up a section of the Watchtower so Firestorm and the Atom can salvage what they can. Element Woman should look like Metamorpho when he changes – her face stretched over the white part – larger than life. There's a BIG SMILE on Element Woman's face. Firestorm is tossing debris over his shoulder – zapping it with a blast from one finger and turning it into gas. The Atom is small and going through debris.

9. ATOM: Batman said to keep our eyes out for anything salvageable from the trophy room, Element Woman.

10. FIRESTORM: I can't believe you stopped Despero all by yourself, Atom.

11. ELEMENT WOMAN: That is the COOLEST thing that's ever happened in the history of happenings.

12. ATOM: Yeah, uh, beginner's luck, I guess.

PANEL FIVE.
FLASHBACK to JUSTICE LEAGUE #20 – the Atom looks up at MARTIAN MANHUNTER who is hunched over DESPERO'S body in the wrecked Watchtower. The Atom gazes over at Manhunter, he gazes back to her.

13. MANHUNTER: Tell no one I was here.

PANEL SIX.
CLOSER ON the Atom, getting a little nervous that they might suspect something – she hides it by calling out as she moves through the wreckage.

14. ATOM: HEY! I think I found something!

PANEL SEVEN.
A WIDESCREEN PANEL ACROSS THE BOTTOM OF THE PAGE

She lifts up a piece of debris and finds a trophy – it's a CHESS SET from the League's original fight with DESPERO. The board is BLACK AND YELLOW CHECKERS. The pieces are lying on the ground – they should look like the oversimplified ones from JUSTICE LEAGUE OF AMERICA #1 (1960s). There's a chessboard and pieces: BATMAN, WONDER WOMAN, THE FLASH, AQUAMAN, GREEN LANTERN, CYBORG and MARTIAN MANHUNTER (in the New 52, this happened when he was on the team). The SUPERMAN piece is MISSING.

The Atom is small, so the pieces should be big – almost as big as her.

15. ATOM: It's a CHESS SET...

PAGE ELEVEN.
PANEL ONE.
CUT BACK TO Superman, Pandora and Diana. Superman walks up to Pandora with Diana, who has put her sword down – not sensing a threat any longer.

1. CAPTION (ATOM): "...but the SUPERMAN piece is MISSING."

2. SUPERMAN: Humans aren't evil because someone opened a MAGIC BOX, Pandora. Whoever told you that--

3. PANDORA: No one TOLD me ANYTHING. I was THERE. I SAW the SEVEN SINS fly out into the world.

4. SUPERMAN: I can't have this conversation. Diana?

5. WONDER WOMAN: That's what happened, Superman. My mother told me the story. Someone TRICKED her into opening the box.

PANEL TWO.
CLOSE ON Pandora, the hood shadowing her face.

6. PANDORA: But there's someone out there that can UNDO what I did. Someone that can OPEN this Box and IMPRISON sin once again.

7. PANDORA: We can FREE humanity from EVIL. And I can be free from my CURSE.

PANEL THREE.
Pandora shoves the Box into Superman's hands – Wonder Woman reaches out for him. Superman recoils in pain.

8. PANDORA: You just need to open the Box. And if ANYONE can SURVIVE its touch, it's SUPERMAN!

9. SUPERMAN (DOUBLE BALLOON): AHH!

PANEL FOUR.
VERY VERY CLOSE ON the FACE OF PANDORA'S BOX – THE THREE EYES.

10. WONDER WOMAN (O/P) (DOUBLE BALLOON): Superman?!

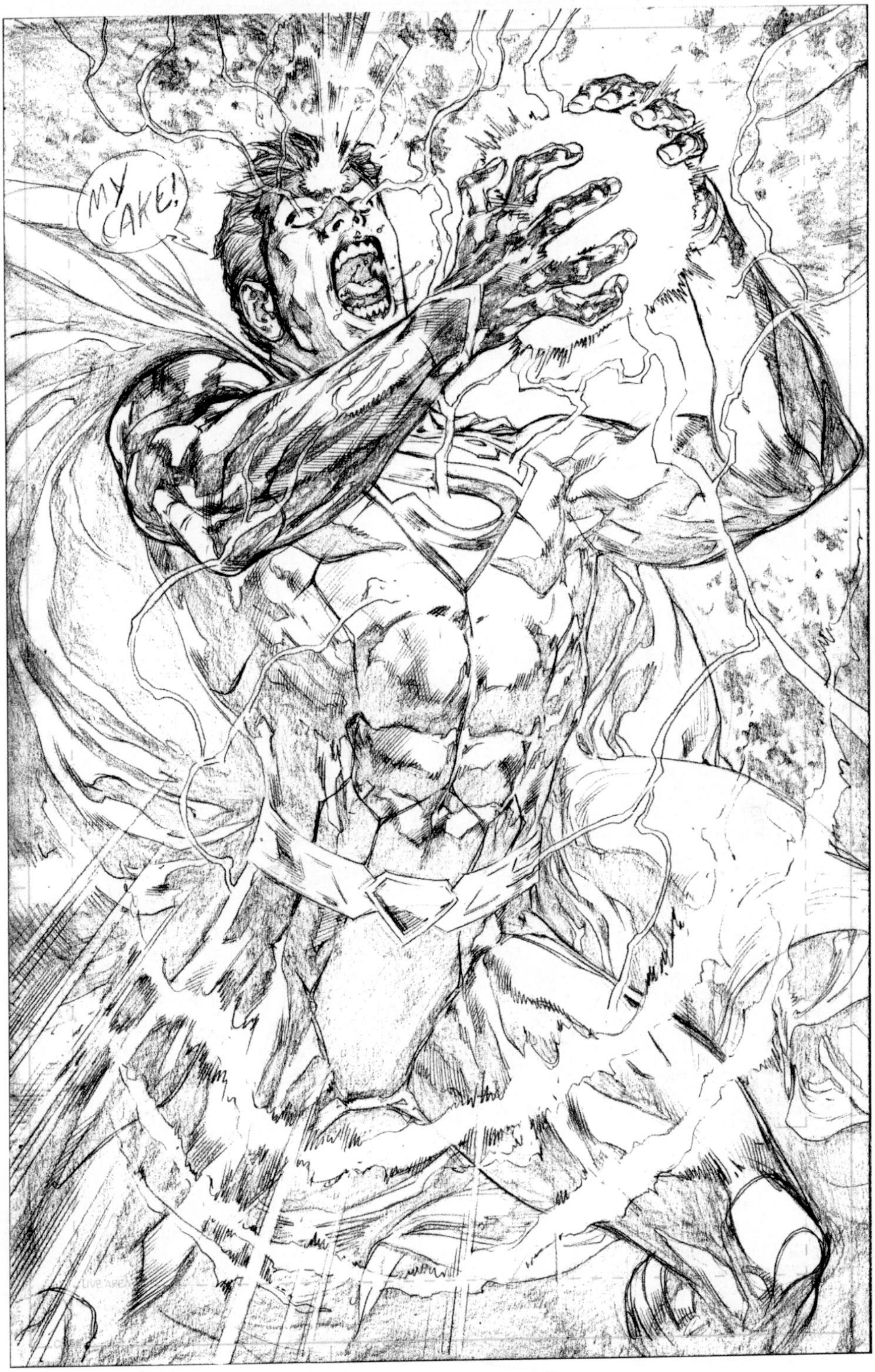
MY CAKE!

PAGE TWELVE.

SPLASH

A FULL FIGURE SHOT of SUPERMAN! Superman touches the Box – and arches back in pain, crying out. His suit goes BLACK. His skin goes PALE. A RED GLOWING SPOT ON THE CENTER OF HIS FOREHEAD – LIKE A THIRD EYE. His eyes glow RED. RED AND BLACK LIGHTNING EXPLODES FROM HIM.

1. SUPERMAN (DOUBLE BALLOON): AAHHHH!

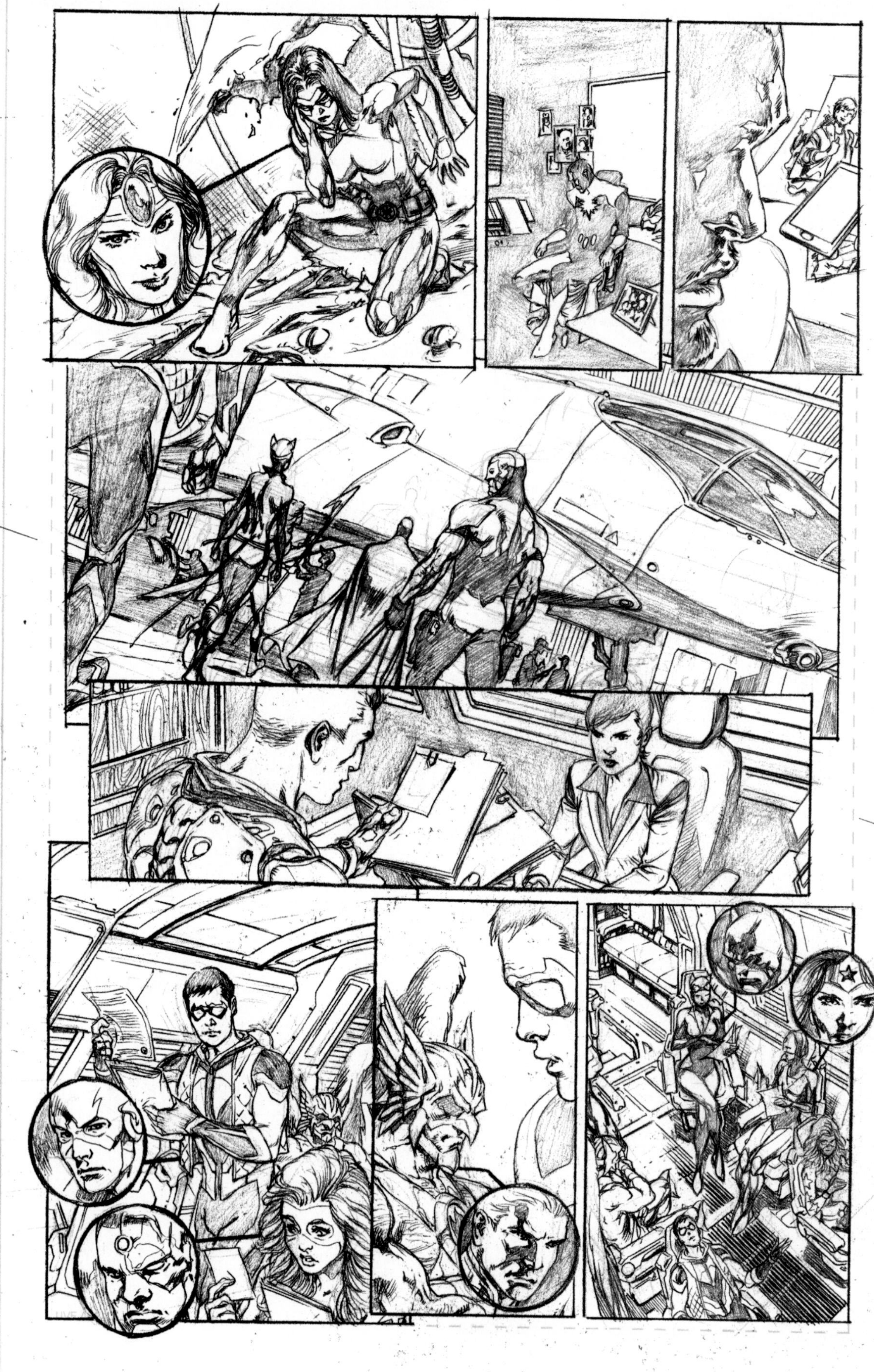
CROP
BLEED

PAGE FIFTEEN.

PANEL ONE.
CUT TO the Atom, very small – hidden among the debris of the Justice League
Watchtower. She speaks, a finger at her ear as she activates her JLA com in her mask. There is a little INSET panel of ELEMENT WOMAN that points to her. (These inset panels are described in greater detail in panel six on this page.)

1. CAPTION (BATMAN): "We're already making a call."

2. ATOM: YES! We're heading into Kahndaq right now, Colonel Trevor.

3. ATOM: What do I do?

PANEL TWO.
CUT BACK TO a sad Doctor Light in his office, his helmet still off and on his desk. He sits in the dark, his head hung low – hands holding it up. He has no one to talk to anymore – he doesn't dare risk contacting his wife about this again.

4. WALLER (ELECTRIC - DISEMBODIED): Doctor Light.

PANEL THREE.
Doctor Light looks over at a JLA COMMUNICATOR (like an iPhone) sitting on his desk by the Firestorm, Ronnie and Jason pictures – beyond it his family photo.

5. WALLER/JLA COMMUNICATOR (ELECTRIC): Get your helmet strapped on and get to the Jet.

PANEL FOUR.
CUT TO the hangar where the Justice League of America keep their INVISIBLE JET, which is a huge military plane that can "cloak" itself invisible.

MARTIAN MANHUNTER leads the Justice League of America to the plane – HAWKMAN, KATANA, CATWOMAN, STARGIRL, VIBE and GREEN LANTERN/SIMON BAZ.

There are A.R.G.U.S. Agents working on the plane.

6. CAPTION (WALLER): "The Justice League is heading into Kahndaq.

7. CAPTION (WALLER): "Your job is to get them OUT by ANY means possible."

8. CAPTION: The JLA's Invisible Jet.

PANEL FIVE.
CUT TO Steve and Waller in Waller's office. Steve is geared up, files of the JUSTICE LEAGUE - including the headshots - in his hands. He's going to pass them to the various members.

9. STEVE: They aren't READY for this, Waller.

10. WALLER: This is an OPPORTUNITY we might not get again, Steve.

11. WALLER: This our chance to go shine a SPOTLIGHT on how UNCONTROLLABLE the Justice League is –

PANEL SIX.
Moving across Vibe who takes a seat with the other Leaguers, sitting next to Stargirl. Vibe is flipping through the Flash file. (Ivan, I'm thinking maybe each member – as we cycle through – has a little square inset panel by them with a line to them – in this panel Vibe would have a little square inset panel of THE FLASH while Stargirl would have a little square inset panel of CYBORG – these would be the same HEADSHOT panels as seen in pages 8/9. Only the JUSTICE LEAGUE have inset square panels, the JLA are in panel.)

12. CAPTION (WALLER): "—and how the JLA is the only team the world can TRUST."

13. VIBE: This is like defcon NEGATIVE ELEVEN, Stargirl.

14. VIBE: Colonel Trevor handed me a FOLDER on THE FLASH and said he was my TARGET. This is CRAZY.

15. STARGIRL: What can I do against Cyborg?

PANEL SEVEN.
Vibe looks over at Hawkman, who is reading Aquaman's file. (And like the above, there's a little inset square panel of AQUAMAN with a line to Hawkman.)

16. VIBE: You got AQUAMAN? You don't, uh, you don't want to TRADE, do you, Hawkman?

17. HAWKMAN: NO.

18. HAWKMAN: But I'll take yours too if you don't think you can handle it.

PANEL EIGHT.
Catwoman is flipping through Batman's file – which to her is incomplete. Katana sitting next to her. (And like the above, we have a little square inset panel of BATMAN with a line to Catwoman and a little square inset panel of WONDER WOMAN with Katana.)

In the back, Vibe notices that the LIGHTS are getting dim.

19. CATWOMAN: Whatever they're doing, if Batman's involved, we should trust them.

20. KATANA: Your personal investment is clouding your judgment, Catwoman.

21. CATWOMAN: Hey, worry about your own target, Katana.

22. CATWOMAN (SMALL): As if that matchup makes ANY sense.

23. VIBE: Hey, why's it getting DARK in here?

24. DOCTOR LIGHT (O/P): This is WRONG.

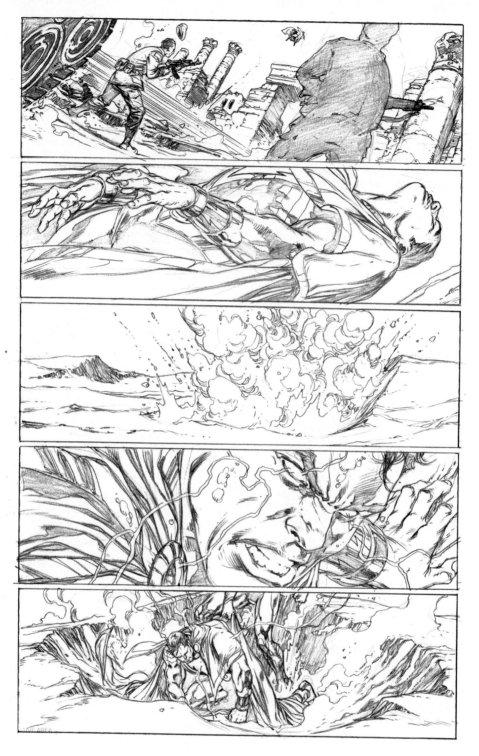

PAGE EIGHTEEN.

PANEL ONE.
But before Shazam can throw his punch he's hit by
something INCREDIBLY STRONG – a BLUR of RED, BLUE
and a tiny bit of YELLOW – Superman, of course – hits him
from left to right. Shazam goes flying. [NO DIALOGUE.]

PANEL TWO.
An extreme longshot of Shazam flying through the air –
into the desert.

[NO DIALOGUE.]

PANEL THREE.
Shazam lands like a BOMB in the desert. He hits a dune –

sending most of it up into the air.

[NO DIALOGUE.]

PANEL FOUR.
CLOSE ON Shazam gazing up, electricity in his eyes.
He's not happy...

1. SHAZAM: Who's asking for a FIGHT?

PANEL FIVE.
Suddenly, something tugs on Shazam's cape.

2. SUPERMAN (O/P): No one wants one.

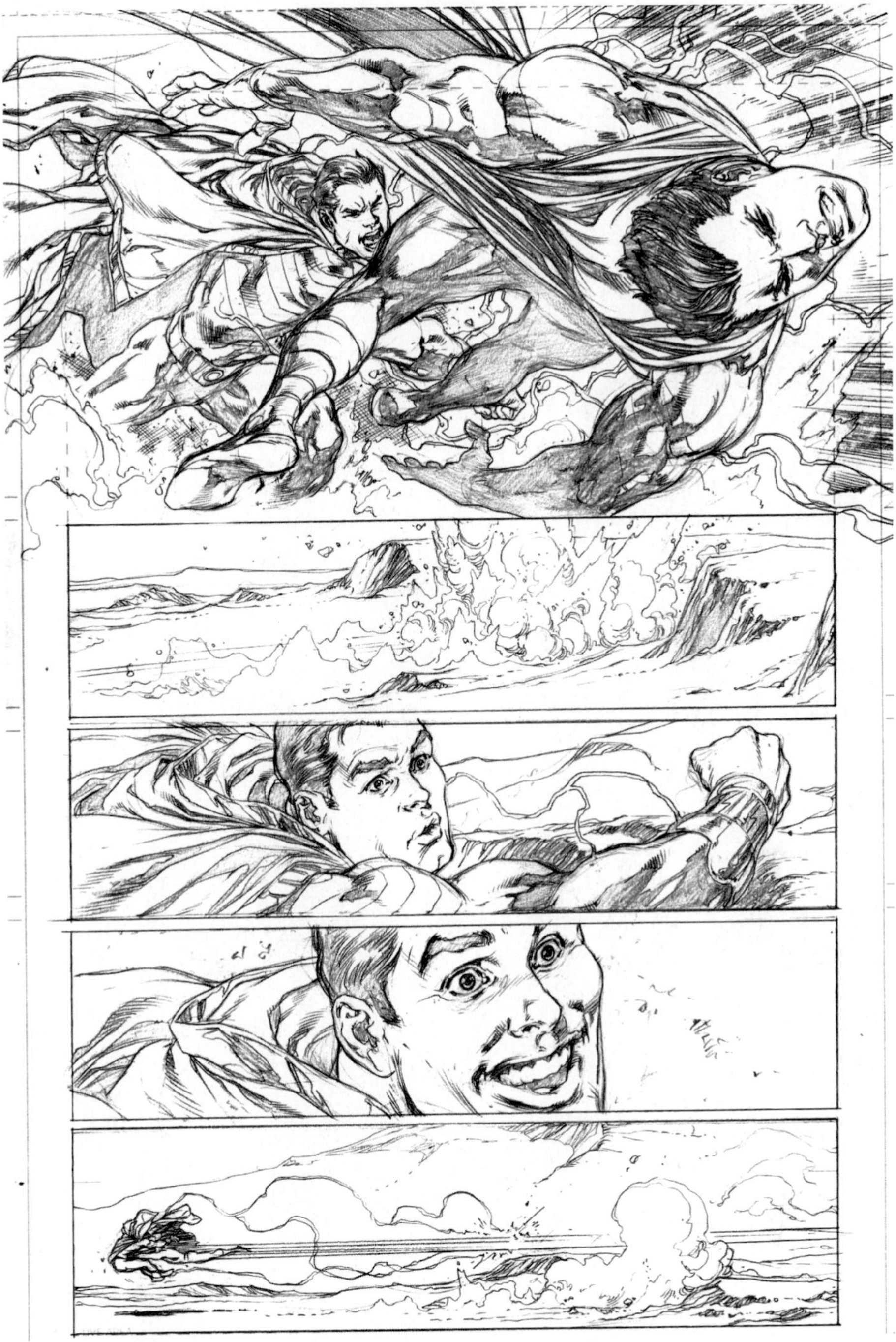

PAGE NINTEEN.
PANEL ONE.

LARGE PANEL
Shazam turns around and swings hard – SLAMMING his fist right into Superman, who is taken aback – and hurt by the MAGIC of it all. Electricity explodes all around!

1. SHAZAM: Then you shouldn't have STARTED it!

PANEL TWO.
Superman slides across the desert – like the space shuttle landing – kicking up sand.

[NO DIALOGUE.]

PANEL THREE.
CLOSE ON Shazam, realizing he just knocked down Superman – UH OH.

2. SHAZAM: SUPERMAN?

3. SHAZAM: I just knocked down Superman.

PANEL FOUR.
SAME EXACT PANEL AS ABOVE, but Shazam realizes HE JUST KNOCKED DOWN SUPERMAN! He smiles.

4. SHAZAM: I JUST KNOCKED DOWN SUPERMAN.

PANEL FIVE.
A WIDESCREEN PANEL ACROSS THE BOTTOM OF THE PAGE

A LONGSHOT of Superman flying from right to left and slamming into Shazam! There's an explosion of lightning! Wind kicks up the sand!

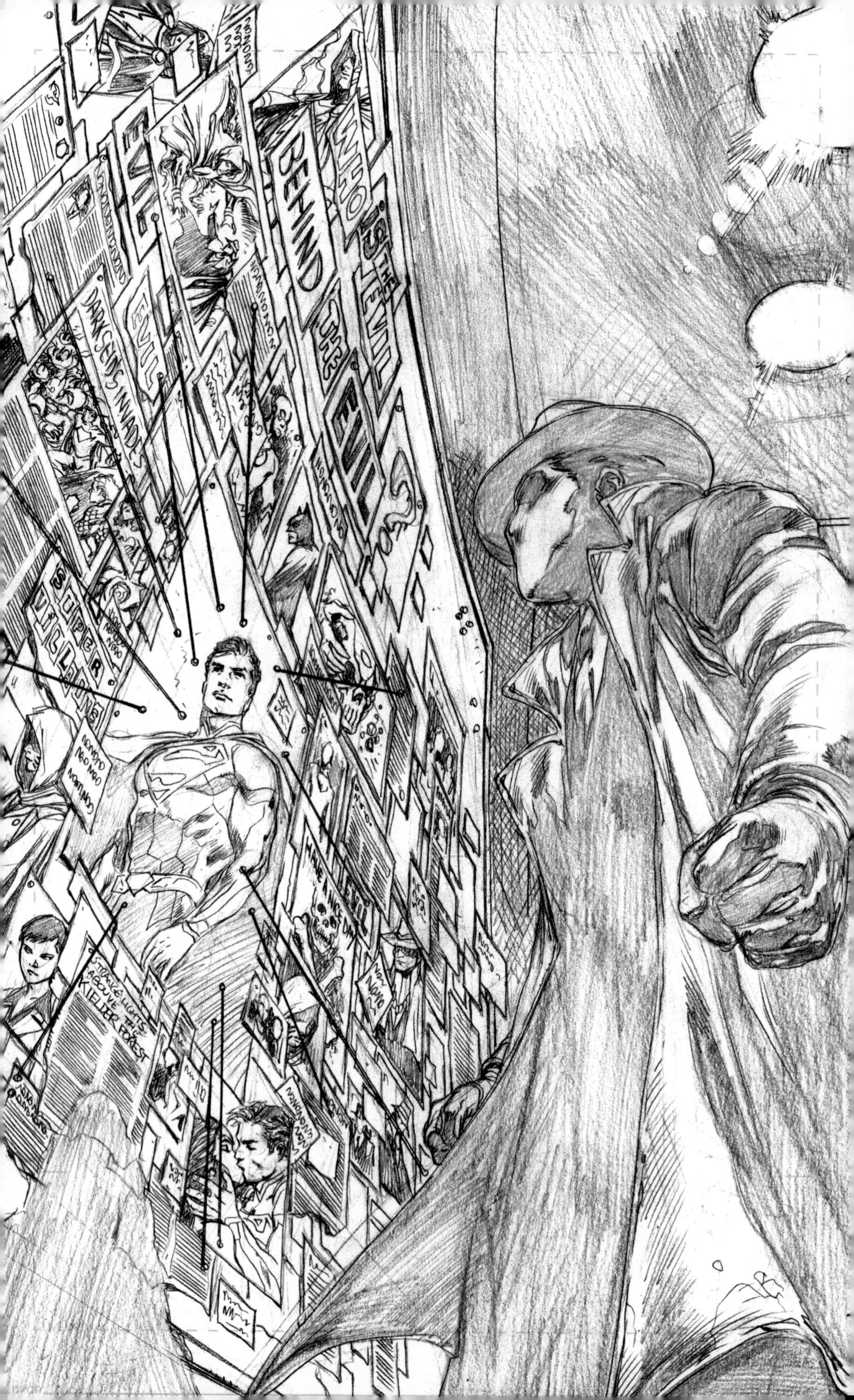
WHO IS THE EVIL BEHIND THE EVIL
SUPER VILLAINS
STRANGE LIGHTS ABOVE KIELDER FOREST

PAGE TWENTY-SIX.

SPLASH

We're standing behind The Question and gazing up at his crazy conspiracy theory board – but it's the entire wall of the warehouse!!! He should be very small, a full figure shot. The wall is full of images and words tied together by strings.

Words from various newspaper articles form a large question on the top of the board:

WHO IS THE EVIL BEHIND THE EVIL?

All the strings point from various Post-Its and photographs of crime scenes, missing persons cases, etc. Some specifics are: an image of Pandora from the bleachers in JUSTICE LEAGUE #1, an image of THE PHANTOM STRANGER as seen battling THE SPECTRE in recent Phantom Stranger issues, an image of SUPERMAN and WONDER WOMAN kissing as seen in JUSTICE LEAGUE OF AMERICA #1, an image of AMANDA WALLER, an image of the screen from the end of JUSTICE LEAGUE #18 with the skull & crossbones and HAVE A NICE DAY written across it, a newspaper article that reads: STRANGE LIGHTS ABOVE THE KIELDER FOREST, a word made up of different letters from various magazines and newspapers – S-U-P-E-R- V-I-L-L-A-I-N-S, a newspaper article that reads: DARKSEID INVADES with an image of the JUSTICE LEAGUE fighting Parademons – AND FINALLY, THERE'S AN IMAGE OF SUPERMAN IN THE VERY CENTER OF THE COLLAGE – ALL THE STRINGS ARE POINTING TOWARD HIM.

1. THE QUESTION: WHO IS THE EVIL BEHIND THE EVIL?

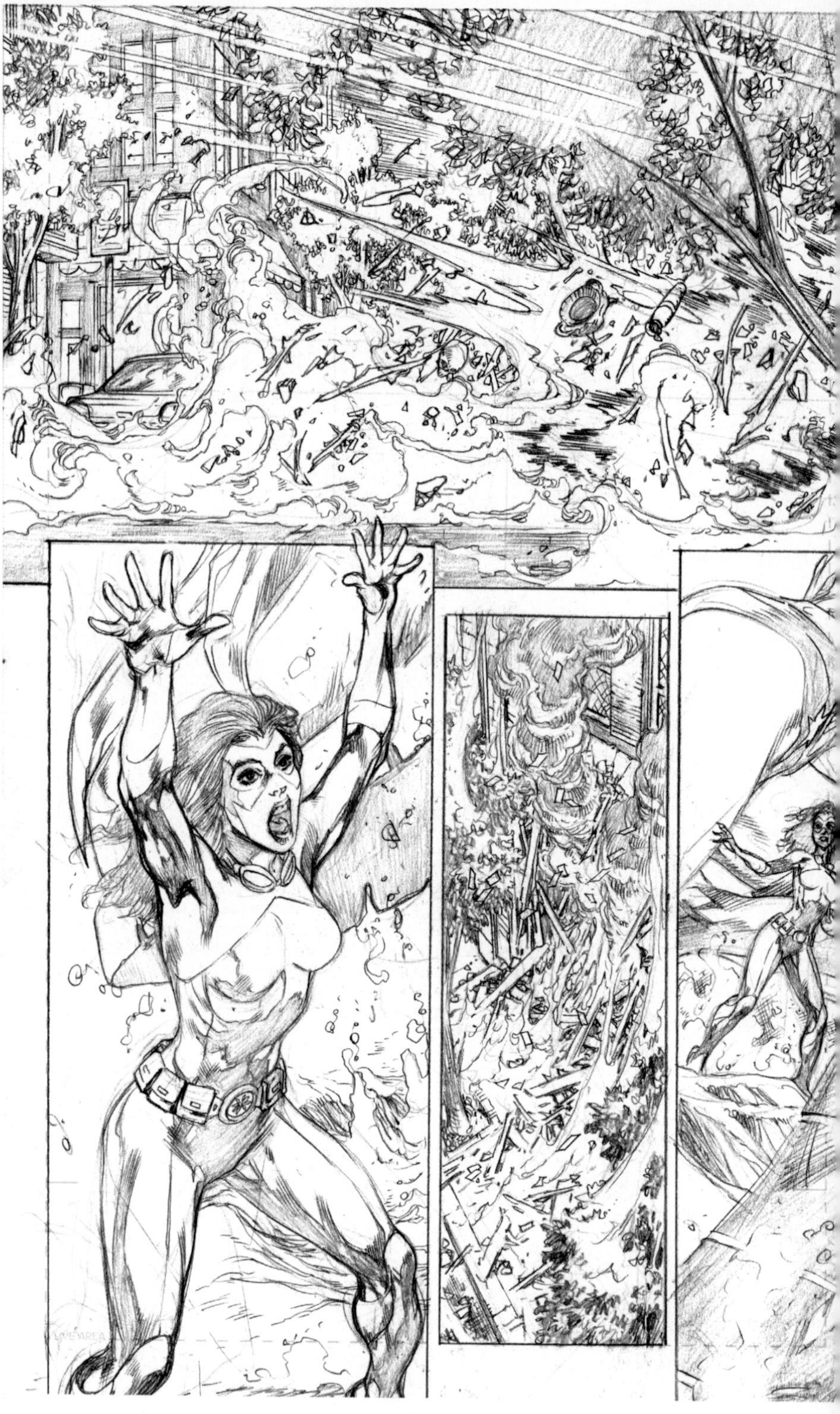

PAGES THIRTY AND THIRTY-ONE.
PANEL ONE.
BIG PANEL ACROSS THE TOP OF THE PAGE

The storefront of Madame Xanadu EXPLODES with ORANGE FIRE – the windows and door incinerated as the powerful flames and force shoot out of the storefront. A passerby is blown backwards.

[NO DIALOGUE.]

PANEL TWO.
CLOSE ON the Atom on the ground, pleading with everyone – fearful and almost in tears. But she's SO SMALL compared to the FEET STOMPING AROUND.

She's almost stepped on by HAWKMAN'S BOOT!

1. ATOM (DOUBLE BALLOON): STOP!

PANEL THREE.
BACK TO the aftermath of the explosion – flames dancing among the debris. The shop and a car outside still burning. Charred tarot cards fluttering down like leaves from a tree – some of them on fire.

[NO DIALOGUE.]

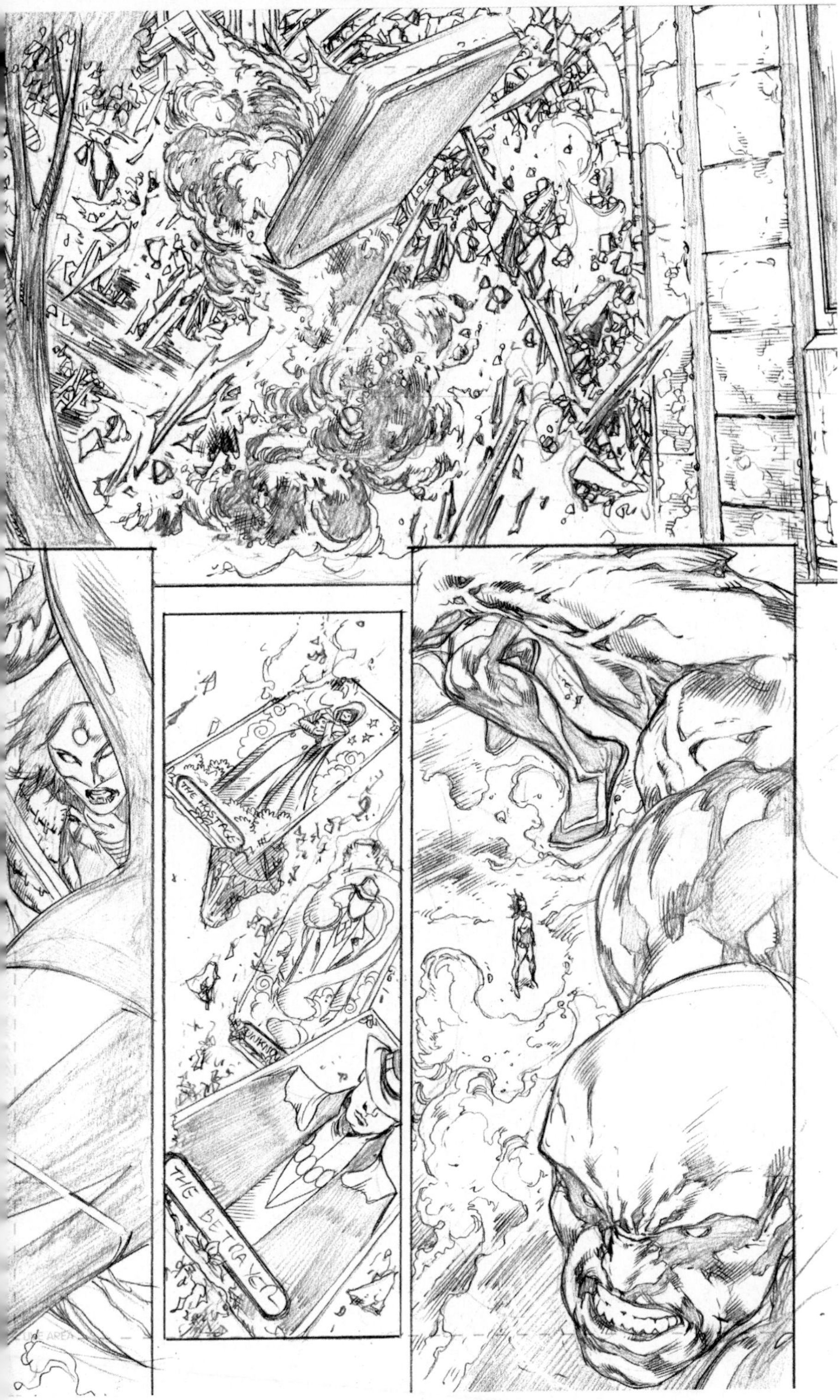
THE HOSTAGE
THE BETRAYER

PANEL FOUR.
Back to panel two's fight, but we PULL BACK FURTHER from the Atom and see PARTS of our heroes fighting. Part of KATANA – Part of WONDER WOMAN. She continues to cry out – her voice being less and less heard.

2. ATOM (SMALLER): Please stop!

PANEL FIVE.
BACK TO the aftermath of the explosion – three cards float down from above – THE TRINITY OF SIN! PANDORA – THE PAWN. THE QUESTION – THE UNKNOWN. And now THE PHANTOM STRANGER – labeled simply THE BETRAYER.

[NO DIALOGUE.]

PANEL SIX.
And now the Atom is extremely small – her voice drowned out by the violence – we barely even see her. We now see MARTIAN MANHUNTER move past her. Again, it's a BLUR of BATTLE.

3. ATOM (EVEN SMALLER): Please!

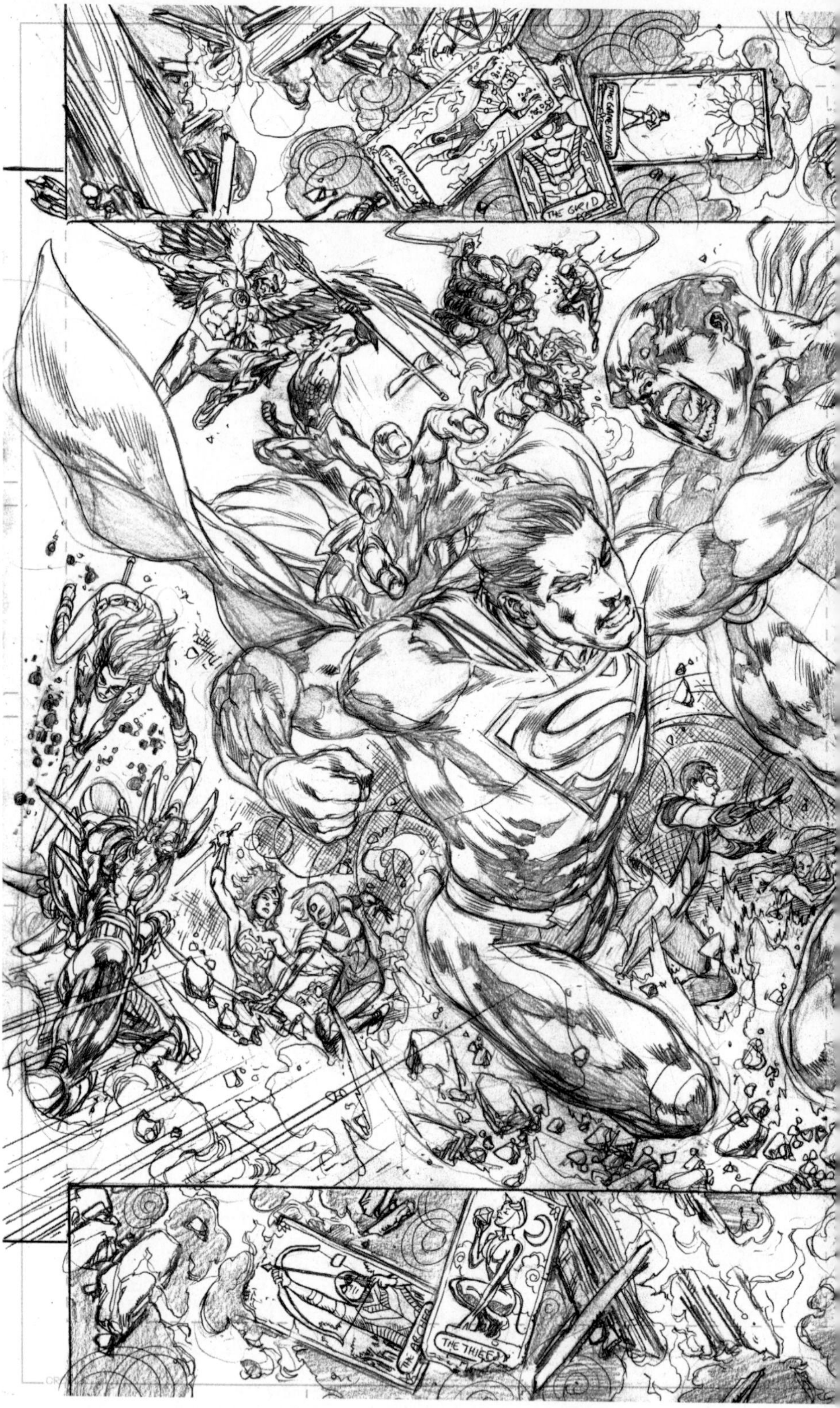
THE GRID

PAGES THIRTY-TWO AND THIRTY-THREE.
PANEL ONE.
A VERY VERY THIN PANEL ACROSS THE TOP TWO PAGES

STRAIGHT DOWN ON SEVERAL OF THE OTHER TAROT CARDS SCATTERED IN THE STREET IN FRONT OF MADAME XANADU'S. Like the others, the pictures are labeled with not their name but a simple descriptor.

CYBORG – THE GRID.
FIRESTORM – THE PRISONER. (though the ER in PRISONER is partly burned/ripped)
THE ATOM – THE GAMEPLAYER.
ELEMENT WOMAN – THE FREAK.
THE FLASH – THE MESSENGER.
AQUAMAN – THE KING.
ZATANNA – THE MAGICIAN.

PANEL TWO.
A DOUBLE-PAGE SPREAD

MOST OF THE TWO PAGES!!!

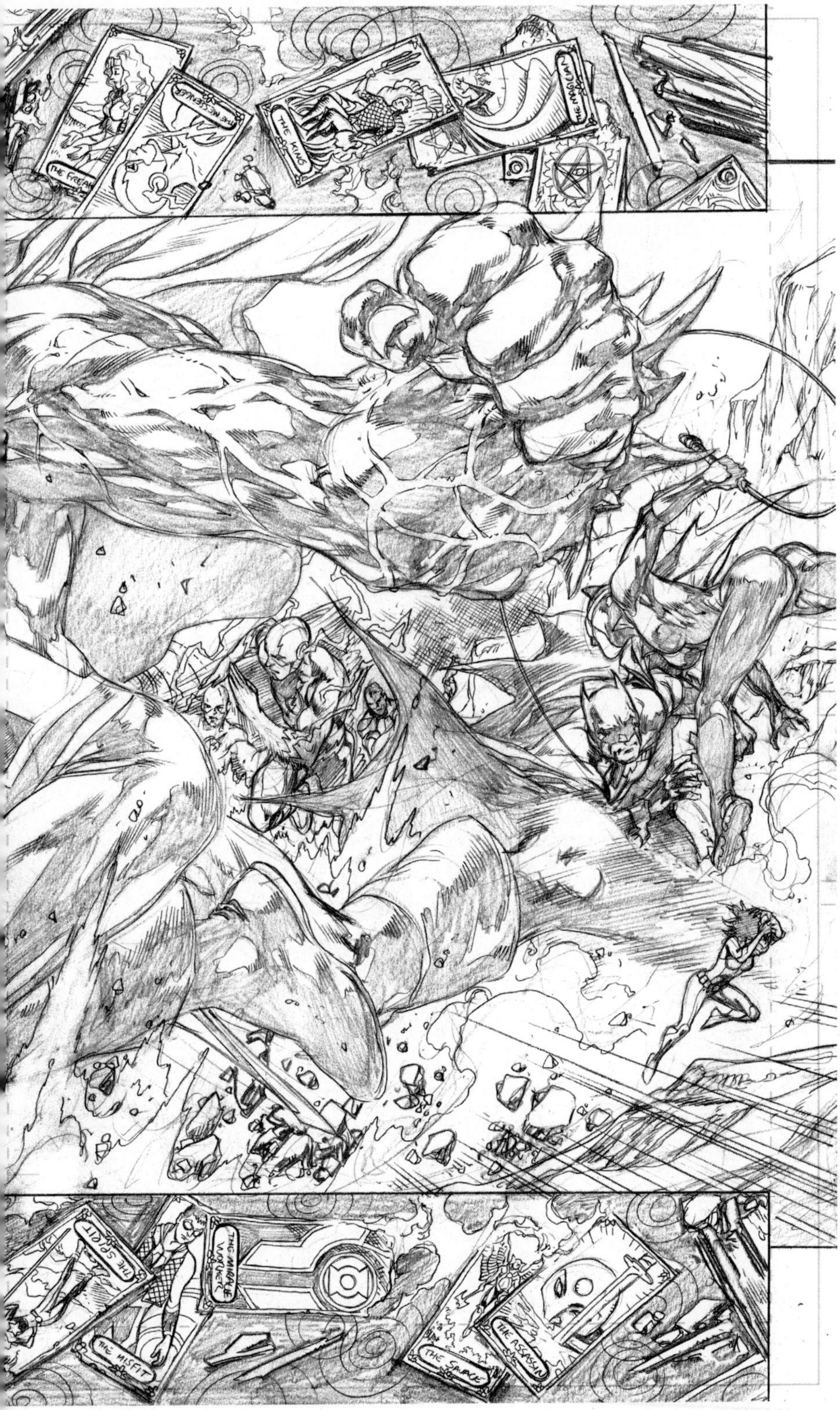
THE MESSENGER
THE KING
THE MAGICIAN
THE SPIRIT
THE MIRACLE WORKER
THE MISFIT
THE SAVAGE
THE ASSASSIN

CUT BACK TO the JUSTICE LEAGUE vs. THE JUSTICE LEAGUE OF AMERICA – it's back on! And in the biggest way – in the main image here of the spread is SUPERMAN vs. MARTIAN MANHUNTER!

The other heroes start attacking their respective members – VIBE blasts THE FLASH – but misses, STARGIRL hits CYBORG, CATWOMAN leaps on BATMAN. [NO DIALOGUE.]

PANEL THREE.
JUST LIKE PANEL ONE – A VERY VERY THIN PANEL ACROSS THE BOTTOM.

STRAIGHT DOWN ON SEVERAL OTHER TAROT CARDS SCATTERED IN THE STREET IN NEW YORK.

GREEN ARROW – THE ARCHER.
CATWOMAN – THE THIEF.
STARGIRL – THE SPIRIT.
SIMON BAZ/GREEN LANTERN – THE MIRACLE WORKER.
VIBE – THE MISFIT.
HAWKMAN – THE SAVAGE.
KATANA – THE ASSASSIN.

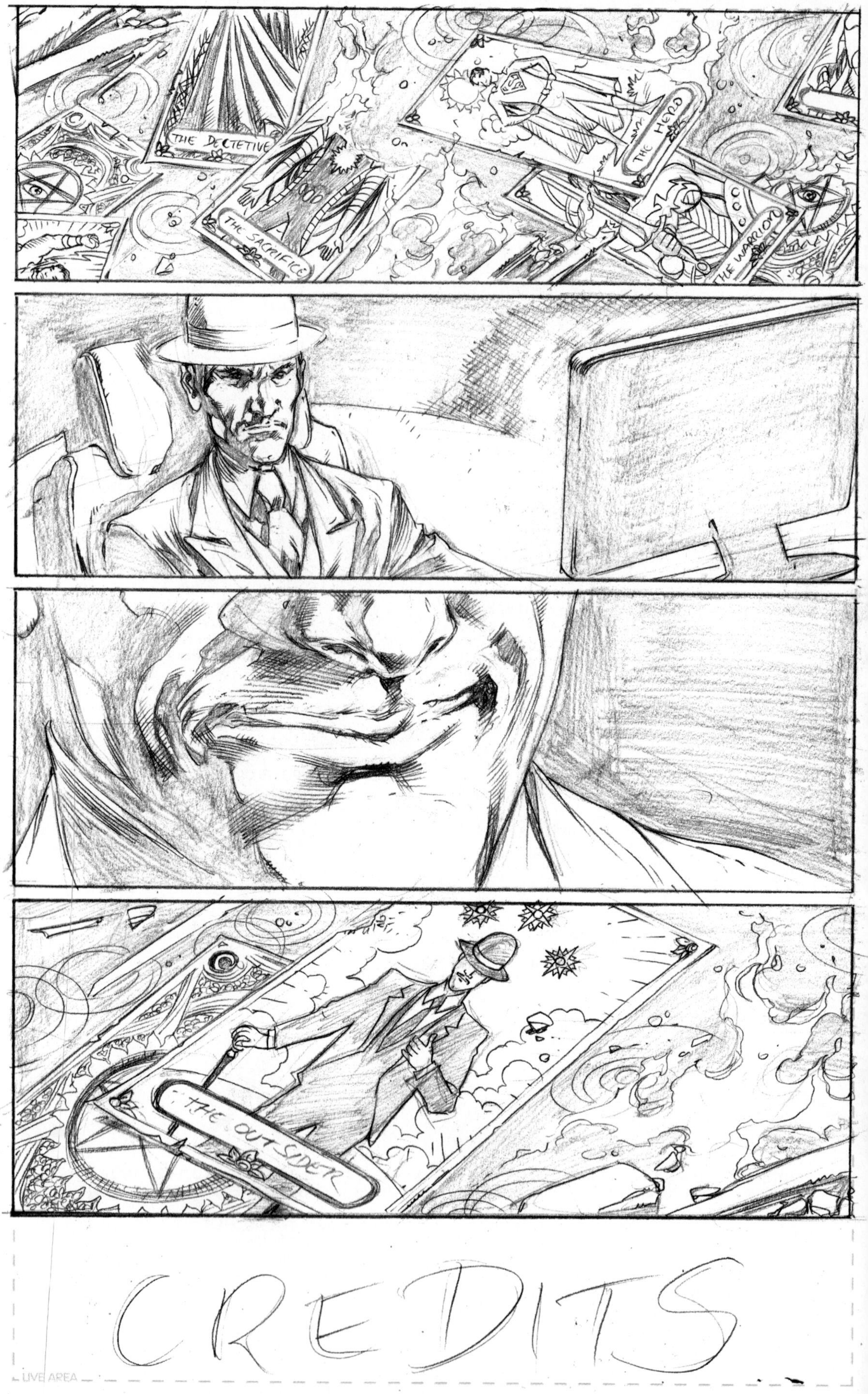
THE DECTETIVE
THE HERO
THE SACRIFICE
THE WARRIOR
THE OUTSIDER
CREDITS
LIVE AREA

PAGE THIRTY-FOUR.
PANEL ONE.

MOST OF THE PAGE

We're on the street outside of Madame Xanadu's shop – looking straight down at the burning debris and among them THREE TAROT CARDS. In the lower center is the card with DOCTOR LIGHT, which is now burned and charred, representing his death. We can read his descriptor underneath it: THE SACRIFICE.

Arching around it are three more cards. To the right of the Doctor Light card is – BATMAN – though it reads THE DETECTIVE – then above the Doctor Light card – SUPERMAN – though it reads THE HERO (though "HERO" has a BLACK SLASH through it) – and then to the right of the Doctor Light card – WONDER WOMAN – though it reads THE WARRIOR.

There are hints of the other cards of each character around them that we've seen throughout the issue.

1. CAPTION (NEWS): "...reports coming in now of an all-out WAR between the
JUSTICE LEAGUE and the JUSTICE LEAGUE OF AMERICA.

2. CAPTION (NEWS): "...ONE CASUALTY already...I'm not sure I believe it...at the hands of SUPERMAN?

PANEL TWO.
CUT TO the Leader of the Secret Society sitting in his chair in his office as established in JUSTICE LEAGUE OF AMERICA #2. He watches a televised report of the battle between the Justice Leagues.

3. NEWS (ELECTRIC): This can't be true.

4. LEADER: Ha.

PANEL THREE.
CLOSE ON the Leader's mouth and chin – a slight smile on his pale skin. WHO IS HE?

5. LEADER: Thanks to ME, everyone will actually BELIEVE that Superman's KILLED Doctor Light.

PANEL FOUR.
And we finally end CLOSE on one of the cards – the silhouette of THE LEADER of the Secret Society with the hat and cane – and his descriptor reads: THE OUTSIDER. There are THREE STARS around the image in the sky – signifying another trinity.

6. CAPTION (LEADER): "And by the time the Justice League figures out what I'm up to, the WORLD will already belong to US."

A BLACK BAR FOR THE CREDITS ALONG THE BOTTOM

TITLE: TRINITY WAR: CHAPTER ONE TITLE:
THE DEATH CARD
WRITER: Geoff Johns
PENCILS: Ivan Reis
INKS: Joe Prado
COLORS: Rod Reis
LETTERS: DC Lettering
ASSISTANT EDITOR: Kate Stewart
SENIOR EDITOR: Brian Cunningham

"Welcoming to new fans looking to get into superhero comics for the first time and old fans who gave up on the funny-books long ago."
—SCRIPPS HOWARD NEWS SERVICE

START AT THE BEGINNING!

JUSTICE LEAGUE
VOLUME 1:ORIGIN

**AQUAMAN
VOLUME 1:
THE TRENCH**

**THE SAVAGE
HAWKMAN VOLUME 1:
DARKNESS RISING**

**GREEN ARROW
VOLUME 1:
THE MIDAS TOUCH**

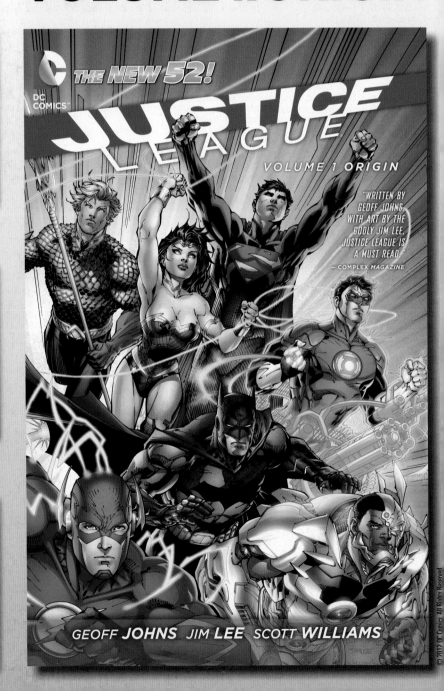

GEOFF **JOHNS** JIM **LEE** SCOTT **WILLIAMS**

"Flash fans should breathe a sigh of relief that the character is 100% definitely in the right hands."
—MTV GEEK

START AT THE BEGINNING!
THE FLASH
VOLUME 1: MOVE FORWARD

JUSTICE LEAGUE INTERNATIONAL VOLUME 1: THE SIGNAL MASTERS

O.M.A.C. VOLUME 1: OMACTIVATE!

CAPTAIN ATOM VOLUME 1: EVOLUTION

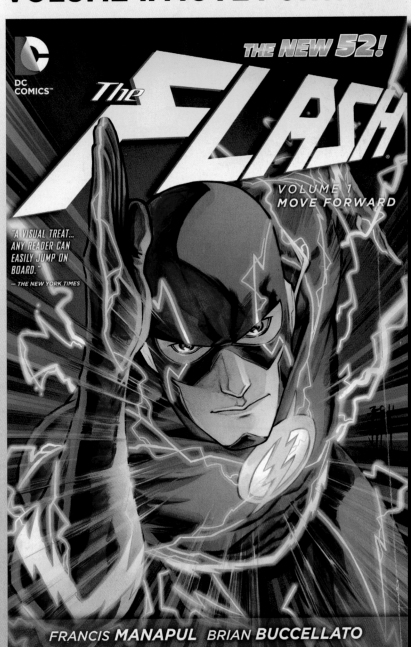

FRANCIS **MANAPUL**   BRIAN **BUCCELLATO**

"Clear storytelling at its best. It's an intriguing concept and easy to grasp."
—NEW YORK TIMES

"Azzarello is rebuilding the mythology of Wonder Woman."
—MAXIM

START AT THE BEGINNING!

WONDER WOMAN VOLUME 1: BLOOD

MR. TERRIFIC
VOLUME 1:
MIND GAMES

BLUE BEETLE
VOLUME 1:
METAMORPHOSIS

THE FURY OF FIRESTORM:
THE NUCLEAR MEN
VOLUME 1:
GOD PARTICLE

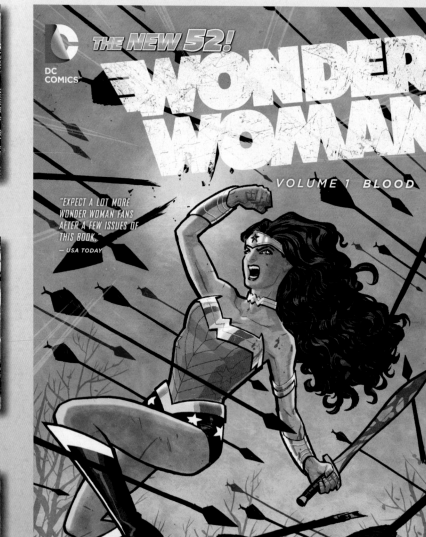

THE NEW 52!

DC COMICS

WONDER WOMAN

VOLUME 1 BLOOD

"EXPECT A LOT MORE WONDER WOMAN FANS AFTER A FEW ISSUES OF THIS BOOK."
— USA TODAY

BRIAN AZZARELLO   CLIFF CHIANG   TONY AKINS

MATH TRAILBLAZERS

Grade 4

Unit Resource Guide
Unit 1
Data About Us

SECOND EDITION

A Mathematical Journey Using Science and Language Arts

KENDALL/HUNT PUBLISHING COMPANY
4050 Westmark Drive   Dubuque, Iowa 52002

A TIMS® Curriculum
University of Illinois at Chicago

UIC The University of Illinois at Chicago

The original edition was based on work supported by the National Science Foundation under grant No. MDR 9050226 and the University of Illinois at Chicago. Any opinions, findings, and conclusions or recommendations expressed in this publication are those of the author(s) and do not necessarily reflect the views of the granting agencies.

ISBN 0-7872-8594-3

Printed in the United States of America

1 2 3 4 5 6 7 8 9 10 07 06 05 04 03

LETTER HOME

Data About Us

Date: ____________________

Dear Family Member:

Welcome to *Math Trailblazers™: A Mathematical Journey Using Science and Language Arts.* Throughout the school year, I will send home letters that provide an overview of each unit.

The first unit, *Data About Us,* addresses ways of collecting, organizing, and studying data. We will study the concept of an average. In your child's everyday world, the word "average" is commonly used. He or she has probably heard the phrases "batting average" or "the average amount of rainfall for the month." Your child will learn how to find a type of average called the median and use it to represent data collected in class.

59 in

Height is one of the variables students measure in this unit.

Your child will also investigate the relationship between the arm span and height of students in class. Can we predict the height of a new fourth grader if we know his or her arm span? To investigate this question, your child will measure classmates' arm spans and heights. Your child will organize this data, make and interpret a graph, and make and check predictions.

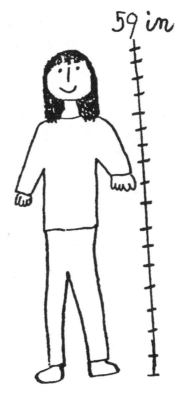

As we explore mathematics concepts in the classroom, you can help by providing additional mathematics opportunities at home. For example:

- Keep an eye out for the words "average" and "median." They may appear on food labels, in weather reports, or in newspapers and magazines. Discuss these averages with your child.
- Your child is reviewing the addition facts in this unit. Help your child review these facts at home. If your child needs more practice, he or she will be given flash cards and games to use at home.

Thank you for taking the time to explore mathematics with your child.

Sincerely,

____

UNIT OUTLINE

UNIT 1

Estimated
Class
Sessions

11–13

Data About Us

Pacing Suggestions

- The pacing schedule for the year assumes that mathematics instruction begins on the first day of school and that students receive 60 minutes of mathematics instruction each day. The first lesson is a data collection activity specifically designed to engage students on the first day of school.

- If students have had *Math Trailblazers* in previous grades, use the minimum number of recommended class sessions as a guide for lesson planning. If students have not had *Math Trailblazers,* use the maximum number of days as a guide.

- Take advantage of connections to science and language arts. Lesson 4 *The Four Servants* is an *Adventure Book* story that reviews the TIMS Laboratory Method in a fairy tale format. Lesson 5 *Arm Span vs. Height* is a laboratory investigation. Students can read the story as part of language arts or collect data for the lab during science time.

- It is not necessary to stop and make sure that students have mastered each skill before moving on to Unit 2, since later units will review and extend the skills and concepts developed in Unit 1. Students will also review skills in the Daily Practice and Problems (in each *Unit Resource Guide*) and Home Practice (in the *Discovery Assignment Book*). The table below shows the location of resources that give information on the development of concepts and skills throughout the year.

Resource	Location
Curriculum Sequence	Selected Lesson Guides (See Unit 1 Lesson 1 for an example.)
Unit Summaries	*Teacher Implementation Guide* Section 4
Unit Scope and Sequence	*Teacher Implementation Guide* Section 5
Daily Practice and Problems and Home Practice Scope and Sequence	*Teacher Implementation Guide* Section 5
Individual Assessment Record Sheet	*Teacher Implementation Guide* Section 8 Part VI

Components Key: SG = Student Guide, DAB = Discovery Assignment Book, AB = Adventure Book, URG = Unit Resource Guide, and DPP = Daily Practice and Problems

	Sessions	Description	Supplies
LESSON 1 **Getting to Know Room 204** SG pages 2–6 URG pages 27–37 DPP A–B	1–2	**ACTIVITY:** Students are introduced to a classroom of fourth graders through a class picture and a data table displaying characteristics of the class. Students investigate categorical variables, organize data in a data table, and make bar graphs.	• easel paper or poster-size graph paper

	Sessions	Description	Supplies
LESSON 2 **Getting to Know Room 204 a Little Better** SG pages 7–11 URG pages 38–49 DPP C–F	2	**ACTIVITY:** Students differentiate between numerical and categorical variables. They investigate a numerical variable that describes themselves. They then collect, organize, and graph data about that variable.	• easel paper or poster-size graph paper
LESSON 3 **An Average Activity** SG pages 12–16 URG pages 50–59 DPP G–J	2	**ACTIVITY:** Students explore the concept of averages. They learn to find the median value of a set of data.	
LESSON 4 **The Four Servants** AB pages 1–14 URG pages 60–70 DPP K–L	1	**ADVENTURE BOOK:** In this fairy tale, four servants solve a puzzle. After collecting pertinent data, they predict the height of a giant from the length of a handprint. The TIMS Laboratory Method is introduced through the story.	
LESSON 5 **Arm Span vs. Height** SG pages 17–23 DAB pages 7–8 URG pages 71–87 DPP M–T	4–5	**LAB:** Students collect, organize, graph, and analyze data using the TIMS Laboratory Method as they explore the relationship between height and arm span. **ASSESSMENT PAGE:** *More Arm Span vs. Height Data,* Unit Resource Guide, page 83.	• metersticks or yardsticks • rulers • calculators • masking tape • poster-size graph paper
LESSON 6 **Solving Problems About Room 204** SG pages 24–25 URG pages 88–94 DPP U–V	1	**ACTIVITY:** Students solve a variety of word problems. The problems require various tools, strategies, skills, and operations.	• calculators

A current list of connections is available at www.mathtrailblazers.com.

Literature

Suggested Titles

- Bishop, Claire Huchet, and Kurt Wiese. *The Five Chinese Brothers.* Coward-McCann, Inc., New York, 1999.

- "How Six Men Traveled Through the Wide World" and "The Six Servants" from *The Complete Grimm's Fairy Tales.* Introduction by Padraic Colum and commentary by Joseph Campbell. Pantheon Books, Inc., New York, 1976.

- "How Six Men Traveled Through the Wide World" in Andrew Lang (Ed.) *The Yellow Fairy Book.* Dover Publications Inc., New York, 1979.

- Mahy, Margaret, and Jean and Mon-Sien Tsaug. *The Seven Chinese Brothers.* Scholastic Inc., New York, 1992.

Software

- *Carmen Sandiego Math Detective* provides practice with math facts, estimation, ordering numbers, and word problems.

- *Graph Master* allows students to organize.data and create graphs.

- *Ice Cream Truck* develops problem solving, money skills, and arithmetic operations.

- *Kid Pix* allows students to create their own illustrations.

- *Math Mysteries Measurement* develops multistep problem solving with distance, weight, and capacity.

- *Math Mysteries: Whole Numbers* is a series of structured word problems dealing with whole numbers.

- *Number Facts Fire Zapper* provides practice with math facts in an arcade-like game.

- *Number Sense—Puzzle Tanks* develops logical thinking while practicing math facts.

- *Ten Tricky Tiles* provides practice with math facts through engaging puzzles.

PREPARING FOR UPCOMING LESSONS

Place pattern blocks, square-inch tiles, and base-ten pieces in a learning center for students to explore.

BACKGROUND

Data About Us

This unit introduces students to fourth-grade mathematics. We want students to learn mathematics by solving problems using a variety of strategies and to be able to communicate both solutions and methods. The content in fourth grade builds upon work in earlier grades.

The first lesson introduces a fictional classroom of students. Students in this Chicago classroom collect and organize data about each other in order to describe themselves to their pen pals in Arizona. Within this context, students learn how to use variables and averages (medians) as they solve problems and review methods for collecting and displaying data.

The TIMS Laboratory Method and the Importance of Variables

This unit reviews (or introduces) the four steps of the TIMS Laboratory Method: drawing a picture, collecting and organizing data in a data table, graphing the data, and analyzing the results. This method is discussed in the TIMS Tutor: *The TIMS Laboratory Method* in the *Teacher Implementation Guide.*

The four steps of the TIMS Laboratory Method will be familiar to students who have had *Math Trailblazers* before. Others may need experiences with the method to get accustomed to the routines. Although we want students eventually to apply this method on their own, many may need to be guided at first. One of your more difficult instructional decisions will be how much guidance to give—how to balance imitation and autonomy. Learning by imitation will make for more orderly lessons, not an unimportant consideration in the beginning of the year. On the other hand, too much imitation can undermine student autonomy and can foster misconceptions about what mathematics and science are. As the year progresses, you will want to see students doing more work on their own with little teacher guidance.

In this unit, students will use bar graphs and point graphs. Since the degree of familiarity with graphing and the TIMS Laboratory Method will vary from class to class, we offer a range of approaches in the first lab, *Arm Span vs. Height.* We build flexibility into the lab so that you can adapt it to the needs of your classroom while you are getting to know your students. One aspect of the method to stress in these early experiments is how the real objects, the picture, the data table(s), and the graph(s) all represent the same situation. Many students benefit from discussions connecting and comparing these various representations.

In this first lab, your students will investigate the relationship between two variables, the arm span and the height of their classmates. Variables are an important part of both mathematics and science. Several TIMS Tutors in the *Teacher Implementation Guide* provide background about different kinds of variables and how to handle them. One of the main variables explored in this unit is length. See the TIMS Tutor: *Length* in the *Teacher Implementation Guide.*

Several basic procedures for handling variables are involved in this unit: distinguishing between variables and values, denoting variables by symbols, and labeling data table columns and graph axes with variable names. Students learn to use more specific terminology for variables—numerical and categorical variables. Variables that have numbers as their values are **numerical;** variables that have nonnumerical values are **categorical.** For example, number of pets and height are numerical variables. Categorical variables your students may study in this first unit are eye color or favorite sport.

Stress that an experiment is an investigation about relationships between variables. For example, in the experiment *Arm Span vs. Height,* students will determine whether they can predict a fourth-grader's height given his or her arm span.

Group Work and Communication

The unit helps establish a classroom atmosphere that promotes working collaboratively, engages students in discourse, and emphasizes the use of manipulatives. Group work enables children to tackle hard problems and generate many solution strategies. We realize teachers may use their own set of structures when organizing student groups. We also know that a strategy that works for one teacher may not be appropriate for another. Therefore, we offer general suggestions for organizing students in groups in the early units. These appear as TIMS Tips in the Lesson Guides.

As students work in groups to solve problems and to collect and organize data, they will talk and write about their methods and solutions including their struggles and successes. Their abilities to communicate both orally and in writing will improve as they practice these skills in their math and language arts classes. Students' early explanations may be brief and poorly stated, but they will become more complete as students continue to talk and write about mathematics. For more information about writing and communication, see the TIMS Tutor: *Journals* in the *Teacher Implementation Guide*.

Review and Practice

Every unit includes a section in the *Unit Resource Guide* called the Daily Practice and Problems (DPP). This set of short exercises provides distributed practice in computation and a structure for the review of the math facts. It develops concepts and skills such as number sense, mental math, telling time, and working with money and reviews topics from earlier units. A Daily Practice and Problems Guide categorizes the items so that you can locate a problem that reviews a specific concept or skill. (See the Daily Practice and Problems Guide for this unit for a description of the math facts work in this unit.) The Daily Practice and Problems is also available on the *Teacher Resource CD*.

Every unit includes a Home Practice section in the *Discovery Assignment Book*. It is a series of problems that supplement the homework included in the lessons. The Home Practice distributes skills practice throughout the units and reviews concepts studied in previous units. At the end of each Lesson Guide in the Suggestions for Teaching the Lesson are suggestions for using both the Daily Practice and Problems and the Home Practice. For more information, see the Scope and Sequence for the Daily Practice and Problems and Home Practice and the *Daily Practice and Problems and Home Practice Guide*. Both documents are in the *Teacher Implementation Guide*.

Resources

- Goldberg, Howard, and F. David Boulanger. "Science for Elementary School Teachers: A Quantitative Approach." *American Journal of Physics* 49 (2), pp. 121–127, 1981.

- Goldberg, Howard, and Philip Wagreich. "A Model Integrated Mathematics and Science Program for the Elementary School." *International Journal of Educational Research* 14 (2), pp. 193–214, 1990.

- Haldane, J.B.S. "On Being the Right Size." In James R. Newman (ed.), *The World of Mathematics, Volume Two.* Simon and Schuster, New York, 1956. (Essay originally published in 1928.)

- Isaacs, Andrew C., and Catherine Randall Kelso. "Pictures, Tables, Graphs, and Questions: Statistical Processes." *Teaching Children Mathematics* 2 (6), pp. 340–345, 1996.

- Isaacs, Andrew C., Philip Wagreich, and Martin Gartzman. "The Quest for Integration: School Mathematics and Science." *American Journal of Education,* 106 (1), pp. 179–206, 1997.

- Kagan, Spencer. *Cooperative Learning.* Kagan Publishing, San Clemente, CA, 1997.

- *Principles and Standards for School Mathematics.* National Council of Teachers of Mathematics, Reston, VA, 2000.

Assessment Indicators

Use these indicators to assess students on the key ideas in this unit. The Assessment Indicators are also listed on the *Observational Assessment Record*. The Assessment section of the *Teacher Implementation Guide* contains a set of blackline masters that list the Assessment Indicators for each unit in order. This set is called the *Individual Assessment Record Sheet*. You can use these blackline masters to document each student's growth over time. The *Individual Assessment Record Sheet* can be included in students' portfolios.

- Can students identify categorical and numerical variables?
- Can students find the median of a data set?
- Can students make and interpret bar graphs?
- Can students make and interpret point graphs?
- Can students use patterns in data tables and graphs to make predictions?
- Can students measure length in inches?
- Do students demonstrate fluency with the addition facts?

OBSERVATIONAL ASSESSMENT RECORD

(A1) Can students identify categorical and numerical variables?

(A2) Can students find the median of a data set?

(A3) Can students make and interpret bar graphs?

(A4) Can students make and interpret point graphs?

(A5) Can students use patterns in data tables and graphs to make predictions?

(A6) Can students measure length in inches?

(A7) Do students demonstrate fluency with the addition facts?

(A8) _____

Name	A1	A2	A3	A4	A5	A6	A7	A8	Comments
1.									
2.									
3.									
4.									
5.									
6.									
7.									
8.									
9.									
10.									
11.									
12.									
13.									

Name	A1	A2	A3	A4	A5	A6	A7	A8	Comments
14.									
15.									
16.									
17.									
18.									
19.									
20.									
21.									
22.									
23.									
24.									
25.									
26.									
27.									
28.									
29.									
30.									
31.									
32.									

Daily Practice and Problems

Data About Us

A DPP Menu for Unit 1

Icons in the Teacher Notes column designate the subject matter of each Daily Practice and Problems (DPP) item. Each item falls into one or more of the categories listed below. A brief menu of the DPP items included in Unit 1 follows.

N Number Sense P, S, U, V	**Computation** B, D, L, N, P	**Time** G, I, O	**Geometry** F, H
Math Facts A–E, K, M	**$ Money** L, N	**Measurement** R, S, V	**Data** J, Q, T, U

The Daily Practice and Problems, found at the beginning of each unit, is a set of short exercises that:

- provides distributed practice in computation and a structure for systematic study of the basic math facts;
- develops concepts and skills such as number sense, mental math, telling time, and working with money throughout the year; and
- reviews topics from earlier units, presenting concepts in new contexts and linking ideas from unit to unit.

There are three types of items: Bits, Tasks, and Challenges. Bits are short and should take no more than five or ten minutes to complete. They usually provide practice with a skill or the basic math facts. Tasks take ten or fifteen minutes to complete. Challenges usually take longer than fifteen minutes to complete, and the problems are more thought-provoking. They can be used to stretch students' problem-solving skills.

Two DPP items are included for each class session listed in the Unit Outline. The first item is always a Bit and the second is either a Task or a Challenge. Refer to the *Daily Practice and Problems and Home Practice Guide* in the *Teacher Implementation Guide* for further information on how and when to use the DPP. A Scope and Sequence Chart for the Daily Practice and Problems for the year can be found in the *Teacher Implementation Guide*.

Practice and Assessment of Math Facts

Students are expected to demonstrate fluency with the math facts according to the following timetable.

- By the end of second grade: addition and subtraction facts
- By the end of third grade: multiplication facts
- By the end of fourth grade: division facts
- During fifth grade: review multiplication and division facts

Many DPP items for this first unit of fourth grade review the addition facts. DPP items for Unit 2 review the subtraction facts. DPP items for Unit 3 begin a systematic review of the multiplication facts and launch a study of the division facts. This work with the facts will continue throughout the DPP in subsequent units.

Aside from reviewing the addition facts, the DPP for this unit includes two diagnostic tests. These tests which are assigned in Bits (items K and M) can be found at the end of the DPP section. The first test, *Doubles, 2s, 3s,* contains those addition facts that can be solved with the strategies using doubles and counting on. The second test, *More Addition Facts,* contains those facts that can be solved using the strategies making a ten, using a ten, and reasoning from known facts. For descriptions of these addition facts strategies, see the TIMS Tutor: *Math Facts* in the *Teacher Implementation Guide*.

These short diagnostic tests, which do not include all of the addition facts, are less threatening and as effective as longer tests. Tests of all the facts for any operation have a very limited role. Since we rarely, if ever, need to recall 100 facts at one time in the real world, overemphasizing tests of all the facts reinforces the notion that math is nothing more than rote memorization and has no connection to the real world. Tests which include a small number of facts give teachers, students, and parents the information needed to continue learning and practicing the facts efficiently. The goal of the math facts assessment program is to determine the degree to which students can find answers to fact problems quickly and accurately and whether they can retain this skill over time. For more information about the distribution of math facts practice and assessment, see the TIMS Tutor: *Math Facts* and the Assessment section in the *Teacher Implementation Guide*.

After you give each diagnostic test to your students, you will be able to identify which students need practice. Those who can find answers quickly and efficiently will continue to practice the addition and subtraction facts throughout the year as they engage in labs, activities, and games, and as they solve problems in the DPP. However, for those students who need extra practice, we have developed the Addition and Subtraction Math Facts Review. This section, which includes games, activities, and flash cards, can be found in the *Grade 4 Facts Resource Guide*. The Teacher Notes for the diagnostic tests in this unit (items K and M) will refer you to the Addition and Subtraction Math Facts Review section and will suggest which activities you should assign after each of the diagnostic tests.

The use of the activities, games, and flash cards in the Addition and Subtraction Math Facts Review should be distributed over time. Practicing small groups of facts often (for short periods of time) is more effective than practicing many facts less often (for long periods of time). Use of strategies, calculators, and printed addition and subtraction tables allows students to continue to develop number sense and work on interesting problems and experiments while they are learning the facts. In this way, students who need extra practice are not prevented from learning more complex mathematics because they do not know all the math facts.

Daily Practice and Problems

Students may solve the items individually, in groups, or as a class. The items may also be assigned for homework.

Student Questions	Teacher Notes

 Triangle Sums 1

What do you notice about the numbers in this triangle?

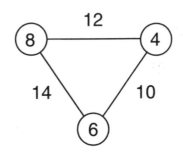

Find the missing numbers in these triangles.

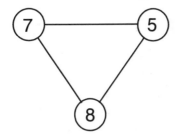

TIMS Bit

Students should see that the numbers in the circles, when added together, result in the number on the line that connects them. These puzzles require both logical thinking and knowledge of addition and subtraction facts.

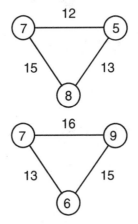

 Addition Practice

1. 20 + 30 + 10 =

2. 40 + 10 + 20 =

3. 50 + 40 + 20 =

4. 60 + 60 + 10 =

5. 70 + 60 + 20 =

TIMS Task

Encourage students to share their strategies. Some students might use paper and pencil to solve the problems while other students solve them in their heads using skip counting and other counting strategies.

1. 60

2. 70

3. 110

4. 130

5. 150

Student Questions	Teacher Notes

C Triangle Sums 2

Find the missing numbers in these triangles.

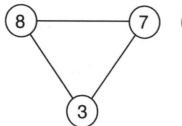

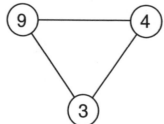

8
7
3

9
4
3

TIMS Bit

15
8
7
11
10
3

13
9
4
12
7
3

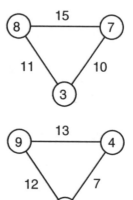

D More Addition Practice

1. 70 + 40 =
2. 60 + 50 + 20 =
3. 80 + 50 =
4. 60 + 90 =
5. 130 + 90 =

TIMS Task

Encourage students to share their strategies. Some students might use paper and pencil to solve the problems while other students solve them in their heads using strategies such as *using a ten, making a ten,* or *reasoning from known facts.* For descriptions of these addition fact strategies, see the TIMS Tutor: *Math Facts* in the *Teacher Implementation Guide.*

1. 110
2. 130
3. 130
4. 150
5. 220

Student Questions	Teacher Notes

 Triangle Sums 3

Notice that numbers in the circles are missing in each of the triangle problems below. Find the missing numbers.

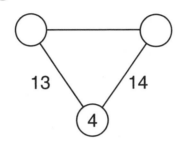

TIMS Bit

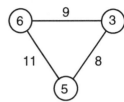

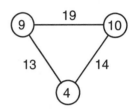

 Counting Squares

How many squares can you find in the figure?

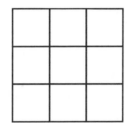

TIMS Task

Size	Number of Squares
1 × 1	9
2 × 2	4
3 × 3	$\dfrac{1}{14}$ = total squares

 Reading Time

Tell what time each clock face is showing.

1.

2.

3.

4.

5.

6.

7.

8.

TIMS Bit

1. 9:00   2. 11:30

3. 12:20   4. 5:00

5. 1:45   6. 4:40

7. 6:30   8. 2:15

Student Questions

H Counting Rectangles

How many rectangles can you find in this figure?

Teacher Notes

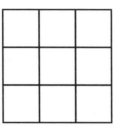

TIMS Challenge

If necessary, remind the students that a square is a special kind of rectangle.

Square rectangles

Size	Number
1×1	9
2×2	4
3×3	1
	14 square rectangles

Non-square rectangles

Size	Number
1×2	6
2×1	6
1×3	3
3×1	3
2×3	2
3×2	2
	22 non-square rectangles

Total:

14 + 22 = 36 rectangles

Student Questions	Teacher Notes
I **Time 1** 1. What is the time now? 2. What time will it be 20 minutes from now? 3. What time will it be $1\frac{1}{2}$ hours from now?	**TIMS Bit** **Answers will vary.**
J **Variables and Values** Mrs. Dewey's class will investigate the variables listed below during its field trip to a baseball game. Decide if each variable is numerical or categorical. Then, name three possible values for each variable. Number of Seats in Each Row Type of Shoe Kind of Drink Size of Drink Type of Food Type of Shirt Class Size	**TIMS Task** **Number of Seats in Each Row: numerical: 15, 20, 30, etc.** **Type of Shoe: categorical: gym shoe, sandal, dress shoe, school shoe** **Kind of Drink: categorical: lemonade, orange drink, cola** **Size of Drink: categorical: small, medium, large; or numerical: 8 oz, 12 oz, 16 oz** **Type of Food: categorical: popcorn, hot dogs, pizza, ice cream** **Type of Shirt: categorical: t-shirt, long-sleeve shirt, sweatshirt** **Class Size: numerical: 25 students, 26 students, 27 students, 33 students, etc., or categorical: small, medium, large**

Student Questions	Teacher Notes
K Addition Test: *Doubles, 2s, 3s* Take the diagnostic test *Doubles, 2s, 3s.* Your teacher will suggest some additional activities if you need more practice.	**TIMS Bit** This diagnostic test, located at the end of this DPP section, will allow you to identify students who need extra practice on the addition facts that can be solved using the strategies *using doubles* and *counting on.* For a description of these strategies, see the TIMS Tutor: *Math Facts* in the *Teacher Implementation Guide.* We recommend 1 minute for this test. Allow students to change pens after the time is up and complete the remaining problems in a different color. Students who need more practice can complete some of the activities provided in the Addition and Subtraction Math Facts Review section in the *Grade 4 Facts Resource Guide.* The games, *Add 1, 2, 3* and *Path to Glory,* provide practice with adding 1, 2, and 3.

Student Questions	Teacher Notes
L Tom's and Tim's Savings	

L Tom's and Tim's Savings

1. Tom wants to buy a book that costs \$2.95. He can save 50¢ a week. How many weeks will he need to save to have enough for the book?
2. Tim is saving to buy a skateboard. He can buy a used one from a friend for \$10. He has \$5.50 now and can save 75¢ a week. How long will it take him to save enough for the skateboard?

TIMS Task

Ask the students to share their solutions. Possible solutions include:

1. **6 weeks; Tom needs almost \$3. It takes 2 weeks to save \$1, so it would take 3 × 2 = 6 weeks to save \$3.**

   Another solution: Skip count by 50 until 300 is reached, and count the number of 50s.
2. **6 weeks; Tim needs \$10.00 − \$5.50 = \$4.50. He can save 75¢ in one week, \$1.50 in 2 weeks, \$3.00 in 4 weeks, and \$4.50 in 6 weeks.**

Student Questions	Teacher Notes

M Addition Test: *More Addition Facts*

Take the diagnostic test *More Addition Facts.* Your teacher will suggest some additional activities if you need more practice.

TIMS Bit

This diagnostic test, located at the end of this DPP section, will allow you to identify students who need extra practice on the "harder" addition facts: 4s, 5s, 6s, 7s, 8s, and 9s. The answers to these facts can be found using strategies such as *using a ten, making a ten,* and *using known facts.* For descriptions of these addition fact strategies, see the TIMS Tutor: *Math Facts* in the *Teacher Implementation Guide.*

We recommend 1 minute for this test. You may want to allow students to change pens after the time is up and complete the remaining problems in a different color.

Students who need more practice can complete some of the activities provided in the Addition and Subtraction Math Facts Review section in the *Grade 4 Facts Resource Guide.* Some appropriate activities are: *Add 4, 5, 6, Addition War, Triangle Flash Cards, Mixed-Up Addition Tables,* and *Line Math.*

Student Questions	Teacher Notes
N Count Your Change You go to the store with \$5.00. You buy 2 items which cost \$1.50 each. You also have to pay sales tax of 7¢ for every dollar spent. How much change will you get back?	**TIMS Task** Items cost a total of \$3.00. Sales tax is 3 × 7¢ = 21¢. Total spent is \$3.21. Change will be \$5.00 − \$3.21 = \$1.79.
O Time 2 1. What is the time now? 2. What time was it 30 minutes ago? 3. What time was it 45 minutes ago?	**TIMS Bit** Answers will vary.

Student Questions	Teacher Notes

P Sharing Pennies

Suppose you had 100 pennies. How can you divide them as evenly as possible into 3 shares? Write a number sentence to go with your answer.

TIMS Task

N

Possible number sentences include: $100 \div 3 = 33$ R1 and $33 + 33 + 33 + 1 = 100$. Ask students to share their strategies. Possible strategies include:

1. **Use base-ten pieces: Deal them out evenly into 3 piles. There will be 3 tens in each pile. The last ten can be broken into 10 ones. Deal these out evenly. Each pile will have 3 tens and 3 ones. There will be one left over.**

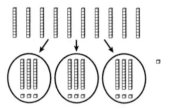

2. **Use shorthand to represent base-ten pieces: Draw three circles. Lines can represent tens, dots can represent ones. Deal lines and dots into circles as described in 1.**
3. **Use pennies or other counters.**
4. **Use a calculator.**

Student Questions | **Teacher Notes**

Q Sandwiches

The school cafeteria asked students how they liked their sandwiches cut. The bar graph displays the data.

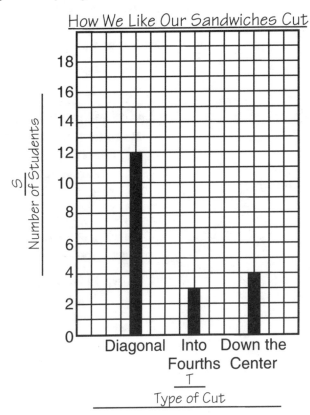

How We Like Our Sandwiches Cut
18
16
14
12
10
8
6
4
2
0
S
Number of Students
Diagonal
Into Fourths
Down the Center
T
Type of Cut

Describe three things that the graph tells you.

TIMS Bit

Answers will vary. Three possible responses are listed below.

1. **The most common type of cut preferred is the diagonal cut.**
2. **The number of students asked is 19.**
3. **The number of students who prefer the diagonal cut is four times as many as those who prefer their sandwich cut into fourths.**

R Measuring

Measure each of the lines below twice. First measure the line to the nearest inch. Then, measure it to the nearest centimeter.

1. ______________________________

2. ____________________

3. _______________________________________

TIMS Task

1. **3 inches; 8 cm**
2. **2 inches; 5 cm**
3. **4 inches; 10 cm**

Student Questions	Teacher Notes

Measurement: Could Be or Crazy

Decide whether each measurement is a "could be" measurement or a "crazy" measurement. No fair measuring! Explain how you decided.

1. The distance from a doorknob to the floor is 30 cm.
2. The distance from a doorknob to the floor is 40 inches.
3. The face of a watch is 3 cm wide.
4. A fourth grader's foot is 20 inches long.
5. A car is 3 meters long.

TIMS Bit

This TIMS bit is a good item to discuss orally. Show students a ruler with centimeters and inches. Point out that the ruler is 12 inches long and about 30 centimeters. They can use the ruler as a point of reference.

1. **Crazy: The number of cm on a 12-inch ruler is 30 cm.**
2. **Could be: Fourth-graders are between 50 and 60 inches tall. A yardstick is 36 inches. A meterstick is about 39 inches.**
3. **Could be: I once measured the width of my wrist and it's about 4 cm.**
4. **Crazy: 20 inches is longer than a 12-inch ruler.**
5. **Could be.**

Name ______________________ Date ______________

Doubles, 2s, 3s

3 + 3 = ______	3 + 6 = ______
5 + 5 = ______	3 + 8 = ______
3 + 5 = ______	9 + 9 = ______
6 + 2 = ______	2 + 4 = ______
3 + 7 = ______	6 + 6 = ______
4 + 4 = ______	3 + 4 = ______
2 + 7 = ______	7 + 7 = ______
8 + 2 = ______	8 + 8 = ______

Name ______________________________ Date ______________

More Addition Facts

5 + 4 = ________ 9 + 5 = ________

6 + 7 = ________ 4 + 6 = ________

4 + 7 = ________ 6 + 8 = ________

8 + 4 = ________ 9 + 4 = ________

9 + 6 = ________ 7 + 8 = ________

7 + 9 = ________ 5 + 6 = ________

5 + 7 = ________ 8 + 9 = ________

8 + 5 = ________ 9 + 3 = ________

10 + 4 = ________ 10 + 9 = ________

LESSON GUIDE 1

Getting to Know Room 204

Estimated Class Sessions: 1–2

Students are introduced to Room 204, a fictional classroom of 22 children, through a class picture, data table, and graph. Students analyze Room 204's data as well as collect, organize, and graph data that describe their own classroom. Students are introduced to the terms variables and values.

Key Content

- Connecting mathematics and science to real-world situations.
- Gathering, organizing, graphing, and analyzing data.
- Making and interpreting bar graphs.
- Establishing norms for working cooperatively.
- Naming values of variables.
- Describing a classroom of students using variables.

Key Vocabulary

bar graph
horizontal axis
value
variable
vertical axis

Daily Practice and Problems:
Bit for Lesson 1

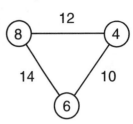

A. Triangle Sums 1 (URG p. 11)

What do you notice about the numbers in this triangle?

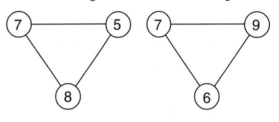

Find the missing numbers in these triangles.

DPP Task is on page 33. Suggestions for using the DPPs are on page 33.

Curriculum Sequence

Before This Unit

Variables and Values. Throughout first, second, and third grades, students in *Math Trailblazers* have identified variables and their values in experiments and activities. See the following lessons in Grade 3 for examples: Unit 1 Lesson 3 and Unit 14 Lesson 4.

Bar Graphs. Since kindergarten, students in *Math Trailblazers* have interpreted data in bar graphs and have collected and displayed their own data using bar graphs. For examples, see Grade 3 Units 1, 5, 14, and 16.

After This Unit

Variables and Values. In Lesson 2 of this unit, students will distinguish between categorical and numerical variables.

Work with variables will appear many times in Grade 4. See the labs in Units 2, 5, and 8 for examples.

Bar Graphs. Students will interpret and create bar graphs in many activities throughout the year. In Units 13 and 14, students will use bar graphs to display their data collected in *TV Survey* and the lab, *Rolling One Number Cube*.

Materials List

Print Materials for Students

	Math Facts and Daily Practice and Problems	Activity	Homework
Student Books — Student Guide		*Getting to Know Room 204* Pages 2–5	*Getting to Know Room 204* Homework Section Pages 5–6
Student Books — Discovery Assignment Book			Home Practice Part 1 Page 3
Teacher Resources — Facts Resource Guide ◎	DPP Items 1A–1B		
Teacher Resources — Unit Resource Guide ◎	DPP Items A–B Page 11		
Teacher Resources — Generic Section ◎		*Centimeter Graph Paper,* 2 per student and *Three-column Data Table,* 1 per student group (optional)	

◎ *available on Teacher Resource CD*

All Transparency Masters, Blackline Masters, and Assessment Blackline Masters in the Unit Resource Guide are on the Teacher Resource CD.

Materials for the Teacher

Bar Graph I: What's Wrong Here? Transparency Master (Unit Resource Guide) Page 36

Observational Assessment Record (Unit Resource Guide, Pages 7–8 and Teacher Resource CD)

For class data tables:

    3 pieces of poster-size graph paper, 3 pieces of easel paper, or several transparencies of the *Three-column Data Table* (Unit Resource Guide, Generic Section)

For class graph:

    1 piece of poster-size graph paper or transparency of *Centimeter Graph Paper* (Unit Resource Guide, Generic Section)

Developing the Activity

Part 1. Identifying Variables and Values

On the *Getting to Know Room 204* Activity Pages in the *Student Guide,* students are introduced to Mrs. Dewey's fourth-grade classroom. Throughout the year, the fictional students in Room 204 will appear in lessons to offer their own data for analysis and to share their ideas and explanations.

In the opening pages, the students in Room 204 discuss what they can share about themselves and what they want to know about their pen pals. Point students' attention to the two-column data table entitled "Room 204's Main Interests." The variable that Room 204 chose to study is main interest. The table also lists values of this variable.

A **variable** is an attribute or quantity that may have one or many different values. Point out that the *variable,* main interest, varies from student to student. The **values** are the possible outcomes for the variable. For example, animals, sports, reading, and music are possible values of the variable, main interest.

> **TIMS Tip**
>
> On the *Getting to Know Room 204* Activity Pages in the *Student Guide,* we offer Room 204's data tables and graph as examples. Adapt this lesson depending upon the needs and interests of your students as well as your own personal teaching style. You may choose to introduce the lesson using the *Student Guide* pages or you may choose to use the pages as closure after your class has collected, organized, and graphed their own data. Reading the *Student Guide* after taking part in the activities is helpful for second language learners and students with limited reading abilities.

In ***Question 1,*** the class makes a table listing variables it can study and possible values for those variables. First, have students work in small groups to gather ideas. Ask them to list variables and values in a data table as shown in Figure 1. Then, pull the class together and list some of their ideas on a class data table. Create a class data table on easel paper, poster-size graph paper, or transparencies of the *Three-column Data Table.* Students experiencing difficulty in understanding the terms variable and value will probably find concrete examples most helpful. See Figure 1 for examples.

> **TIMS Tip**
>
> Save the class data table created in ***Question 1*** for further discussion later in the activity and for use in Lesson 2. In Lesson 2 the third column will be filled in.

Getting to Know Room 204

The class picture at the beginning of this unit shows Mrs. Dewey's fourth-grade class. Their classroom is Room 204 in the Bessie Coleman Elementary School in Chicago, Illinois. Mrs. Dewey's class wants to share information about themselves with their pen pals at Westmont School in Phoenix, Arizona. They also want to get to know their pen pals.

Mrs. Dewey asked her class what they would like to know about their new pen pals. Tanya said, "I'd like to know what they are interested in. I love to read. I can recommend some really good books!"

Roller blading

Jessie said, "I wonder if they have some really cool trails in Arizona! I love to ride my bike and roller blade!"

Keenya said, "I'll probably ask my pen pal to tell me about her favorite food, her favorite holiday, and her favorite color. I'll also ask if she plays an instrument. I'm learning to play a keyboard."

Keyboard

"I'll ask my pen pal about the color of his hair and eyes, and whether he is short or tall," said Jerome.

John said, "I'll ask my pen pal what his favorite sport is. I like soccer and basketball."

2 SG · Grade 4 · Unit 1 · Lesson 1 Getting to Know Room 204

***Student Guide* - Page 2**

Values and Variables

The students in Room 204 decided to collect data they would like to share about their class. They started by making a list of things they wanted to learn about one another. They made the following chart of the variables they chose to study and possible values for each variable. A **variable** is an attribute or quantity that may have one or many different values. The possible outcomes for each variable are called **values.**

Variables and Possible Values

Variable	Possible Values
Interests	Sports, Reading, Outdoor Activities, Playing Games, Music, Animals, etc.
Eye color	Blue, Hazel, Green, Brown
Favorite food	Pizza, Tacos, Liver, Chicken

Mrs. Dewey's class decided to collect data about the variable, main interest. The main interests in Room 204 varied from student to student. Some students chose reading as their main interest, while others chose animals, sports, music, outdoor activities, or playing games. These possible outcomes are the values of the variable.

Discuss

1. What would you like to learn about the students in your class? Make a table like the one above, listing variables you can study about your classmates and possible values for each of the variables.

Room 204's Main Interests

Name	Interest
Linda	Animals
John	Sports
Tanya	Reading
Shannon	Reading
Jerome	Games
Romesh	Animals
Ana	Outdoors
Jackie	Sports
Nicholas	Animals
Ming	Sports
Luis	Music
Jacob	Reading
Jessie	Sports
Keenya	Music
Nila	Sports
Michael	Reading
Roberto	Outdoors
Irma	Reading
Maya	Sports
Lee Yah	Sports
Frank	Music
Grace	Sports

Getting to Know Room 204 SG · Grade 4 · Unit 1 · Lesson 1 3

***Student Guide* - Page 3**

Since students will often work in groups throughout the year, introduce routines that encourage effective group work as part of these first activities. For example, to generate a list of variables, groups can use a cooperative learning structure known as Roundtable. Give each group a copy of a *Three-column Data Table*. (See Figure 1 for table headings.) To begin, one group member writes a variable in the left-hand column of the data table, and the other members take turns listing possible values for the variable. As discussion continues, each member of the group has a chance to write a variable in the data table as well as to add possible values. If a student cannot think of a variable or value, he or she may ask for help from the rest of the group.

A whole-class discussion of the reports from the groups should follow. Use the class data table to record students' ideas.

Part 2. Collecting, Graphing, and Exploring the Data

After students have generated a list of variables and their possible values, ask them to choose one variable to study *(Question 2)*. Some variables listed in your table might have values that are numbers, such as number of people in your family or height in inches. Choose a variable that does *not* have numerical values such as main interest or eye color. Students will work with numerical values in Lesson 2. Students will collect data on the chosen variable, organize the data, and make a bar graph.

It is important that the variable you choose to study be well-defined and that it involves quick and easy data collection. For example, if you are studying students' birth places, define what is meant by birth place. The values of the variable, birth place, could be the states in which the students were born, the countries in which they were born, or the actual place their mothers gave birth (e.g., home, hospital, or ambulance). Some students might not even know

Variables	Possible Values	
Number of People in Family	2, 3, 4, 5, 6, 7, etc.	
Languages Spoken	Spanish, Polish, English	
Birthday Month	January, February, etc.	
Number of Blocks from School	1, 2, 3, etc.	
Height	49 in, 50 in, 51 in, 52 in, etc.	
Eye Color	Brown, Blue, Hazel, Green	
Length of Hair	Short, Medium, Long	
Hand Length	13 cm, 14 cm, 15 cm, etc.	
Main Interest	Animals, Sports, Reading, Music, etc.	
Favorite Color	Blue, Green, Orange, etc.	
Favorite Playground Game	Hopscotch, Jump rope, Tag, etc.	
Proudest Achievement	Learning how to swim, Running a mile, Performing at a recital, Making pancakes for the first time, Getting good grades	

Figure 1: *Sample table of variables and values*

that may be asked to guide such a discussion. ***Question 7*** asks students to describe their graphs. Possible descriptions of the graph of the Room 204 data in Figure 4 include the following:

- The most common eye color is brown.
- Almost half of the class has brown eyes.
- Almost the same number of students have hazel, green, and blue eyes.
- If a new student came to our class, I might predict that he or she has brown eyes.

Questions 8–10 ask similar questions about the graph for Room 204's Main Interests. The students in Room 204 graphed the variable, Main Interest, on the horizontal axis and the variable, Number of Students, on the vertical axis ***(Question 8).*** The tallest bar tells us that sports is the most common main interest in Room 204 ***(Question 9).*** Four more students prefer to read than play games ***(Question 10).***

Suggestions for Teaching the Lesson

Math Facts

- Students using *Math Trailblazers* are expected to demonstrate fluency with all the math facts by the end of fourth-grade. Fluency with the addition and subtraction facts was assessed in second grade and fluency with the multiplication facts was assessed in third grade. Beginning in Unit 3, the fourth grade materials review the multiplication facts and begin work on the division facts.

  In Unit 1, DPP items K and M provide opportunities to identify students who do not yet have fluency with the addition facts. For those students who do need extra practice with these facts, use the Addition and Subtraction Math Facts Review section in the *Grade 4 Facts Resource Guide.* This section includes diagnostic tests, activities, and games to identify and practice the facts they need to learn. Students should work on these facts using the suggested sequence of activities at home with their families or in school with resource teachers or parent volunteers. At the same time they should continue with the normal fourth-grade lessons using strategies, calculators, and printed facts tables to assist them as they solve problems. In this way they will not be prevented from learning more rigorous mathematics while they are working on the math facts.
- DPP Bit A uses puzzles to provide practice with addition facts. DPP Task B provides more practice with addition facts using multiples of ten.

Explore

3. What variable is on the horizontal axis (⟷) on your graph?
4. What variable is on the vertical axis (↕) on your graph?
5. A. Which bar is the tallest on your graph?
   B. What does the tallest bar represent?
6. A. Which bar is the shortest on your graph?
   B. What does the shortest bar represent?
7. What else does your graph tell you about your class?
8. A. Look back at Room 204's graph. Which variable did they graph on the horizontal axis?
   B. Which variable did they graph on the vertical axis?
9. What does the tallest bar on their graph represent?
10. How many more students prefer to read than play games?

Homework

You will need a sheet of *Centimeter Graph Paper* to complete Question 6.

1. Another fourth grade class at Bessie Coleman School, Mrs. Cook's class, collected data to share with their pen pals. What variable did they study?
2. What does the tallest bar on their graph represent?
3. What do the shortest bars on Room 206's graph represent?
4. How many more students speak Spanish as their primary language than Assyrian?
5. What else does this graph tell you about Mrs. Cook's class?

Languages Spoken in 206
Number of People
N
English
Urdu
Spanish
Romanian
Hebrew
Greek
Assyrian
Korean
Gujarati
Primary Language Spoken
L

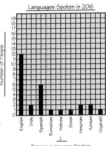

Getting to Know Room 204 SG • Grade 4 • Unit 1 • Lesson 1 5

***Student Guide* - Page 5**

Daily Practice and Problems: Task for Lesson 1

B. Task: Addition Practice (URG p. 11)

1. 20 + 30 + 10 =
2. 40 + 10 + 20 =
3. 50 + 40 + 20 =
4. 60 + 60 + 10 =
5. 70 + 60 + 20 =

Dear Family Member:

Your child is learning about his or her classmates by collecting data and displaying the data in a bar graph. Use the graph on the previous page as a model for graphing the data in Question 6. Remind your child to title the graph and label the axes.

6. Room 204's pen pals in Phoenix sent back data on their favorite subjects. Use the data to create a bar graph. Remember to label the axes and title your graph.

7. A. What variable is on the horizontal axis?
   B. What variable is on the vertical axis?

8. Answer the following questions based on the graph you created in Question 6.
   A. What is the most common favorite subject?
   B. What is the least common favorite subject?
   C. Which of the subjects in the data table is your favorite?
   D. How many of the Phoenix pen pals have the same favorite subject as you do?

9. How many students are in the Phoenix class? Explain how you know.

Favorite Subjects

Favorite Subject	Number of Students
Writing	2
Social Studies	3
Math	8
Reading	2
Spelling	6
Science	7

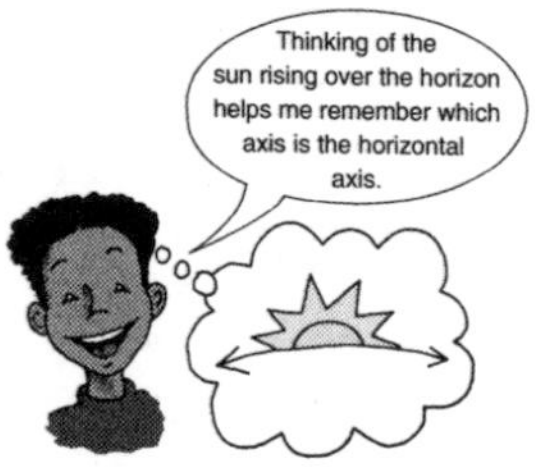
Thinking of the sun rising over the horizon helps me remember which axis is the horizontal axis.

6 SG · Grade 4 · Unit 1 · Lesson 1 Getting to Know Room 204

***Student Guide* - Page 6**

Name ______________________ Date ____________

Unit 1: Home Practice

Part 1 Practice

Solve the following addition problems. Try to solve the problems without paper and pencil. Be prepared to share your solution strategies.

1. 8 + 3 + 5 = ________
2. 9 + 7 + 5 = ________
3. 6 + 8 + 6 = ________
4. 4 + 8 + 9 = ________
5. 70 + 30 = ________
6. 60 + 20 + 30 = ________
7. 50 + 70 = ________
8. 30 + 50 + 70 = ________
9. 20 + 85 = ________
10. 10 + 80 + 15 = ________

Part 2 Variables and Values

Look around your home and find four variables. Find two numerical variables and two categorical variables. Then, name some values for each of your variables. Be prepared to discuss and compare your findings. For example: Type of drinks is a categorical variable. Some values for this variable are iced tea, milk, and fruit juice.

1. Variable: ______________ numerical or categorical (circle one)
   Values of your variable:
2. Variable: ______________ numerical or categorical (circle one)
   Values of your variable:
3. Variable: ______________ numerical or categorical (circle one)
   Values of your variable:
4. Variable: ______________ numerical or categorical (circle one)
   Values of your variable:

DATA ABOUT US DAB · Grade 4 · Unit 1 3

***Discovery Assignment Book* - Page 3**

Suggestions for Teaching the Lesson *(continued)*

Homework and Practice

- Assign the Homework section of the *Getting to Know Room 204* Activity Pages. Students will need a copy of *Centimeter Graph Paper.*
- Assign Part 1 of the Home Practice. It provides mental math practice.

Answers for Part 1 of the Home Practice can be found in the Answer Key at the end of this lesson and at the end of this unit.

Assessment

Use the *Observational Assessment Record* to document students' abilities to make and interpret bar graphs. Observe students as they are working or use their homework as an assessment. Students' abilities to interpret bar graphs can be assessed as they discuss ***Question 7*** in the Explore section in the *Student Guide.*

Extension

Collect data for other variables that describe the students in your class. Then, students can make bar graphs using the data.

Software Connection

Use on-line services or email with other classes to collect data from other classes around the country.

AT A GLANCE

Math Facts and Daily Practice and Problems

DPP items A and B provide practice with addition.

Part 1. Identifying Variables and Values

1. Read the first page of the *Getting to Know Room 204* Activity Pages in the *Student Guide.*
2. Using the data table Room 204's Main Interests, discuss **variables** and **values.**
3. Create a table listing variables your class can study and possible values for these variables. *(Question 1)*

Part 2. Collecting, Graphing, and Exploring the Data

1. The class chooses one variable from the class data table to study. *(Question 2)*
2. Create a raw data table for the class. In the first column, list students' names. The heading for the second column should be the name of the variable you are studying. (See Figure 2.)
3. Record each student's value for the variable in the second column.
4. Create a three-column data table using these headings: the name of the variable you are studying, Tally, and Number of Students. In the first column list all the values of the variable that appeared in the raw data table. Complete the data table as shown in Figure 3.
5. Create a class graph of the data. (optional)
6. Discuss the following before students create their own graphs: giving the graph a title, labeling and scaling axes, and drawing the bars.
7. Use the transparency *Bar Graph 1: What's Wrong Here?* in your discussion.
8. Students make their own bar graphs on *Centimeter Graph Paper.*
9. Discuss *Questions 3–10* in the Explore section in the *Student Guide.*

Homework

1. Assign *Questions 1–9* in the Homework section. Students need one sheet of *Centimeter Graph Paper.*
2. Assign Part 1 of the Home Practice.

Assessment

Use the *Observational Assessment Record* to document students' abilities to make and interpret bar graphs.

Notes:

Bar Graph 1: What's Wrong Here?

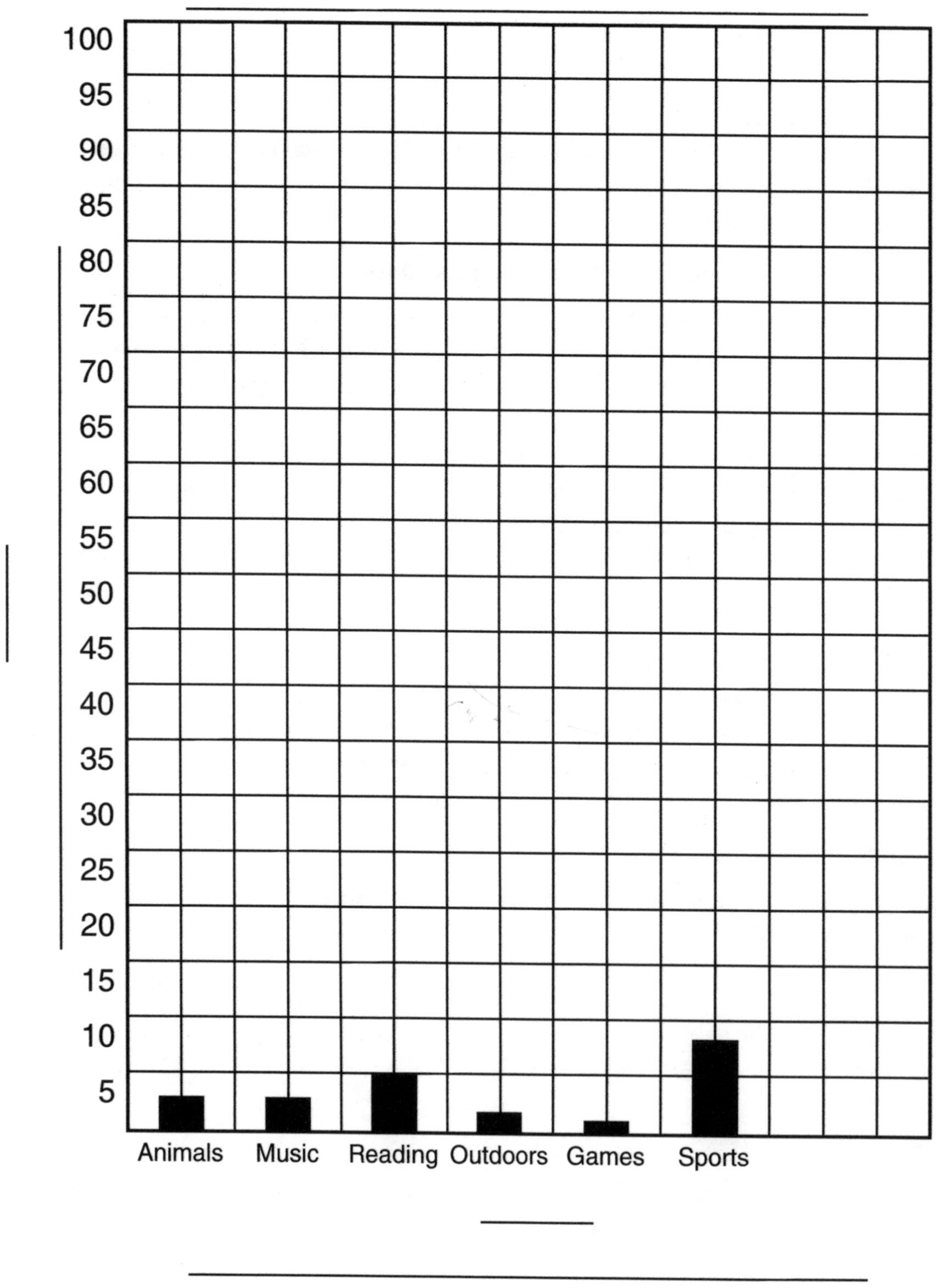
100
95
90
85
80
75
70
65
60
55
50
45
40
35
30
25
20
15
10
5
Animals
Music
Reading
Outdoors
Games
Sports

Student Guide

Questions 1–10 (SG pp. 3–5)

1.–2. *Answers will vary. See Figure 1 in Lesson Guide 1 for a sample table.

*The answers to ***Questions 3–7*** are based on the sample data tables and graph in Figures 2–4 in Lesson Guide 1. Answers will vary depending on your class data.

3. Eye Color

4. Number of Students

5. **A.** brown

B. Brown is the most common eye color.

6. **A.** blue

B. Blue is the least common eye color in Room 204.

7. Answers will vary. Brown is the most common eye color. The other three colors occur almost the same number of times in Room 204. Five more students have brown eyes than hazel eyes.

8. **A.** Main Interests

B. Number of Students

9. 8 students in the class have a main interest in sports.

10. 4 students

Homework (SG pp. 5–6)

Questions 1–9

1. primary language spoken

2. The tallest bar is English. The bar denotes that the most common primary language spoken in Room 204 is English.

3. The shortest bars are Romanian, Hebrew, Greek, and Gujarati. These bars denote the least common languages spoken in Room 204.

4. 4 students

5. Answers will vary. Room 204 has a mix of nationalities and native languages. English is the most common, followed by Spanish. Each of the other languages is spoken by only 1 or 2 students.

6.

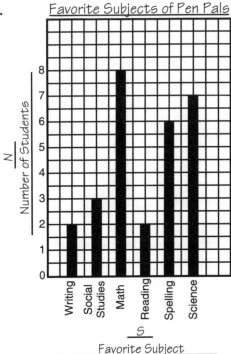

Favorite Subjects of Pen Pals
N
Number of Students
0
1
2
3
4
5
6
7
8
Writing
Social Studies
Math
Reading
Spelling
Science
S
Favorite Subject

7. **A.** Favorite Subject

B. Number of Students

8. **A.** Math

B. Writing and Reading

C. Answers will vary.

D. Answers will vary.

9. 28 students; add up the number of students in all.

Discovery Assignment Book

****Home Practice (DAB p. 3)**

Part 1. Practice

Questions 1–10

1. 16

2. 21

3. 20

4. 21

5. 100

6. 110

7. 120

8. 150

9. 105

10. 105

***Answers and/or discussion are included in the Lesson Guide.**

****Answers for all the Home Practice in the *Discovery Assignment Book* are at the end of the unit.**

Daily Practice and Problems: Bits for Lesson 2

C. Triangle Sums 2 (URG p. 12)

Find the missing numbers in these triangles.

8
7
3
9
4
3

E. Triangle Sums 3 (URG p. 13)

Notice that numbers in the circles are missing in each of the triangle problems below. Find the missing numbers.

6
9
11
13
14
4

DPP Tasks are on page 44. Suggestions for using the DPPs are on page 43.

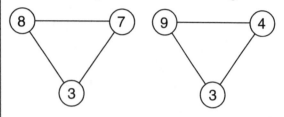

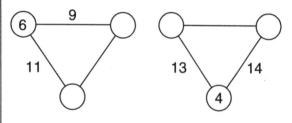

LESSON GUIDE 2

Getting to Know Room 204 a Little Better

Estimated Class Sessions: 2

Students distinguish between categorical and numerical variables. They collect, organize, and graph numerical data that describe themselves.

Key Content

- Connecting mathematics and science to real-world situations.
- Naming values of variables.
- Distinguishing between categorical and numerical variables.
- Describing a classroom of students using numerical variables.
- Collecting, organizing, graphing, and analyzing data.
- Making and interpreting bar graphs.

Key Vocabulary

bar graph
categorical variable
horizontal axis
numerical variable
value
variable
vertical axis

Materials List

Print Materials for Students

		Math Facts and Daily Practice and Problems	Activity	Homework
Student Books	Student Guide		*Getting to Know Room 204 a Little Better* Pages 7–10	*Getting to Know Room 204 a Little Better* Homework Section Pages 10–11
	Discovery Assignment Book			Home Practice Part 2 Page 3
Teacher Resources	Facts Resource Guide	DPP Items 1C–1E		
	Unit Resource Guide	DPP Items C–F Pages 12–13		
	Generic Section		*Centimeter Graph Paper,* 2 per student and *Three-column Data Table,* 1 per student group (optional)	

available on Teacher Resource CD

All Transparency Masters, Blackline Masters, and Assessment Blackline Masters in the Unit Resource Guide are on the Teacher Resource CD.

Materials for the Teacher

Bar Graph II: What's Wrong Here? Transparency Master (Unit Resource Guide) Page 46
Bar Graph III: What's Wrong Here? Transparency Master (Unit Resource Guide) Page 47
Observational Assessment Record (Unit Resource Guide, Pages 7–8 and Teacher Resource CD)
The class-generated data table, *Variables and Possible Values,* from Lesson 1
For class data table:
    2 pieces of poster-size graph paper, 2 pieces of easel paper, or several transparencies of the *Three-column Data Table* (Unit Resource Guide, Generic Section)
For class graph:
    transparency of *Centimeter Graph Paper* (Unit Resource Guide, Generic Section) or 1 piece of poster-size graph paper

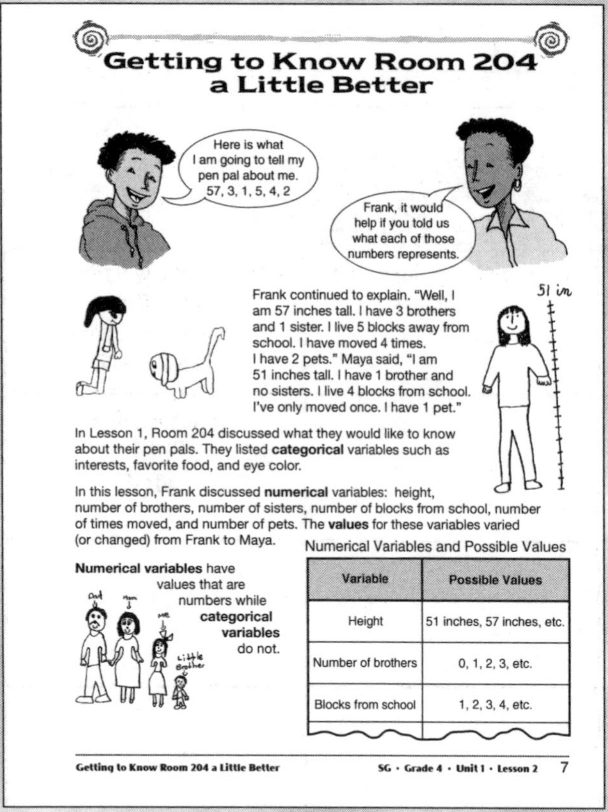

Getting to Know Room 204 a Little Better

Here is what I am going to tell my pen pal about me. 57, 3, 1, 5, 4, 2

Frank, it would help if you told us what each of those numbers represents.

Frank continued to explain. "Well, I am 57 inches tall. I have 3 brothers and 1 sister. I live 5 blocks away from school. I have moved 4 times. I have 2 pets." Maya said, "I am 51 inches tall. I have 1 brother and no sisters. I live 4 blocks from school. I've only moved once. I have 1 pet."

51 in

In Lesson 1, Room 204 discussed what they would like to know about their pen pals. They listed **categorical** variables such as interests, favorite food, and eye color.

In this lesson, Frank discussed **numerical** variables: height, number of brothers, number of sisters, number of blocks from school, number of times moved, and number of pets. The **values** for these variables varied (or changed) from Frank to Maya.

Numerical variables have values that are numbers while **categorical variables** do not.

Dad Mom Me Little Brother

Numerical Variables and Possible Values

Variable	Possible Values
Height	51 inches, 57 inches, etc.
Number of brothers	0, 1, 2, 3, etc.
Blocks from school	1, 2, 3, 4, etc.

Getting to Know Room 204 a Little Better SG • Grade 4 • Unit 1 • Lesson 2 7

***Student Guide* - Page 7**

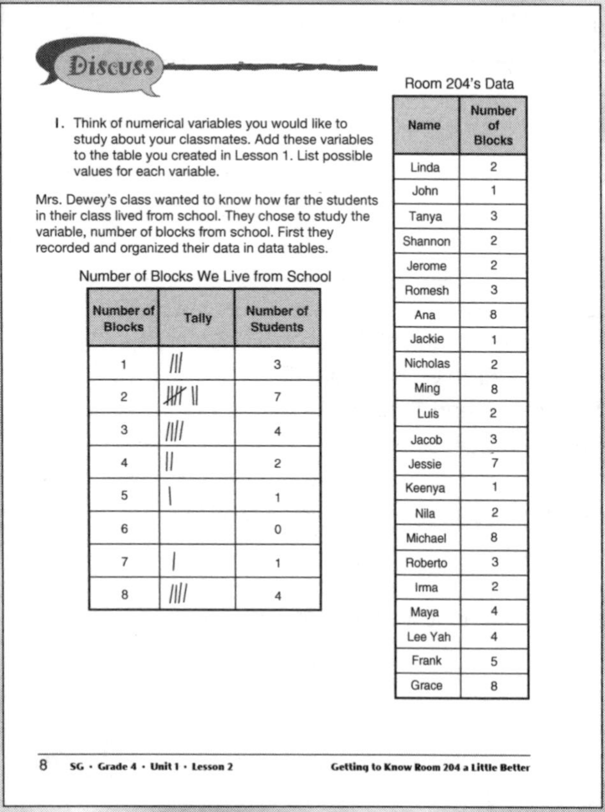

Discuss

1. Think of numerical variables you would like to study about your classmates. Add these variables to the table you created in Lesson 1. List possible values for each variable.

Mrs. Dewey's class wanted to know how far the students in their class lived from school. They chose to study the variable, number of blocks from school. First they recorded and organized their data in data tables.

Number of Blocks We Live from School

Number of Blocks	Tally	Number of Students
1	///	3
2	𝍸 //	7
3	////	4
4	//	2
5	/	1
6		0
7	/	1
8	////	4

Room 204's Data

Name	Number of Blocks
Linda	2
John	1
Tanya	3
Shannon	2
Jerome	2
Romesh	3
Ana	8
Jackie	1
Nicholas	2
Ming	8
Luis	2
Jacob	3
Jessie	7
Keenya	1
Nila	2
Michael	8
Roberto	3
Irma	2
Maya	4
Lee Yah	4
Frank	5
Grace	8

8 SG • Grade 4 • Unit 1 • Lesson 2 Getting to Know Room 204 a Little Better

***Student Guide* - Page 8**

Developing the Activity

Part 1. Categorical and Numerical Variables

Read together the first page of the *Getting to Know Room 204 a Little Better* Activity Pages in the *Student Guide.* Compare the types of variables that Room 204 discussed in the vignette in Lesson 1 (e.g., main interest, favorite holiday, eye color, hair color) to those mentioned here (e.g., height, number of brothers, number of sisters, number of pets, number of times moved). Those discussed in Lesson 1 are **categorical variables.** In this lesson we will focus on **numerical variables.** Numerical variables have **values** that are numbers while categorical variables do not.

Question 1 asks students to think of numerical variables they would like to study in order to get to know their classmates. Refer back to the Variables and Possible Values Data Table students generated in Lesson 1. See Figure 1 in Lesson Guide 1. Some variables your class listed in Lesson 1 may be numerical variables. Title the third column, Type of Variable (categorical or numerical). Ask students to name whether each variable is categorical or numerical and add their responses to the third column of the data table. For example, height and hand length are numerical variables. Eye color and length of hair are categorical. (If the length of hair was actually measured, we could have numbers for its values and then it would be considered a numerical variable.) Brainstorm a few more variables with the class to ensure they understand the difference between categorical and numerical variables.

Students may work in groups to generate more numerical variables for the table. Give each group a copy of a *Two-column Data Table.* Ask students to record numerical variables and values that correspond to each variable. Some common examples of numerical variables are number of family members, number of pets, height, and number of times moved. The values of these variables are numbers (e.g., the number of pets could be 0, 1, 2, 3, etc.). After students have been given ample time to think of different numerical variables, pull the class together and add some of their ideas to the class data table (Variables and Possible Values).

As in Lesson 1, two sample data tables and a graph are provided on the *Getting to Know Room 204 a Little Better* Activity Pages. These display Room 204's data on the number of blocks they live from school. Discuss Room 204's sample data before your class chooses a variable ***(Question 2)*** and collects data.

Question 2 asks your class to choose a numerical variable to study. It is important that the variable you choose involves quick and easy data collection. For instance, if you choose number of pencils in your desk as the numerical variable you can easily ask each student to count his or her pencils and tell you the number. A numerical variable such as number of pets may be a good choice for your classroom to study. However, the number of pets may not vary much in some classrooms. (Many students might not have any pets or they may have only 1 or 2.) Choosing height, hand area, or the number of windows in students' homes would require more time since students would need to gather data.

The numerical variable you select must be well-defined. If you collect data on family size, you will need to define this variable. A student's definition of family could include members outside the immediate family, especially if relatives such as a grandmother or an uncle reside in the home. Decide upon a definition such as the following: As long as the person lives in the student's home full-time, he or she could be considered part of the family. Number of pets is another variable that may need some definition. Does a student who has an aquarium count all the fish in his or her tank or do fish count as one pet?

Part 2. Collecting, Organizing, and Graphing the Data

Before collecting the raw data on the variable your class has chosen, create a class data table on large paper or several transparencies of the *Three-column Data Table.* In the first column of the data table, list students' names. In the heading of the second column, list the name of the variable you are studying. Then, record each student's individual data beside his or her name. Room 204's data on the number of pets is shown in Figure 5.

Name	Number of Pets	
Linda	2	
Grace	0	
Ming	1	
Frank	0	

Figure 5: *Raw data for Room 204's pet data*

TIMS Tip

Some teachers choose to engage their students in the actual data collection before reviewing the student pages. These teachers may discuss the sample data tables and graphs in the *Student Guide* to provide closure to the activity.

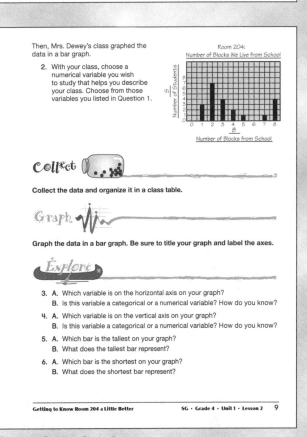

Then, Mrs. Dewey's class graphed the data in a bar graph.

2. With your class, choose a numerical variable you wish to study that helps you describe your class. Choose from those variables you listed in Question 1.

Room 204:
Number of Blocks We Live from School
S
Number of Students
0
1
2
3
4
5
6
7
8
0 1 2 3 4 5 6 7 8
B
Number of Blocks from School

Collect

Collect the data and organize it in a class table.

Graph

Graph the data in a bar graph. Be sure to title your graph and label the axes.

Explore

3. A. Which variable is on the horizontal axis on your graph?
   B. Is this variable a categorical or a numerical variable? How do you know?
4. A. Which variable is on the vertical axis on your graph?
   B. Is this variable a categorical or a numerical variable? How do you know?
5. A. Which bar is the tallest on your graph?
   B. What does the tallest bar represent?
6. A. Which bar is the shortest on your graph?
   B. What does the shortest bar represent?

***Student Guide* - Page 9**

Next, your class needs to organize the data by creating a new table like that in Figure 6. Make another three-column data table. Label the three headings as follows: the name of the variable you are studying, Tally, and Number of Students. In the first column list all of the values that appeared in your raw data table in numerical order. Then, using the raw data, tally the number of students that have the same value for the variable. Once all the data has been tallied, the marks are counted and the total for each row is recorded in the third column. The total number of all of the tally marks should equal the number of students in the class. The organized data can then be graphed.

Number of Pets	Tally	Number of Students
0	//	
1	/	
2	\	

Figure 6: *Number of pets data table*

Number of Pets in Room 204
S
Number of Students
0
1
2
3
4
5
6
7
8
9
10
0
1
2
3
4
5
6
P
Number of Pets

Figure 7: *Sample bar graph*

Use a transparency of *Centimeter Graph Paper* to model setting up a bar graph. Be sure to discuss the following before students create their own graphs: giving the graph a title, labeling and scaling axes, and drawing the bars. (See Figure 7 for a sample graph of the pets data.)

The Transparency Masters *Bar Graph II* and *III: What's Wrong Here?* show incorrect bar graphs of the data Room 204 collected on the number of blocks they live from school. Students may compare the correct bar graph in the *Student Guide* with the graphs on the transparencies.

In *Bar Graph II: What's Wrong Here?* the student listed each individual name and graphed a bar for each person's individual data. This does not organize the data any better than the raw data table. Also, the two variables we want to graph are not name and number of blocks but rather number of students and number of blocks. These may be considered mistakes in data analysis rather than in graphing.

Bar Graph III: What's Wrong Here? does not list the values in order on the horizontal axis which makes the graph harder to read than the graph in the *Student Guide.* Although we found out that no students live

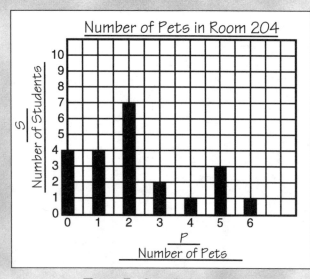

6 blocks away from school, *Bar Graph III* does not display this information. A place-holder on the horizontal axis for 6 blocks from school should be included on the graph. A small line, the width of a bar, can be placed on the horizontal axis above the 6 to denote that no students live 6 blocks away from school.

Students are now ready to graph the data they have collected. While students graph the data on *Centimeter Graph Paper,* create a class graph of the data on a transparency or poster-size graph paper. This class graph will serve as a reference for class discussion. Use ***Questions 3–6*** to start a discussion about what you have learned about your class. ***Questions 7–10*** ask similar questions about Room 204's data.

Question 8 asks students if Room 204's graph would be as easy to read if the numbers (values) on the horizontal axis were not in numerical order. Students might recall that the *Bar Graph III: What's Wrong Here?* transparency gave an example of such a graph. It is much easier to read and interpret a graph when the values on the horizontal axis are in numerical order. The shape of Room 204's graph in the *Student Guide* tells us more when the numbers are in order. The graph tells us ***(Question 9)*** that the majority of the students in Room 204 live near school—3 blocks or closer. Not as many students live between 5 and 7 blocks away. Then, the final bar shows that several students live quite far. These students might get to school by bus.

Suggestions for Teaching the Lesson

Math Facts

- DPP Bits C and E are triangle puzzles that provide practice with addition facts. Bit E requires reasoning and problem-solving skills.
- Task D provides practice with addition facts in the context of adding tens.

Homework and Practice

- Students complete the Homework section on the *Getting to Know Room 204 a Little Better* Activity Pages. Each student will need one piece of *Centimeter Graph Paper* to complete the assignment.
- DPP Task F requires students to solve a problem by reasoning from a geometric figure.

7. A. Look back at Room 204's graph called Number of Blocks We Live from School. Is the variable they graphed on the horizontal axis numerical or categorical?
   B. Is the variable they graphed on the vertical axis numerical or categorical?
8. A. Would Room 204's graph be as easy to read if the numbers (values) on the horizontal axis were not in order? Explain.
   B. Does it matter in what order you label the horizontal axis when the variable is categorical? Refer back to Room 204's Main Interests graph in Lesson 1.
9. What story does the graph tell you about the students in Room 204?
10. A. How many students in Room 204 live 3 blocks or less from school?
    B. Is this more or less than half the class?

Homework

You will need one sheet of *Centimeter Graph Paper* to complete this homework.

1. Room 204's Phoenix pen pals sent back the following data on the number of times their families have moved. Use the data to create a bar graph. Remember to label the axes and title your graph.
2. Answer the following questions using the bar graph you drew in Question 1.
   A. Is the variable on your horizontal axis numerical or categorical?
   B. Is the variable on your vertical axis numerical or categorical?
   C. Which is the tallest bar on the graph? What does it tell you?
   D. What is the most number of times any student has moved?
   E. Describe the shape of your graph.

Number of Times Families Moved

Number of Times Moved	Number of Students
0	0
1	3
2	7
3	7
4	3
5	2
6	2
7	2
8	1
9	1
10	0

10 SG • Grade 4 • Unit 1 • Lesson 2 Getting to Know Room 204 a Little Better

***Student Guide* - Page 10**

3. What story does the graph tell you about the Phoenix pen pals?
4. Decide whether each of the variables below is a numerical or categorical variable. Then, name three possible values for each variable.
   A. ice cream flavors
   B. number of telephones in homes
   C. heights of tables at home
   D. favorite kind of movie
   E. weights of newborn babies
   F. foot size
   G. types of vehicles

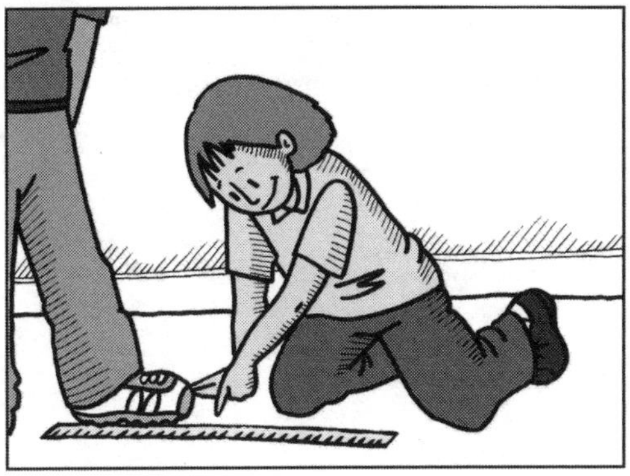

Getting to Know Room 204 a Little Better SG • Grade 4 • Unit 1 • Lesson 2 11

***Student Guide* - Page 11**

Daily Practice and Problems: Tasks for Lesson 2

D. Task: More Addition Practice (URG p. 12)

1. 70 + 40 =
2. 60 + 50 + 20 =
3. 80 + 50 =
4. 60 + 90 =
5. 130 + 90 =

F. Task: Counting Squares (URG p. 13)

How many squares can you find in the figure?

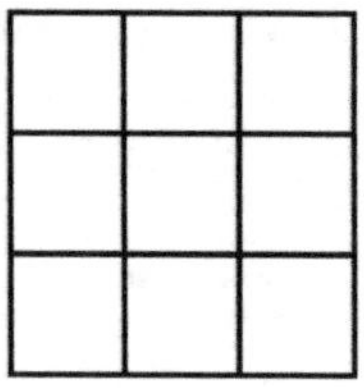

Suggestions for Teaching the Lesson *(continued)*

- Part 2 of the Home Practice provides additional practice with the terms numerical, categorical, and values.

Answers for Part 2 of the Home Practice can be found in the Answer Key at the end of this lesson and at the end of this unit.

Assessment

- Use the *Observational Assessment Record* to record students' progress in identifying categorical and numerical variables.
- Use ***Question 1*** of the homework to assess students' abilities to make a bar graph.

Extension

Collect data for other variables that describe the students in your class. Students can make bar graphs of both numerical and categorical data.

Software Connection

Use on-line services or email to collect data from other classes around the country.

Name ______________________ Date ______________

Unit 1: Home Practice

Part 1 Practice

Solve the following addition problems. Try to solve the problems without paper and pencil. Be prepared to share your solution strategies.

1. 8 + 3 + 5 = ________
2. 9 + 7 + 5 = ________
3. 6 + 8 + 6 = ________
4. 4 + 8 + 9 = ________
5. 70 + 30 = ________
6. 60 + 20 + 30 = ________
7. 50 + 70 = ________
8. 30 + 50 + 70 = ________
9. 20 + 85 = ________
10. 10 + 80 + 15 = ________

Part 2 Variables and Values

Look around your home and find four variables. Find two numerical variables and two categorical variables. Then, name some values for each of your variables. Be prepared to discuss and compare your findings. For example: Type of drinks is a categorical variable. Some values for this variable are iced tea, milk, and fruit juice.

1. Variable: ________________ numerical or categorical (circle one)

   Values of your variable:

2. Variable: ________________ numerical or categorical (circle one)

   Values of your variable:

3. Variable: ________________ numerical or categorical (circle one)

   Values of your variable:

4. Variable: ________________ numerical or categorical (circle one)

   Values of your variable:

DATA ABOUT US DAB • Grade 4 • Unit 1 3

Discovery Assignment Book - Page 3

AT A GLANCE

Math Facts and Daily Practice and Problems

DPP items C, D, and E provide practice with addition facts. DPP Task F provides practice analyzing a geometric figure.

Part 1. Categorical and Numerical Variables

1. Read the first page of the *Getting to Know Room 204 a Little Better* Activity Pages.
2. Discuss the terms **numerical** and **categorical variables** using the vignettes in Lessons 1 and 2 in the *Student Guide.*
3. Refer to the Variables and Possible Values Data Table generated in Lesson 1. Ask students to name those variables that are categorical and those that are numerical.
4. Working in groups, students think of more numerical variables and list possible values for each.
5. The class adds more numerical variables to the class list. *(Question 1)*
6. The class chooses a numerical variable to study. *(Question 2)*

Part 2. Collecting, Organizing, and Graphing the Data

1. Create a raw data table for the class. In the first column, list students' names. In the heading of the second column, list the name of the variable you are studying.
2. Record individual data beside each student's name.
3. Create a three-column data table. Label the three headings as follows: the name of the variable you are studying, Tally, and Number of Students.
4. In the first column, list all the values that appeared in your raw data table in numerical order. Tally the number of students that have the same value for the variable. Record the total for each row in the third column.
5. Use a transparency of *Centimeter Graph Paper* to model setting up a graph. Discuss giving the graph a title, labeling and scaling axes, and drawing the bars.
6. Use the *Bar Graph II and III: What's Wrong Here?* Transparency Masters in your discussion of bar graphs.
7. Students graph the class data on *Centimeter Graph Paper.* Make a graph of the class data on a transparency of *Centimeter Graph Paper.*
8. Use *Questions 3–10* on the *Getting to Know Room 204 a Little Better* Activity Pages to discuss the class data.

Homework

1. Assign the Homework section on the *Getting to Know Room 204 a Little Better* Activity Pages. Students need a piece of *Centimeter Graph Paper.*
2. Assign Part 2 of the Home Practice.

Assessment

1. Use the *Observational Assessment Record* to document students' progress in identifying categorical and numerical variables.
2. Use *Question 1* of the Homework section to assess students' abilities to create a bar graph.

Notes:

Bar Graph II: What's Wrong Here?

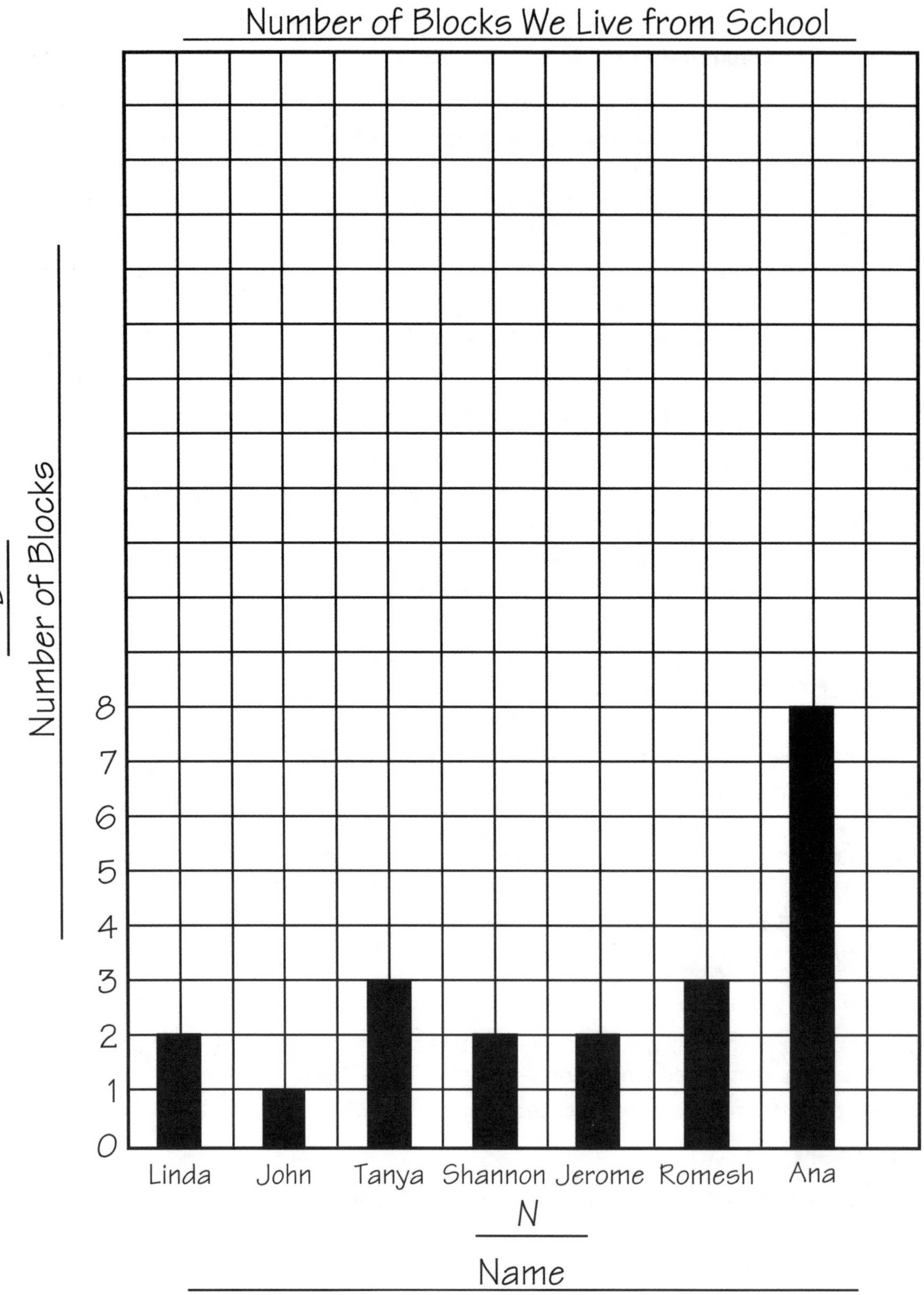
Number of Blocks We Live from School
B
Number of Blocks
8
7
6
5
4
3
2
1
0
Linda
John
Tanya
Shannon
Jerome
Romesh
Ana
N
Name

Bar Graph III: What's Wrong Here?

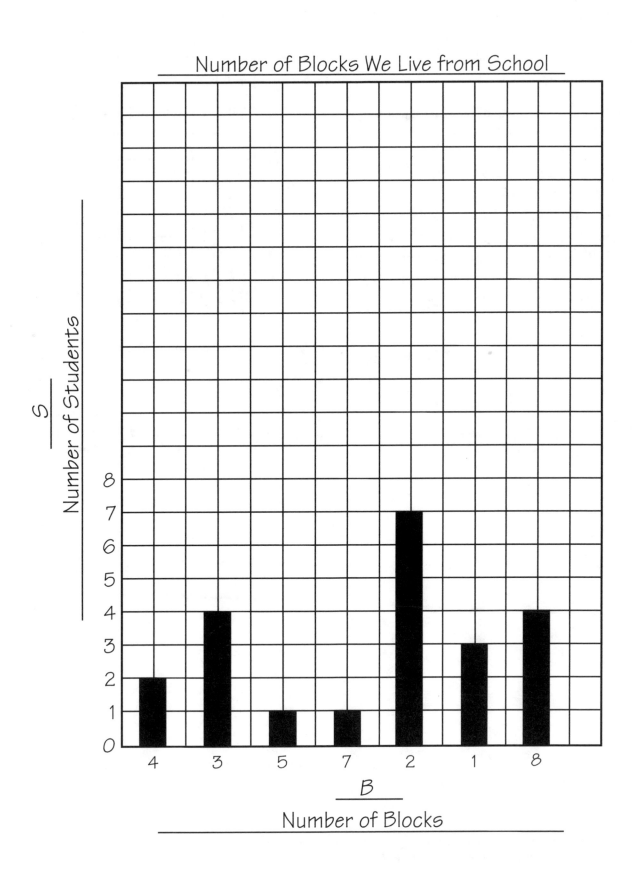

Number of Blocks We Live from School

$\frac{S}{\text{Number of Students}}$

Number of Students: 8, 7, 6, 5, 4, 3, 2, 1, 0

Number of Blocks: 4, 3, 5, 7, 2, 1, 8

$\frac{B}{}$

Number of Blocks

Student Guide

Questions 1–10 (SG pp. 8–10)

1.–2. *Answers will vary. See Figure 1 in Lesson Guide 1 for a sample table.

*The answers to **Questions 3–6** are based on the sample data tables and graph in Figures 5–7 in Lesson Guide 2. Answers for these questions will vary depending on your class data.

3. **A.** Number of Pets

   B. numerical; the values are numbers.

4. **A.** Number of Students

   B. numerical; the values are numbers.

5. **A.** The bar for 2 pets is the tallest.

   B. It shows that the most common number of pets in a household is 2 pets.

6. **A.** The bar for 4 pets and the bar for 6 pets are the shortest bars.

   B. These bars show that the least common number of pets in a household are 4 pets and 6 pets.

7. **A.** numerical

   B. numerical

8. **A** *No; The shape of the graph tells us more when the values are in order.

   B. No.

9. *Answers will vary. Most of the students live near the school—3 blocks or closer.

10. **A.** 14 students

    B. More than half

Homework (SG pp. 10–11)

Questions 1–4

1.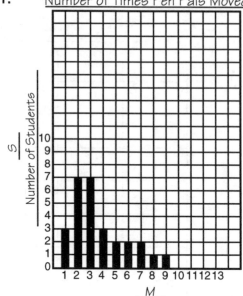

   Number of Times Pen Pals Moved

   Number of Times Moved

2. **A.** numerical

   B. numerical

   C. The bar that shows that seven students moved twice. The bar that shows that seven students moved three times. These two bars represent the most common number of times students have moved—2 or 3 times.

   D. 9 times (only 1 student moved this many times)

   E. Answers will vary. The graph looks like a roller coaster. First it is not going up much, then it goes up high, and then it gradually decreases in height.

---

*Answers and/or discussion are included in the Lesson Guide.

**Answers for all the Home Practice in the *Discovery Assignment Book* are at the end of the unit.

3. Answers will vary. It is most common for a student in the Phoenix classroom to have moved 2 or 3 times. Every student has moved at least once.

4. Answers will vary.

   A. categorical: vanilla, chocolate, mint

   B. numerical: 1, 2, 3

   C. categorical or numerical: short, medium, tall or 30 inches, 31 inches, 32 inches

   D. categorical: horror, drama, comedy

   E. numerical: 7 lbs, 8 lbs, 9 lbs

   F. categorical or numerical: small, medium, large or 5, 6, 7

   G. categorical: small, medium, large or trucks, cars, airplanes, trains

Discovery Assignment Book

**Home Practice (DAB p. 3)

Part 2. Variables and Values

Questions 1–4

Answers will vary. An example of a categorical variable is type of drinks. Values for this variable are iced tea, milk, and fruit juice. An example of a numerical variable is number of windows in each room. Values for this variable are 0, 1, 2, 3, etc.

*Answers and/or discussion are included in the Lesson Guide.

**Answers for all the Home Practice in the *Discovery Assignment Book* are at the end of the unit.

Daily Practice and Problems: Bits for Lesson 3

G. Reading Time (URG p. 13)

Tell what time each clock face is showing.

1. 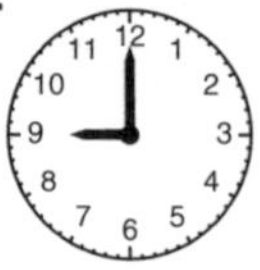
2. 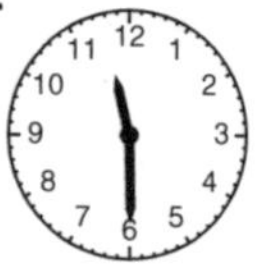
3. 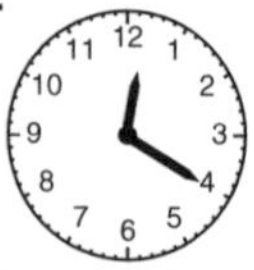
4. 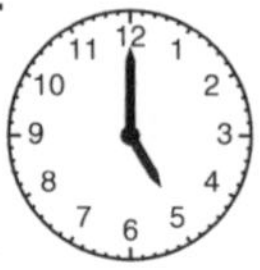
5. 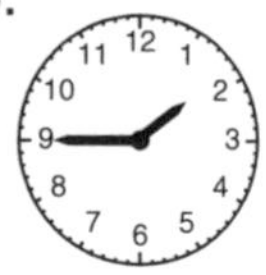
6. 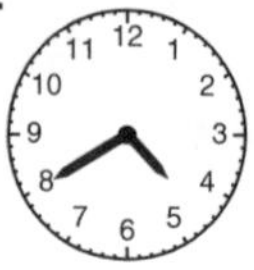
7. 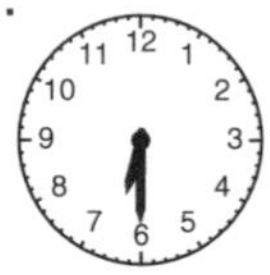
8. 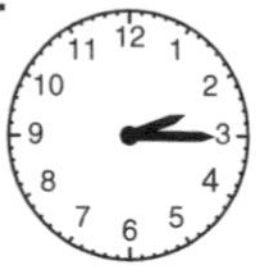

I. Time 1 (URG p. 15)

1. What is the time now?
2. What time will it be 20 minutes from now?
3. What time will it be $1\frac{1}{2}$ hours from now?

DPP Task and Challenge are on page 56. Suggestions for using the DPPs are on pages 56–57.

LESSON GUIDE 3

An Average Activity

Estimated Class Sessions: 2

Students investigate averages using data about the students in Room 204 and their own classroom. They use the median to average data.

Key Content

- Connecting mathematics and science to real-world situations.
- Investigating the concept of average as a representative value for a data set.
- Averaging: finding the median.

Key Vocabulary

average
median

Curriculum Sequence

Before This Unit

Averages. Students have used medians to describe data sets collected in labs in Grades 1, 2, and 3. See Unit 5 in Grade 3 for an example.

After This Unit

Averages. The mean is introduced and the median is reviewed in Unit 5 Lessons 2 and 3. Students will continue to use averages in labs and activities throughout the year. (See Units 5, 10, 13, and 15 for specific examples.)

Materials List

Print Materials for Students

		Math Facts and Daily Practice and Problems	Activity	Homework	Written Assessment
Student Books	**Student Guide**		*An Average Activity* Pages 12–15	*An Average Activity* Homework Section Page 16	
	Discovery Assignment Book				Home Practice Part 3 Page 4
Teacher Resource	**Unit Resource Guide**	DPP Items G–J Pages 13–15 ⊙			DPP Item J *Variables and Values* Page 15 ⊙

⊙ *available on Teacher Resource CD*

All Transparency Masters, Blackline Masters, and Assessment Blackline Masters in the Unit Resource Guide are on the Teacher Resource CD.

Materials for the Teacher

Observational Assessment Record (Unit Resource Guide, Pages 7–8 and Teacher Resource CD)
class data table *(Variables and Possible Values)* from Lesson 2
class graph from Lesson 2

An Average Activity

Mrs. Dewey's class was collecting data on the heights of fourth graders. She asked a doctor to talk to the class about how children grow and develop. One of the things Dr. Solinas talked about was the average height of ten-year-olds. What does "average" mean?

- "It was just an average day."
- "The doctor said my height is above average for kids my age."
- "We really need rain. Rainfall this year has been well below average."
- "My average grade in spelling is 75 percent."
- "Our soccer team averages about three goals per game."

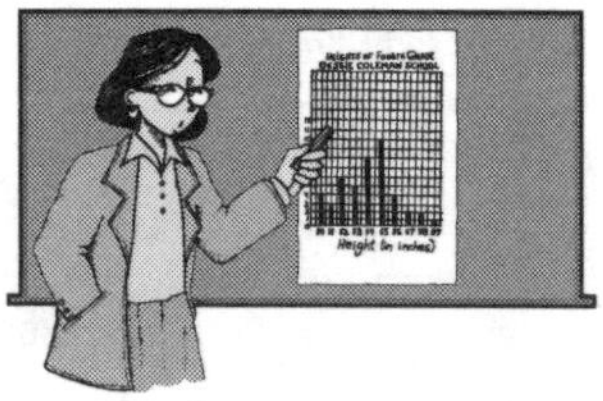

Height (in inches)

Each sentence describes what is usual or typical for the situation.

Scientists and mathematicians use averages to help them describe data they have collected. Doctors who study how children grow measure the heights of many children. Then, they use this data to find the average height for different age groups. They use one number, an average, to represent the heights of a whole group.

The average value for any set of numbers, such as the average height of fourth graders, can be calculated in more than one way. In this lesson you will learn about one kind of average: the median. You can find the median of a set of numbers easily and use it to describe the data you collect. Later this year, you will learn to calculate another kind of average.

12 SG • Grade 4 • Unit 1 • Lesson 3 An Average Activity

***Student Guide* - Page 12**

Developing the Activity

Begin by exploring medians using data about the students in your class as described in Part 1 below. Then use the discussion about Room 204 on the *An Average Activity* Activity Pages in the *Student Guide* to review terms and formalize procedures. Alternatively, you can begin with the *Student Guide* and use the information and examples involving data from Room 204 as background for the activities in Part 1.

Part 1. Exploring Medians Using Data About Us
Ask:

- *When have you heard the term average?*

This should generate a list of responses that may include batting average, average rainfall, grade point average, average student, and average height. These averages indicate what is representative or typical in a given situation. Advise students that they will learn how to use one number to describe what is typical in a set of numbers. For example, when a student says that she averages about three goals per game, she doesn't mean that she scores three goals every game. She means that the typical number of goals she scores is three.

Review the data your class collected and graphed in Lesson 2 along with the list of numerical variables your class generated at the beginning of that lesson. Choose two or three numerical variables and tell students that they are going to find an average or typical value for each variable that you choose. Choose numerical variables with values that students can easily report and that have a relatively wide range of values. Height is a good variable for this activity since it is easy to recognize the median height of a group of students when they are standing in a line in order from shortest to tallest. If you use the variable your class graphed in Lesson 2, you will be able to find the median on your class graph as well as through the procedure described below. In this discussion we will use the following variables as examples: height, number of pets, and number of pencils in your desk.

Ask students to write the number of pets on one side of a piece of paper as large as possible and the number of pencils in their desks on the other side. (Make sure students label the numbers so they know which is which.) Define the variables precisely. For example, the number of pencils in a desk will probably not include pens or markers.

Tell students that the median is one kind of average and that they are going to find the median value for each variable. Define the **median** as the value exactly in the middle of the data. Ultimately, you will find medians for the whole class, but first demonstrate the procedure using five students lined up in front of the room. Choose five students with varying heights and ask them to arrange themselves in order from shortest to tallest. The third student in line—the student in the middle—is the student with the median height. Note that this is one example where we only have to measure the middle data point.

Content Note

Average. In everyday language we use average to describe what is normal or typical. In mathematics, the **average** is a single value that is used to represent a set of numbers. For example, the average grade for a student is one number that is used to represent all of his or her grades. In fourth grade, students will find two types of averages: the mean and the median.

The arithmetic mean is the most commonly used average. In fact, frequently the term average is used interchangeably with mean. However in *Math Trailblazers* we use average to describe measures of central tendency. The mean is one measure of central tendency. For example, if a student spells 18, 19, 10, 14, and 19 words correctly on a series of five spelling tests, the student's **mean** number correct is $(18 + 19 + 10 + 14 + 19) \div 5$ which equals 16. Students will learn to find means in Unit 5.

In this unit students find the median values of sets of data. The **median** is the number exactly in the middle of the scores. To find the median of an odd number of scores, arrange the scores from smallest to largest and choose the middle number. The median score for the above data (10, 14, 18, 19, 19) is 18 since there are two values smaller than 18 and two values larger than 18. If a student takes an even number of tests, the median is not as obvious since there is not one middle piece of data. If a student earns scores of 10, 14, 18, and 19 on four tests, his or her median score is 16. In this case, we look at the two middle pieces of data (14 and 18) and the median is the number which is halfway between these two numbers. If a student earns scores of 10, 13, 18, and 19 on the four tests, the median score is 15.5 since it is midway between the 13 and 18. (See the TIMS Tutor: *Averages* for more detailed information on means and medians, including a discussion on the appropriate uses of each.)

TIMS Tip

If height is a sensitive issue for any of the students in your class, you can choose another variable. For example, students can compare the length of their hands or the length of their arm spans instead of their heights.

Finding Medians

Mrs. Dewey asked five students to stand in front of the room to show the class how to find medians. Jerome, Ana, Grace, Roberto, and Shannon stood in a line from shortest to tallest. The **median** is the number that is exactly in the middle of the data.

Discuss

1. A. Which student has the median height in Jerome's group?
   B. Does it make sense to say that this student's height is the "typical" height for this group? Why or why not?
2. A. Use the information in the table to find the median height for Keenya's group. Put the numbers in order from smallest to largest. The median height will be in the middle of the data.
   B. When you have found the median, look back at the data. An **average** is one number that can be used to represent all the data. Does your answer make sense?

Keenya's Group: Our Heights

Name	Height in inches
Keenya	55 in
Nila	50 in
John	57 in
Michael	54 in
Luis	58 in
Jackie	54 in
Lee Yah	52 in

An Average Activity SG • Grade 4 • Unit 1 • Lesson 3 13

***Student Guide* - Page 13**

Number of Pets in Room 204
These 2 values are in the middle. 2 is the median number of pets.
S
Number of Students
P
Number of Pets
0
1
2
3
4
5
6
7
8
9
10

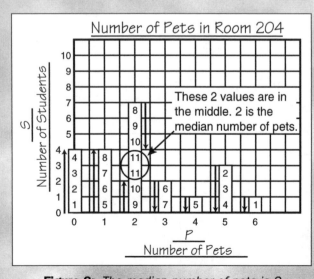

Figure 8: *The median number of pets is 2.*

Next, find the median value for one of the other variables such as number of pets. Have the five students show the number of pets they own by holding up the data they wrote on pieces of paper. The students rearrange themselves in order with the student with the smallest number of pets at one end of the line and the student with the largest number of pets at the other end of the line. The student in the middle of the line is holding the median number of pets. Note that more than one student may have the median number of pets. If the students in the line have 0, 1, 1, 2, and 2 pets, respectively, the median is 1 pet. Repeat the procedure to find the median number of pencils in the students' desks.

Demonstrate how to find the median of an even number of values. Ask six students to show their data for the number of pencils in their desks. Here are three possible data sets and the corresponding medians.

Data Set A: 0, 1, 3, 5, 6, 10
The median is 4 pencils. Since there is not one middle data point, look at the numbers the two students in the middle of the line are holding (3 and 5). The median (4) is the number halfway between these two numbers.

Data Set B: 0, 1, 2, 2, 5, 6
The median is 2 pencils, since the two middle data points are both 2.

Data Set C: 0, 1, 3, 4, 6, 10
The median is $3\frac{1}{2}$ pencils, since $3\frac{1}{2}$ is midway between the two middle data points (3 and 4).

Once the students understand the process, ask all of them to stand with their data. First, students find the median height by comparing heights with one another, arranging themselves in order from smallest to largest, and identifying the student or students with the median height. Then, students find the medians for the other two variables in a similar fashion using the numbers they have written down.

The graphs your class made in Lesson 2 can be used to find the medians and reinforce the concept that the median is in the center of the data. The Number of Pets graph in Figure 8 illustrates how to find the median of a set of data using a graph. To find the middle value, count off each piece of data, one from the left and one from the right, until you reach the middle. Since the two middle values fall on the bar for 2 pets, 2 is the median number of pets for this class.

Part 2. Exploring Medians Using Data About Room 204

The concept of average is described briefly in *An Average Activity* in the *Student Guide.* ***Questions 1–5*** review (or introduce) procedures for finding the median and explore the uses of averages in describing a set of data. To answer ***Question 1A,*** students identify the child with the median height in an illustration of five students lined up in a row. Grace has the median height because she is standing in the middle of the line. ***Question 1B*** asks students to reflect on the idea that the average height is the typical height for the group. If students do not agree with the idea that the middle height is the average or typical height, ask them which height would represent the heights of the group better. If they can use just one height to represent the heights of the students in the group, which height would they choose? Students should come to realize from this discussion and later examples that using the middle height does make sense.

Question 2 provides practice finding the median of an odd number of values. ***Questions 3 and 4*** provide practice finding the median of an even number of values.

Question 5 asks students to find the median number of blocks the students in Room 204 live from school using the data table or the graph. Students can either count off each tally mark, one at the top of the table and one at the bottom, until they reach the center or count the number of blocks represented by each bar in the graph. Figure 9 shows that the middle two values are both on the bar representing 3 blocks from school, so the median number of blocks is 3.

Journal Prompt

What is an average?

3. Keenya, Maya, Jessie, and Shannon all walk to school together.
   - Jessie lives 7 blocks from school.
   - Shannon lives 2 blocks from school.
   - Maya lives 4 blocks from school.
   - Keenya lives 1 block from school.

   Jessie said, "The median number of blocks that the four of us walk to school is 3 blocks." Is she correct? Why or why not? (*Hint:* Find the number halfway between the middle two values.)

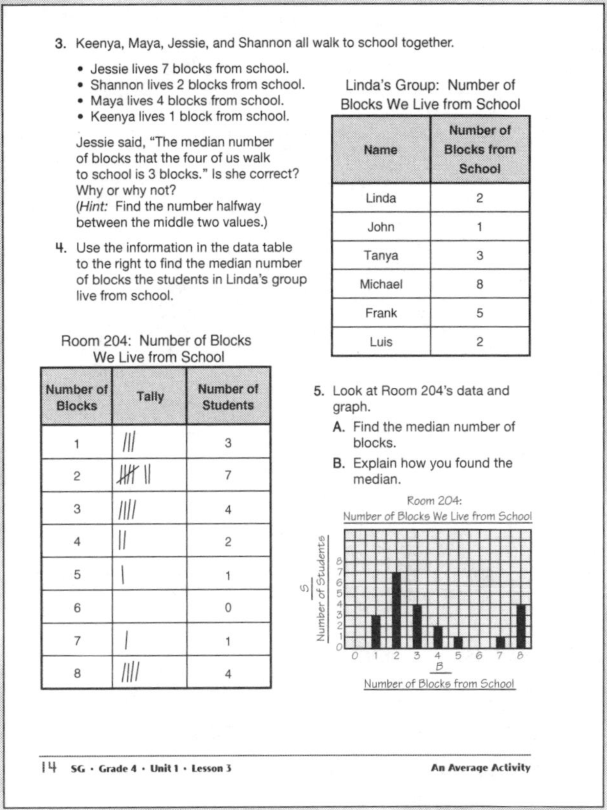

4. Use the information in the data table to the right to find the median number of blocks the students in Linda's group live from school.

Linda's Group: Number of Blocks We Live from School

Name	Number of Blocks from School
Linda	2
John	1
Tanya	3
Michael	8
Frank	5
Luis	2

Room 204: Number of Blocks We Live from School

Number of Blocks	Tally	Number of Students
1	|||	3
2	~~||||~~ ||	7
3	||||	4
4	||	2
5	|	1
6		0
7	|	1
8	||||	4

5. Look at Room 204's data and graph.
   A. Find the median number of blocks.
   B. Explain how you found the median.

Room 204:
Number of Blocks We Live from School
S
Number of Students
B
Number of Blocks from School

***Student Guide* - Page 14**

Room 204: Number of Blocks We Live from School

Number of Blocks	Tally	Number of Students
1	|||	3
2	~~||||~~ ||	7
3	(||)||	4
4	||	2
5	|	1
6		0
7	|	1
8	||||	4

The 2 circled tally marks are the 11th and 12th tallies.

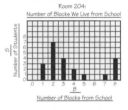

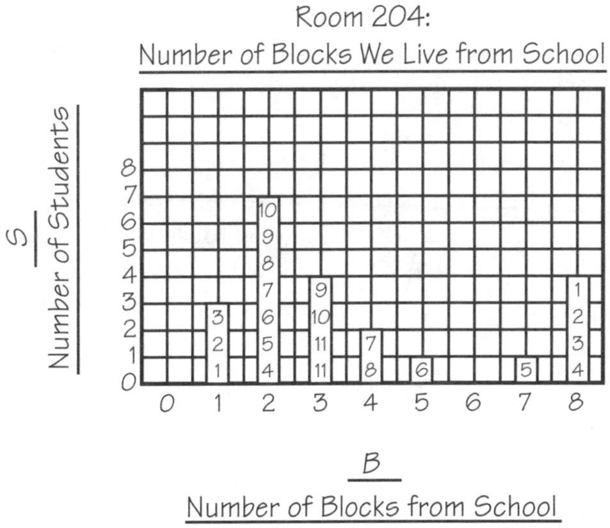

Room 204:
Number of Blocks We Live from School
S
Number of Students
B
Number of Blocks from School

Figure 9: *Using a data table or graph to find the median. The median is 3 blocks.*

Explore

6. The students in Room 204 collected data on the number of times their families had moved. The data for Ming's group is in the table to the right. Find the median number of times the students in his group have moved.
7. Jerome's baseball team has played eight games. Here are the number of runs they scored: 1, 3, 5, 3, 2, 7, 2, 4. Find the median number of runs they scored.
8. John, Shannon, and Tanya made paper airplanes. They had a contest to see who made the best airplane. Each airplane was flown three times.
   A. Find the median distance for each student's airplane.
   B. Who do you think should win the contest? Justify your choice.

Ming's Group: Number of Times We Moved

Name	Number of Times Moved
Ming	2
Irma	1
Nicholas	5
Romesh	0
Linda	3

Name	Distance in cm			
	Trial 1	Trial 2	Trial 3	Median
John	410 cm	390 cm	640 cm	
Shannon	250 cm	230 cm	290 cm	
Tanya	420 cm	590 cm	600 cm	

An Average Activity SG • Grade 4 • Unit 1 • Lesson 3 15

***Student Guide* - Page 15**

Daily Practice and Problems: Task and Challenge for Lesson 3

H. Challenge: Counting Rectangles
(URG p. 14)

How many rectangles can you find in this figure?

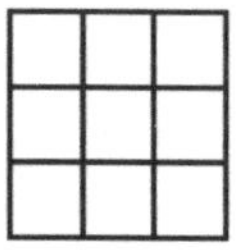

J. Task: Variables and Values
(URG p. 15)

Mrs. Dewey's class will investigate the variables listed below during its field trip to a baseball game. Decide if each variable is numerical or categorical. Then, name three possible values for each variable.

Number of Seats in Each Row

Type of Shoe

Kind of Drink

Size of Drink

Type of Food

Type of Shirt

Class Size

At this point, students can work in pairs to solve the remaining problems. ***Questions 6 and 7*** provide more practice finding medians. ***Question 8A*** asks students to find medians of values recorded in a data table similar to the *Three-trial Data Tables* they used in earlier grades. In this data table, three students from Room 204 recorded the distances their paper airplanes flew in a contest. Each airplane was flown three times. ***Question 8B*** asks which student should win the contest. Some students may argue that since the average distance can represent all the flights, Tanya should be the winner because her plane had the largest median. Others may argue that John should be the winner since his plane flew the farthest. Both arguments have merit, and students should be encouraged to justify their choices and clearly communicate their reasoning.

TIMS Tip

Working in pairs at the beginning of the year is a good way for students to start working in small groups. To encourage pairs to work together, tell students that you will only answer team questions. That is, you will not answer an individual's question unless he or she has discussed the question with his or her partner. If both partners agree that they cannot answer the question, then both students should raise their hands to let you know that they have both considered the question and that they still need your help.

Suggestions for Teaching the Lesson

Homework and Practice

- Assign ***Questions 1–3*** in the Homework section. ***Question 3*** asks students to measure the hand lengths of friends and members of their families, record the data in a table, and find the median hand length. This activity will introduce students to the Adventure Book in Lesson 4 *The Four Servants.*
- DPP Bits G and I provide practice with telling time and calculating elapsed time. DPP Challenge H is a geometry problem that involves squares and rectangles. This problem is an extension of the problem in Task F.

Journal Prompt

This lesson is called *An Average Activity.* Is this a good name for this lesson? Why or why not?

Assessment

- Use ***Questions 7–8*** in the Explore section of the *Student Guide* to assess students' abilities to find the median of a set of data and interpret the meaning of an average value. ***Questions 1–2*** in the Homework section are also appropriate assessment items.
- Use DPP Task J to assess students' abilities to identify categorical and numerical variables and to name possible values.
- Use Part 3 of the Home Practice to assess students' abilities to find the median of a data set. Use the *Observational Assessment Record* to document students' progress.

Answers for Part 3 of the Home Practice can be found in the Answer Key at the end of this lesson and at the end of this unit.

Homework

1. Romesh took a survey on his block and recorded his data in the table shown at the right. Find the median number of pets on his block.

Pets Survey

Family	Number of Pets
Bailey	2
Johnson	0
Cruz	5
Kanno	3
Holt	4
Elkins	1
Roberts	2

2. Ana and her two brothers play soccer. They all play on different teams. Find the median number of goals for each team.
   A. Ana's team has played 6 games. Here are the number of goals her team has scored in the six games: 4, 4, 0, 3, 2, 5.
   B. David's team has played 5 games. Here are the number of goals his team has scored: 2, 1, 3, 2, 3.
   C. Tony's team has played 4 games. Here are the number of goals his team has scored: 1, 0, 3, 6.
   D. Ana claims that her team is the best. Do you agree? Why or why not?

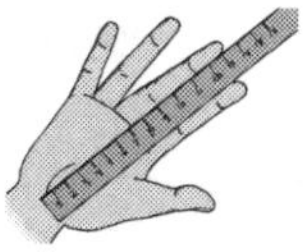

3. A. Make a data table like the one shown below. Measure the length of your hand and the hands of your family and friends. Measure at least five hands including your own. Carefully measure from the wrist to the end of the longest finger. Measure to the nearest centimeter.
   B. Record your data in the data table.
   C. Find the median value for your hand length data.

Hand Length Data

Name	Hand Length in cm

16 SG · Grade 4 · Unit 1 · Lesson 3 — An Average Activity

***Student Guide* - Page 16**

Name ____________________ Date ____________

Part 3 **Finding the Median**

1. Mr. Lewis's fourth-grade class did an experiment with colored candies. Five students took a handful of candy. They pulled 12, 6, 5, 3, and 7 pieces of candy. What is the median number of candies pulled? Show how you decided.

2. Lee Yah measured the hand lengths of the people in her family. Her grandmother's hand measured 15 cm in length. Her two sisters' hand lengths were 12 cm and 10 cm. Her mother's hand length was 14 cm. Her father's hand length was 18 cm. Lee Yah's hand measured 12 cm. What is the median hand length in Lee Yah's family? Show how you decided.

3. The fourth-grade soccer team at Bessie Coleman School practices after school. This week they practiced for 45 minutes on Monday, 30 minutes on Tuesday, an hour on Thursday, and 40 minutes on Friday. They skipped practice on Wednesday. What is the median number of minutes they practiced for the five days? Show how you decided.

4. Eight of Mrs. Dewey's students stayed after school to help her decorate her bulletin boards. She gave each student a box of raisins as a treat. Each student counted the number of raisins in his or her box. Here is their data: 23, 27, 22, 26, 21, 27, 25, and 23. Based on the students' data, what is the median number of raisins found in a box? Show how you decided.

4 DAB · Grade 4 · Unit 1 — DATA ABOUT US

***Discovery Assignment Book* - Page 4**

AT A GLANCE

Math Facts and Daily Practice and Problems

DPP Bits G and I provide practice with telling time. DPP Challenge H is a geometry problem. Task J provides practice with variables and values.

Part 1. Exploring Medians Using Data About Us

1. Discuss the term average.
2. Choose two or three numerical variables of interest to your students to use in examples as they learn to find medians. Height, number of pets, and number of pencils in your desk will be used as examples here.
3. Students write the number of pets they own and the number of pencils in their desks on a sheet of paper.
4. Define the median as the value exactly in the middle of the data.
5. Illustrate how to find the median by asking five students to line up in front of the class from shortest to tallest. The student in the middle of the line has the median height.
6. Use a similar procedure to find the medians of the other variables you chose to study.
7. Show how to find the median of an even number of values using six students.
8. Ask all the students to stand with their data. Use the procedure described above to find the median values for height and the other two variables you chose.
9. Demonstrate how to find the median on a bar graph. Find the median value on the class graph you made in Lesson 2.

Part 2. Exploring Medians Using Data About Room 204

1. Read and discuss the information on the *An Average Activity* Activity Pages.
2. Use *Questions 1–5* to guide a class discussion on medians.
3. Students work in pairs to answer *Questions 6–8*.

Homework

Assign *Questions 1–3* in the Homework section.

Assessment

1. Use *Questions 7–8* from the Explore section as assessment.
2. Use *Questions 1–2* from the Homework section in the *Student Guide* as an assessment.
3. Use DPP Task J to assess students' understanding of variables and values.
4. Use Home Practice Part 3 as an assessment.
5. Use the *Observational Assessment Record* to document students' abilities to find a median.

Notes:

Student Guide

Questions 1–8 (SG pp. 13–15)

1. **A.** *Grace

   B. *Yes; typical implies average

2. **A.** 54 inches

   B. Yes

3. Yes; 3 is halfway between 1 and 4.

4. $2\frac{1}{2}$ blocks

5. **A.** *3 blocks

   B. *Students might use the data table or graph to find the median. For example, students can count off each tally mark, one at the top of the table and one at the bottom, until they reach the center.

6. 2 moves

7. 3 runs

8. **A.** *John: 410 cm, Shannon: 250 cm, Tanya: 590 cm

   B. *Answers will vary. Students may feel that Tanya should win because her plane had the largest median flight, 590 cm. This average distance can represent all her flights. Other students may feel that John should win because he had the longest flight, 640 cm.

Homework (SG p. 16)

Questions 1–3

1. 2 pets

2. **A.** 3.5 goals

   B. 2 goals

   C. 2 goals

   D. Answers will vary. Students may feel that Ana's team is the best because her median number of goals (3.5 goals) is the highest or students may feel that Tony's team is the best because his team has the highest number of goals in all of the games (6 goals).

3. Answers will vary. See the *Arm Span vs. Height* Lab Pages in the *Student Guide* for a sample data table.

Discovery Assignment Book

**Home Practice (DAB p. 4)

Part 3. Finding the Median

Questions 1–4

1. 6 pieces of candy; Arrange the numbers in order and select the middle number.

2. 13 cm; Arrange the numbers in order, select the two middle numbers, and find the number halfway between the two middle numbers.

3. 40 minutes; The five numbers are: 0, 30, 40, 45, and 60. The median is 40 minutes.

4. 24 raisins; Arrange the numbers in order. The two middle numbers are 23 and 25, so the median is 24 raisins.

*Answers and/or discussion are included in the Lesson Guide.

**Answers for all the Home Practice in the *Discovery Assignment Book* are at the end of the unit.

Daily Practice and Problems: Bit for Lesson 4

K. Addition Test: ***Doubles, 2s, 3s***
(URG p. 16)

Take the diagnostic test *Doubles, 2s, 3s.* Your teacher will suggest some additional activities if you need more practice.

DPP Task is on page 68. Suggestions for using the DPPs are on page 68.

LESSON GUIDE 4

The Four Servants

Estimated Class Sessions: 1

Four servants (Artist, Table-Maker, Grapher, and Answerer) help a young prince find the golden bird that will save his father's life. The story is a variation on several magical helper folk tales. The story reviews (or introduces) the TIMS Laboratory Method.

Key Content

- Using the TIMS Laboratory Method to solve problems.
- Using patterns in data tables and graphs to make predictions.
- Solving problems in more than one way.
- Connecting mathematics and language arts.

Key Vocabulary

horizontal axis
vertical axis

Curriculum Sequence

Before This Unit

TIMS Laboratory Method. Students used the TIMS Laboratory Method as they conducted experiments in first, second, and third grades. In third grade they made point graphs, drew lines to fit the points, and used the lines to make predictions in Units 7, 9, 10, 15, and 20.

After This Unit

TIMS Laboratory Method. More detailed instruction on the use of data tables and graphs to make predictions will be presented in Lesson 5 of this unit and in Units 2 and 5. Units 8, 10, 14, 15, and 16 will include experiments in which students use the TIMS Laboratory Method.

Materials List

Print Materials for Students

		Math Facts and Daily Practice and Problems	Activity	Homework	Written Assessment
Student Books	**Adventure Book**		*The Four Servants* Pages 1–14		
Student Books	**Discovery Assignment Book**			Home Practice Parts 4 & 5 Page 5	
Teacher Resources	**Facts Resource Guide**	DPP Item 1K			DPP Item 1K *Addition Test: Doubles, 2s, 3s*
Teacher Resources	**Unit Resource Guide**	DPP Items K–L Pages 16–17			DPP Item K *Addition Test: Doubles, 2s, 3s* Page 16

available on Teacher Resource CD

All Transparency Masters, Blackline Masters, and Assessment Blackline Masters in the Unit Resource Guide are on the Teacher Resource CD.

The Four Servants

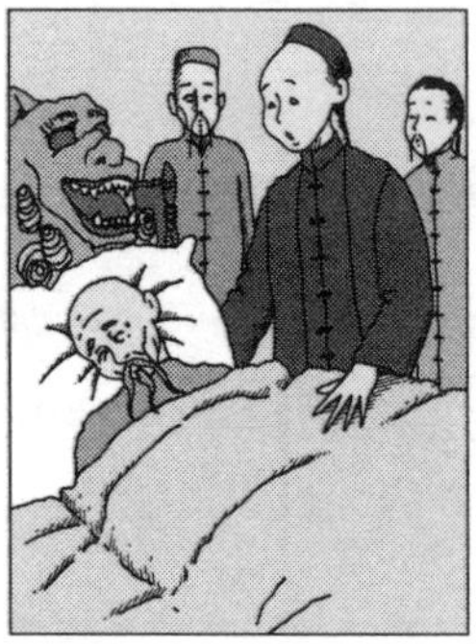

Once there was a king who was very sick, so sick he was about to die. All the wise men and women of the kingdom agreed that only the golden bird's singing could save him. But no one knew where to find the golden bird.

Now the king had a son who loved his father dearly. "I will find the golden bird," said the prince.

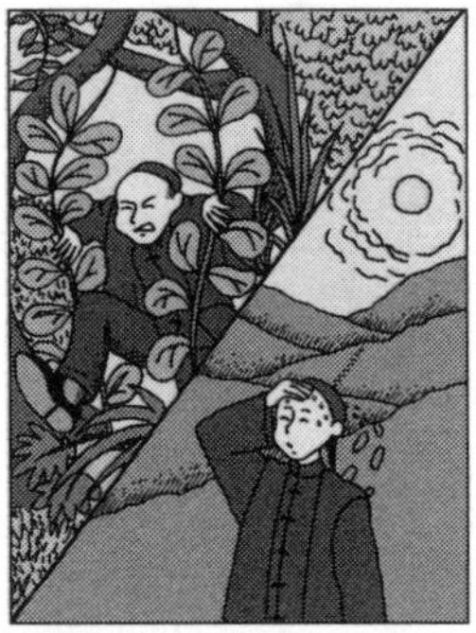

So the young prince set out to find the golden bird and save his father's life.

2 AB • Grade 4 • Unit 1 • Lesson 4

***Adventure Book* - Page 2**

The Four Servants

Before long the prince came upon a girl with a pencil in her hand. The girl was surrounded by papers filled with beautiful drawings.

"What are you doing?" asked the prince.

"I am drawing pictures," answered the girl. "I can draw anything so that it looks as real as life. Do you think I could be of use to you as a servant?"

"What a wonderful skill!" said the prince. "Come along and follow me. Who knows if drawing pictures may not be useful?"

And so Artist followed the prince as his servant.

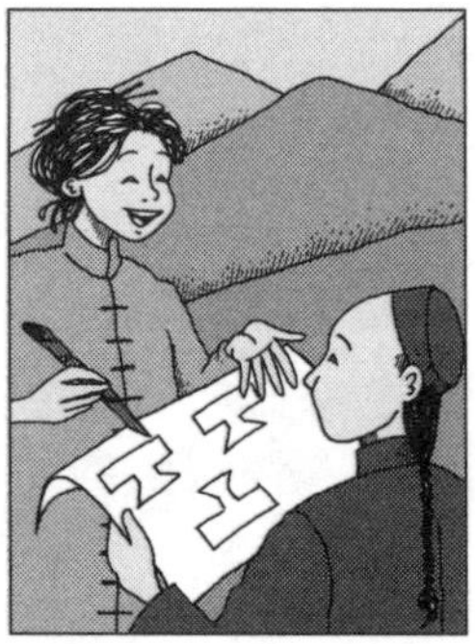

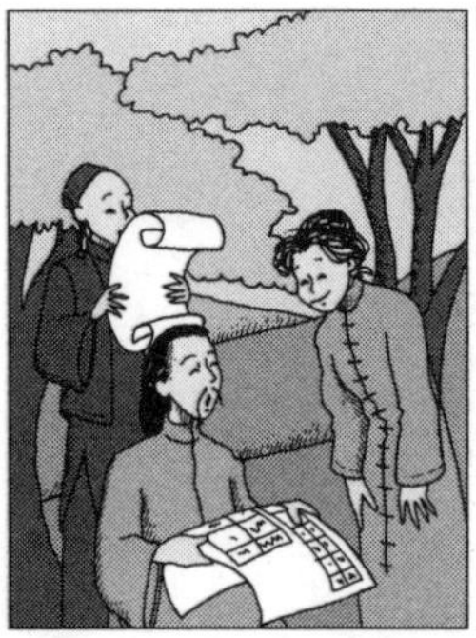

Before long they came upon a fellow who was also surrounded by papers. These papers were filled with tables of data.

"What are you doing, sir?" asked the prince.

"Why, I am taking data and organizing it into tables," replied the fellow. "Give me any amount of information and I will sort it out and organize it in a data table. Could you use a fellow like me?"

"Come along," said the prince. "Who knows if table-making may not be useful?"

And so Table-Maker followed the prince too.

AB • Grade 4 • Unit 1 • Lesson 4 3

***Adventure Book* - Page 3**

Before the Activity

Some of the key action in this story parallels what students do in Lesson 5 *Arm Span vs. Height,* so it may be helpful to read through that lab before you teach this Adventure Book.

Discussion Prompts

Page 2

- *The theme of going on a quest for a magical object is common in folk literature. The search for the Holy Grail is the most famous quest tale, but such stories abound in collections like those from the Brothers Grimm and Andrew Lang.*

Page 3

- *Does the picture that Artist is making look familiar?*

Artist is drawing a picture that may remind your students of *Stencilrama,* a lab they did in Grade 3 Unit 10. In that lab, students study the relationship between the number of times an index card stencil is used and the length of the resulting pattern.

- *What is Table-Maker doing?*

Table-Maker is organizing data in a table.

Discussion Prompts

Page 4

- *Does the graph that Grapher is plotting look familiar?*

Answers will vary. Students using *Math Trailblazers* in third grade made point graphs similar to this.

- *How would you answer the question, "How many clouds are in the sky?"*

This is a very hard question to answer. Clouds form and disappear. Not all places in the world have clouds at the same time or have clouds in the same quantity. Students might suggest counting the number of clouds in a small section and using it to generalize the amount of clouds all over the world.

Questions like this one—questions with answers that are difficult or impossible to verify—are sometimes called Fermi questions after the great physicist Enrico Fermi. One of Fermi's favorites was, *"How many piano tuners are there in Chicago?"* Another example is, *"How many leaves are on a fully grown elm tree?"* Fermi questions can help students improve their estimation skills.

Page 5

- *About how many meters tall would you guess the giant is?*

Answers will vary. Later in the story the giant is found to be about $4\frac{1}{2}$ m tall, but at this point accept any reasonable answer.

- *How would you figure out the giant's height?*

Answers will vary. The approach taken by the prince and his servants is to find the relationship between hand length and height and then to use this relationship to find the giant's height. Other approaches are plausible, particularly if they depend on scaling up from humans to the giant.

The Four Servants

A little farther along they came upon yet another fellow surrounded by papers. But these papers were filled with numbers, lines, and points.

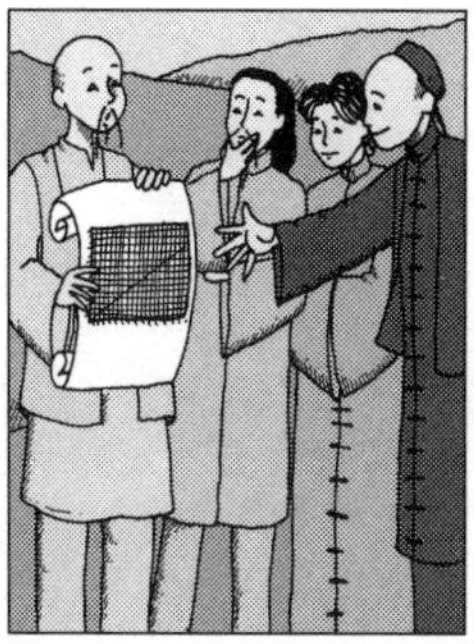

"Who are you and what are you doing?" asked the prince.

"I am making graphs," replied this fellow. "Give me any data and I will graph it so that anyone can understand it. Do you think you could use a fellow like me as a servant?"

"Why not?" replied the prince. "Who knows but that graphing might not be useful?"

And so Grapher joined the others following the prince.

Yet a little farther along the prince saw a girl lying on the grass looking up into the sky.

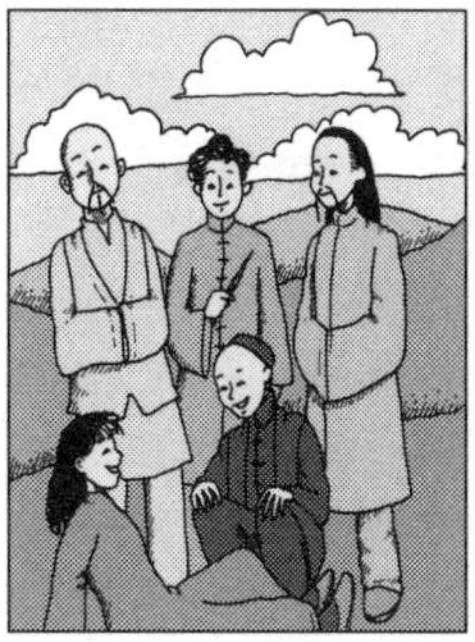

"What are you doing?" asked the prince.

"What an easy question!" answered the girl. "I was just thinking about some hard questions. How many clouds are in the sky? I love to answer hard questions. Could you use someone like me for a servant?"

"Why not?" said the prince. "Who knows when we might need to have a hard question answered? In truth, I have a hard question right now. Where can I find the golden bird?"

"I don't know where the golden bird is," said Answerer, "but we could ask Mother Hollah for help. I have heard that she is the wisest woman in the land."

4 AB • Grade 4 • Unit 1 • Lesson 4

***Adventure Book* - Page 4**

The Four Servants

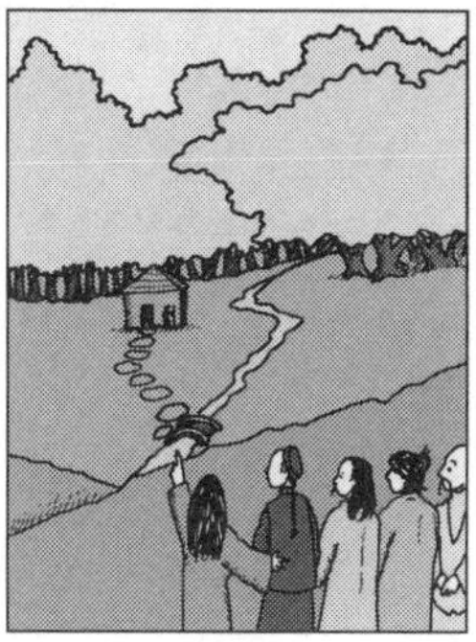

So the prince set off to see Mother Hollah. Artist, Table-Maker, Grapher, and Answerer followed. When they arrived at Mother Hollah's hut, the old woman was waiting for them.

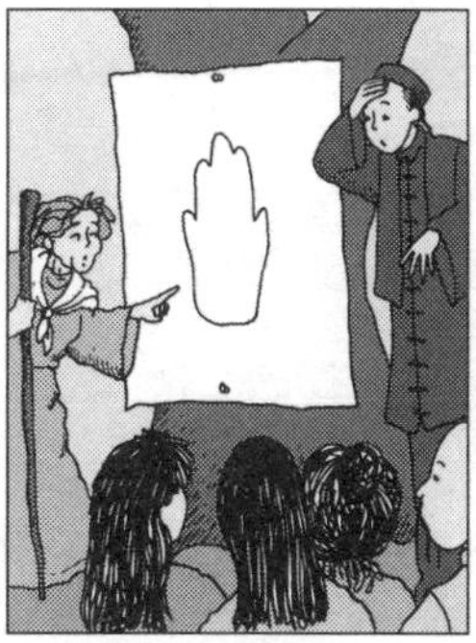

"So, you are looking for the golden bird," said Mother Hollah. "If you can solve my puzzle, then I will tell you where to find the golden bird. My puzzle is, 'How tall is the giant who made this handprint?'"

And Mother Hollah showed the prince and his servants a huge handprint.

"What a monster that giant must be!" exclaimed the prince. "How are we ever to find how tall such a creature is?"

AB • Grade 4 • Unit 1 • Lesson 4 5

***Adventure Book* - Page 5**

But Artist was already at work.

"Look here," she said. "I have drawn the giant, whose height we don't know, and the handprint, which is here in front of us. We want to know the height, *H*. We can measure the length of the hand print, *L*."

"That's true," said the prince. "We have to find the giant's height. We can measure the length of the handprint, but will that help us find the height?"

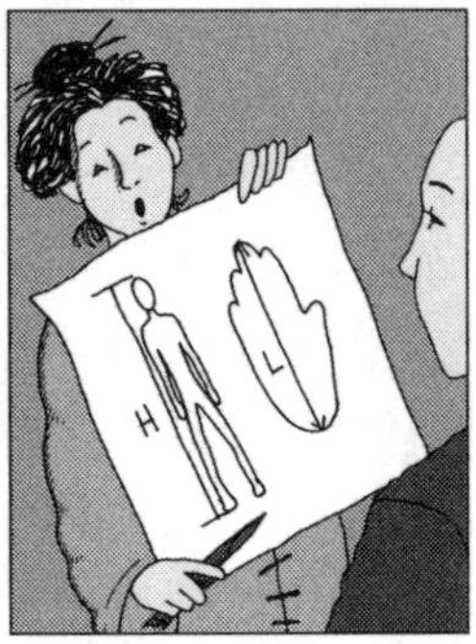
H
L

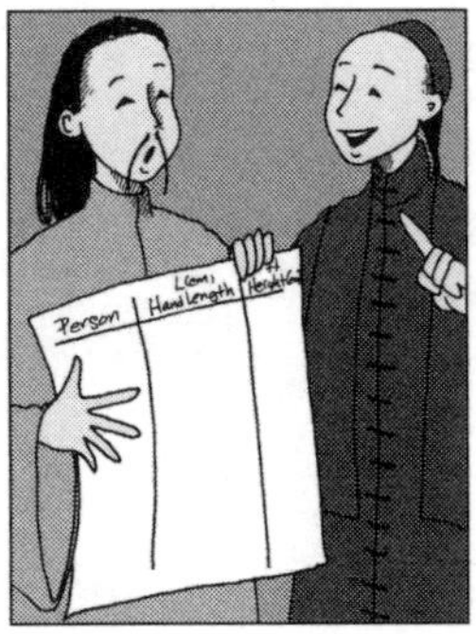
Person

Table-Maker had an idea. "Let's gather some data. We will measure the length of our hands and our height. We'll organize our data in a table. Maybe that will tell us something, but even if it doesn't, we'll have fun!"

"Good idea, Table-Maker," said the prince.

***Adventure Book* - Page 6**

So the prince and his four servants began to make measurements. To find their heights, they worked in pairs. One in each pair stood against a wall, and the other used a meterstick to measure the height.

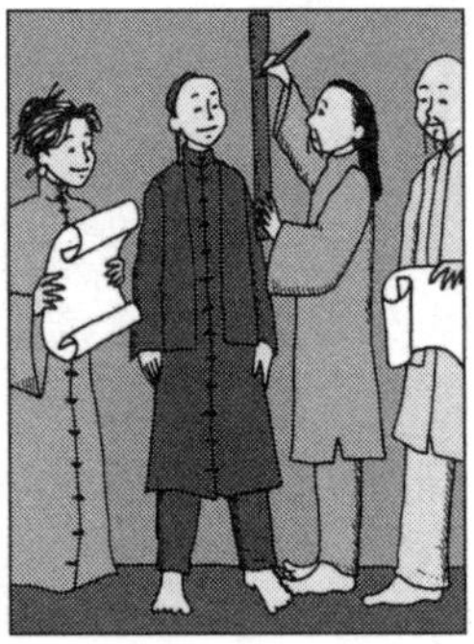

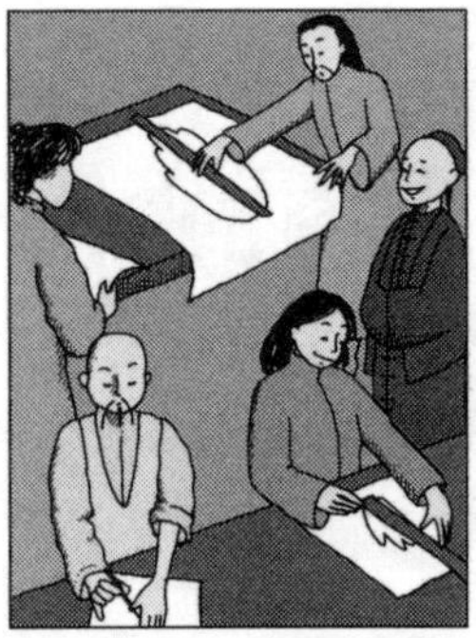

To measure the length of their handprints, first they traced their hands on paper. Then, they measured the lengths from the wrists to the middle fingertip.

So the prince and his four servants measured their heights and the lengths of their handprints.

***Adventure Book* - Page 7**

Discussion Prompts

Page 6

- *What are the two variables that Artist has identified?*

Hand length *(L),* and height *(H).*

Page 7

- *Would knowing the length of someone's hand help you predict that person's height? Why?*

Yes. Because people with longer hands are usually taller.

- *Would knowing the length of someone's name help you predict that person's height? Why not?*

No. Because there is no relationship between a person's name length and his or her height.

Discussion Prompts

Page 8

- *What patterns do you notice in Table-Maker's table?*

Answers will vary. The most important pattern for the purpose of the story is the relationship that exists between hand length and height. Whenever one of these doubles or triples, for example, the other does too.

Page 9

- *Compare the graph and the data table. Which one would you use to solve the problem?*

Answers will vary. The idea that the graph makes the pattern clearer should come up.

 The Four Servants

"We should try to measure very big and very small people, too," said Table-Maker. "That will make any patterns in the data show up more clearly."

So the prince and his servants measured people on the road and in the village. They measured carefully because they knew the king's life depended on them.

Person	L Hand Length (cm)	H Height (cm)
Newborn	5	46
Baby Carrie	8	74
Toddler	10	92
Answerer	14	129
Prince	15	135
Shepherd Girl	16	148
Artist	16	150
Table-Maker	18	170
Grapher	20	183
Peddler Woman	21	191
Tall Man	25	223
Giant	50	

Finally, they measured the length of the giant's handprint. Table-Maker organized all the data in a table.

"That was fun," said the prince. "And this data table seems to be helping. But the pattern is not clear to me. I still don't know the giant's height."

8   AB · Grade 4 · Unit 1 · Lesson 4

Adventure Book - Page 8

The Four Servants

"I can help," said Grapher. "I'll plot the data. Then maybe we'll understand better."

In a moment, Grapher had made a clear graph. He saw that the data points were close to a straight line, so he drew a straight line that fit the pattern of the points.

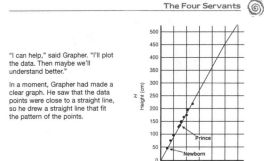

"I think this graph will help us answer Mother Hollah's riddle," said Answerer.

"Well, maybe," said the prince. "But I don't understand it. Can someone explain it to me?"

AB · Grade 4 · Unit 1 · Lesson 4   9

Adventure Book - Page 9

The Four Servants

"The points on this graph stand for the people we measured," said Grapher. "See, this point is for you; your hand length is 15 cm and your height is 135 cm. This point here is for the newborn: hand length 5 cm and height 46 cm. Every point is for a person we measured."

"All right," said the prince, "but why did you draw a line?"

"The line shows where points for people we didn't measure would probably be," said Grapher.

H
Height (cm)
500
450
400
350
300
250
200
150
100
50
0
Prince
Newborn
0 10 20 30 40 50 60
L
Hand Length (cm)

H
Height (cm)
500
450
400
350
300
250
200
150
100
50
0
0 10 20 30 40 50 60
L
Hand Length (cm)

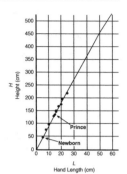

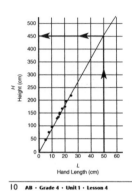

"I can see now that it's a very fine graph," said the prince, "but I still don't understand how it helps us find the giant's height."

"Look again," said Answerer. "Since all our points fall close to a line, the giant's point will be close to the line too. Since we know that the length of the giant's hand is 50 cm, we will use that to predict the height. Find L = 50 cm on the horizontal axis, go up to the best-fit line, and go over to the vertical axis. This shows us that the giant's height is probably about 450 cm."

10 AB · Grade 4 · Unit 1 · Lesson 4

***Adventure Book* - Page 10**

The Four Servants

"That's four and a half meters. That makes sense as a giant's height," said the prince, "but I would feel better if we could solve the problem in another way too."

"Good idea," said Answerer. "It's always better to solve an important problem another way. Tell me, Prince, do you see any patterns in our data table?"

"Well," said the prince, "it seems that when hand length gets bigger, so does height."

L
Hand Length (cm)

Person	L Hand Length (cm)	H Height (cm)
Newborn	5	46
Baby Carrie	8	74
Toddler	10	92
Answerer	14	129
Prince	15	135
Shepherd Girl	16	148
Artist	16	150
Table-Maker	18	170
Grapher	20	183
Peddler Woman	21	191
Tall Man	25	223
Giant	50	

"Very good," said Answerer, "but there's more of a pattern than just that. Look at the data in the hand length column for the newborn and for the toddler. What do you notice?"

"The toddler's hand is twice as long as the newborn's," answered the prince.

"Right," said Answerer. "Now, what about the height for the newborn and the toddler?"

"It looks as though the height about doubles, too," said the prince.

AB · Grade 4 · Unit 1 · Lesson 4 11

***Adventure Book* - Page 11**

Discussion Prompts

Page 10

- *Use the graph to predict the giant's height. Remember the giant's hand length is 50 cm.*

About 450 cm. If your students are unfamiliar with this procedure, use the story as a quick introduction to the idea that graphs are useful for making predictions and solving problems. Students will have many opportunities to make predictions from graphs in succeeding units.

- *Would the giant be able to stand up straight in the classroom?*

No, 450 cm is 4.5 meters or about 15 feet tall.

Page 11

- *What patterns do you notice in the data table?*

There are many. One is the relationship between the data for Baby Carrie and the Shepherd Girl. The Shepherd Girl has a hand that is twice as long as Baby Carrie's and is also twice as tall.

Encourage students to look across the rows of the table, as well as down the columns. Some may notice that the heights are about nine times the hand lengths.

Discussion Prompts

Page 13

- *Did the prince and his servants find the exact height of the giant? Was their answer close enough?*

Using the graph, the prince predicted that the giant would be about 450 cm tall and using patterns in the data table, he predicted that the giant would be 446 cm. These estimates are very close to the giant's height of 448 cm.

The Four Servants

Mother Hollah smiled when the prince gave her the giant's height. "You have used your tools well to make a good prediction. Here is the giant. If you will measure her height, you will find that she is 448 cm tall."

"The golden bird is on top of the golden mountain," said Mother Hollah. "The way is far, but the giant will carry you."

The giant carried the prince to the golden mountain. There the prince found a golden cage and in it the golden bird. The prince took the bird and cage and returned to his father's kingdom. His four faithful servants went with him.

AB · Grade 4 · Unit 1 · Lesson 4   13

Adventure Book - Page 13

Page 14

- *What do the four servants have to do with the TIMS Laboratory Method?*

The four servants embody the four steps in the TIMS Laboratory Method.

- *Can you think of other problems the four servants could help solve?*

Answers will vary, but the scientific method is a powerful approach to many problems.

 The Four Servants

As soon as the bird came into the palace, it began to sing the most beautiful songs. Right away the king began to feel better. Before long he was stronger and healthier than ever.

Now the four servants were not idle either. They carried out many experiments and discovered many interesting and useful things. They helped to make the kingdom a rich and happy place.

After many years, the old king died and the prince became King. And if he hasn't died yet, why he's still King today!

14   AB · Grade 4 · Unit 1 · Lesson 4

Adventure Book - Page 14

Daily Practice and Problems:
Task for Lesson 4

L. Task: Tom's and Tim's Savings
(URG p. 17)

1. Tom wants to buy a book that costs $2.95.
He can save 50¢ a week. How many weeks
will he need to save to have enough for
the book?

2. Tim is saving to buy a skateboard. He can
buy a used one from a friend for $10. He
has $5.50 now and can save 75¢ a week.
How long will it take him to save enough
for the skateboard?

Name _____ Date _____

Part 4 **Measuring in Inches**
You will need an inch ruler to complete this assignment. Estimate the length
in inches of four objects in your home. Then, measure each object to the
nearest inch. Complete the data table below.

Object	Estimate (in inches)	Actual (in inches)

Part 5 **Inches and Centimeters**
You will need a ruler that measures inches and centimeters for this part.

1. Which is longer, 1 centimeter or 1 inch? _____ Using a ruler,
draw a line that is 1 centimeter long. Draw another line, 1 inch long.
Label each line with its measurement.

2. Which is longer, 5 centimeters or 3 inches? _____ Using a ruler,
draw a line that is 5 centimeters long. Draw another line, 3 inches long.
Label each line with its measurement.

3. **A.** Which is longer, 40 centimeters or 13 inches? _____
B. How did you decide?

DATA ABOUT US   **DAB · Grade 4 · Unit 1**   **5**

Discovery Assignment Book **- Page 5**

Suggestions for Teaching the Lesson

Math Facts

DPP Bit K is a written assessment of addition facts:
Doubles, 2s, and 3s. For students who need extra
practice with these facts, use the Addition and
Subtraction Math Facts Review section in the
Grade 4 Facts Resource Guide.

Homework and Practice

- Students might enjoy reading and discussing the
story with an adult at home.

- DPP Task L provides practice solving word
problems. The students must analyze the problems and determine what operations will be useful. Solving the problems will require repeated
addition, skip counting, multiplication,
or subtraction.

- Parts 4 and 5 of the Home Practice review measurement concepts and practice measuring skills.
This review will help students prepare for the
work they will do in Lesson 5.

*Answers for Parts 4 and 5 of the Home Practice can be
found in the Answer Key at the end of this lesson and at
the end of this unit.*

Extension

Gather hand length and height data from some students and adults. Check to see if the data points fall
on or near the line in the graph in the story.

Language Arts Connection

Students might enjoy writing another adventure for
the four servants. They might base their story on a
pizza (or ice cream) manufacturer trying to decide
how many of each of several types of pizza (or ice
cream) to make.

Literature Connection

For the Student

There are several folk stories in which servants with incredible abilities play a prominent role. We like "How Six Men Traveled Through the Wide World" and "The Six Servants" by the Brothers Grimm, and "How Six Men Traveled Through the Wide World" in *The Yellow Fairy Book* by Andrew Lang. *The Five Chinese Brothers* and *The Seven Chinese Brothers* are similar in that brothers with special powers save the day.

- Bishop, Claire Huchet, and K. Wiese. *The Five Chinese Brothers*. Coward-McCann, Inc., New York, 1999.

- "How Six Men Traveled Through the Wide World" and "The Six Servants" from *The Complete Grimm's Fairy Tales*. Pantheon Books, Inc., New York, 1976.

- "How Six Men Traveled Through the Wide World" in Andrew Lang (Ed.), *The Yellow Fairy Book*. Dover Publications Inc., New York, 1979.

- Mahy, Margaret, and J. & M.S. Tsang. *The Seven Chinese Brothers*. Scholastic Inc., New York, 1992.

For the Teacher

Haldane, J.B.S. "On Being the Right Size." In James R. Newman (ed.), *The World of Mathematics, Volume Two*. Simon and Schuster, New York, 1956. (Essay originally published in 1928.)

Discovery Assignment Book

**Home Practice (DAB p. 5)

Part 4. Measuring in Inches

Answers will vary.

Part 5. Inches and Centimeters

Questions 1–3

I. 1 inch

 _____ 1 cm

 _____ 1 inch

2. 3 inches

 _____ 5 cm

 _____ 3 inches

3. **A.** 40 centimeters
 B. Answers will vary. Students might draw the
 lines and compare them.

*Answers and/or discussion are included in the Lesson Guide.

**Answers for all the Home Practice in the *Discovery Assignment Book* are at the end of the unit.

70 **URG · Grade 4 · Unit 1 · Lesson 4 · Answer Key**

LESSON GUIDE 5

Arm Span vs. Height

Estimated Class Sessions: 4–5

Students use the TIMS Laboratory Method to investigate the relationship between the arm span and height of their classmates.

Key Content

- Connecting mathematics and science to real-world situations.
- Investigating the relationship between arm span and height.
- Translating between graphs and real-world data.
- Measuring length in inches.
- Representing data in a point graph.
- Using patterns in tables and graphs to make predictions.

Key Vocabulary

fixed variables
point graph

Curriculum Sequence

Before This Unit

Point Graphs. Students learned to make point graphs in third grade. See Grade 3 Unit 7 *Lemonade Stand* for examples.

After This Unit

Point Graphs. Students will plot points in a variety of graphing activities in fourth grade. For example, students will create line graphs in laboratory investigations in Units 2, 5, 8, 10, 15, and 16.

Daily Practice and Problems: Bits for Lesson 5

M. Addition Test: *More Addition Facts* (URG p. 18)

Take the diagnostic test *More Addition Facts.* Your teacher will suggest some additional activities if you need more practice.

O. Time 2 (URG p. 19)

1. What is the time now?
2. What time was it 30 minutes ago?
3. What time was it 45 minutes ago?

Q. Sandwiches (URG p. 21)

The school cafeteria asked students how they liked their sandwiches cut. The bar graph displays the data.

How We Like Our Sandwiches Cut
S
Number of Students
0
2
4
6
8
10
12
14
16
18
Diagonal
Into Fourths
Down the Center
T
Type of Cut

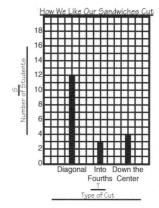

Describe three things that the graph tells you.

S. Measurement: Could Be or Crazy (URG p. 22)

Decide whether each measurement is a "could be" measurement or a "crazy" measurement. No fair measuring! Explain how you decided.

1. The distance from a doorknob to the floor is 30 cm.
2. The distance from a doorknob to the floor is 40 inches.
3. The face of a watch is 3 cm wide.
4. A fourth grader's foot is 20 inches long.
5. A car is 3 meters long.

DPP Tasks are on page 80. Suggestions for using the DPPs are on page 80.

Materials List

Print Materials for Students

	Math Facts and Daily Practice and Problems	Lab	Homework	Written Assessment
Student Books — Student Guide		*Arm Span vs. Height* Pages 17–23	*Arm Span vs. Height* Homework Section Page 23	
Student Books — Discovery Assignment Book		*Plotting Points Pictures* Pages 7–8		
Teacher Resources — Facts Resource Guide ⊙	DPP Item 1M			DPP Item 1M *Addition Test: More Addition Facts*
Teacher Resources — Unit Resource Guide	DPP Items M–T Pages 18–23 ⊙			DPP Item M *Addition Test: More Addition Facts* Page 18, and DPP Item T *Favorite Sandwiches* Page 23 ⊙ *More Arm Span vs. Height Data* Page 83, 1 per student
Teacher Resources — Generic Section ⊙		*Centimeter Grid Paper* (optional) and *Centimeter Graph Paper*, 2 per student, and *Three-column Data Table*, 1 per student group		

⊙ available on Teacher Resource CD

All Transparency Masters, Blackline Masters, and Assessment Blackline Masters in the Unit Resource Guide are on the Teacher Resource CD.

Supplies for Each Student Group

4 yardsticks or metersticks at each station (at least 3 stations are recommended)
rulers
calculators

Materials for the Teacher

Jerome's Family: Hand Lengths and Heights Transparency Master (Unit Resource Guide) Page 84
Transparencies of *Three-column Data Table* (Unit Resource Guide, Generic Section) number of copies depends on the number of students in your class or 1 class data table on poster-size graph paper
Point Graph: What's Wrong Here? Transparency Master (Unit Resource Guide) Page 85
Transparency of *Centimeter Graph Paper* (Unit Resource Guide, Generic Section) or 1 sheet of poster-size graph paper for class graph
Observational Assessment Record (Unit Resource Guide, Pages 7–8 and Teacher Resource CD)
Individual Assessment Record Sheet (Teacher Implementation Guide, Assessment section and Teacher Resource CD)
masking tape

Before the Lab

Set up at least three *Arm Span vs. Height* stations for your students to collect data. Since you will measure in inches, you may use either yardsticks or metersticks that have inches on one side. At each station, tape two metersticks vertically on a wall for measuring height. Tape two metersticks horizontally for measuring arm span. Make the height of the horizontal metersticks appropriate to the heights of your students' shoulders.

One way to tape the metersticks is shown in Figure 10. In this case, students must add the reading on one meterstick to the length (to the nearest inch) on the other meterstick. The reading on one meterstick will be 39 inches, which must be added to the reading on the second meterstick. While measuring height and arm span, students are also practicing addition. If you want the computation to be easy, line up the edge of the second meterstick with the 30-inch mark on the first meterstick. (If yardsticks are used, they may be lined up edge-to-edge. Students must add the reading on the second yardstick to 36 inches.)

Figure 10: *Setting up measurement stations with metersticks*

Create a three-column data table on poster-size graph paper or on transparencies of a *Three-column Data Table*. Label the columns with the following headings: Name, Arm Span, and Height. Post this in a convenient location where students can easily record their data.

If your students have not had many opportunities to plot points, provide students with two sheets of *Centimeter Grid Paper* and the *Plotting Points Pictures* Activity Pages in the *Discovery Assignment Book*. Using these pages students plot points both on

TIMS Tip

Plot the points to make the pictures on the *Plotting Points Pictures* Activity Pages. Then, make a transparency of the picture. You can lay the transparency over students' pictures to see where they had difficulty plotting points.

Name _____ Date _____

Plotting Points Pictures

Number the axes on a sheet of *Centimeter Grid Paper* by ones. Plot the data shown below. Use a ruler to connect the points with lines as you plot each point. When the data table says stop, start at the next new point, but do not connect the previous point.

Picture 1

Horizontal Axis	Vertical Axis	Horizontal Axis	Vertical Axis	Horizontal Axis	Vertical Axis
1	1	14	13	0	10
2	3	12	13	0	5
4	5	10	11	2	9
5	7	11	13	3	10
6	8	15	15	5	9
5	6	10	15	4	8
5	4	9	13	3	6
3	3	8	14	1	4
2	1	8	16	1	1
4	2	10	17	S T O P	
6	2	12	16	12	12
7	5	15	17	10	10
8	3	12	18	10	8
7	0	10	19	12	6
10	3	7	18	S T O P	
9	6	6	16	13	11
10	4	6	14	12	11
12	2	7	12	12	10
15	1	6	13	13	10
14	3	4	17	13	11
12	4	2	19	S T O P	
11	5	0	19	13	8
10	7	3	16	12	8
12	5	5	12	12	7
14	5	6	11	13	7
15	7	4	12	13	8
15	11	2	12	S T O P	

Arm Span vs. Height   DAB · Grade 4 · Unit 1 · Lesson 5   7

Copyright © Kendall/Hunt Publishing Company

Discovery Assignment Book - Page 7

Name _____ Date _____

Number the axes on a sheet of *Centimeter Grid Paper* by tens. The horizontal axis must go up to 150 and the vertical axis must go up to 200. Plot the data shown below on grid paper. Use a ruler to connect the points with lines as you plot each point.

Picture 2

Horizontal Axis	Vertical Axis
45	0
85	0
125	40
130	80
70	80
70	90
150	90
70	180
105	185
70	200
70	80
60	80
60	200
0	90
60	90
60	80
0	80
5	40
45	0

8   DAB · Grade 4 · Unit 1 · Lesson 5   Arm Span vs. Height

Copyright © Kendall/Hunt Publishing Company

Discovery Assignment Book - Page 8

Arm Span vs. Height

The TIMS Laboratory Method

Irma and Jerome noticed that the Adventure Book story *The Four Servants* took place in China. All the measurements were of Chinese people. They wondered if the four servants would have found the same results if they had measured the people in Irma and Jerome's neighborhood.

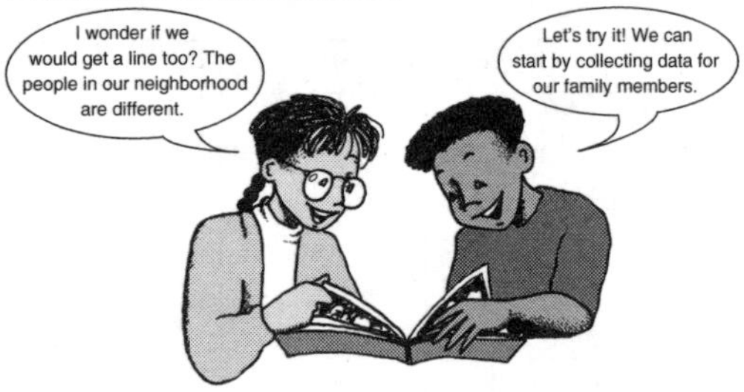
I wonder if we would get a line too? The people in our neighborhood are different.
Let's try it! We can start by collecting data for our family members.

Irma and Jerome decided to use the TIMS Laboratory Method to help them solve problems involving hand length and height in their neighborhood. The four servants used this four-step method. First, Irma and Jerome **drew a picture** of the steps they would follow in the experiment. Irma's picture is shown below.

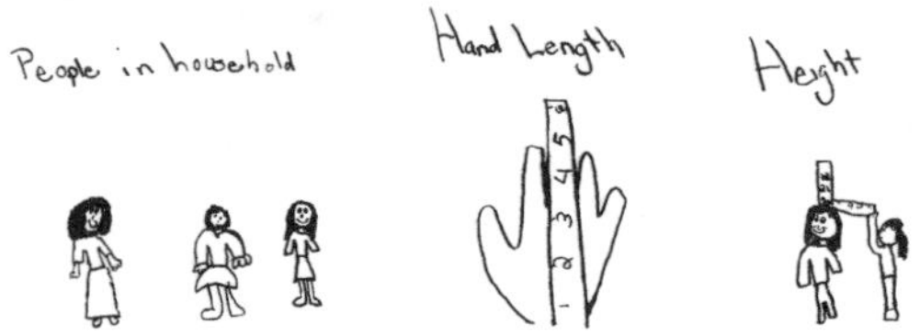
People in household
Hand Length
Height

Arm Span vs. Height SG · Grade 4 · Unit 1 · Lesson 5 17

***Student Guide* - Page 17**

Notice that Irma showed the people in her household, how she was going to measure hand length, and how she was going to measure height. Irma labeled the variables in her experiment, Hand Length and Height.

Irma and Jerome then **collected and organized** the data in a data table. Below is the data Jerome collected from his family:

Jerome's Family Table

Name	Hand Length (in cm)	Height (in cm)
Peter	12 cm	102 cm
Abby	13 cm	110 cm
Timothy	15 cm	124 cm
Jerome	14 cm	127 cm
Jenny	16 cm	147 cm
Mom		

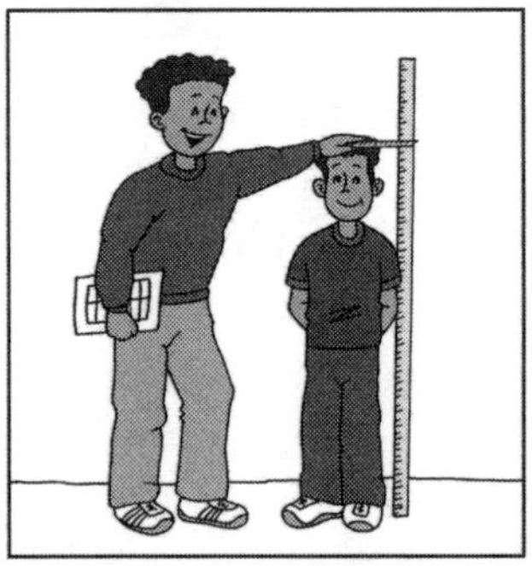

18 SG · Grade 4 · Unit 1 · Lesson 5 Arm Span vs. Height

***Student Guide* - Page 18**

and between the lines. You can quickly ascertain which students can plot data from the pictures that result. Student groups can work on these activity pages while other groups collect their data. Students can finish the activity pages at home.

Developing the Lab

Part 1. Launching the Lab

The *Arm Span vs. Height* Lab Pages in the *Student Guide* outline the four steps of the TIMS Laboratory Method. These steps were reviewed in the Adventure Book *The Four Servants* in Lesson 4. Irma and Jerome use the TIMS four-step method to solve a problem.

Jerome collected data from his family on their hand lengths and heights and graphed the data as a point graph. Use the *Jerome's Family: Hand Lengths and Heights* Transparency Master to show how points are plotted. Tell students that a common way to plot a data point is to locate the horizontal measurement first, in this case, hand length. (You may say, "Go to the ladder, then climb up.") The measurement graphed on the vertical axis, height, is located second. To check the location of each of Jerome's points, one student can locate the hand length on the horizontal axis and another student can locate the height on the vertical axis. As the first student begins tracing his finger straight up the graph, the other traces his finger to the right. Where the two fingers meet, the point is plotted. This is shown in Figure 11.

TIMS Tip

If students have difficulty tracing the lines to a point with their fingers, you may want them to use two rulers to show the point of the intersection of the lines.

Notice that Jerome measured hand length and height in centimeters. It is important to label both axes and include the units when recording measurements. Encourage students to identify some of the points on the graph. Students should see that some of the hand lengths and heights do not fall on the intersection of the graph's lines.

Describe and discuss the investigation *Arm Span vs. Height.* Each group will measure and record the height and arm span of each of its members. Before they collect the data, ask:

- *Do you think we can predict the height of a fourth grader if we know his or her arm span?*

This question will be asked again in the Explore questions.

Model the measurement procedure. Ask questions such as:

- *What should we do to measure accurately?*
- *What variables should we keep fixed?*

The class as a group will need to decide upon some rules that will make the measurement consistent across the class.

For example, the class might decide that everyone should:

1. Remove their shoes.
2. Stand straight and place their feet together when they are being measured.
3. Place a ruler flat on the top of the head of the classmate being measured, touch the ruler to the meterstick, and measure to the nearest inch.
4. Start at the edge of the first meterstick when arm span is being measured. (The tip of the longest finger should line up with the edge of the first meterstick.) Students have a tendency to lean up against the metersticks and spread their arms out without touching the edge or 0. Refer to Figure 10.

Jerome's Family Graph
Dad
Mom
Jenny
Jerome
Timothy
Abby
Peter
H
Height (in centimeters)
0
10
20
30
40
50
60
70
80
90
100
110
120
130
140
150
160
170
180
0 4 8 12 16 20 24 28 32 36
L
Hand Length (in centimeters)

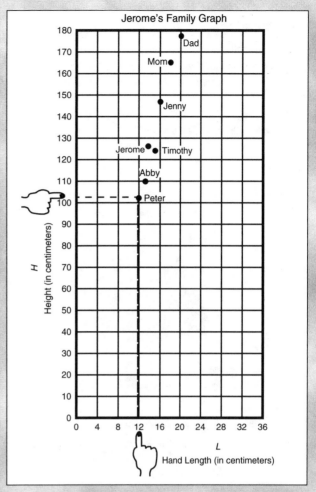

Figure 11: *Plotting a point*

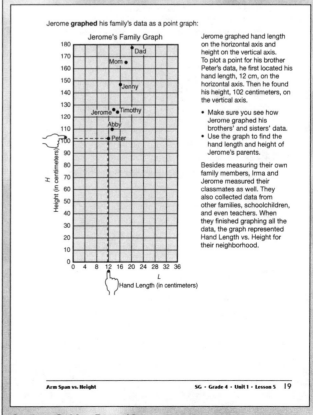

Jerome **graphed** his family's data as a point graph:

Jerome's Family Graph
Dad
Mom
Jenny
Jerome
Timothy
Abby
Peter
H
Height (in centimeters)
0 4 8 12 16 20 24 28 32 36
L
Hand Length (in centimeters)

Jerome graphed hand length on the horizontal axis and height on the vertical axis. To plot a point for his brother Peter's data, he first located his hand length, 12 cm, on the horizontal axis. Then he found his height, 102 centimeters, on the vertical axis.

- Make sure you see how Jerome graphed his brothers' and sisters' data.
- Use the graph to find the hand length and height of Jerome's parents.

Besides measuring their own family members, Irma and Jerome measured their classmates as well. They also collected data from other families, schoolchildren, and even teachers. When they finished graphing all the data, the graph represented Hand Length vs. Height for their neighborhood.

Arm Span vs. Height SG • Grade 4 • Unit 1 • Lesson 5 19

***Student Guide* - Page 19**

TIMS Tip

During the activity, take time out to ask the groups how well they are working together. Concentrate the discussion on one of the following questions: *"Did your group take turns? Did your group stay on task? Did everyone participate?"* If any group answers, "No," then encourage the group to make a plan to take turns, stay on task, or to include everyone.

Finally, when their graph was finished, they **analyzed and discussed** their results.

Irma and Jerome chose to investigate the two variables, hand length and height. You, like Irma and Jerome, will investigate two variables which describe your class. The arm span and height of each student in your class will be measured. Your job is to find out whether you can predict a fourth-grade student's height if you know his or her arm span.

We never measured the principal's hand length and height.
It looks like she's in a hurry. Let's ask her if we can measure her hand. We can use our graph to predict her height.

You will begin by drawing a picture of what you will do in the experiment. Then, collect and organize data in a table. Next, you will make a graph of the data. Finally, you will explore the data by looking for patterns.

Draw

Draw a picture of the setup for your experiment. Show the variables Arm Span (*S*) and Height (*H*) in your picture. Use Irma's hand length and height picture to help you draw a picture of your *Arm Span vs. Height* experiment. Remember to label the variables.

Discuss

1. A. Is arm span a categorical or a numerical variable?
   B. Is height a categorical or a numerical variable? Explain how you know.
2. What is the same about all the people you measured for this experiment?

20 SG • Grade 4 • Unit 1 • Lesson 5 Arm Span vs. Height

***Student Guide* - Page 20**

TIMS Tip

Students can fold a piece of paper into thirds to create a *Three-column Data Table.*

TIMS Tip

A teacher who had a student in class who was confined to a wheelchair assigned the data collection as homework. All the children were measured at home. The child who used a wheelchair was measured by his parents as he was lying down.

Part 2. Drawing the Picture and Collecting Data

Students draw a picture of the investigation. Discuss what goes in the picture: the main variables of the experiment and the procedure. Figure 12 is a sample picture which clearly shows the two main numerical variables, arm span and height. Use Irma's picture of her experiment in the *Student Guide* to illustrate what should be in the picture. Discuss with students some additional pieces that can be added to their pictures. For example, the sample picture in the *Student Guide* does not show how the metersticks are aligned for measuring height. Discuss any additional steps or variables that illustrate the measurement procedure. Then, ask students to begin drawing their pictures. While some groups draw their pictures, others may collect and record their data or complete the *Plotting Points Pictures* Activity Pages.

H
S

Figure 12: *Sample picture*

The two main variables, arm span and height, are numerical variables ***(Question 1)***. ***Question 2*** asks what is the same about all the people students measured in the experiment. If students measured their classmates, they should realize that their ages are the same. All the measurements in this lab are of fourth graders—generally speaking, nine- or ten-year-olds. Age therefore is a fixed variable. **Fixed variables** are variables in an experiment that are held constant or not changed.

Students should work in groups to collect and organize their data on a *Three-column Data Table*.

After the groups have collected their data, one student from each group should transfer their data onto the class data table. Discuss any patterns students see. Ask:

- *Who has the longest arm span?*
- *Who is the tallest?*
- *How many people have the same arm span as height?*
- *How many people have an arm span and height that differ only by one inch? Two inches? Three inches?* (Usually you will find that a person's arm span and height are within one or two inches of each other.)

Part 3. Graphing and Analyzing the Data

Before graphing, discuss how to set up the graph on *Centimeter Graph Paper.* Include titling the graph, labeling and scaling the axes, and remembering the units. When reviewing how to plot a point, be sure to include points that do not lie on grid lines.

To reinforce graphing techniques, display the *Point Graph: What's Wrong Here?* transparency. This transparency shows a student's graph that has several errors. Students may notice that:

- The title is wrong on the graph. (It is labeled "Data Table" instead of "Graph.")
- There are no units labeled for the measurements, i.e., inches or centimeters.
- The numbering on the vertical axis is incorrect. (The zero starts on the 10 line.)
- The points are not spread apart as well as they could be by scaling the axes. This makes it difficult to plot all the points. Ask students how they could change the scale to spread the data out more. Scaling by fives works well.

Several options follow for graphing the class data since some students will be more familiar with graphing points and the TIMS Laboratory Method.

Measure the arm span and height of each person in your group to the nearest inch. Record your group's data in a data table like the one at the right. Discuss with your group what the letters *S* and *H* stand for.

Discuss any patterns you see in the data table.

Arm Span vs. Height Data Table

Name	S Arm Span (in inches)	H Height (in inches)

- Graph your group's data. Plot arm span on the horizontal axis and height on the vertical axis. Scale your horizontal axis to at least 75 inches and the vertical axis to at least 100 inches. Remember to label each axis.
- A class graph of *Arm Span vs. Height* will provide more data for you to analyze. Plot one point, your own data, for arm span and height on the class graph.

Explore

Use your class data and your graphs to help you and your group answer the following questions. Include units with your answers. Be ready to share your answers with the entire class.

3. A. Describe your group's graph. What do you notice about the points?
   B. Describe the class graph. What do you notice about the points?

4. Compare your group's graph and the class graph. How are they alike and how are they different?

Arm Span vs. Height   SG · Grade 4 · Unit 1 · Lesson 5   21

Student Guide - Page 21

Journal Prompt

Did you make sure everyone in your group had a job when collecting data for *Arm Span vs. Height?* If so, what jobs did you do? If not, explain how your group collected the data.

Option A

If your class does not need practice plotting points, ask each student to plot only his or her data on a class graph. Students should work in pairs. After one child has plotted his or her point, the partner can check its placement. The class graph may be made on a transparency of *Centimeter Graph Paper* or on poster-size graph paper. A sample graph is shown in Figure 13.

Arm Span vs. Height
H
Height (inches)
100
95
90
85
80
75
70
65
60
55
50
45
40
35
30
25
20
15
10
5
0
0 5 10 15 20 25 30 35 40 45 50 55 60 65 70 75
S
Arm Span (inches)
estimated average

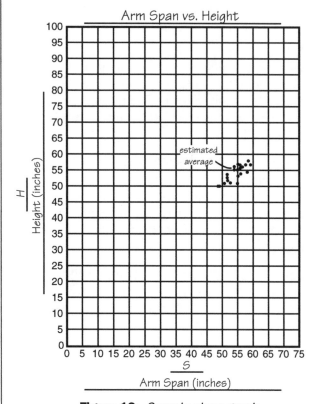

Figure 13: *Sample class graph*

Option B

Have each student graph his or her group's data on a sheet of *Centimeter Graph Paper.* Encourage students to scale their vertical axes so that the data is spread out as much as possible. Numbering by fives usually works well to help spread apart the data. Students may label each point with initials. Group members should compare graphs to check where the points were plotted. After each student in the group has graphed the group data, individuals plot their own data on a class graph. The instructions in the *Student Guide* describe this approach.

Option C

Make copies of the class data table and distribute one to each student. Then, each student graphs all of the class data. You can begin graphing some of these data points in class and then assign the remainder for homework. As a reference for class discussion, make a transparency from a copy of a student's graph or graph the data on poster-size graph paper.

Note that the graph for students' data will result in a cluster of points. Students do not need to fit a best-fit line through these points. Best-fit lines will be reviewed in a later unit.

Have students work in their groups to answer *Questions 3–6.* Ask the groups to report their answers during the class discussion. For *Question 3,* students may say that the data points are "clumped together" or "they form a group." In some cases, as in Figure 13, a student might even say the data points "run diagonally."

Question 5B asks if a student can make a prediction about another fourth grader's height, given his or her arm span. Although we cannot predict precisely where a person's data point will lie, we do know with high certainty that it will fall within the cluster. By referring to the data table and graph, students should recognize that the height of a student and his or her arm span are usually within two inches or so of one another. Discuss the range of arm spans and the range of heights in your class. A new fourth grader's measurements will probably fall somewhere within these ranges.

Encourage students to give their answers with units. Students should have labeled their graphs with units of measurement, so their answers should also include units.

Part 4. Continuing to Analyze the Data

Verify students' understanding of the data displayed on the graph by discussing circumstances where arm spans and heights may not be approximately equivalent. For example, in *Question 6B,* students find where a kangaroo might fall on their graph. Kangaroos have significantly shorter arm spans than heights. Therefore, the data for kangaroos would fall above and to the left of the fourth-grader data. You might also discuss where data would fall for snakes and basketball players. Snakes have no arms, so their data would be along the vertical axis. Basketball players have long arms and tall heights, so their data would fall above and to the right of the fourth-grade data.

If you assign *Questions 7–10* for group discussion, make sure students have the class graph available.

Questions 7–10 involve estimating and finding medians. A point in the center of the clump is representative of a student with the average arm span and height for the class. Use the class data table and graph to estimate the average arm span and height. Refer again to Figure 13.

Question 9A asks students to find the median height. Remind students that to do so they must first rank the heights. As you did in Lesson 3, have students

---

5. A. If you measured a new classmate's arm span and height, where do you think his or her data would lie?
   B. If a fourth grader from another classroom had an arm span of 53 inches, what would you predict about his or her height?
6. A. In which part of the graph would first-grade data cluster in comparison to fourth-grade data—in the area marked A, B, or C?
   B. In which cluster would a kangaroo's data fall—in the area marked A, B, or C?

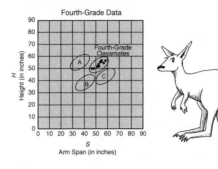

Fourth-Grade Data

Discuss

Use your class graph to discuss the following.

7. Use your graph to estimate the average arm span of your classmates. (*Hint:* This is a number that represents all the arm spans in your classroom.)

8. Use your graph to estimate the average height of your classmates.

22   SG · Grade 4 · Unit 1 · Lesson 5   Arm Span vs. Height

Student Guide - Page 22

---

9. A. Find the median height in your class.
   B. Find the median arm span in your class.
   C. Compare with your estimate. Were you close?
10. A. Use a red pen or marker to plot the data point for the median height and arm span on your graph.
    B. Where is the data point for the median values compared to the other data points on the graph?

Homework

1. The data table shows data for three groups of students in Room 204. Graph *Arm Span vs. Height* for these groups on a sheet of *Centimeter Graph Paper.* Title the graph so that you know it is not your class data. Plot arm span on the horizontal axis and height on the vertical axis. Remember to label your axes and include units.

2. A. Estimate the average arm span of the groups using the graph.
   B. Estimate the average height using your graph.
   C. How does the groups' data compare to your class data?

3. If a new fourth grader who entered Mrs. Dewey's classroom had an arm span of 54 inches, what would you predict about the student's height?

4. If you measured the arm spans and heights of the parents of classmates in Mrs. Dewey's classroom, where would the data cluster? Show your answer on your graph of *Arm Span vs. Height* for the groups in Room 204.

Room 204 Arm Span and Height Data Table

Name	S Arm Span (in inches)	H Height (in inches)
Linda	51	51
Romesh	52	53
Nicholas	56	54
Jerome	49	50
Keenya	54	55
Frank	59	57
Luis	58	58
Roberto	55	57
Ana	52	52
Jacob	56	56
Grace	55	55
Lee Yah	53	52

Arm Span vs. Height   SG · Grade 4 · Unit 1 · Lesson 5   23

Student Guide - Page 23

Daily Practice and Problems:
Tasks for Lesson 5

N. Task: Count Your Change
(URG p. 19)

You go to the store with $5.00. You buy 2 items which cost $1.50 each. You also have to pay sales tax of 7¢ for every dollar spent. How much change will you get back?

P. Task: Sharing Pennies (URG p. 20)

Suppose you had 100 pennies. How can you divide them as evenly as possible into 3 shares? Write a number sentence to go with your answer.

R. Task: Measuring (URG p. 21)

Measure each of the lines below twice. First measure the line to the nearest inch. Then, measure it to the nearest centimeter.

1. _____

2. _____

3. _____

T. Task: Favorite Sandwiches (URG p. 23)

A classroom of students were asked to name their favorite sandwich. The following data was collected.

1. Complete the third column of the table.

Type of Sandwich	Tally	Number of Students
Cheese	⑷Ⱶ	
Ham	⑷Ⱶ ||||	
Turkey	/||	
Peanut Butter	⑷Ⱶ ⑷Ⱶ /|	
Baloney	⑷Ⱶ /	

2. How many students are in the class?

3. Which sandwich did students pick as their favorite most often?

---

line up in order by height. The student in the middle has the median height. Students might want to repeat the exercise with arm spans.

Suggestions for Teaching the Lesson

Math Facts

DPP Bit M is another written assessment of addition facts, this time assessing those facts not included in the DPP Bit K assessment. For students who need extra practice, use the Addition and Subtraction Math Facts Review section in the *Grade 4 Facts Resource Guide.*

Homework and Practice

- The Homework section on the *Arm Span vs. Height* Lab Pages asks students to repeat the investigation using data from groups from Mrs. Dewey's fourth grade classroom. Students will need a piece of *Centimeter Graph Paper* to complete this assignment.

- If students did not complete the *Plotting Points Pictures* Activity Pages in class, assign them as homework.

- DPP Tasks N and P provide practice in computation. Bit O provides practice with measuring time. Items R and S develop students' abilities to measure accurately and to estimate measurement. DPP Bit Q provides a graphical depiction of a set of data which students are asked to analyze.

Assessment

- Use some of the questions in the Homework section of the *Arm Span vs. Height* Lab Pages for assessment.

- Use the *More Arm Span vs. Height Data* Assessment Blackline Master to assess students' abilities to estimate medians in data and to plot points accurately.

- DPP Task T may be used as an assessment of students' abilities to create bar graphs. Make a copy of the data table and ask students to graph the data in a bar graph on a piece of *Centimeter Graph Paper.*

- Observe students as they gather the data for the lab. Check to see if students can measure length in inches. Record your observations on the *Observational Assessment Record.*

- Transfer appropriate documentation from the Unit 1 *Observational Assessment Record* to students' *Individual Assessment Record Sheets.*

Extension

Several schools have extended this lab by investigating the relationship between arm span and height in their entire school. They made a large graph and posted it on a wall in a main hallway of the school. Each student and teacher in the school plotted his or her own arm span and height data on the graph using a small sticker. Figure 14 is a sample school graph which was completed by the students and teachers in a Chicago elementary school. The teacher included a professional basketball player's data on the graph as well as her 1-year-old nephew's data.

If it is inappropriate for everyone in the school to participate, invite a first grade classroom, an eighth-grade classroom, and several teachers to graph their data.

Software Connection

If you have a spreadsheet software package available, your class can use it throughout the year to enter data, calculate averages, and graph the data. We recommend that you introduce the features of the spreadsheet one at a time. For this lab, students can enter the arm span and height data in a spreadsheet and use the computer to find the median.

Height (in inches)
90
85
80
75
70
65
60
55
50
45
40
35
30
25
20
15
10
5
0
0 5 10 15 20 25 30 35 40 45 50 55 60 65 70 75 80 85 90
Arm Span (in inches)
★ Fourth Grade
◇ Second Grade
○ Sixth Grade
△ Eighth Grade
● 1 year old
■ Pro basketball player

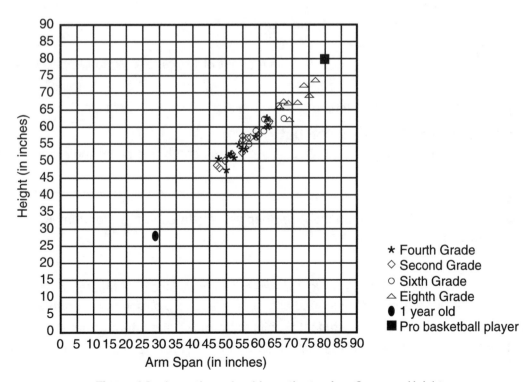

Figure 14: *An entire school investigates* Arm Span vs. Height

AT A GLANCE

Math Facts and Daily Practice and Problems

DPP Bit M assesses addition facts. Tasks N and P are problems involving money. Bit O practices telling time. Items Q–T provide practice with bar graphs and measurement concepts.

Before the Lab

Students can practice plotting points using the *Plotting Points Pictures* Activity Pages in the *Discovery Assignment Book*.

Part 1. Launching the Lab

1. Students are introduced to the four steps of the TIMS Laboratory Method on the *Arm Span vs. Height* Lab Pages in the *Student Guide*. These pages present the context of the lab.

2. Introduce students to plotting points (point graphs) by discussing the graph *Jerome's Family: Hand Lengths and Heights*.

3. Model the procedures for collecting data for *Arm Span vs. Height*.

Part 2. Drawing the Picture and Collecting Data

1. Discuss the variables and components that should be included in students' pictures.

2. Student groups draw their pictures of the lab while other groups collect data or complete the *Plotting Points Pictures* Activity Pages.

3. The class discusses the answers to *Questions 1–2* on the *Arm Span vs. Height* Lab Pages.

Part 3. Graphing and Analyzing the Data

1. Students discuss the setup of the graph including labeling and scaling the axes.

2. Use the *Point Graph: What's Wrong Here?* transparency to alert students to some possible graphing errors.

3. Each student graphs the group data on a sheet of *Centimeter Graph Paper*.

4. Each student plots a point for his or her individual data on the class graph.

5. Student groups answer *Questions 3–6* on the *Arm Span vs. Height* Lab Pages.

Part 4. Continuing to Analyze the Data

Student groups answer *Questions 7–10* using the class graph and share their responses in a class discussion.

Homework

Assign the Homework section on the *Arm Span vs. Height* Lab Pages for homework or assessment.

Assessment

1. Use the *More Arm Span vs. Height Data* Assessment Blackline Master to assess students' abilities to estimate medians in data and to plot points accurately.

2. Use DPP Task T to assess students' abilities to make and interpret bar graphs.

3. Use the *Observational Assessment Record* to note students' abilities to measure length in inches.

4. Transfer appropriate documentation from the Unit 1 *Observational Assessment Record* to students' *Individual Assessment Record Sheets*.

Notes:

Name ______________________ Date ______________

More Arm Span vs. Height Data

1. The data below is taken from another fourth-grade classroom. Estimate the average height and arm span for a fourth-grader from this class.

   Average Height __________ Average Arm Span __________

Fourth-Grade Data
90
80
70
60
50
40
30
20
10
0
H
Height (in inches)
0 10 20 30 40 50 60 70 80 90
S
Arm Span (in inches)

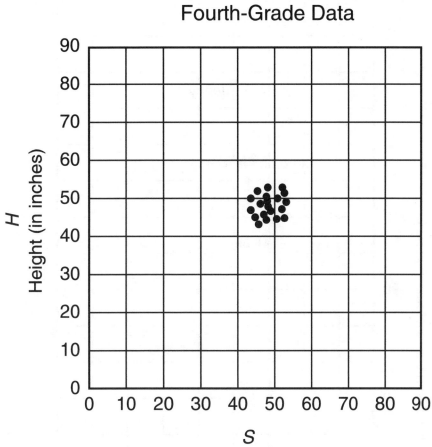

2. Suppose Jack, whose height is 45 inches, joins this fourth-grade classroom. What would you predict about his arm span?

3. Maria is in sixth grade. Her arm span measures 62 inches. Her height measures 63 inches. Add her point to the graph.

Jerome's Family: Hand Lengths and Heights

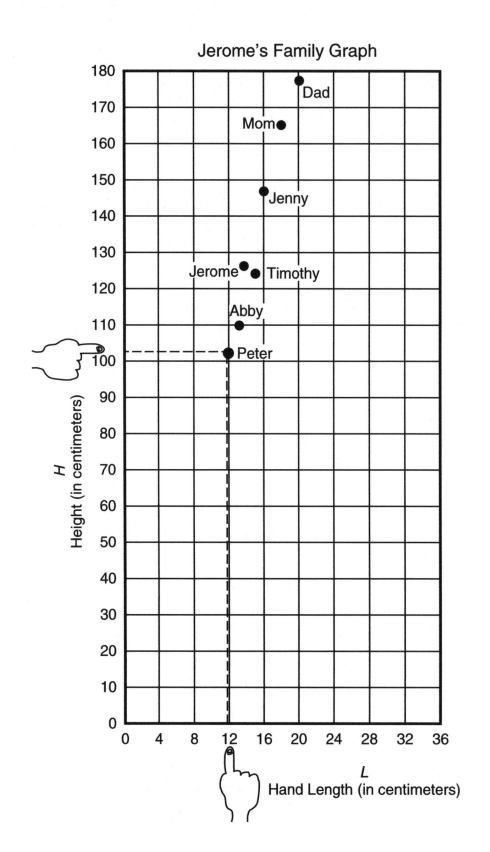

Jerome's Family Graph
180
170
160
150
140
130
120
110
100
90
80
70
60
50
40
30
20
10
0
H
Height (in centimeters)
Dad
Mom
Jenny
Jerome
Timothy
Abby
Peter
0
4
8
12
16
20
24
28
32
36
L
Hand Length (in centimeters)

Point Graph: What's Wrong Here?

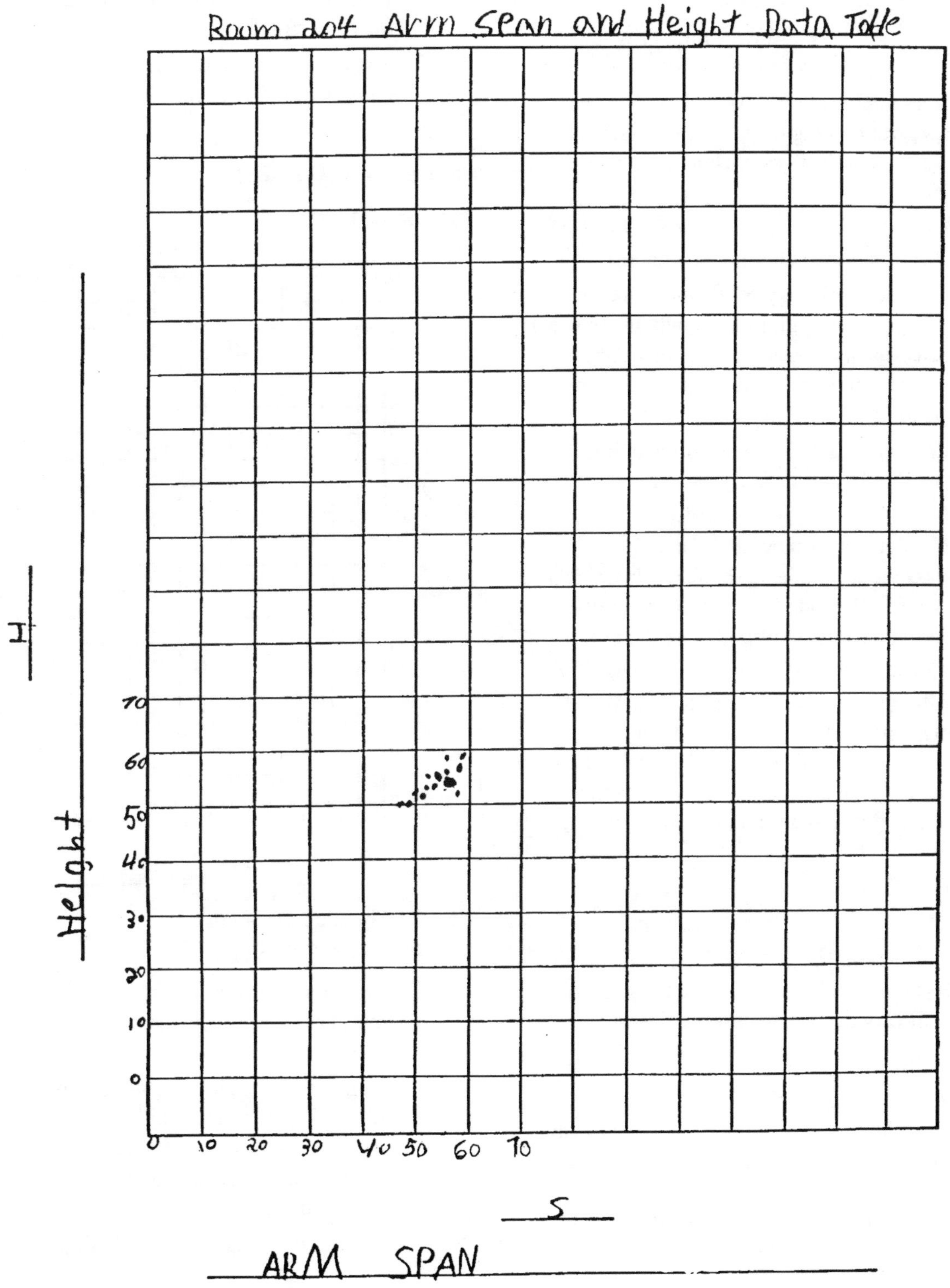

Room 204 Arm Span and Height Data Table
H
Height
70
60
50
40
30
20
10
0
0
10
20
30
40
50
60
70
S
ARM SPAN

Student Guide

Questions 1–10 (SG pp. 20–23)

1. **A.** numerical

   B. numerical; The values are numbers.

2. Answers will vary. Students might say that they measured only fourth graders.

*The answers to ***Questions 3–6*** are based on the sample class graph in Figure 13 in the Lesson Guide. Figure 12 in the Lesson Guide provides a sample picture.

3. **A.** *Answers will vary. Students might say the data points are "clumped together."

   B. *Answers will vary. Students might say the data points are "clumped together." In some cases, as in the graph in Figure 13 of the Lesson Guide, the data points may "run diagonally."

4. Answers will vary. The data points in both graphs should cluster fairly close to one another.

5. **A.** *Students may show their answer using the class graph. Students should realize that a new fourth grader's data point should lie within the cluster of points on the graph.

   B. *The height and arm span are usually within two inches or so of one another. If the new fourth grader had an arm span of 53 inches, his height would probably be in the range of 51–55 inches. Discuss the range of arm spans and the range of heights in your class.

6. **A.** B

   B. *A

*The answers to ***Questions 7 and 8*** are based on the sample class graph in Figure 13 in the Lesson Guide. Answers will vary depending on your class data.

7. 54 inches

8. 55 inches

9. **A.–B.** *Answers will vary. Students may line up in order by height. The student in the middle has the median height. Students may repeat the exercise with arm spans.

   C. Students should compare the answers to ***Questions 9A and 9B*** to their estimates in ***Questions 7 and 8.***

10. **A.** Answers will vary. Plot the points from your answers to ***Questions 9A and 9B*** on the class graph.

    B. The data point for the median values should be in the middle of the cluster.

Homework (SG p. 23)

Questions 1–4

1.

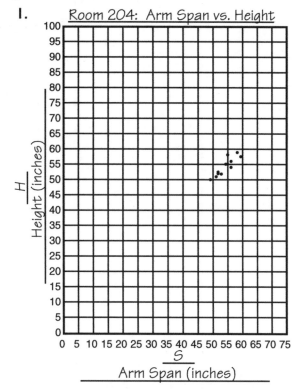

Room 204: Arm Span vs. Height
100
95
90
85
80
75
70
65
60
55
50
45
40
35
30
25
20
15
10
5
0
H
Height (inches)
0 5 10 15 20 25 30 35 40 45 50 55 60 65 70 75
S
Arm Span (inches)

2. **A.** About 53 or 54 cm

   B. About 53 or 54 cm

   C. The group's graph should look similar to your class graph. The data points should form a cluster.

3. Answers will vary. Height and arm span are usually within two inches or so of one another. The student's arm span could be in the range of 52–56 inches. His height could be the same as his arm span—54 inches.

4. Above and to the right of the fourth-grade data.

***Answers and/or discussion are included in the Lesson Guide.**

****Answers for all the Home Practice in the *Discovery Assignment Book* are at the end of the unit.**

Discovery Assignment Book

Plotting Points Pictures (DAB pp. 7–8)

Picture 1 is an octopus or spider.

Picture 2 is a sailboat.

Unit Resource Guide

More Arm Span vs. Height Data (URG p. 83)

1. Answers will vary; approximately 48 cm for height and 48 cm for arm span.
2. Answer will vary; his arm span could be equivalent to his height or it could be within 2 inches of his height—43–47 inches are acceptable answers.
3.

Fourth-Grade Data
H
Height (in inches)
0
10
20
30
40
50
60
70
80
90
S
Arm Span (in inches)

*Answers and/or discussion are included in the Lesson Guide.

**Answers for all the Home Practice in the *Discovery Assignment Book* are at the end of the unit.

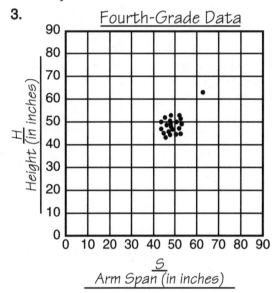

Daily Practice and Problems:
Bit for Lesson 6

U. More on Median (URG p. 23)

1. Romesh is 53 inches tall. Grace is 55 inches tall. Their two team members, Jerome and John, are 50 and 57 inches tall. What is the median height of these four students?

2. Irma is 51 inches tall. Tanya is 56 inches tall. Their two team members, Roberto and Ana, are 57 and 52 inches tall. What is the median height of these four students?

DPP Challenge is on page 92. Suggestions for using the DPPs are on page 92.

LESSON GUIDE

Solving Problems About Room 204

> **Estimated Class Sessions: 1**

Students make estimates and find solutions for word problems about Mrs. Dewey's class. The problems require various strategies, skills, and operations. Students decide when it is appropriate to calculate with paper-and-pencil methods, find an estimate, or use a calculator. Students use estimation to check the reasonableness of their results.

Key Content

- Solving multistep word problems.
- Estimating quantities.
- Choosing appropriate methods and tools to calculate (calculator, pencil and paper, or mental math).
- Communicating solutions orally and in writing.

Key Vocabulary

convenient numbers
estimation
reasonable

Curriculum Sequence

Before This Unit

Calculators. *Math Trailblazers* introduces calculators beginning in first grade and encourages appropriate calculator use throughout the curriculum. Students who have previous experience with the curriculum should have a basic working knowledge of the keyboard and function keys.

Estimation. Estimation strategies are presented in every grade. Beginning in kindergarten, students estimate measurements and quantities. They make predictions using data they collect. Third-grade students find the closest ten or hundred as a number that is convenient for a mental calculation. See Grade 3 Unit 6 Lesson 5.

After This Unit

Calculators. In fourth grade, students continue to use calculators as one method of computation. They choose an appropriate method (paper-and-pencil procedures, calculators, mental math, or estimation) for each problem-solving situation.

Estimation. Fourth grade students use a variety of estimation strategies to predict and check their answers. The use of convenient numbers in this lesson is intended only to be a quick review. A more formal discussion of convenient numbers is included in Unit 6 Lesson 6.

Word Problems. Many units include a lesson that is a set of word problems similar to this one. See Units 3, 4, 5, 7, 10, 11, 13, 14, 15, and 16. The Home Practice in the *Discovery Assignment Book* also includes a set of word problems for most units.

Materials List

Print Materials for Students

	Math Facts and Daily Practice and Problems	Activity	Homework
Student Books — Student Guide		*Solving Problems About Room 204* Pages 24–25	
Student Books — Discovery Assignment Book			Home Practice Part 6 Page 6
Teacher Resource — Unit Resource Guide	DPP Item U–V Pages 23–24 ⊙		

⊙ *available on Teacher Resource CD*

All Transparency Masters, Blackline Masters, and Assessment Blackline Masters in the Unit Resource Guide are on the Teacher Resource CD.

Supplies for Each Student

calculator

Content Note

Calculator Use. Calculator use in this lesson requires only the number and function keys (+, −, ×, ÷). However, if your students have not had experience using calculators, these problems provide a good setting for establishing your general classroom procedures and expectations for their use as well as basic techniques.

Before you introduce calculators into your classroom, plan how you will deal with the issues of storage, variation in the features and functions among different models, and how you will help students understand the proper use and care of their calculators.

Storage. Some teachers have students keep calculators in their desks so that they can be accessed quickly. Other teachers prefer a central storage system. Whichever you choose, make sure that calculators are generally accessible to students when they wish to use them. Calculator availability should be the norm in the class. You can then specify when you want an activity to be done without using a calculator.

Features. Different brands of calculators often have slightly different features and functions. We strongly recommend that every student in the class use the same type of calculator. This allows the class to share keystroke sequences for solving problems.

Care. Students also need to know how to care for their calculators properly. They are not waterproof and the solar cell now found at the top of many calculators is easily broken if the calculator is not covered or stored where it is protected. (In other words, don't jam an uncovered calculator into your backpack with your pens, leaky water bottle, or heavy books and expect it to work when you take it out!) Students should not use pencils or other sharp objects to press the keys. They should also avoid pressing on the display window and the solar cell.

Developing the Activity

Throughout the year, students will solve many problems in activities, labs, and problem sets such as this one. This set of problems can be used in several ways. Students can work on the problems individually, in pairs, or in groups, then come together to discuss the methods they used.

Some of the problems simply provide practice choosing and applying appropriate operations given a real-life setting. Other problems encourage students to use estimation strategies. Many problems will challenge students to use their knowledge of mathematics in a new situation. We provide a variety of problems by design—we want students to think through each problem individually rather than simply to apply the same procedure to several problems in a row. The National Council of Teachers of Mathematics' *Principles and Standards for School Mathematics* states,

"Part of being able to compute fluently means making smart choices about which tools to use and when. Students should have experiences that help them learn to choose among mental computation, paper-and-pencil strategies, estimation, and calculator use. The particular context, the question, and the numbers involved all play roles in those choices. . . . Students should evaluate problem situations to determine whether an estimate or an exact answer is needed, using their number sense to advantage, and be able to give a rationale for their decision." (NCTM, 2000, p. 36)

For more information on word problems, see the TIMS Tutor: *Word Problems* in the *Teacher Implementation Guide.*

Since students may choose to use calculators to solve these problems, distribute calculators and briefly review the use of different keys with one or two sample problems before students work independently. A quick sketch of the calculator on the overhead can help clarify communication.

Students learn a great deal when solutions are discussed, explained, compared, and contrasted. Therefore, it is important that students take part in a class discussion about the problems they have solved. Such discussions remind children that there are often many ways to solve a problem and that while accuracy is important, communicating a solution path can be equally important. From listening to others, they may hear that although problems are difficult, sticking with a problem by trying different strategies often results in a solution. These are high expectations for students. At the beginning of the year, students may struggle with problem solving and communicating solutions, but as they continue to solve and discuss problems through-out the year, they will become more confident and successful thinkers and communicators.

To begin this lesson, have students read the first paragraph of the *Solving Problems About Room 204* Activity Pages in the *Student Guide.* Briefly review with students how to choose **convenient numbers** when estimating. Ask them to suggest a convenient number for 345. Make sure that students understand that 300 or 350 are both good choices. Convenient numbers are chosen so that you can easily work with them "in your head." Different people may find dif-ferent numbers convenient in different situations.

In discussing the problems in this activity we include sample strategies that can be used. Students are likely to come up with other ways to solve these problems. Use *Question 1* as part of the introduction to this les-son. Discuss various strategies for approaching this problem. To solve the problem, students must find the difference between the number of students in two schools. They must subtract 396 from 509. They can use their calculators or a pencil-and-paper method. They can also use a counting-up strategy. Beginning with 396, they can count up 4 to 400, 100 more to 500, and then 9 more to 509 for a total 113. Estimation strategies should be discussed as a way of checking the reasonableness of either a paper-and-pencil calculation or a calculator answer.

Even if every student agrees on the answer for this problem, be sure to ask:

- *How can we test to see if this is a reasonable answer?*

If students are unable to propose an estimation strat-egy, suggest that they look for a convenient number that is close to each of the numbers in the problem. For example, 396 is close to 400, 509 is close to 500, so the difference is close to 100.

Questions 2A and 2B ask students to calculate the answers to very similar problems. In *Question 2C,* by using convenient numbers, students might suggest the following: 22 is about 20 and 20 times 5 is 100. The number of books Mrs. Dewey passed out was about 100. At Westmont there are 28 students. Students might choose the convenient number 30 and estimate that there are 150 textbooks. Another way to do this is to use the number 25. Since 25 cents is a familiar quantity, students may be able to mentally calculate the value of five quarters ($1.25). 25 can be used as a convenient number for both 22 and 28. Then, they can estimate that each classroom has about 5 × 25 or 125 textbooks. Point out to students that the word "about" encourages an estimation.

Solving Problems About Room 204

Mrs. Dewey asked her students to solve some problems comparing Bessie Coleman School to Westmont School. She asked them to check their calculations by estimating a reasonable answer to each problem. She reminded them that sometimes using a convenient number that is easier to calculate in your head helps to make a quick estimate.

Solve the following problems Mrs. Dewey gave her class. Show how you solved each problem. Be ready to explain how you estimated your answers.

1. There are 396 students at Bessie Coleman School. At Westmont School in Phoenix, there are 509 students. How many more students go to Westmont School?

2. There are 22 students in Mrs. Dewey's fourth-grade class at Bessie Coleman School. At Westmont School, the fourth-grade class has 28 students.
   A. On the first day of school, Mrs. Dewey gave each of her students five textbooks. How many textbooks did she pass out?
   B. If each student in fourth grade at Westmont has 5 textbooks, how many textbooks do the Westmont fourth graders have in their classroom?
   C. Look back at your answers. Explain why you think they are reasonable.

3. Milk at both schools costs 25¢.
   A. If 20 students in Room 204 at the Bessie Coleman School bought milk, how much money did Mrs. Dewey collect?
   B. In the Westmont fourth-grade class, the total cost for milk was $5.25. How many students bought milk in this fourth-grade class?

4. Each of the 22 students in Mrs. Dewey's class sent a letter to their pen pal at Westmont School. Find the cost of the stamps.

5. In music class at Bessie Coleman School, Lee Yah, Roberto, Grace, and Luis lined up across the front of the room to demonstrate a folk dance. They began with their arms outstretched and their fingers just touching. They could just reach across the room. Since the average arm span of the students in Room 204 is 54 inches, about how wide is the room?

24   SG · Grade 4 · Unit 1 · Lesson 6   Solving Problems About Room 204

Student Guide - Page 24

6. Bessie Coleman School begins its school day at 8:30 A.M. and ends at 3:00 P.M. Jerome stays for lunch. How long is he at school?

7. The distance between Phoenix and Chicago is 1816 miles.
   A. If you traveled from Chicago to Phoenix and back again, how many miles would you travel?
   B. Make sure your answer in Question 7A is correct. Explain how you can make a quick estimate of the total distance to see if your answer is reasonable.

Solving Problems About Room 204   SG · Grade 4 · Unit 1 · Lesson 6   25

Student Guide - Page 25

Journal Prompt

What did you learn about your new class by using data in this unit?

Daily Practice and Problems:
Challenge for Lesson 6

V. Challenge: Best Guess (URG p. 24)

1. Make your best guess for the length and width of your classroom. Make sure to include the unit of measurement you choose.

2. Measure the length and width of the classroom. Remember to include units.

Name _____ Date _____

Part 6 The Students in Room 204

Solve each of the following problems. Show how you solved each problem. If you need additional space, use a clean sheet of paper.

1. Ming said, "I collect baseball cards. If I collect 30 more, I'll have 250 cards." How many cards does Ming have now?

2. Keenya likes to listen to music while she practices her tumbling routines for gymnastics class. She listened to two complete cassette tapes while practicing today. There are about 10 songs on each tape, and each song is between 2 and 3 minutes long. About how long did Keenya practice?

3. Irma likes to read. She has two weeks to read the books she took out from the library. One book has 158 pages. The other book has 76 pages.
   A. How many pages are in the two books?
   B. If she reads about ten pages a day, can she finish the two books in two weeks?

4. Maya's family went on a three-day bike trip last week. They biked 36 miles on Friday, 33 on Saturday, and 45 on Sunday. How many miles did they bike in all?

5. It is 4:30 now. Nila's dinner will be ready at 5:15. Nila wants to play her new computer basketball game for twenty minutes. However, she needs fifteen minutes to walk the dog and about seven minutes to set the table. Will Nila be ready for dinner on time? Explain your answer.

6. Write a word problem that describes something about yourself. Write the answer and show how you solved the problem.

6   DAB · Grade 4 · Unit 1   DATA ABOUT US

Copyright © Kendall/Hunt Publishing Company

Discovery Assignment Book - Page 6

To answer **Question 3A,** a calculator or paper-and-pencil approach is appropriate. To help students conceptualize this process, again quarters may be useful. Students might draw pictures of the coins and group them by fours to count the number of dollars.

Question 3B asks for the number of students that bought milk in the fourth-grade class at Westmont School. A complicated calculation is not necessary. The students at Westmont bought 1 more carton of milk than the students at Bessie Coleman; therefore, 21 students bought milk. If students drew the quarters for **Question 3A,** they should quickly see that $5.25 means one more quarter and one more student. As always, other approaches should be encouraged.

Question 4 is an example of an everyday problem people solve in which more information is needed. Students must determine the current cost of a postage stamp. If necessary ask:

- *Where can you find the information you need to solve this problem?*

This will help students see that at times they will need to seek out more information to solve a problem. Using a calculator is appropriate here once they have determined the cost of one stamp.

Question 5 encourages students to estimate the sum of four arm spans. Since a fourth-grader's arm span is approximately 50 inches, a rough estimate would be 200 inches. You may wish to discuss other methods of finding the estimate with the class.

Suggestions for Teaching the Lesson

Homework and Practice

- Assign unfinished problems for homework. Ask students to choose one of the problems they worked on and explain why they think their solution is a reasonable answer.

- DPP Bit U provides review and practice finding the median for a set of data. DPP Challenge V provides practice in estimating and measuring distances.

- Part 6 of the Home Practice continues student work with word problems.

Answers for Part 6 of the Home Practice can be found in the Answer Key at the end of this lesson and at the end of this unit.

Assessment

Use student responses for **Question 7B** as an informal assessment of how well students understand the concept of estimation.

AT A GLANCE

Math Facts and Daily Practice and Problems

DPP items U and V provide practice with finding medians and measuring length.

Developing the Activity

1. Review calculator use and procedures.
2. Review estimation strategies by discussing *Question 1*.
3. Students use estimation, calculators, paper-and-pencil methods, and mental calculation to solve word problems presented on the *Solving Problems About Room 204* Activity Pages.
4. Students discuss their solution strategies with the class.
5. Use the Journal Prompt to help students summarize what they learned in Unit 1.

Homework

Part 6 of the Home Practice continues work solving word problems.

Notes:

Student Guide

Questions 1–7 (SG pp. 24–25)

1. 113 students

2. **A.** 110 textbooks

   B. 140 textbooks

3. **A.** $5.00

   B. 21 students

4. $8.14 (using 37¢ as the cost of 1 stamp)

5. About 200 inches

6. $6\frac{1}{2}$ hours

7. **A.** 3632 miles

   B. 2000 + 2000 = 4000 miles; The actual answer should be less than 4000 miles.

Discovery Assignment Book

**Home Practice (DAB p. 6)

Part 6. The Students in Room 204

Questions 1–6

1. 220 cards; 250 cards − 30 cards = 220 cards

2. About 50 minutes; Keenya listened to 20 songs. 2 minutes per song × 20 songs = 40 minutes; 3 minutes per song × 20 songs = 60 minutes, halfway between 40 minutes and 60 minutes is 50 minutes.

3. **A.** 234 pages; 158 pages + 76 pages = 234 pages.

   B. No; two weeks is 14 days; 14 × 10 = 140 pages

4. 114 miles; 36 miles + 33 miles + 45 miles = 114 miles

5. Yes; 20 minutes + 15 minutes + 7 minutes = 42 minutes. There are 45 minutes between 4:30 and 5:15.

6. Answers will vary.

*Answers and/or discussion are included in the Lesson Guide.

**Answers for all the Home Practice in the *Discovery Assignment Book* are at the end of the unit.

Discovery Assignment Book

Part 1. Practice

Questions 1–10 (DAB p. 3)

1. 16
2. 21
3. 20
4. 21
5. 100
6. 110
7. 120
8. 150
9. 105
10. 105

Part 2. Variables and Values

Questions 1–4 (DAB p. 3)

Answers will vary. An example of a categorical variable is type of drinks. Values for this variable are iced tea, milk, and fruit juice. An example of a numerical variable is number of windows in each room. Values for this variable are 0, 1, 2, 3, etc.

Part 3. Finding the Median

Questions 1–4 (DAB p. 4)

1. 6 pieces of candy; Arrange the numbers in order and select the middle number.
2. 13 cm; Arrange the numbers in order, select the two middle numbers, and find the number halfway between the two middle numbers.
3. 40 minutes; The five numbers are: 0, 30, 40, 45, and 60. The median is 40 minutes.
4. 24 raisins; Arrange the numbers in order. The two middle numbers are 23 and 25, so the median is 24 raisins.

Part 4. Measuring in Inches (DAB p. 5)

Answers will vary.

Part 5. Inches and Centimeters

Questions 1–3 (DAB p. 5)

1. 1 inch

   _____ 1 cm

   _____ 1 inch

2. 3 inches

   _____ 5 cm

   _____ 3 inches

3. **A.** 40 centimeters
   B. Answers will vary. Students might draw the lines and compare them.

Part 6. The Students in Room 204

Questions 1–6 (DAB p. 6)

1. 220 cards; 250 cards − 30 cards = 220 cards
2. About 50 minutes; Keenya listened to 20 songs. 2 minutes per song × 20 songs = 40 minutes; 3 minutes per song × 20 songs = 60 minutes, halfway between 40 minutes and 60 minutes is 50 minutes.
3. **A.** 234 pages; 158 pages + 76 pages = 234 pages.
   B. No; two weeks is 14 days; 14 × 10 = 140 pages
4. 114 miles; 36 miles + 33 miles + 45 miles = 114 miles
5. Yes; 20 minutes + 15 minutes + 7 minutes = 42 minutes. There are 45 minutes between 4:30 and 5:15.
6. Answers will vary.

*Answers and/or discussion are included in the Lesson Guide.